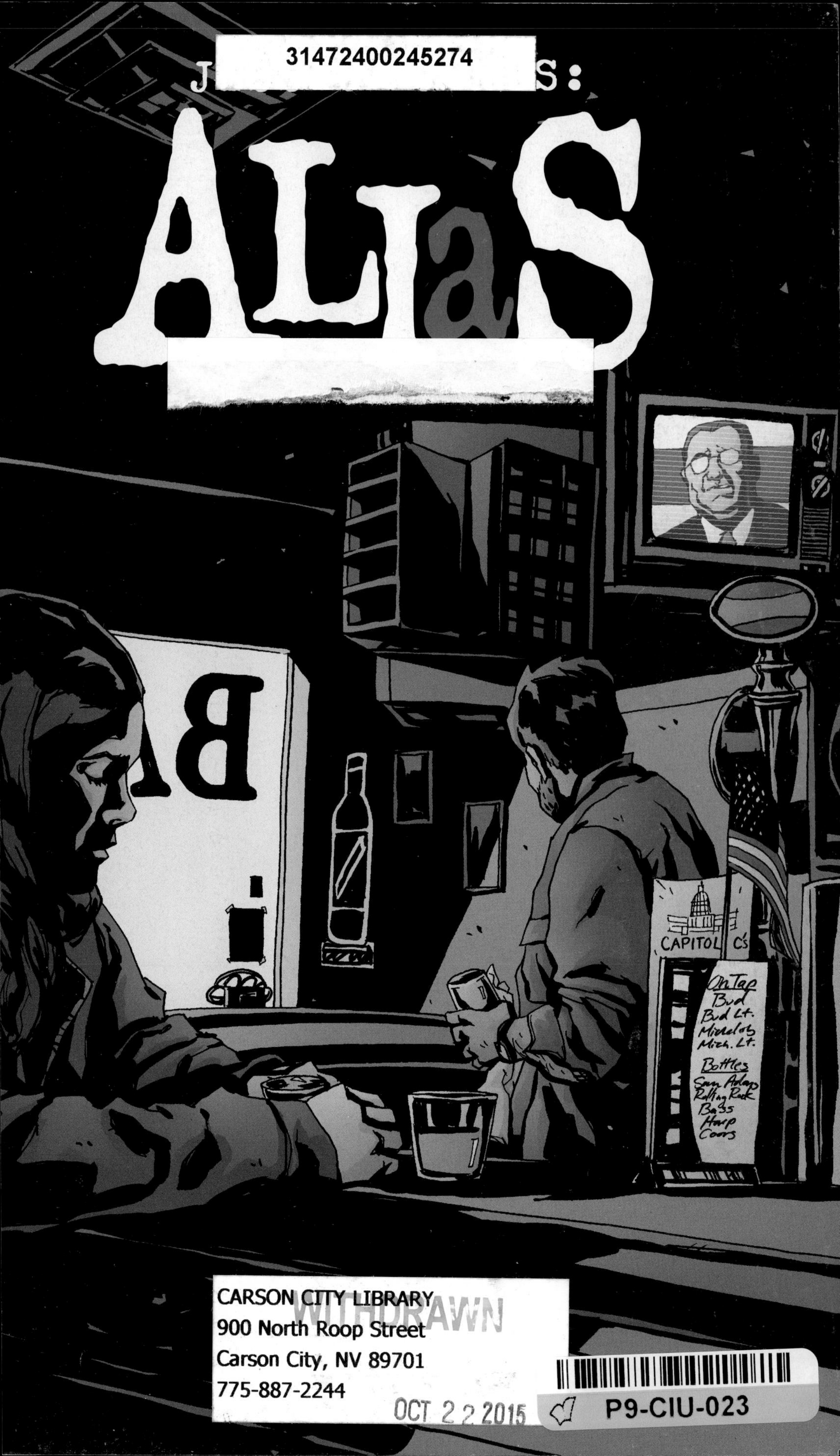
ALIAS
CAPITOL C's
On Tap
Bud
Bud Lt.
Michelob
Mich. Lt.
Bottles
Sam Adams
Rolling Rock
Bass
Harp
Coors

ALIAS
ESTIGATIONS

Collection Editor: **Jennifer Grünwald**
Assistant Editor: **Sarah Brunstad**
Associate Managing Editor: **Alex Starbuck**
Editor, Special Projects: **Mark D. Beazley**
Senior Editor, Special Projects: **Jeff Youngquist**
SVP Print, Sales & Marketing: **David Gabriel**
Book Designer: **Jay Bowen**

Editor in Chief: **Axel Alonso**
Chief Creative Officer: **Joe Quesada**
Publisher: **Dan Buckley**
Executive Producer: **Alan Fine**

JESSICA JONES: ALIAS VOL. 1. Contains material originally published in magazine form as ALIAS #1-9. First printing 2015. ISBN# 978-0-7851-9855-0. Published by MARVEL WORLDWIDE, INC., a subsidiary of MARVEL ENTERTAINMENT, LLC. OFFICE OF PUBLICATION: 135 West 50th Street, New York, NY 10020. Copyright © 2015 MARVEL No similarity between any of the names, characters, persons, and/or institutions in this magazine with those of any living or dead person or institution is intended, and any such similarity which may exist is purely coincidental. **Printed in the U.S.A.** ALAN FINE, President, Marvel Entertainment; DAN BUCKLEY, President, TV, Publishing and Brand Management; JOE QUESADA, Chief Creative Officer; TOM BREVOORT, SVP of Publishing; DAVID BOGART, SVP of Operations & Procurement, Publishing; C.B. CEBULSKI, VP of International Development & Brand Management; DAVID GABRIEL, SVP Print, Sales & Marketing; JIM O'KEEFE, VP of Operations & Logistics; DAN CARR, Executive Director of Publishing Technology; SUSAN CRESPI, Editorial Operations Manager; ALEX MORALES, Publishing Operations Manager; STAN LEE, Chairman Emeritus. For information regarding advertising in Marvel Comics or on Marvel.com, please contact Jonathan Rheingold, VP of Custom Solutions & Ad Sales, at jrheingold@marvel.com. For Marvel subscription inquiries, please call 800-217-3158. Manufactured between 7/10/2015 and 8/17/2015 by R.R.

JESSICA JONES:

Brian Michael Bendis
WRITER

Michael Gaydos
ARTIST

Matt Hollingsworth
COLORIST

Bill Sienkiewicz
"SIDEKICK" ART

Richard Starkings and
Comicraft's Wes Abbott & Oscar Gongora
LETTERERS

David Mack
COVER ART

Stuart Moore
EDITOR

Kelly Lamy
ASSOCIATE MANAGING EDITOR

Nanci Dakesian
MANAGING EDITOR

ALIaS CREATED BY BRIAN MICHAEL BENDIS & MICHAEL GAYDOS

FUCK.

I'm sorry, I know that may have startled some of you. Or even offended you. I didn't mean to upset you, but it is quite remarkable how a simple word — a four-letter word — can bring about such a reaction. Or, in the case of the book you are holding, a revolution.

Seeing that word on the first page and the first line of the first chapter of *Alias* wasn't the first time I had seen it in a comic book. Certainly, it wasn't the first time I had seen it in print or even heard it. So, what was the big deal?

I don't remember seeing it in a Marvel comic book.

The same folks who had thrilled me with Spider-Man and the Fantastic Four were taking me on a bold new adventure into something they called "the MAX line."

To put it simply, just as there have been G-rated and PG-rated movies in the United States for years, there are also R-rated films. These are more adult in nature, both in theme and in language. They are intended to reach out to an older audience; over 17 is the idea.

Welcome to MAX, the comic-book line for over-17-year-olds.

Alias heralded the coming of MAX and remains, in my opinion, the best of the bunch. That may or may not have something to do with the guy who has made his reputation on being something of a revolutionary himself, *Alias*'s creator and writer, Brian Michael Bendis.

If you don't know Bendis (that's what you call him), you will now. Bendis uses words the way they are meant to be in stories like these — as bullets that pierce your imagination and get stuck in your brain until he decides to operate on you with his next installment.

In *Alias*, Jessica Jones is a not-so-hardboiled detective whose life as a former super hero is both a blessing and a curse. In the opening scene, in a delightful homage to the classic film *Chinatown*, a husband finds out his wife has a secret through Jessica's detective work. Jessica isn't happy about this type of job — but like many gumshoes, it pays the bills. The scene plays much like you'd expect, but then Bendis throws you a fastball that's just his style. Oh, and you're not supposed to be able to hit Bendis's fastballs — you get hit by them.

Don't worry. Bendis goes just as hard on his characters as he will on you. Jessica's world isn't pretty. There are no capes here. No secret headquarters. Just the underbelly of the Marvel Universe cut open for all of us to be amazed by. There are twists and double crosses — and just when you think you've got it all figured out, forget it. Bendis is so far ahead of you, the only way to catch up is to turn the page — and even then, good luck.

In the 1950s, these types of tales were called "Film Noir." They were tales of bad men — and often, worse women — who started out at the bottom of the well, only to find there was much farther to fall. Bendis has created something here for Marvel we should call "comic-book noir."

His vision is executed by an extraordinary team of artists and editors. They are the filmmakers to his screenplay. Michael Gaydos pencils and inks each tale with all the grit and texture of the words, bringing life to Jessica and the less-than-lovely city in which she works. Matt Hollingsworth's colors then enhance the mood, drowning you in somber tones that match the images with perfection. Richard Starkings and Comicraft's Wes Abbott carve out Bendis's words so neatly, you almost can hear him reading them to you. Or barking at you, as the case may be. And it's all kept under the watchful eyes of editors Stuart Moore, Kelly Lamy and Nanci Dakesian.

Like I said, *Alias* isn't pretty. But it sure as hell is fun.

Welcome to the Revolution!

Jeph Loeb

Jeph Loeb
Los Angeles, 2002

JEPH LOEB IS AN EMMY AWARD-NOMINATED AND EISNER AWARD-WINNING WRITER/PRODUCER. IN TELEVISION, HIS MANY CREDITS INCLUDE *MARVEL'S AGENTS OF S.H.I.E.L.D.*, *HEROES*, *LOST* AND *SMALLVILLE*; AND IN FILM, *TEEN WOLF* AND *COMMANDO*. JEPH HAS WRITTEN NEARLY EVERY MAJOR COMICS ICON INCLUDING THE AVENGERS, HULK, IRON MAN, SPIDER-MAN, CAPTAIN AMERICA, BATMAN AND SUPERMAN. SINCE 2010, HE HAS BEEN MARVEL'S EXECUTIVE VICE PRESIDENT, HEAD OF TELEVISION, AND HE IS EXECUTIVE PRODUCING FIVE SERIES FOR NETFLIX INCLUDING *JESSICA JONES*.

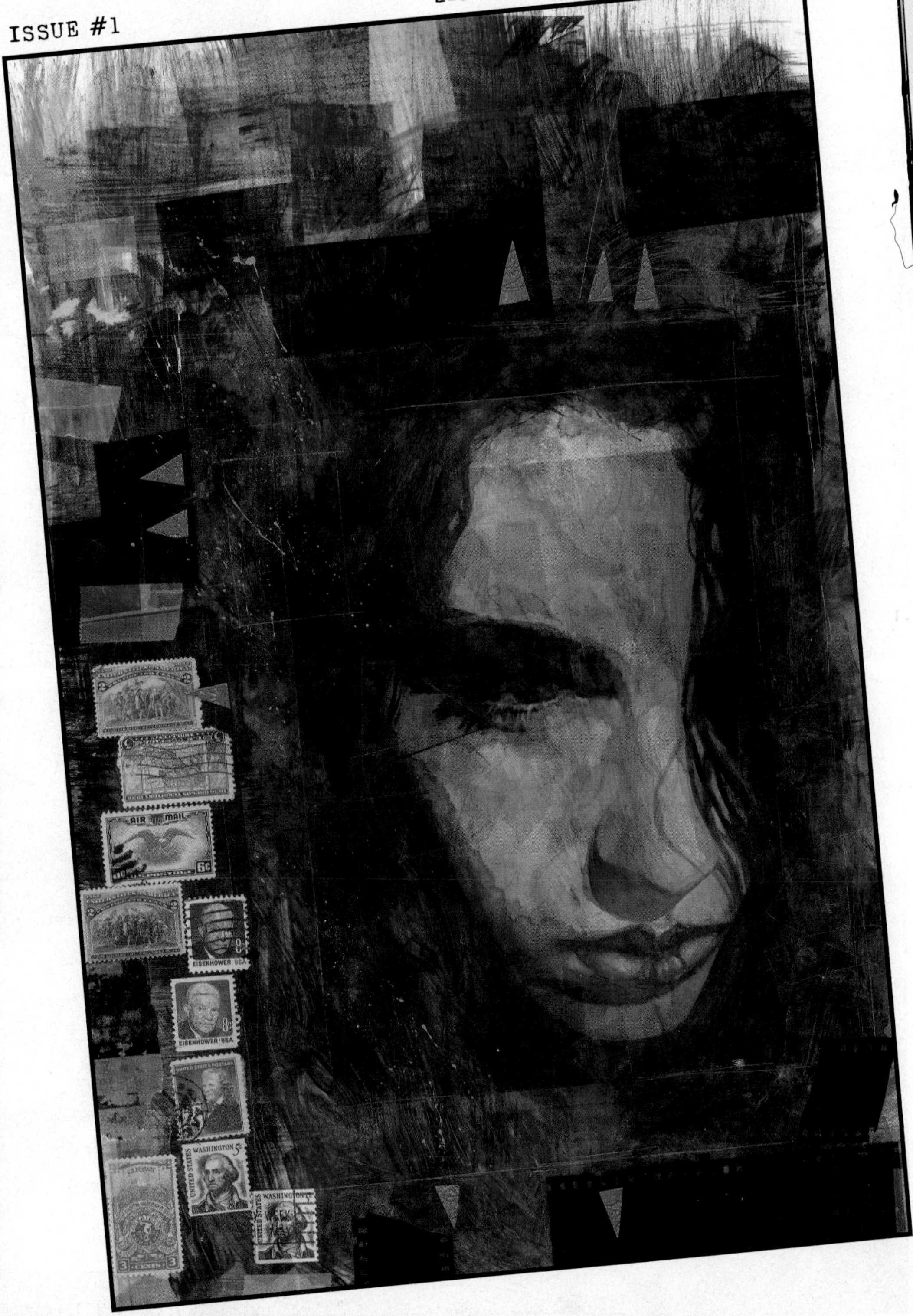

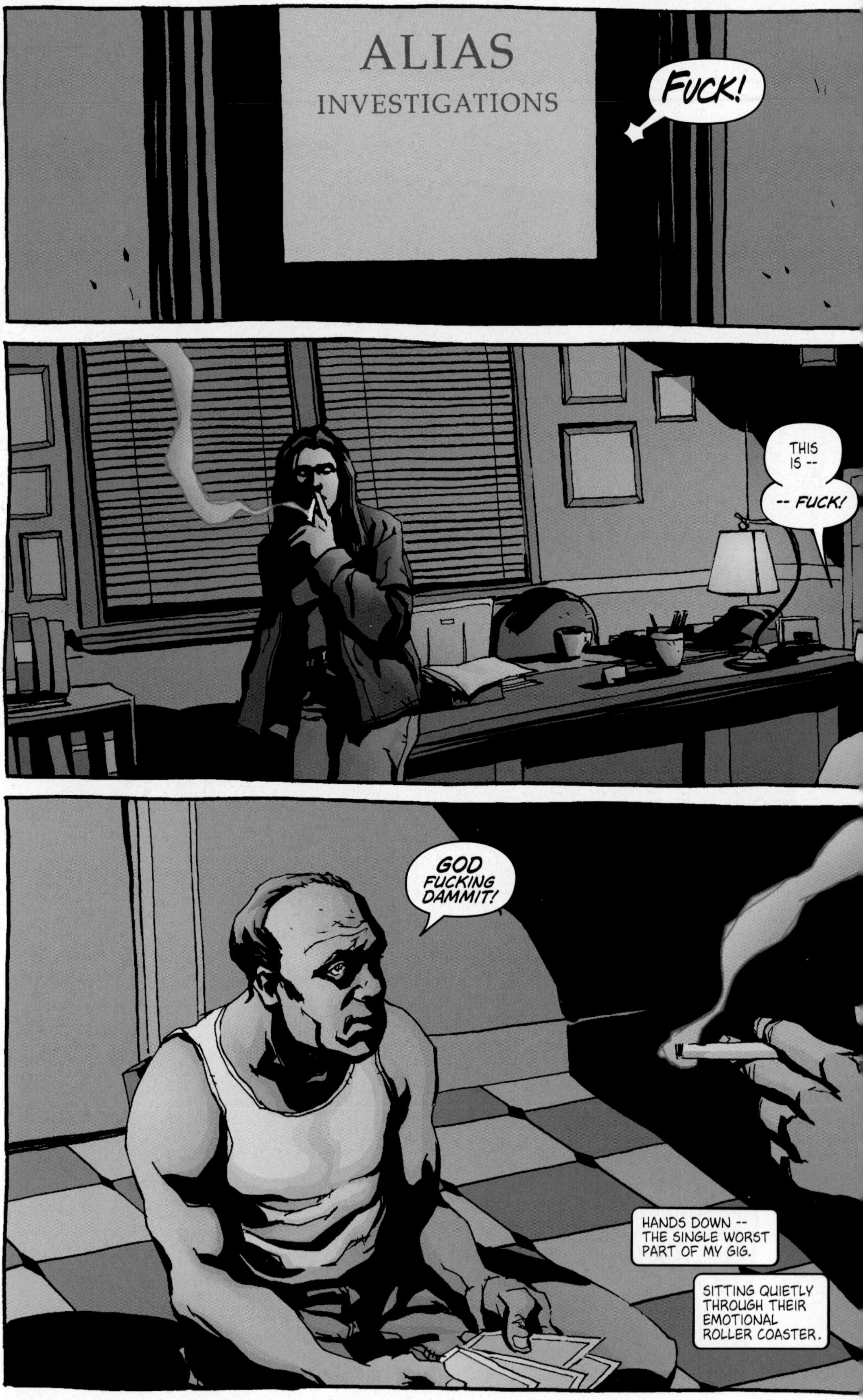

ALIAS
INVESTIGATIONS
FUCK!
THIS IS --
-- FUCK!
GOD FUCKING DAMMIT!
HANDS DOWN -- THE SINGLE WORST PART OF MY GIG.
SITTING QUIETLY THROUGH THEIR EMOTIONAL ROLLER COASTER.

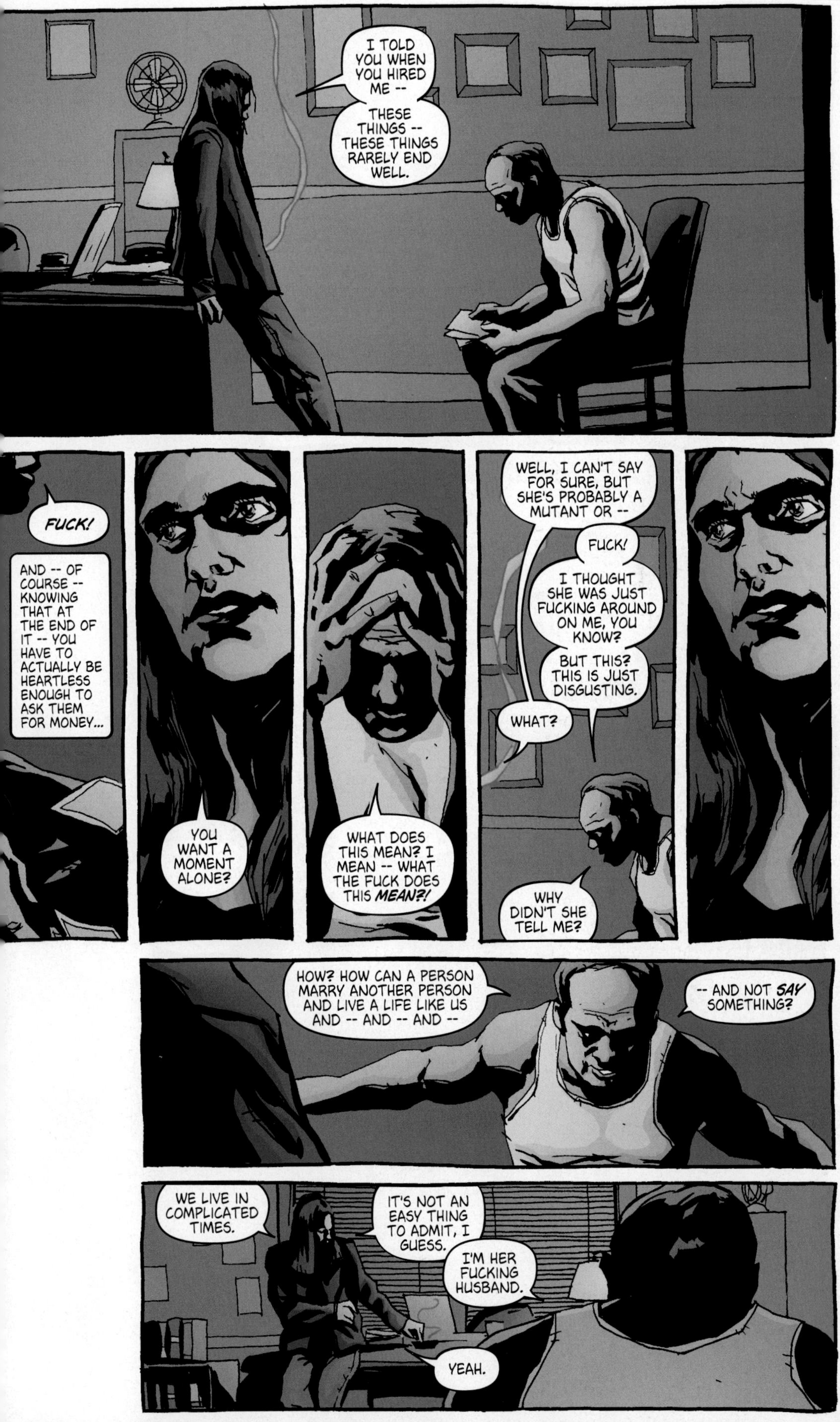
I TOLD YOU WHEN YOU HIRED ME --
THESE THINGS -- THESE THINGS RARELY END WELL.
FUCK!
AND -- OF COURSE -- KNOWING THAT AT THE END OF IT -- YOU HAVE TO ACTUALLY BE HEARTLESS ENOUGH TO ASK THEM FOR MONEY...
YOU WANT A MOMENT ALONE?
WHAT DOES THIS MEAN? I MEAN -- WHAT THE FUCK DOES THIS *MEAN?!*
WELL, I CAN'T SAY FOR SURE, BUT SHE'S PROBABLY A MUTANT OR --
FUCK!
I THOUGHT SHE WAS JUST FUCKING AROUND ON ME, YOU KNOW?
BUT THIS? THIS IS JUST DISGUSTING.
WHAT?
WHY DIDN'T SHE TELL ME?
HOW? HOW CAN A PERSON MARRY ANOTHER PERSON AND LIVE A LIFE LIKE US AND -- AND -- AND --
-- AND NOT *SAY* SOMETHING?
WE LIVE IN COMPLICATED TIMES.
IT'S NOT AN EASY THING TO ADMIT, I GUESS.
I'M HER FUCKING HUSBAND.
YEAH.

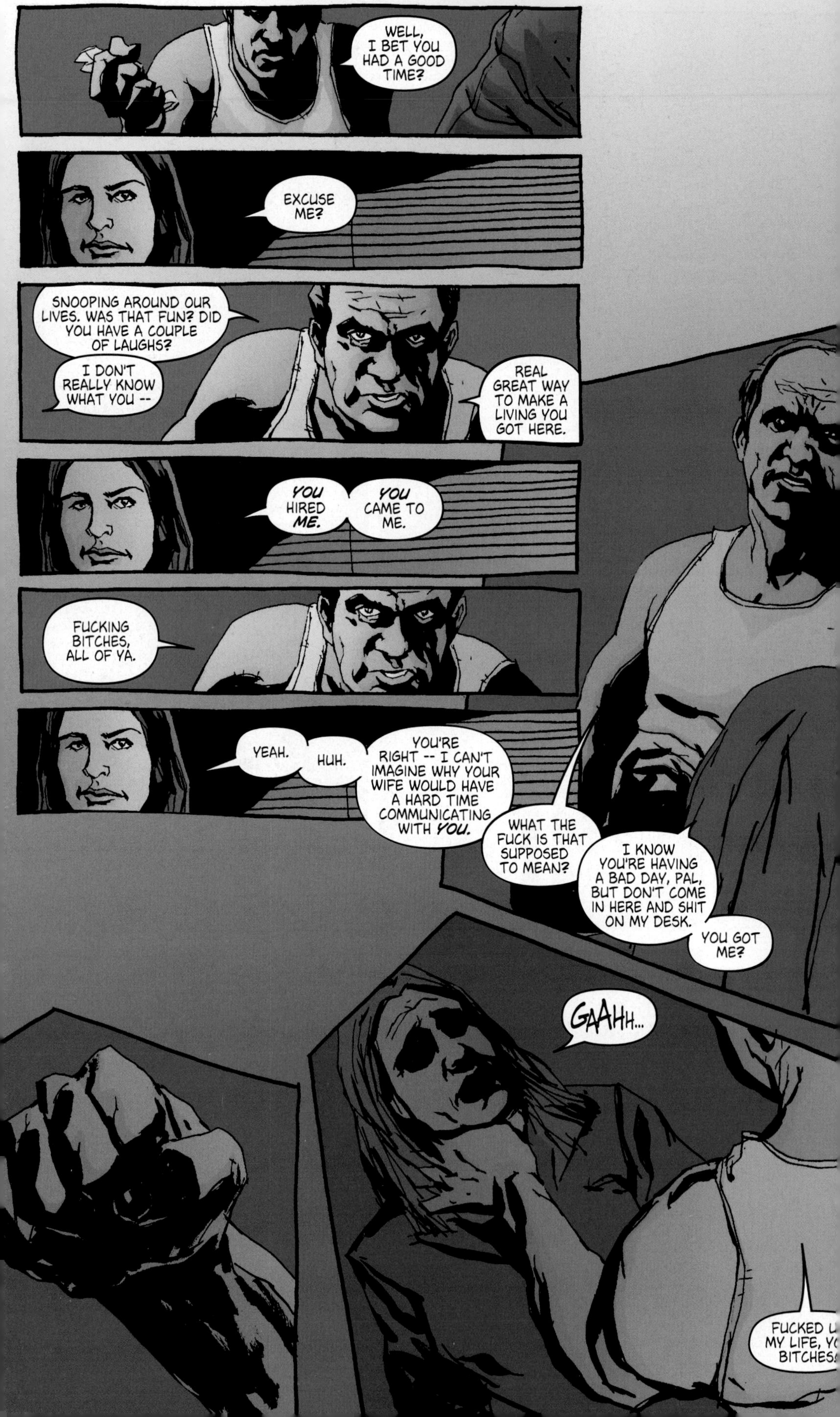
WELL, I BET YOU HAD A GOOD TIME?
EXCUSE ME?
SNOOPING AROUND OUR LIVES. WAS THAT FUN? DID YOU HAVE A COUPLE OF LAUGHS?
I DON'T REALLY KNOW WHAT YOU --
REAL GREAT WAY TO MAKE A LIVING YOU GOT HERE.
YOU HIRED ME.
YOU CAME TO ME.
FUCKING BITCHES, ALL OF YA.
YEAH.
HUH.
YOU'RE RIGHT -- I CAN'T IMAGINE WHY YOUR WIFE WOULD HAVE A HARD TIME COMMUNICATING WITH YOU.
WHAT THE FUCK IS THAT SUPPOSED TO MEAN?
I KNOW YOU'RE HAVING A BAD DAY, PAL, BUT DON'T COME IN HERE AND SHIT ON MY DESK.
YOU GOT ME?
GAAHH...

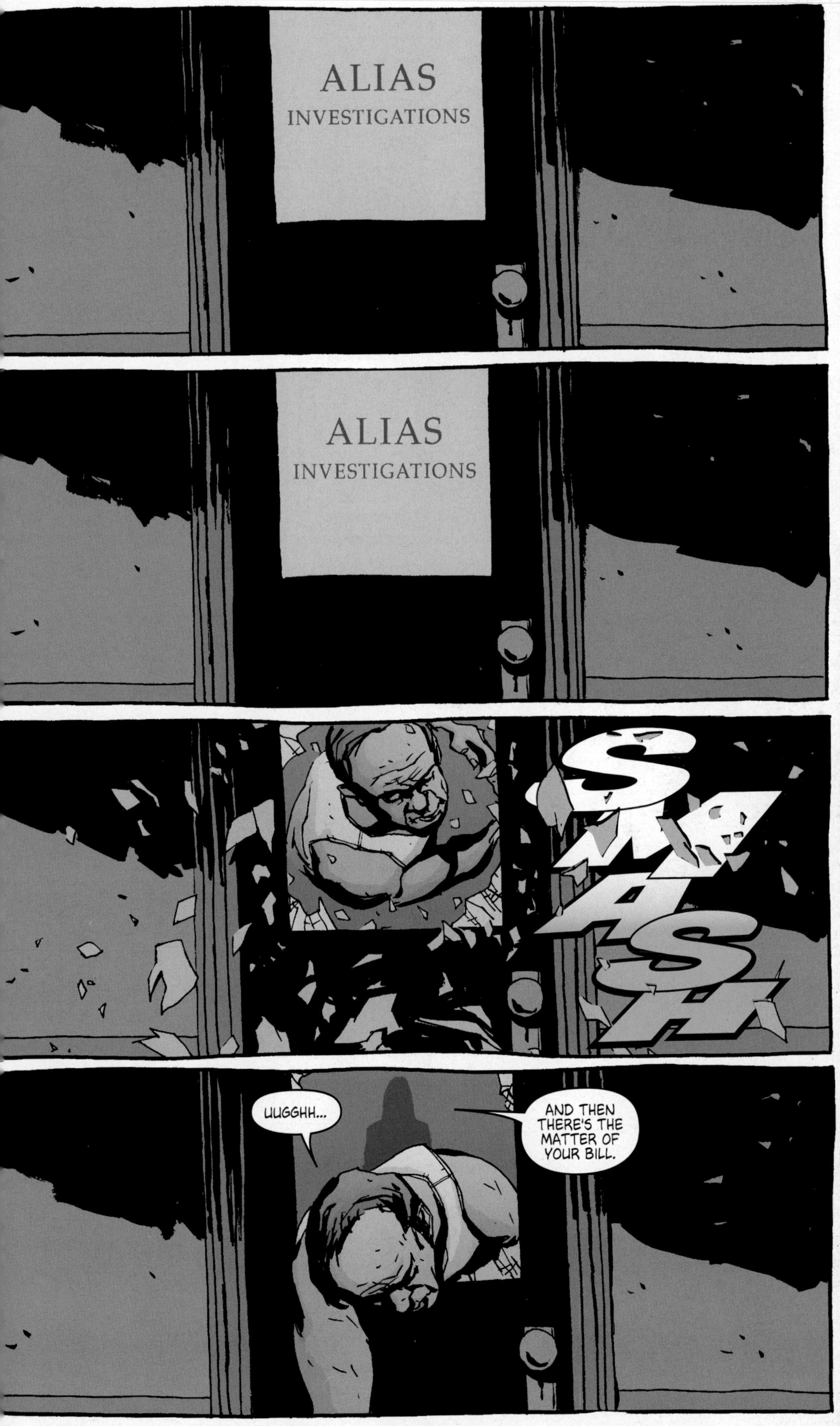
ALIAS
INVESTIGATIONS
ALIAS
INVESTIGATIONS
SMASH
UUGGHH...
AND THEN THERE'S THE MATTER OF YOUR BILL.

AND YOU ARE JESSICA JONES?

YES.

ANYONE ELSE WORK HERE?

NO.

YOU KNOW, YOU CAN'T GO TOSSING GUYS THROUGH WINDOWS.

I WASN'T AIMING.

I WAS JUST TRYING TO, YOU KNOW, NOT GET HIT IN THE FACE.

GUY HIRED YOU -- THEN ATTACKED YOU?

I FOUND OUT SOMETHING ABOUT HIS WIFE FOR HIM.

HE DIDN'T LIKE WHAT HE HEARD.

I ASSUME ALL YOUR LICENSES AND PAPERWORK ARE IN ORDER.

YEAH. OF COURSE.

HEY, YOU KNOW THEM OR SOMETHING?

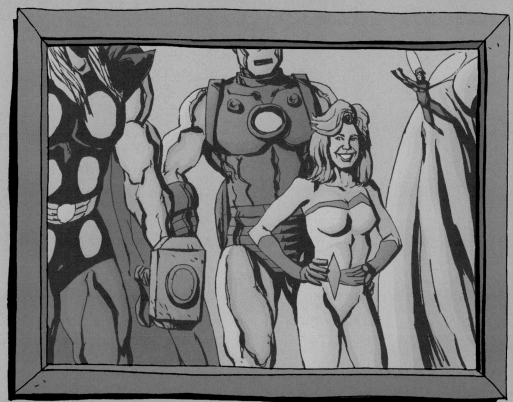

USED TO.

NO SHIT.

WHICH ONE?

IS THAT YOU?

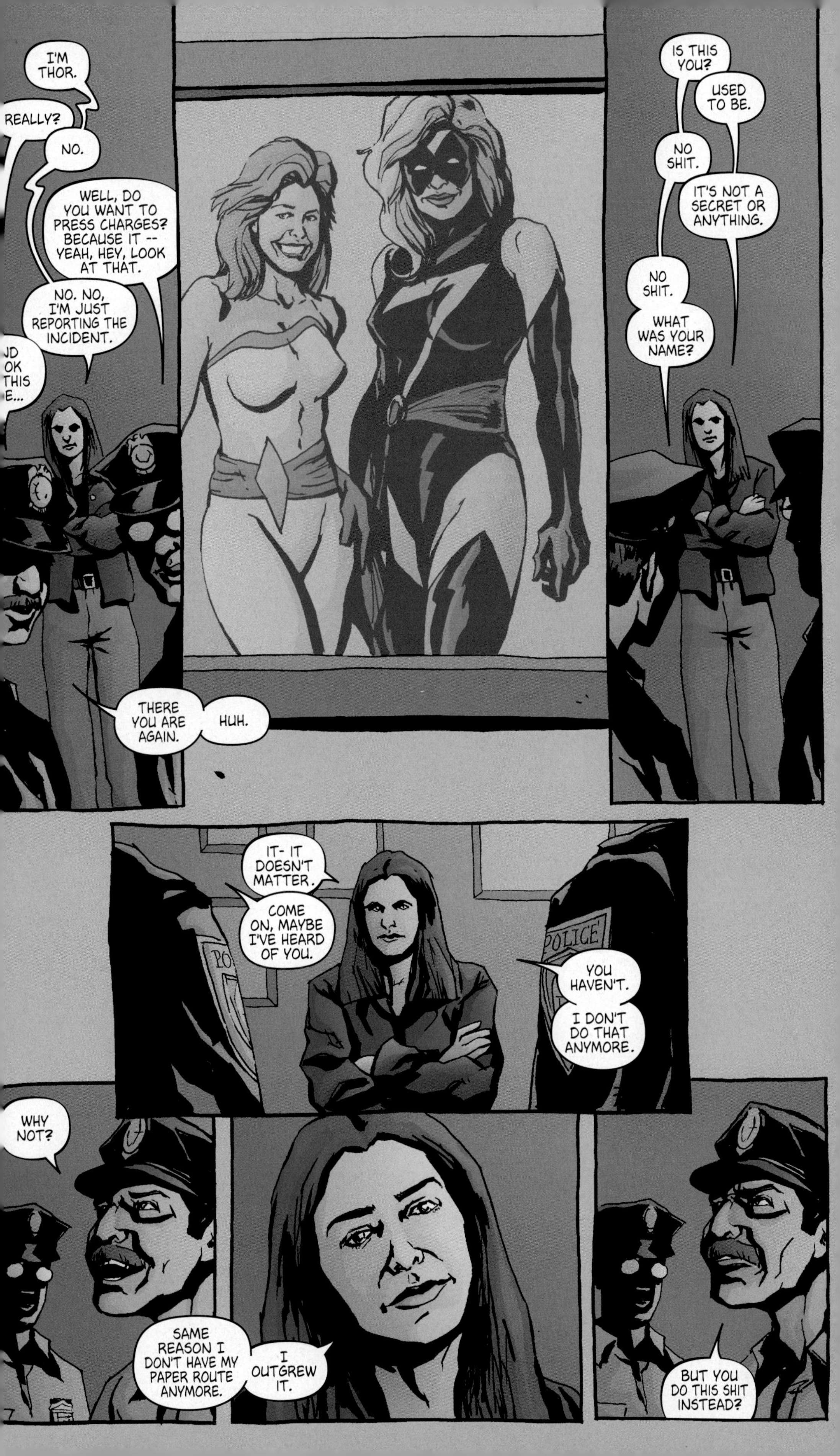

I'M THOR.
REALLY?
NO.
WELL, DO YOU WANT TO PRESS CHARGES? BECAUSE IT -- YEAH, HEY, LOOK AT THAT.
NO. NO, I'M JUST REPORTING THE INCIDENT.
THERE YOU ARE AGAIN.
HUH.
IS THIS YOU?
USED TO BE.
NO SHIT.
IT'S NOT A SECRET OR ANYTHING.
NO SHIT.
WHAT WAS YOUR NAME?
IT- IT DOESN'T MATTER.
COME ON, MAYBE I'VE HEARD OF YOU.
POLICE
YOU HAVEN'T.
I DON'T DO THAT ANYMORE.
WHY NOT?
SAME REASON I DON'T HAVE MY PAPER ROUTE ANYMORE.
I OUTGREW IT.
BUT YOU DO THIS SHIT INSTEAD?

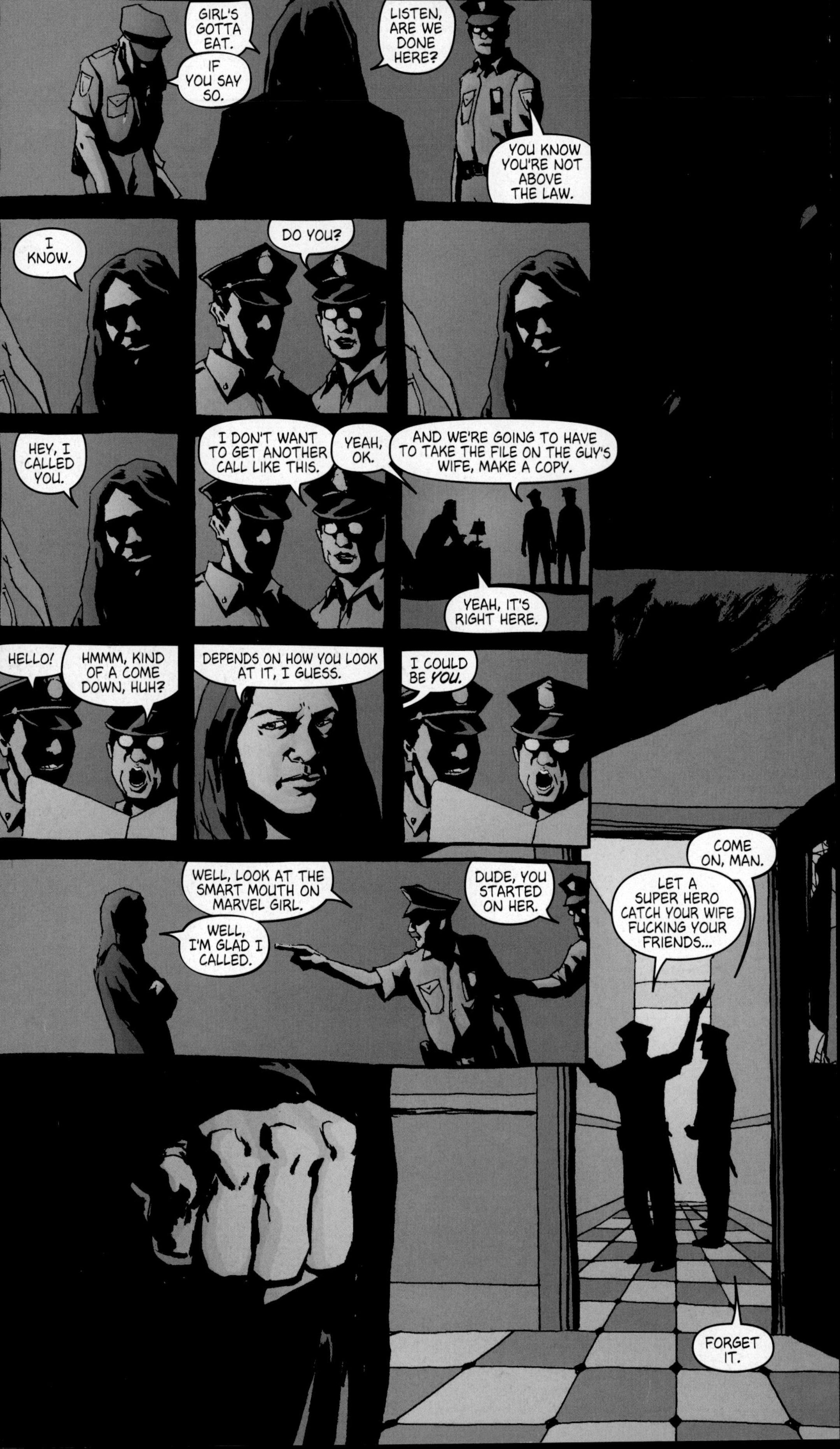
GIRL'S GOTTA EAT.
IF YOU SAY SO.
LISTEN, ARE WE DONE HERE?
YOU KNOW YOU'RE NOT ABOVE THE LAW.
I KNOW.
DO YOU?
HEY, I CALLED YOU.
I DON'T WANT TO GET ANOTHER CALL LIKE THIS.
YEAH, OK.
AND WE'RE GOING TO HAVE TO TAKE THE FILE ON THE GUY'S WIFE, MAKE A COPY.
YEAH, IT'S RIGHT HERE.
HELLO!
HMMM, KIND OF A COME DOWN, HUH?
DEPENDS ON HOW YOU LOOK AT IT, I GUESS.
I COULD BE YOU.
WELL, LOOK AT THE SMART MOUTH ON MARVEL GIRL.
WELL, I'M GLAD I CALLED.
DUDE, YOU STARTED ON HER.
COME ON, MAN.
LET A SUPER HERO CATCH YOUR WIFE FUCKING YOUR FRIENDS...
FORGET IT.

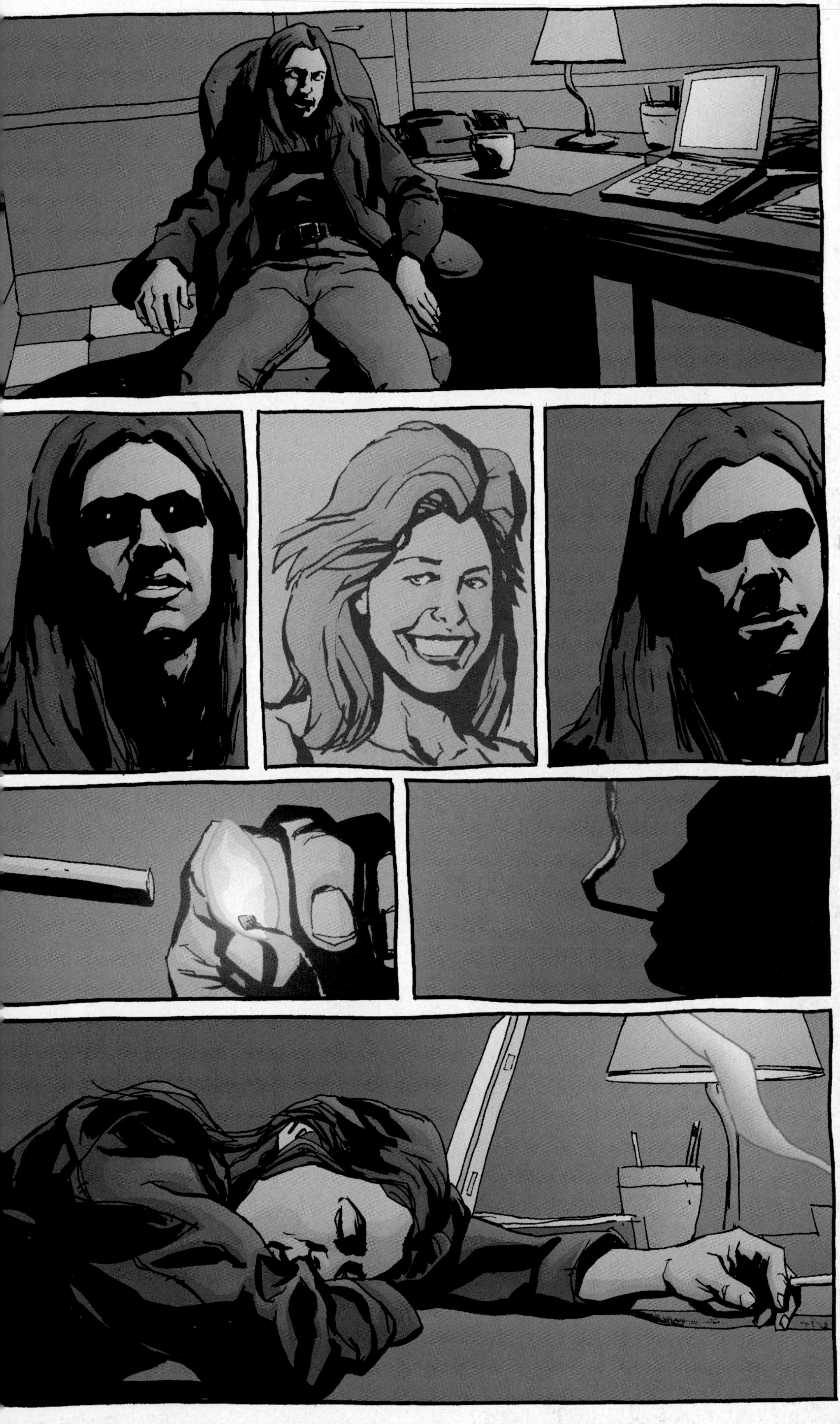

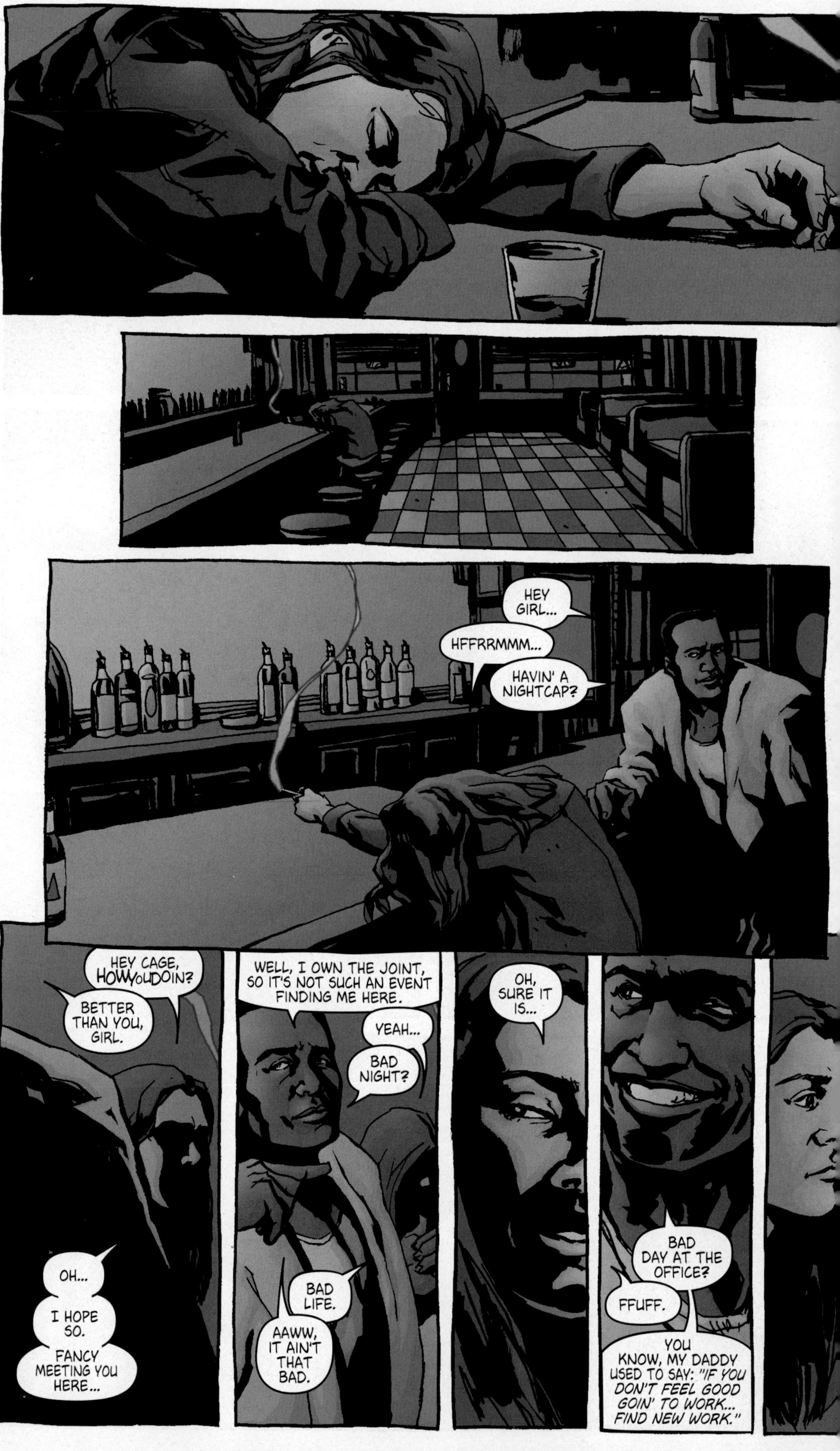

HEY GIRL...
HFFRRMMM...
HAVIN' A NIGHTCAP?
HEY CAGE, HOWYOUDOIN?
BETTER THAN YOU, GIRL.
OH...
I HOPE SO.
FANCY MEETING YOU HERE...
WELL, I OWN THE JOINT, SO IT'S NOT SUCH AN EVENT FINDING ME HERE.
YEAH...
BAD NIGHT?
BAD LIFE.
AAWW, IT AIN'T THAT BAD.
OH, SURE IT IS...
BAD DAY AT THE OFFICE?
FFUFF.
YOU KNOW, MY DADDY USED TO SAY: "IF YOU DON'T FEEL GOOD GOIN' TO WORK... FIND NEW WORK."

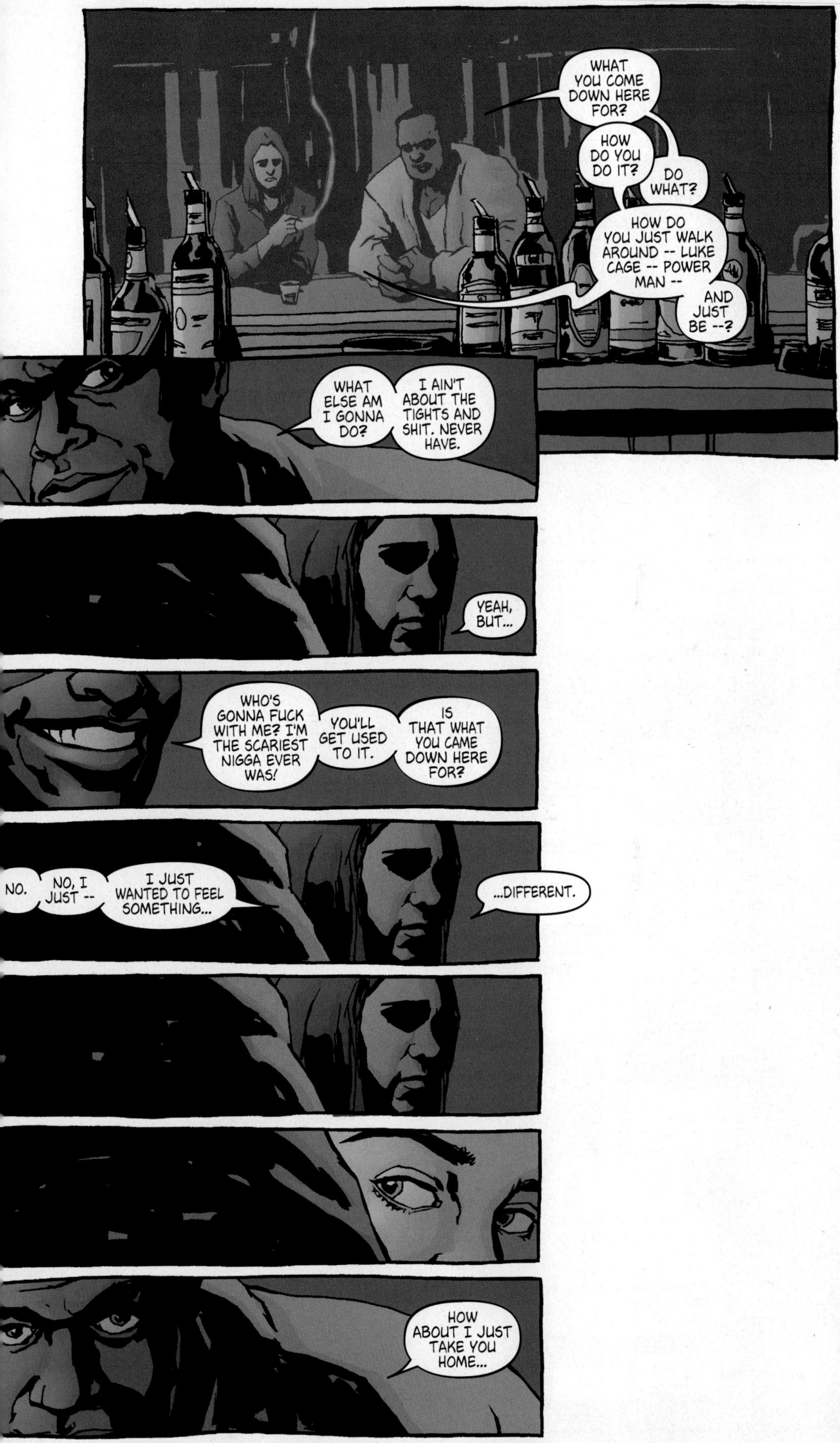
WHAT YOU COME DOWN HERE FOR?
HOW DO YOU DO IT?
DO WHAT?
HOW DO YOU JUST WALK AROUND -- LUKE CAGE -- POWER MAN --
AND JUST BE --?
WHAT ELSE AM I GONNA DO?
I AIN'T ABOUT THE TIGHTS AND SHIT. NEVER HAVE.
YEAH, BUT...
WHO'S GONNA FUCK WITH ME? I'M THE SCARIEST NIGGA EVER WAS!
YOU'LL GET USED TO IT.
IS THAT WHAT YOU CAME DOWN HERE FOR?
NO.
NO, I JUST --
I JUST WANTED TO FEEL SOMETHING...
...DIFFERENT.
HOW ABOUT I JUST TAKE YOU HOME...

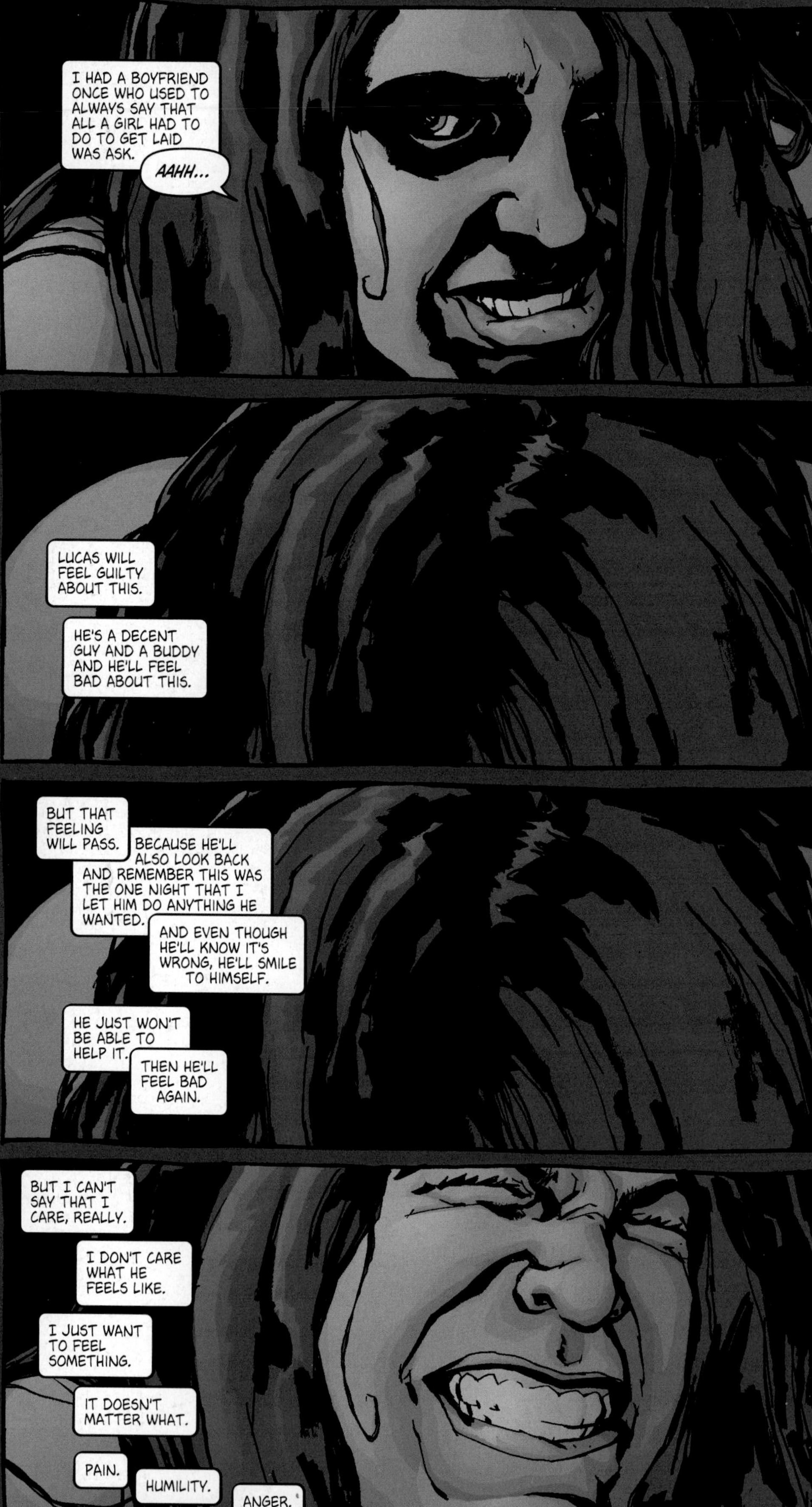
I HAD A BOYFRIEND ONCE WHO USED TO ALWAYS SAY THAT ALL A GIRL HAD TO DO TO GET LAID WAS ASK.
AAHH...
LUCAS WILL FEEL GUILTY ABOUT THIS.
HE'S A DECENT GUY AND A BUDDY AND HE'LL FEEL BAD ABOUT THIS.
BUT THAT FEELING WILL PASS.
BECAUSE HE'LL ALSO LOOK BACK AND REMEMBER THIS WAS THE ONE NIGHT THAT I LET HIM DO ANYTHING HE WANTED.
AND EVEN THOUGH HE'LL KNOW IT'S WRONG, HE'LL SMILE TO HIMSELF.
HE JUST WON'T BE ABLE TO HELP IT.
THEN HE'LL FEEL BAD AGAIN.
BUT I CAN'T SAY THAT I CARE, REALLY.
I DON'T CARE WHAT HE FEELS LIKE.
I JUST WANT TO FEEL SOMETHING.
IT DOESN'T MATTER WHAT.
PAIN.
HUMILITY.
ANGER.

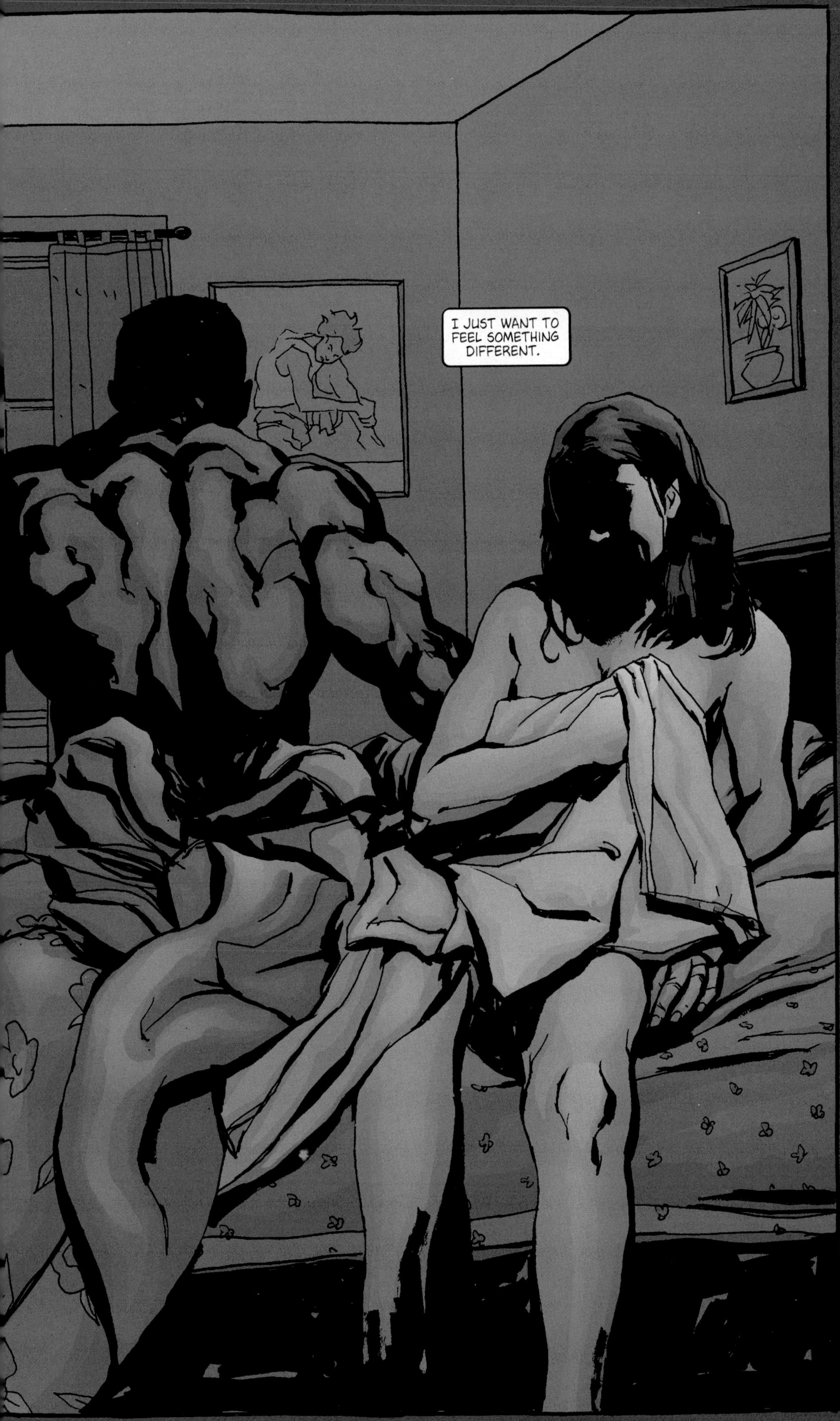
I JUST WANT TO FEEL SOMETHING DIFFERENT.

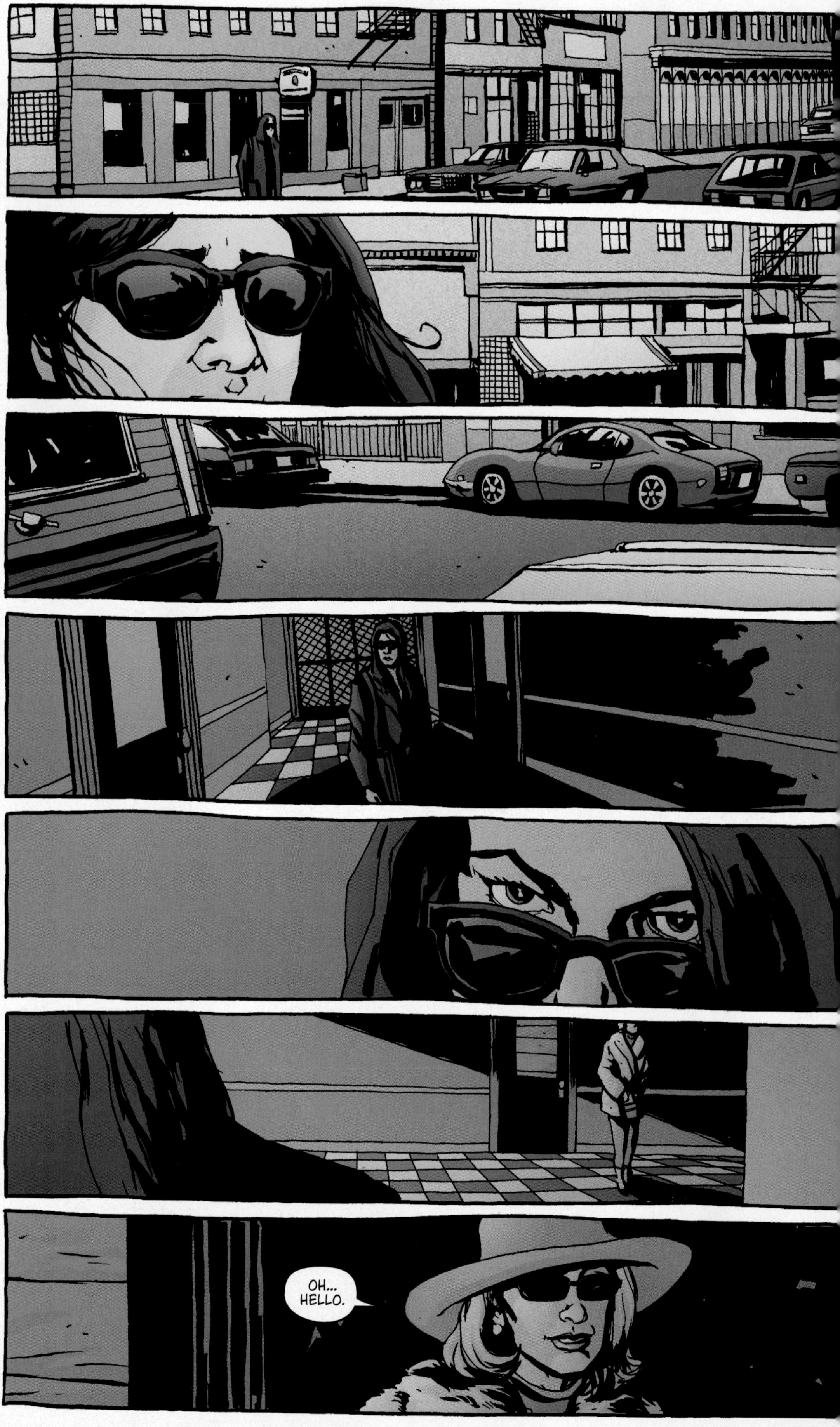
OH... HELLO.

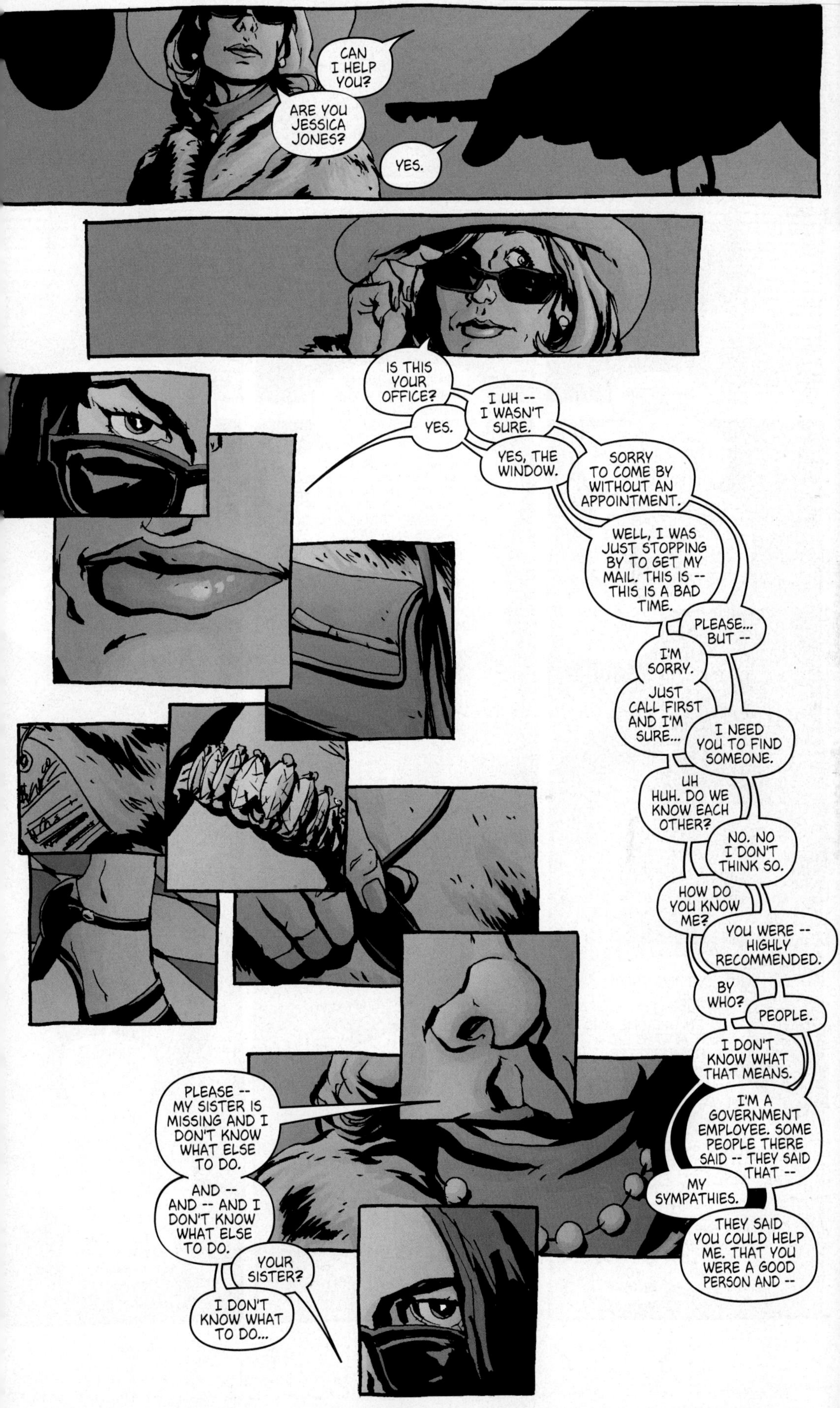
CAN I HELP YOU?
ARE YOU JESSICA JONES?
YES.
IS THIS YOUR OFFICE?
YES.
I UH -- I WASN'T SURE.
YES, THE WINDOW.
SORRY TO COME BY WITHOUT AN APPOINTMENT.
WELL, I WAS JUST STOPPING BY TO GET MY MAIL. THIS IS -- THIS IS A BAD TIME.
PLEASE... BUT --
I'M SORRY.
JUST CALL FIRST AND I'M SURE...
I NEED YOU TO FIND SOMEONE.
UH HUH. DO WE KNOW EACH OTHER?
NO. NO I DON'T THINK SO.
HOW DO YOU KNOW ME?
YOU WERE -- HIGHLY RECOMMENDED.
BY WHO?
PEOPLE.
I DON'T KNOW WHAT THAT MEANS.
I'M A GOVERNMENT EMPLOYEE. SOME PEOPLE THERE SAID -- THEY SAID THAT --
MY SYMPATHIES.
THEY SAID YOU COULD HELP ME. THAT YOU WERE A GOOD PERSON AND --
PLEASE -- MY SISTER IS MISSING AND I DON'T KNOW WHAT ELSE TO DO.
AND -- AND -- AND I DON'T KNOW WHAT ELSE TO DO.
YOUR SISTER?
I DON'T KNOW WHAT TO DO...

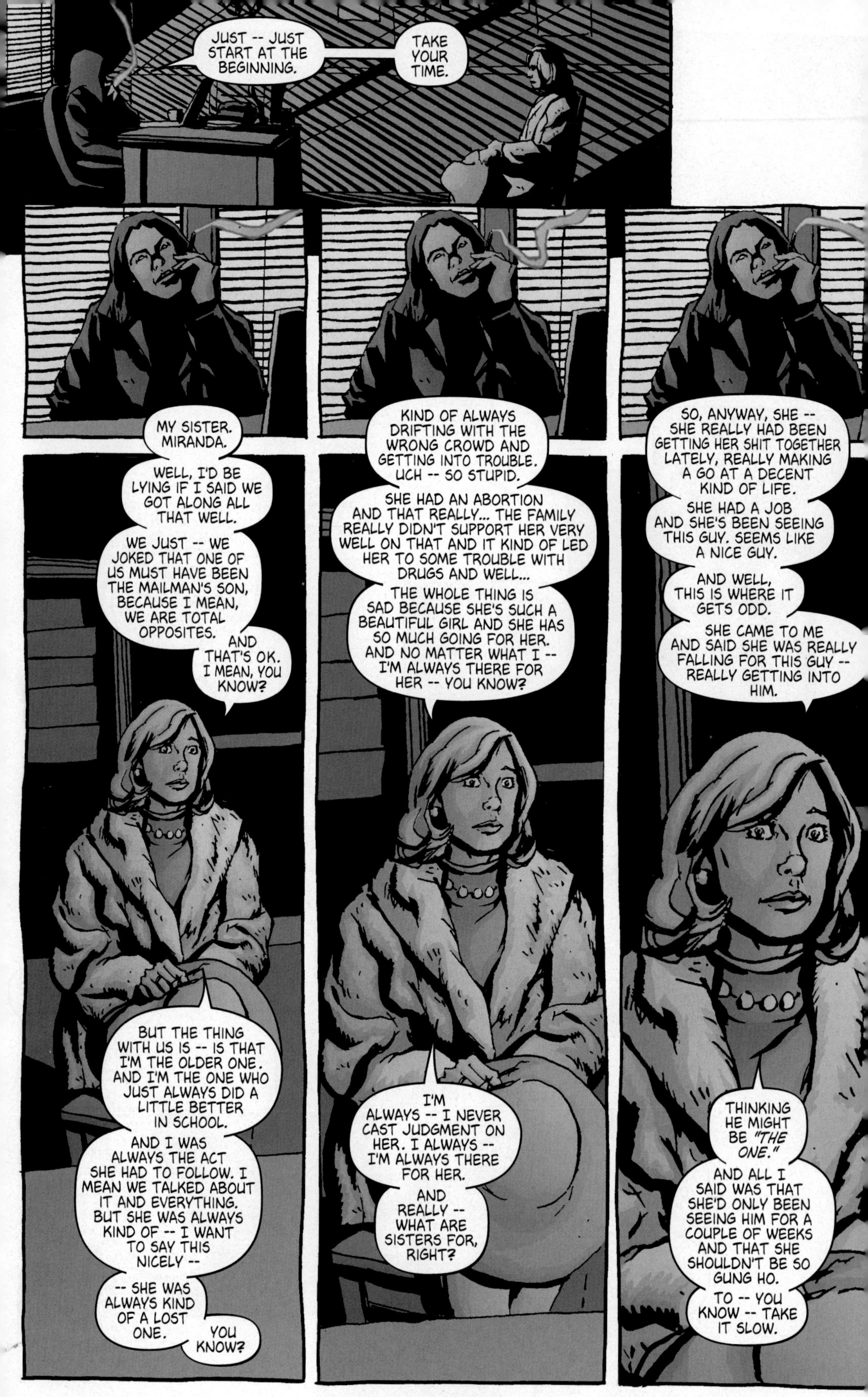

JUST -- JUST START AT THE BEGINNING.
TAKE YOUR TIME.
MY SISTER. MIRANDA.
WELL, I'D BE LYING IF I SAID WE GOT ALONG ALL THAT WELL.
WE JUST -- WE JOKED THAT ONE OF US MUST HAVE BEEN THE MAILMAN'S SON, BECAUSE I MEAN, WE ARE TOTAL OPPOSITES.
AND THAT'S OK. I MEAN, YOU KNOW?
BUT THE THING WITH US IS -- IS THAT I'M THE OLDER ONE. AND I'M THE ONE WHO JUST ALWAYS DID A LITTLE BETTER IN SCHOOL.
AND I WAS ALWAYS THE ACT SHE HAD TO FOLLOW. I MEAN WE TALKED ABOUT IT AND EVERYTHING. BUT SHE WAS ALWAYS KIND OF -- I WANT TO SAY THIS NICELY --
-- SHE WAS ALWAYS KIND OF A LOST ONE.
YOU KNOW?
KIND OF ALWAYS DRIFTING WITH THE WRONG CROWD AND GETTING INTO TROUBLE. UCH -- SO STUPID.
SHE HAD AN ABORTION AND THAT REALLY... THE FAMILY REALLY DIDN'T SUPPORT HER VERY WELL ON THAT AND IT KIND OF LED HER TO SOME TROUBLE WITH DRUGS AND WELL...
THE WHOLE THING IS SAD BECAUSE SHE'S SUCH A BEAUTIFUL GIRL AND SHE HAS SO MUCH GOING FOR HER. AND NO MATTER WHAT I -- I'M ALWAYS THERE FOR HER -- YOU KNOW?
I'M ALWAYS -- I NEVER CAST JUDGMENT ON HER. I ALWAYS -- I'M ALWAYS THERE FOR HER.
AND REALLY -- WHAT ARE SISTERS FOR, RIGHT?
SO, ANYWAY, SHE -- SHE REALLY HAD BEEN GETTING HER SHIT TOGETHER LATELY, REALLY MAKING A GO AT A DECENT KIND OF LIFE.
SHE HAD A JOB AND SHE'S BEEN SEEING THIS GUY. SEEMS LIKE A NICE GUY.
AND WELL, THIS IS WHERE IT GETS ODD.
SHE CAME TO ME AND SAID SHE WAS REALLY FALLING FOR THIS GUY -- REALLY GETTING INTO HIM.
THINKING HE MIGHT BE *"THE ONE."*
AND ALL I SAID WAS THAT SHE'D ONLY BEEN SEEING HIM FOR A COUPLE OF WEEKS AND THAT SHE SHOULDN'T BE SO GUNG HO.
TO -- YOU KNOW -- TAKE IT SLOW.

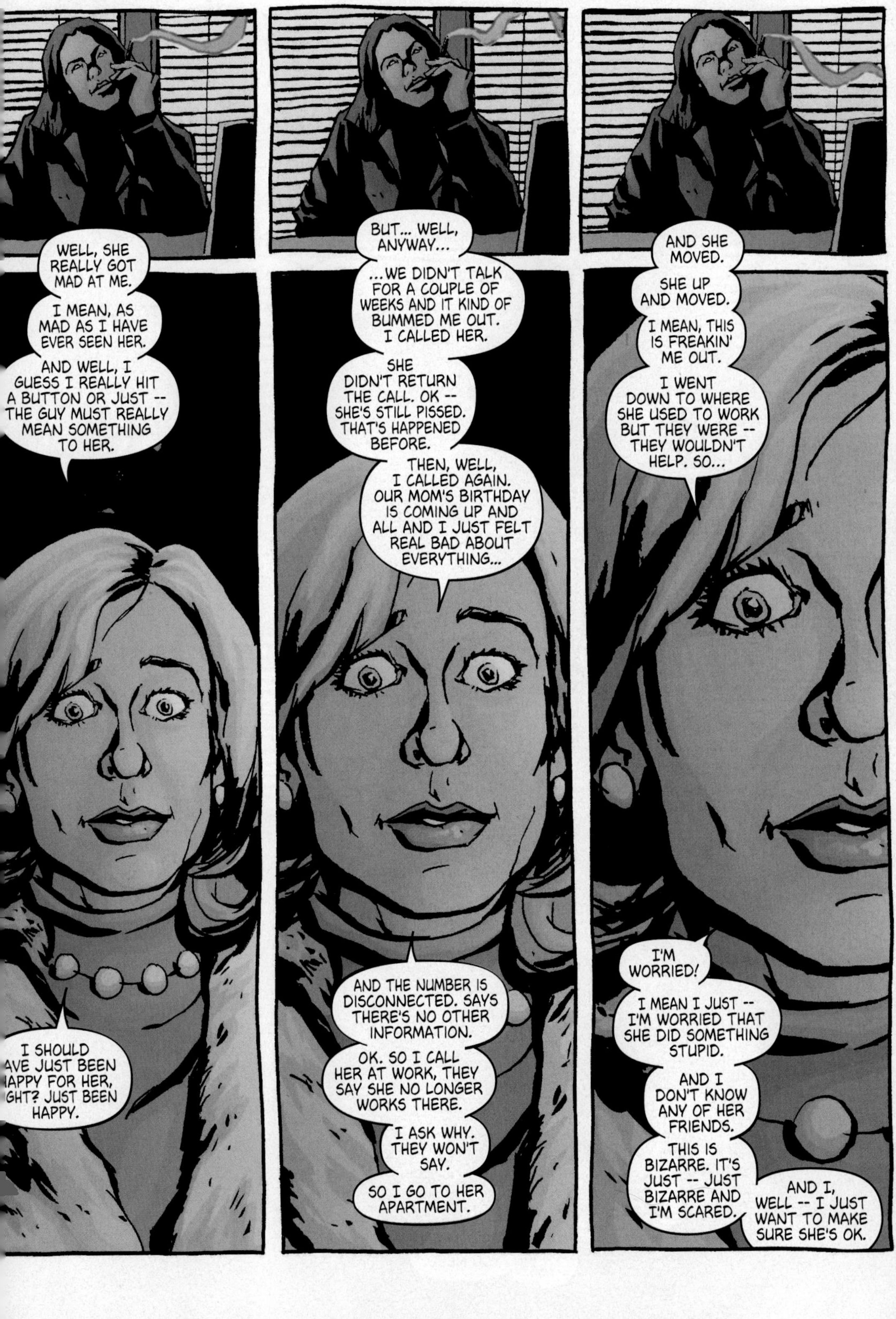
WELL, SHE REALLY GOT MAD AT ME.
I MEAN, AS MAD AS I HAVE EVER SEEN HER.
AND WELL, I GUESS I REALLY HIT A BUTTON OR JUST -- THE GUY MUST REALLY MEAN SOMETHING TO HER.
I SHOULD AVE JUST BEEN APPY FOR HER, GHT? JUST BEEN HAPPY.
BUT... WELL, ANYWAY...
...WE DIDN'T TALK FOR A COUPLE OF WEEKS AND IT KIND OF BUMMED ME OUT. I CALLED HER.
SHE DIDN'T RETURN THE CALL. OK -- SHE'S STILL PISSED. THAT'S HAPPENED BEFORE.
THEN, WELL, I CALLED AGAIN. OUR MOM'S BIRTHDAY IS COMING UP AND ALL AND I JUST FELT REAL BAD ABOUT EVERYTHING...
AND THE NUMBER IS DISCONNECTED. SAYS THERE'S NO OTHER INFORMATION.
OK. SO I CALL HER AT WORK, THEY SAY SHE NO LONGER WORKS THERE.
I ASK WHY. THEY WON'T SAY.
SO I GO TO HER APARTMENT.
AND SHE MOVED.
SHE UP AND MOVED.
I MEAN, THIS IS FREAKIN' ME OUT.
I WENT DOWN TO WHERE SHE USED TO WORK BUT THEY WERE -- THEY WOULDN'T HELP. SO...
I'M WORRIED!
I MEAN I JUST -- I'M WORRIED THAT SHE DID SOMETHING STUPID.
AND I DON'T KNOW ANY OF HER FRIENDS.
THIS IS BIZARRE. IT'S JUST -- JUST BIZARRE AND I'M SCARED.
AND I, WELL -- I JUST WANT TO MAKE SURE SHE'S OK.

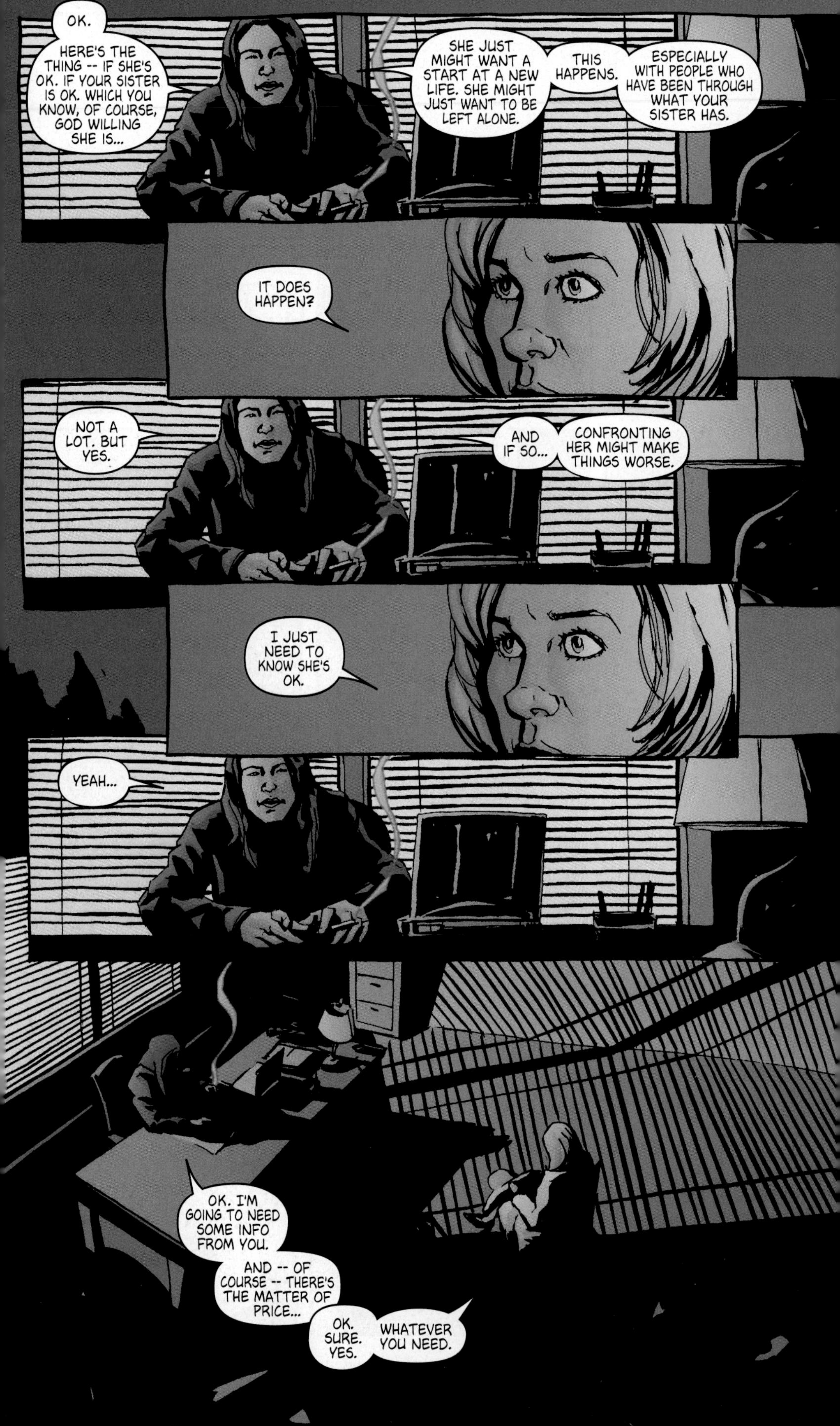
OK.
HERE'S THE THING -- IF SHE'S OK. IF YOUR SISTER IS OK. WHICH YOU KNOW, OF COURSE, GOD WILLING SHE IS...
SHE JUST MIGHT WANT A START AT A NEW LIFE. SHE MIGHT JUST WANT TO BE LEFT ALONE.
THIS HAPPENS.
ESPECIALLY WITH PEOPLE WHO HAVE BEEN THROUGH WHAT YOUR SISTER HAS.
IT DOES HAPPEN?
NOT A LOT. BUT YES.
AND IF SO...
CONFRONTING HER MIGHT MAKE THINGS WORSE.
I JUST NEED TO KNOW SHE'S OK.
YEAH...
OK. I'M GOING TO NEED SOME INFO FROM YOU.
AND -- OF COURSE -- THERE'S THE MATTER OF PRICE...
OK. SURE. YES.
WHATEVER YOU NEED.

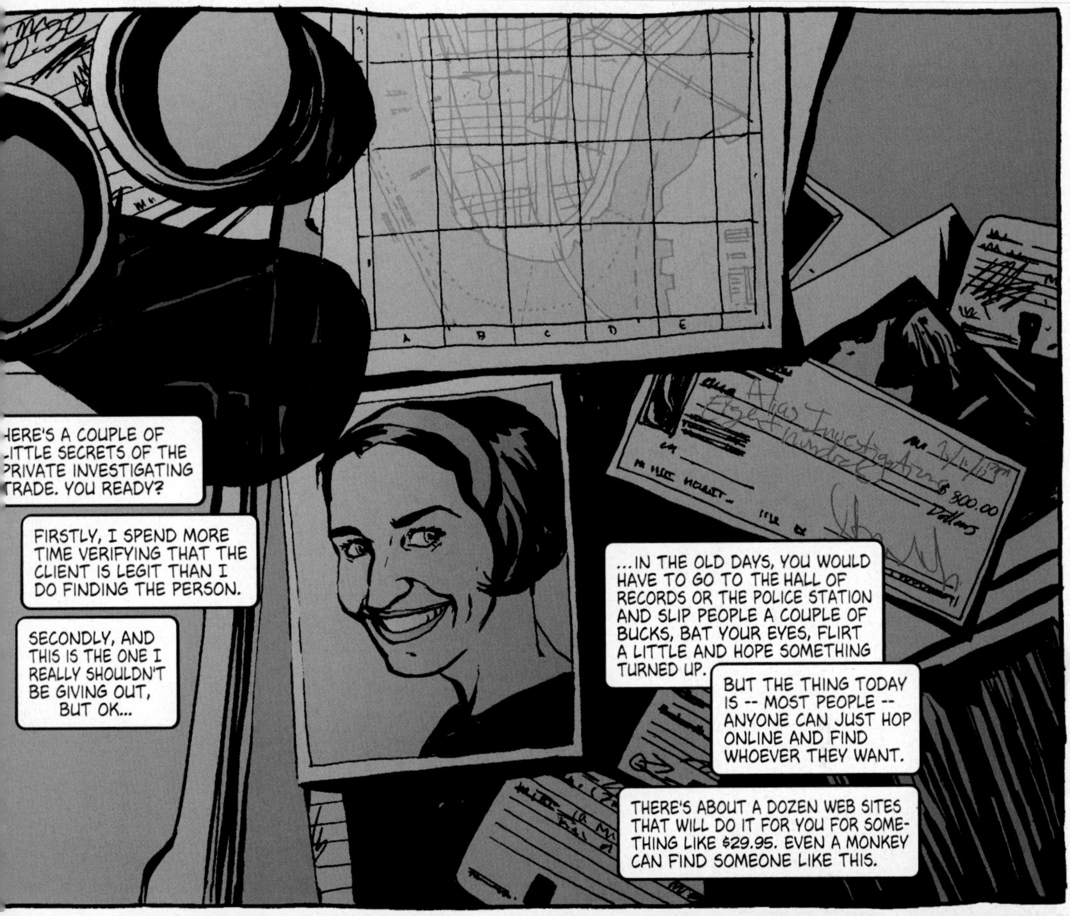
HERE'S A COUPLE OF LITTLE SECRETS OF THE PRIVATE INVESTIGATING TRADE. YOU READY?
FIRSTLY, I SPEND MORE TIME VERIFYING THAT THE CLIENT IS LEGIT THAN I DO FINDING THE PERSON.
SECONDLY, AND THIS IS THE ONE I REALLY SHOULDN'T BE GIVING OUT, BUT OK...
...IN THE OLD DAYS, YOU WOULD HAVE TO GO TO THE HALL OF RECORDS OR THE POLICE STATION AND SLIP PEOPLE A COUPLE OF BUCKS, BAT YOUR EYES, FLIRT A LITTLE AND HOPE SOMETHING TURNED UP.
BUT THE THING TODAY IS -- MOST PEOPLE -- ANYONE CAN JUST HOP ONLINE AND FIND WHOEVER THEY WANT.
THERE'S ABOUT A DOZEN WEB SITES THAT WILL DO IT FOR YOU FOR SOMETHING LIKE $29.95. EVEN A MONKEY CAN FIND SOMEONE LIKE THIS.

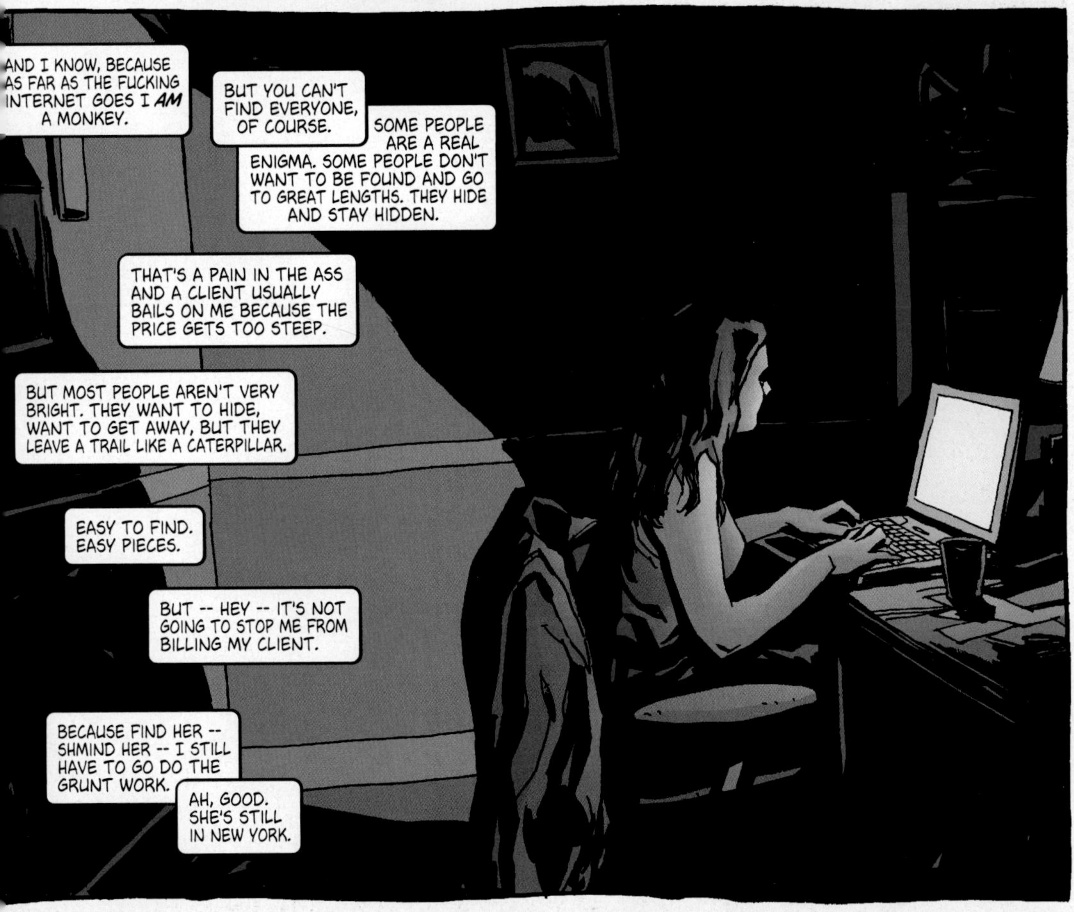
AND I KNOW, BECAUSE AS FAR AS THE FUCKING INTERNET GOES I *AM* A MONKEY.
BUT YOU CAN'T FIND EVERYONE, OF COURSE.
SOME PEOPLE ARE A REAL ENIGMA. SOME PEOPLE DON'T WANT TO BE FOUND AND GO TO GREAT LENGTHS. THEY HIDE AND STAY HIDDEN.
THAT'S A PAIN IN THE ASS AND A CLIENT USUALLY BAILS ON ME BECAUSE THE PRICE GETS TOO STEEP.
BUT MOST PEOPLE AREN'T VERY BRIGHT. THEY WANT TO HIDE, WANT TO GET AWAY, BUT THEY LEAVE A TRAIL LIKE A CATERPILLAR.
EASY TO FIND. EASY PIECES.
BUT -- HEY -- IT'S NOT GOING TO STOP ME FROM BILLING MY CLIENT.
BECAUSE FIND HER -- SHMIND HER -- I STILL HAVE TO GO DO THE GRUNT WORK.
AH, GOOD. SHE'S STILL IN NEW YORK.

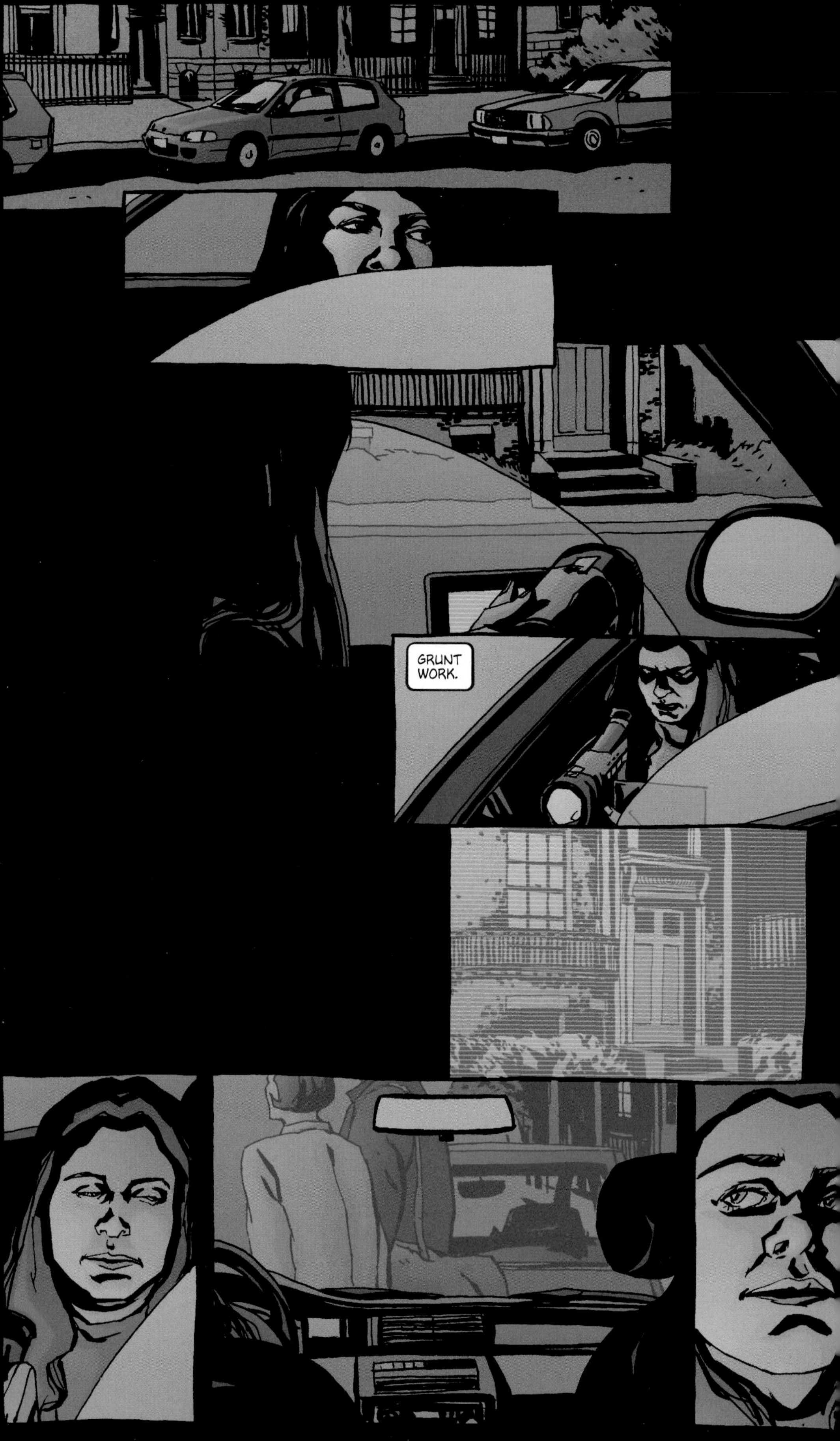
GRUNT WORK.

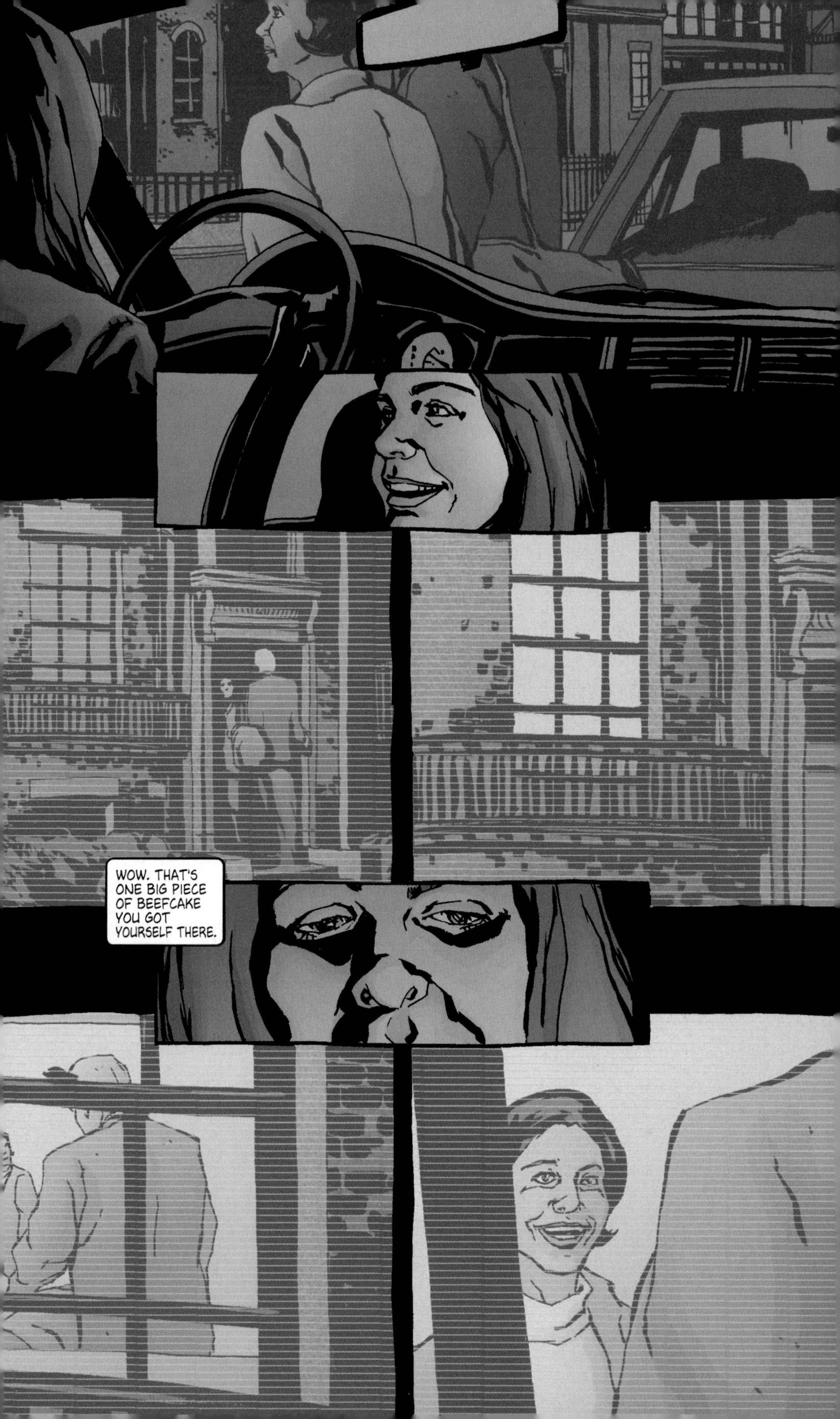
WOW. THAT'S ONE BIG PIECE OF BEEFCAKE YOU GOT YOURSELF THERE.

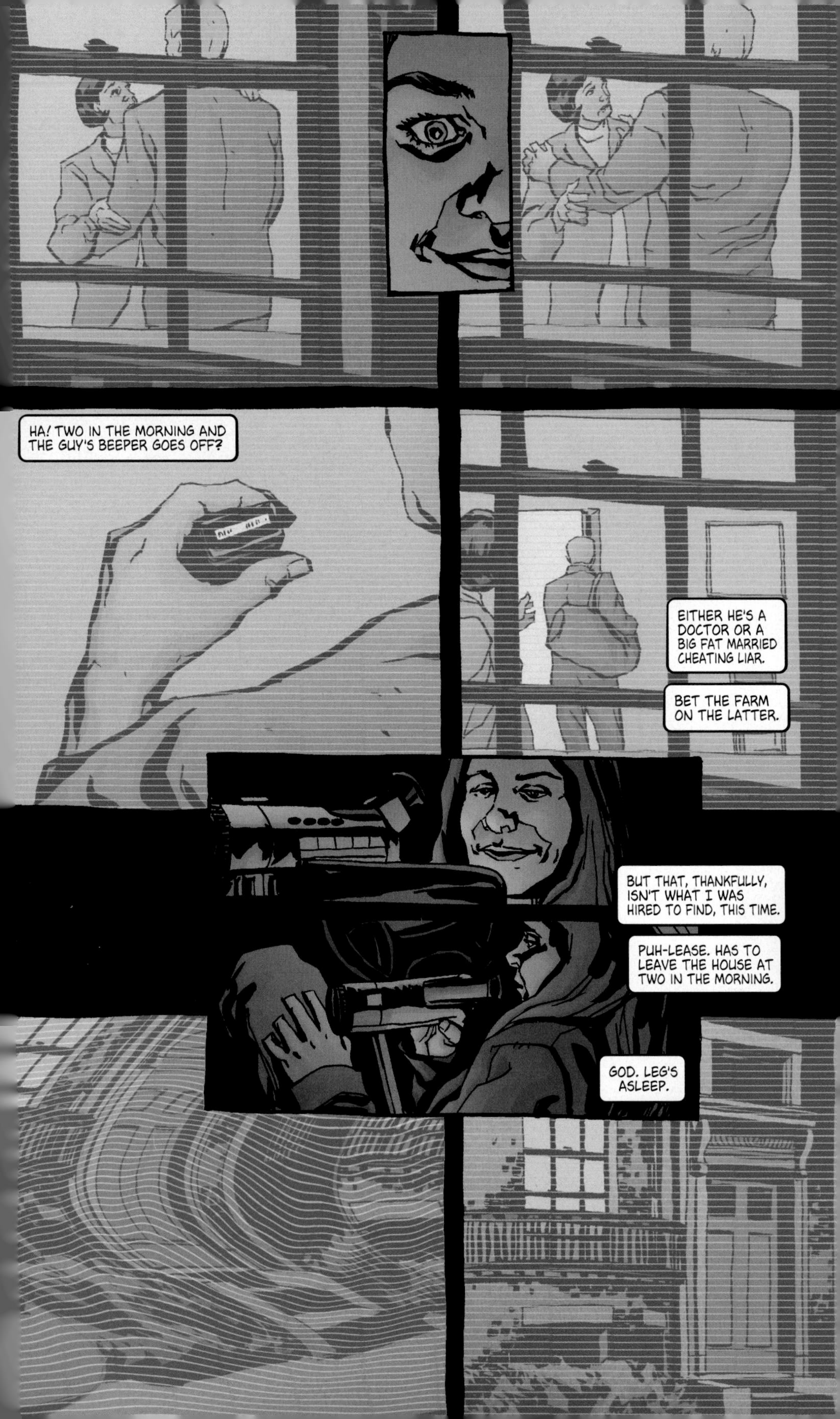
HA! TWO IN THE MORNING AND THE GUY'S BEEPER GOES OFF?
EITHER HE'S A DOCTOR OR A BIG FAT MARRIED CHEATING LIAR.
BET THE FARM ON THE LATTER.
BUT THAT, THANKFULLY, ISN'T WHAT I WAS HIRED TO FIND, THIS TIME.
PUH-LEASE. HAS TO LEAVE THE HOUSE AT TWO IN THE MORNING.
GOD. LEG'S ASLEEP.

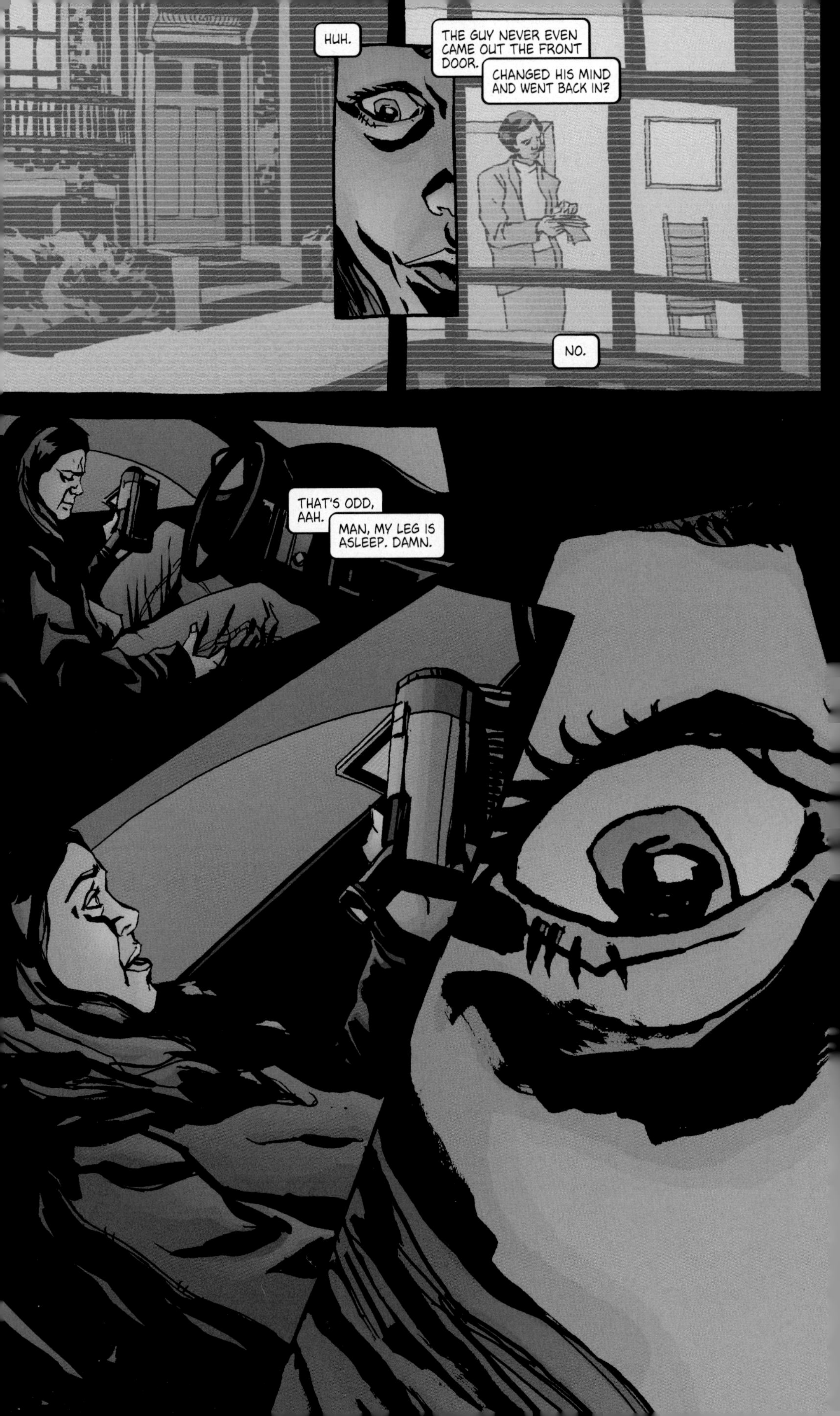
HUH.
THE GUY NEVER EVEN CAME OUT THE FRONT DOOR.
CHANGED HIS MIND AND WENT BACK IN?
NO.
THAT'S ODD, AAH.
MAN, MY LEG IS ASLEEP. DAMN.

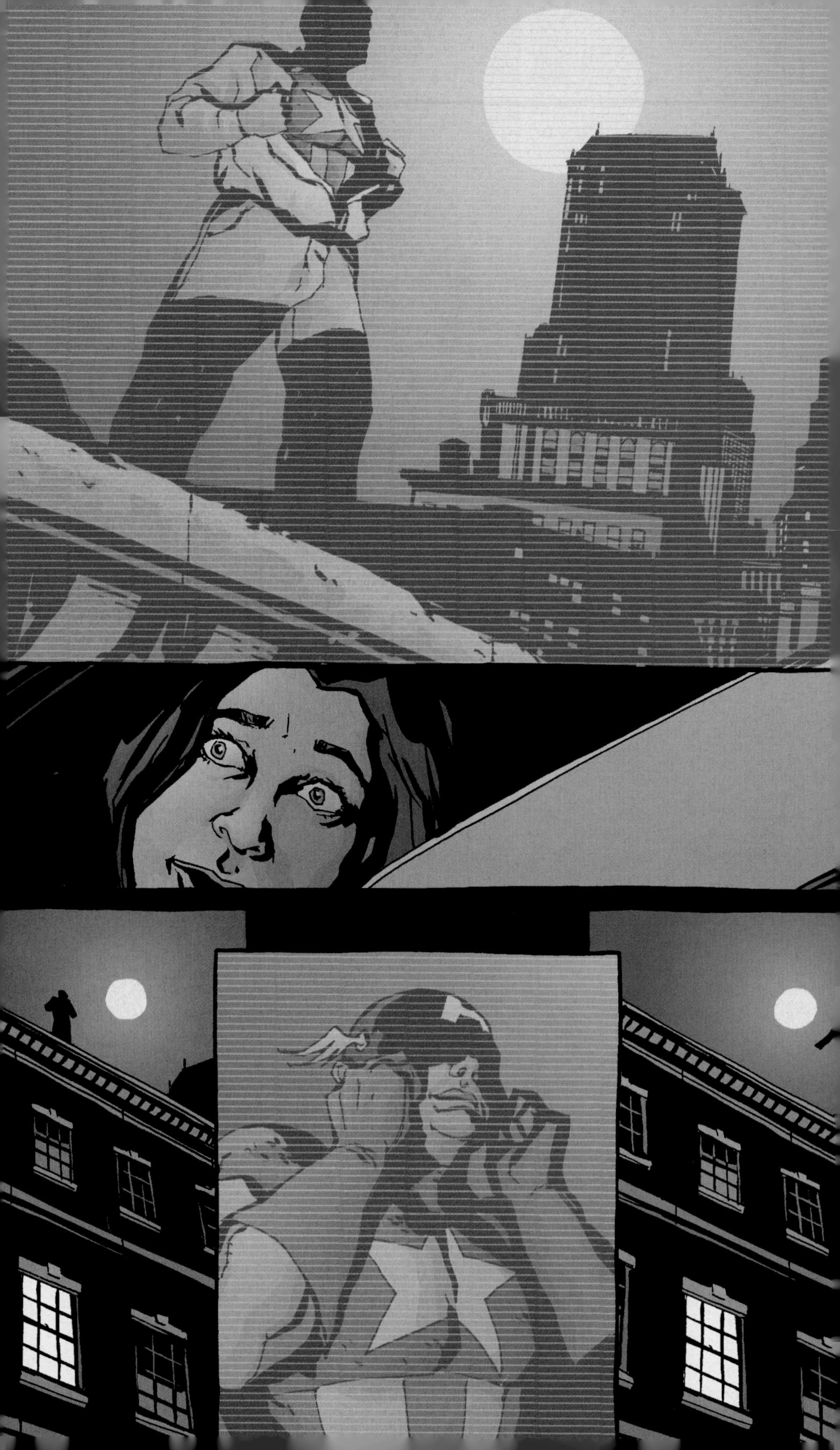

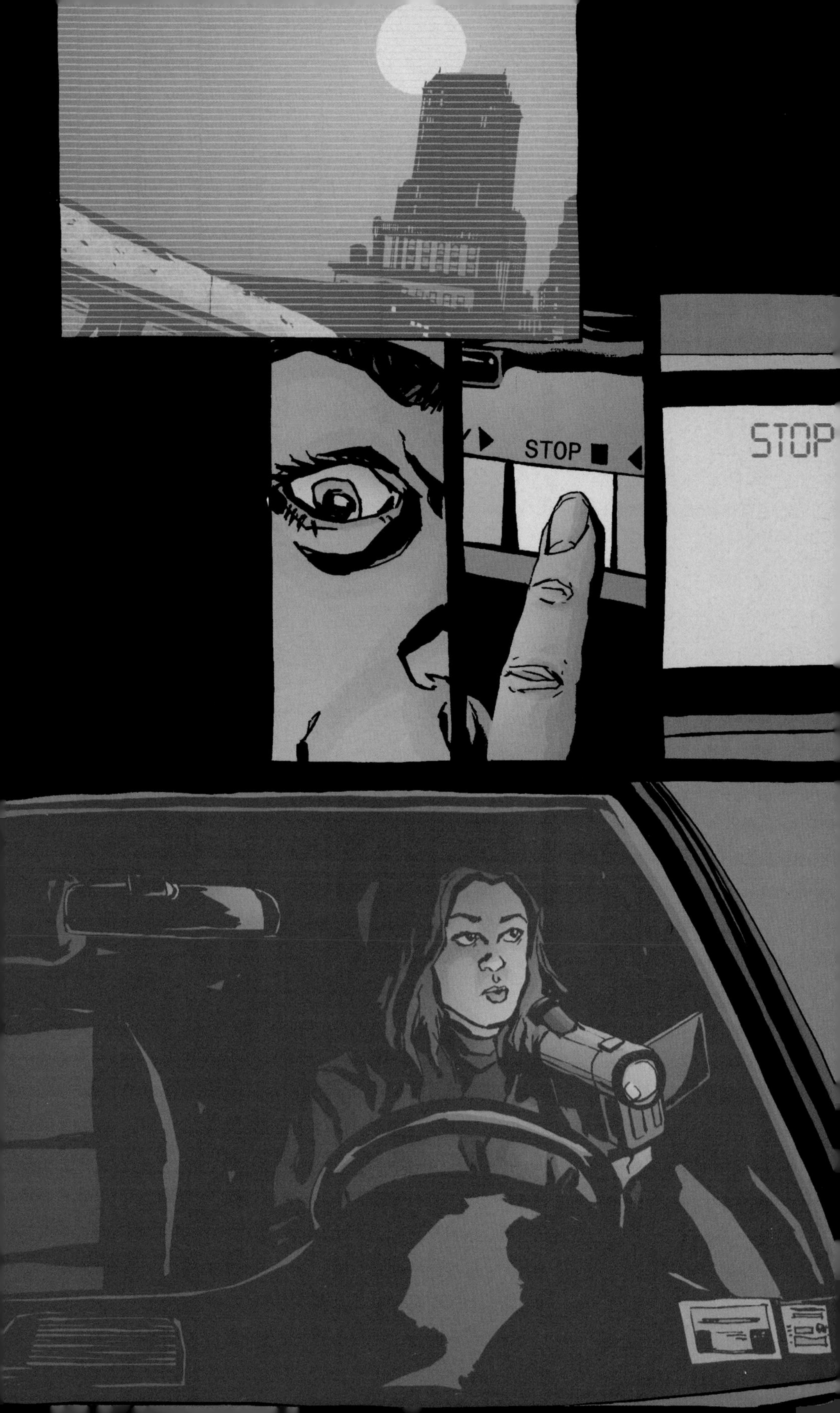
STOP
STOP

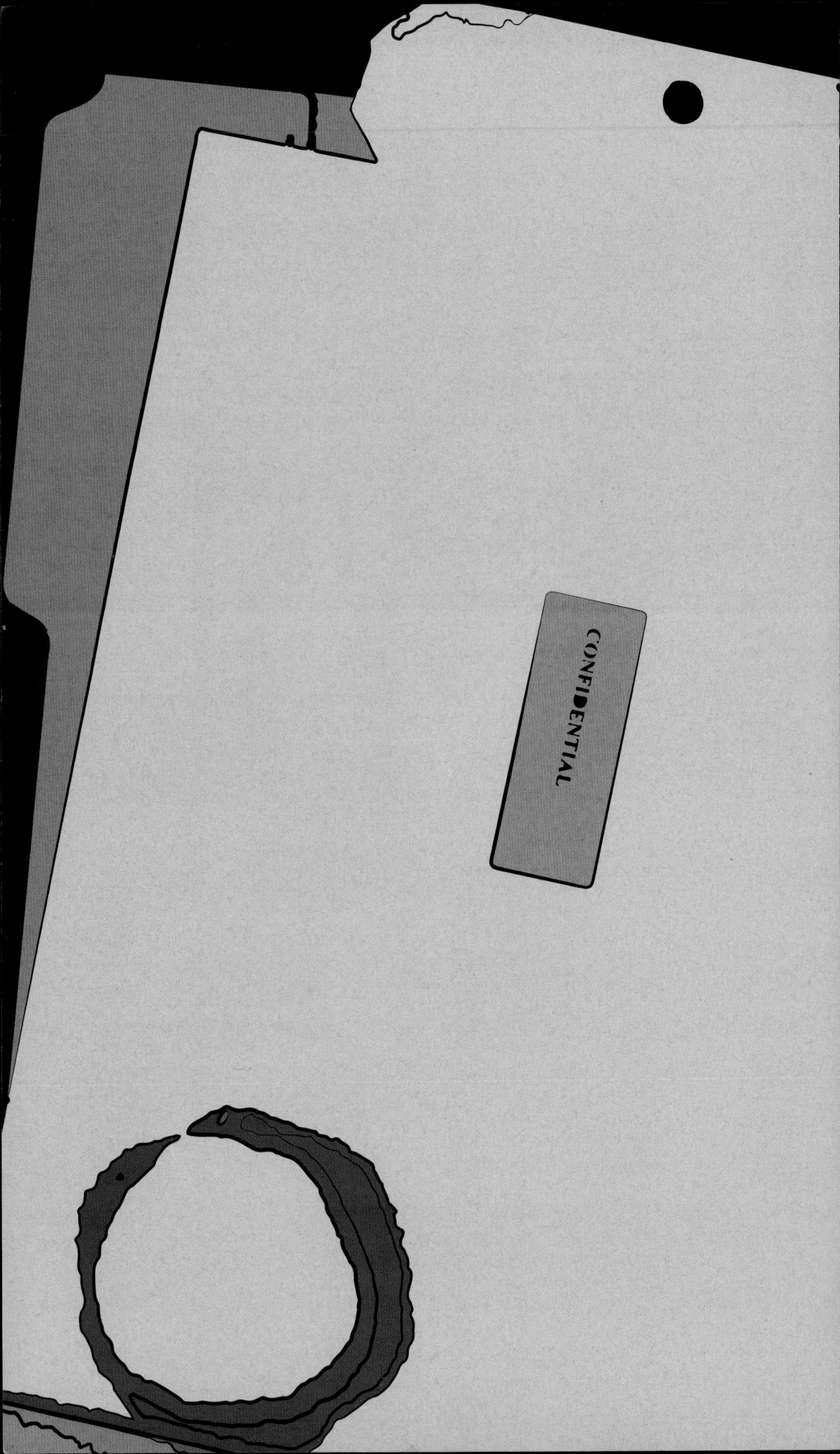
CONFIDENTIAL

ISSUE #2 BE[redacted]

[redacted]2

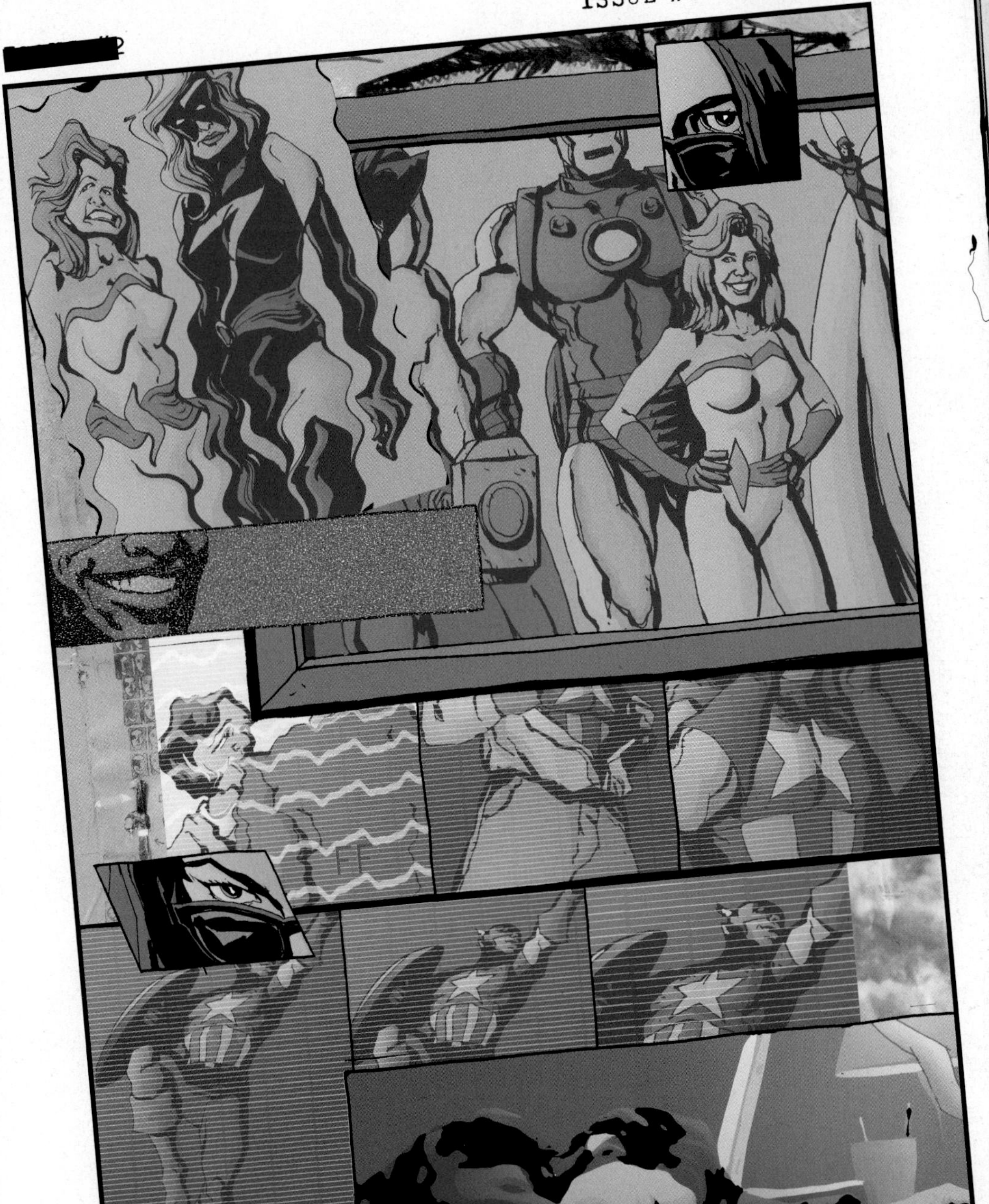

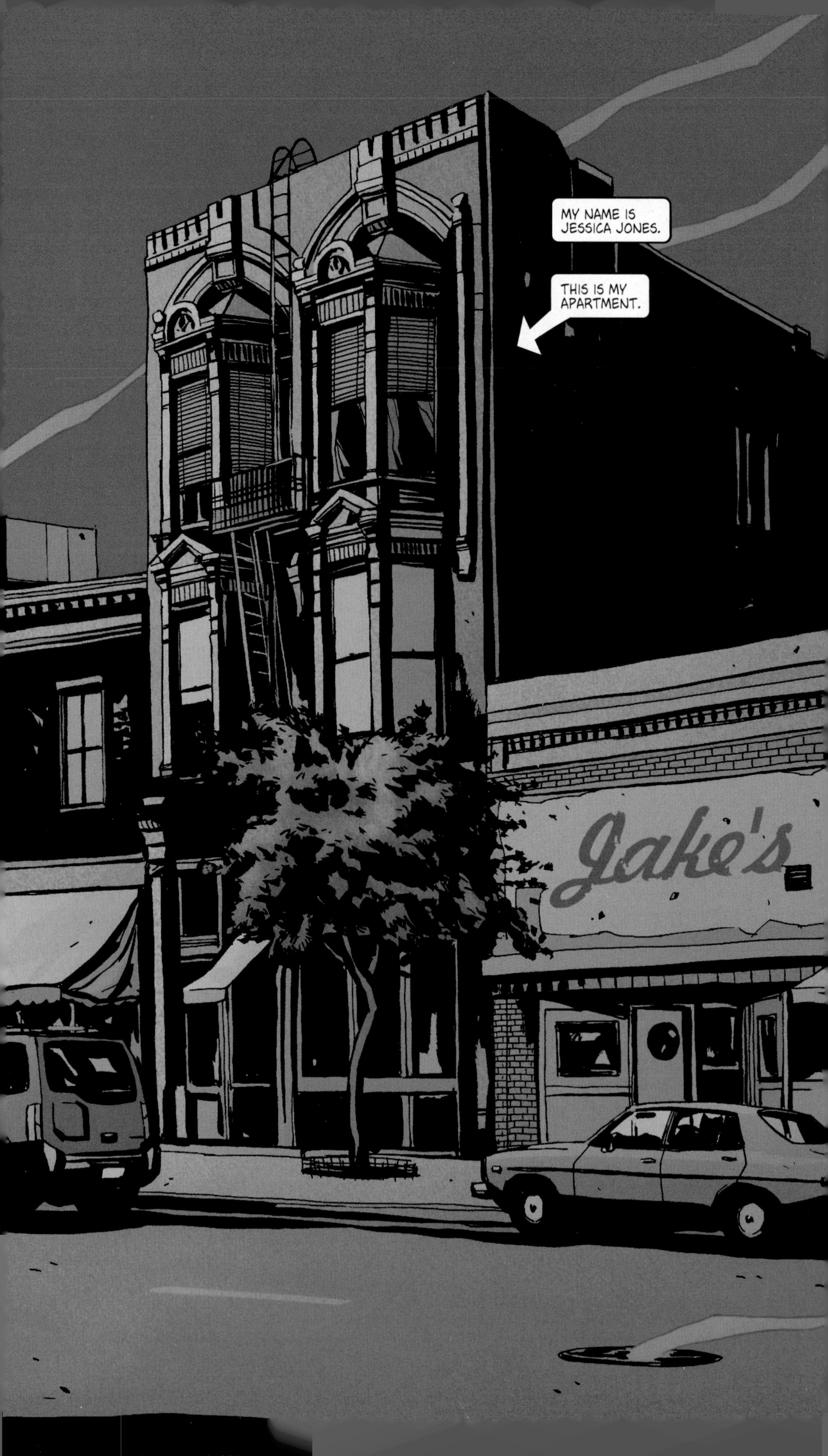
MY NAME IS JESSICA JONES.
THIS IS MY APARTMENT.
Jake's

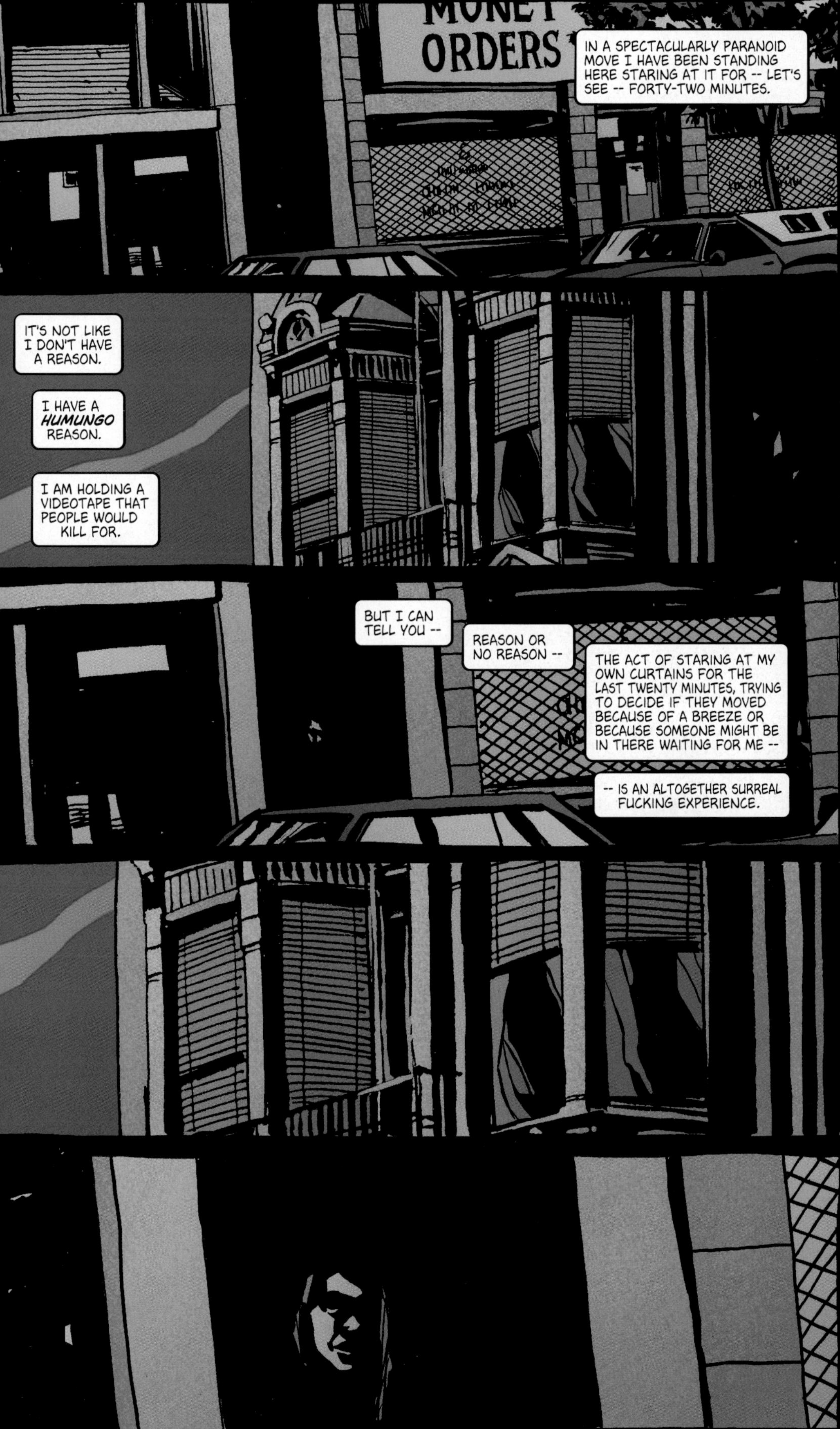
MONEY ORDERS
IN A SPECTACULARLY PARANOID MOVE I HAVE BEEN STANDING HERE STARING AT IT FOR -- LET'S SEE -- FORTY-TWO MINUTES.
IT'S NOT LIKE I DON'T HAVE A REASON.
I HAVE A *HUMUNGO* REASON.
I AM HOLDING A VIDEOTAPE THAT PEOPLE WOULD KILL FOR.
BUT I CAN TELL YOU --
REASON OR NO REASON --
THE ACT OF STARING AT MY OWN CURTAINS FOR THE LAST TWENTY MINUTES, TRYING TO DECIDE IF THEY MOVED BECAUSE OF A BREEZE OR BECAUSE SOMEONE MIGHT BE IN THERE WAITING FOR ME --
-- IS AN ALTOGETHER SURREAL FUCKING EXPERIENCE.

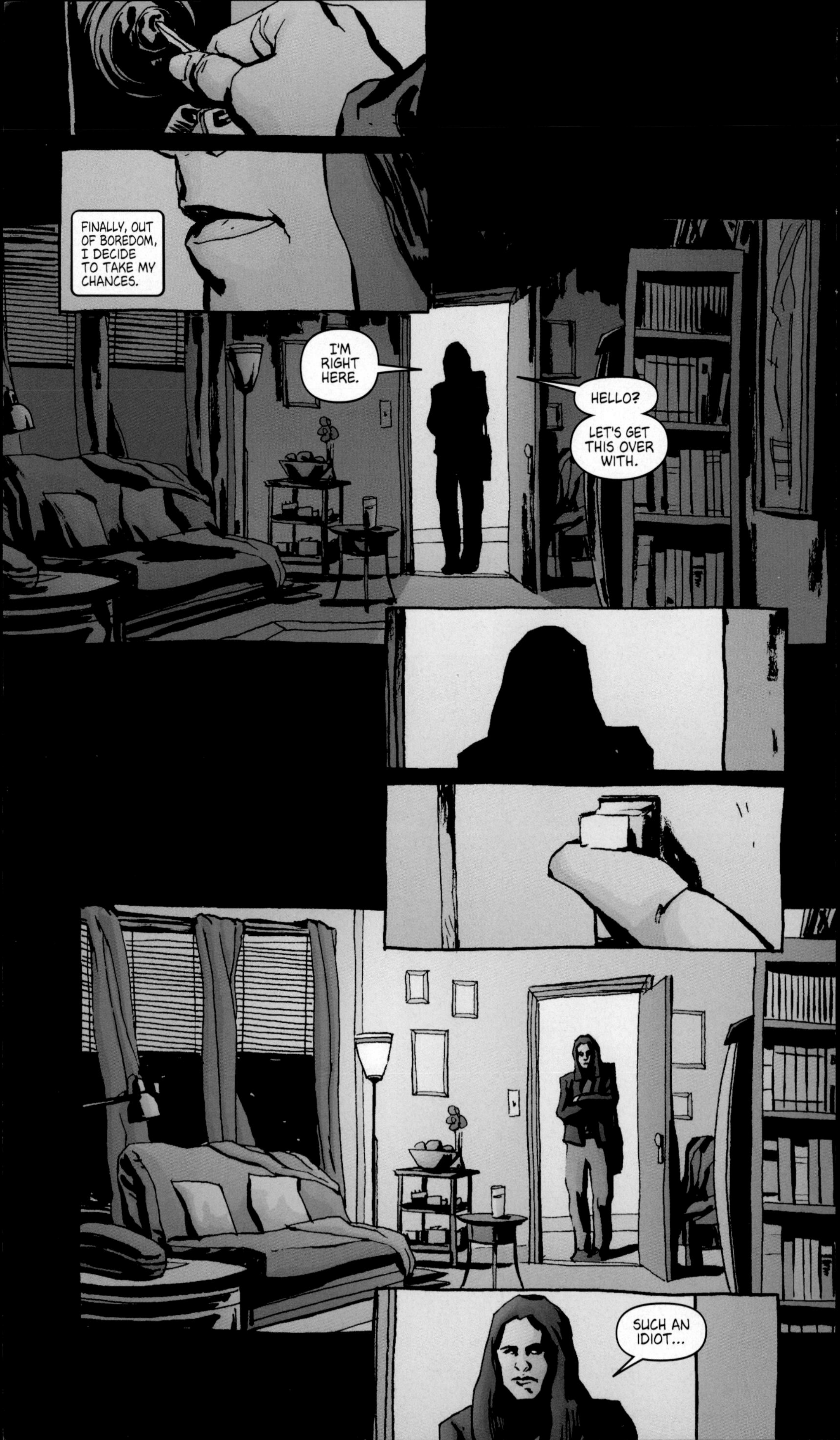
FINALLY, OUT OF BOREDOM, I DECIDE TO TAKE MY CHANCES.
I'M RIGHT HERE.
HELLO?
LET'S GET THIS OVER WITH.
SUCH AN IDIOT...

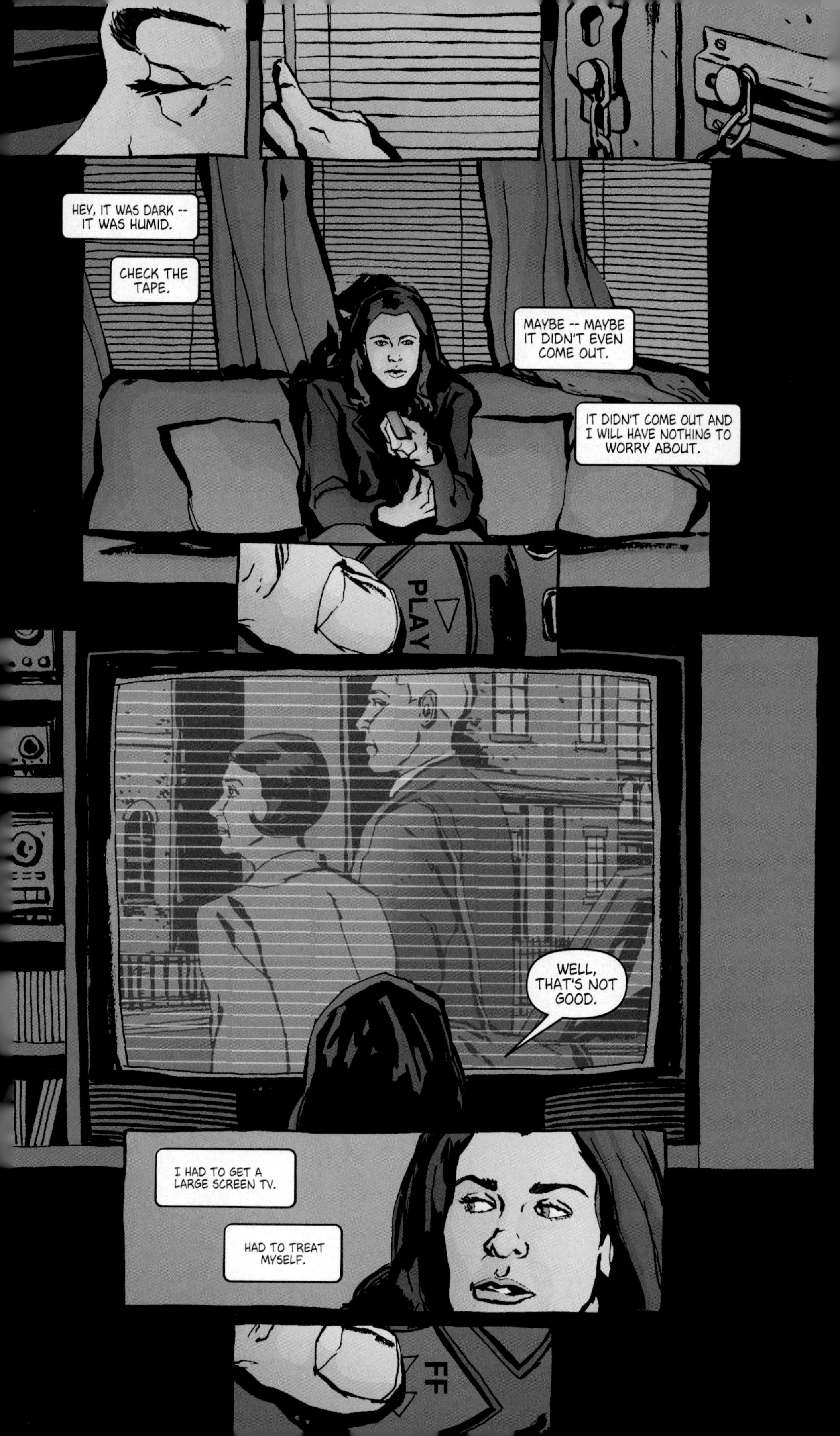
HEY, IT WAS DARK -- IT WAS HUMID.
CHECK THE TAPE.
MAYBE -- MAYBE IT DIDN'T EVEN COME OUT.
IT DIDN'T COME OUT AND I WILL HAVE NOTHING TO WORRY ABOUT.
PLAY
WELL, THAT'S NOT GOOD.
I HAD TO GET A LARGE SCREEN TV.
HAD TO TREAT MYSELF.
FF

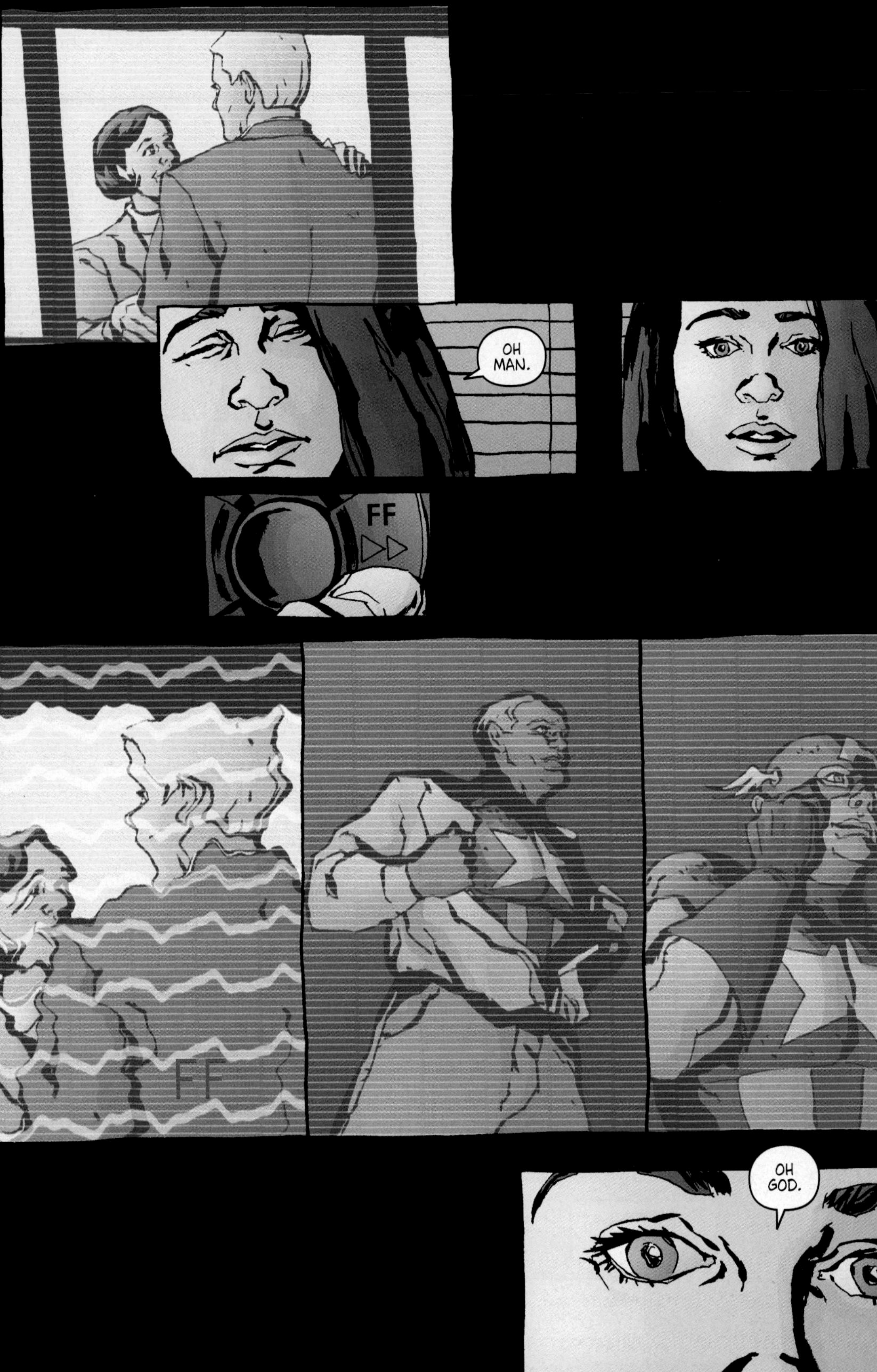
OH MAN.
FF
FF
OH GOD.

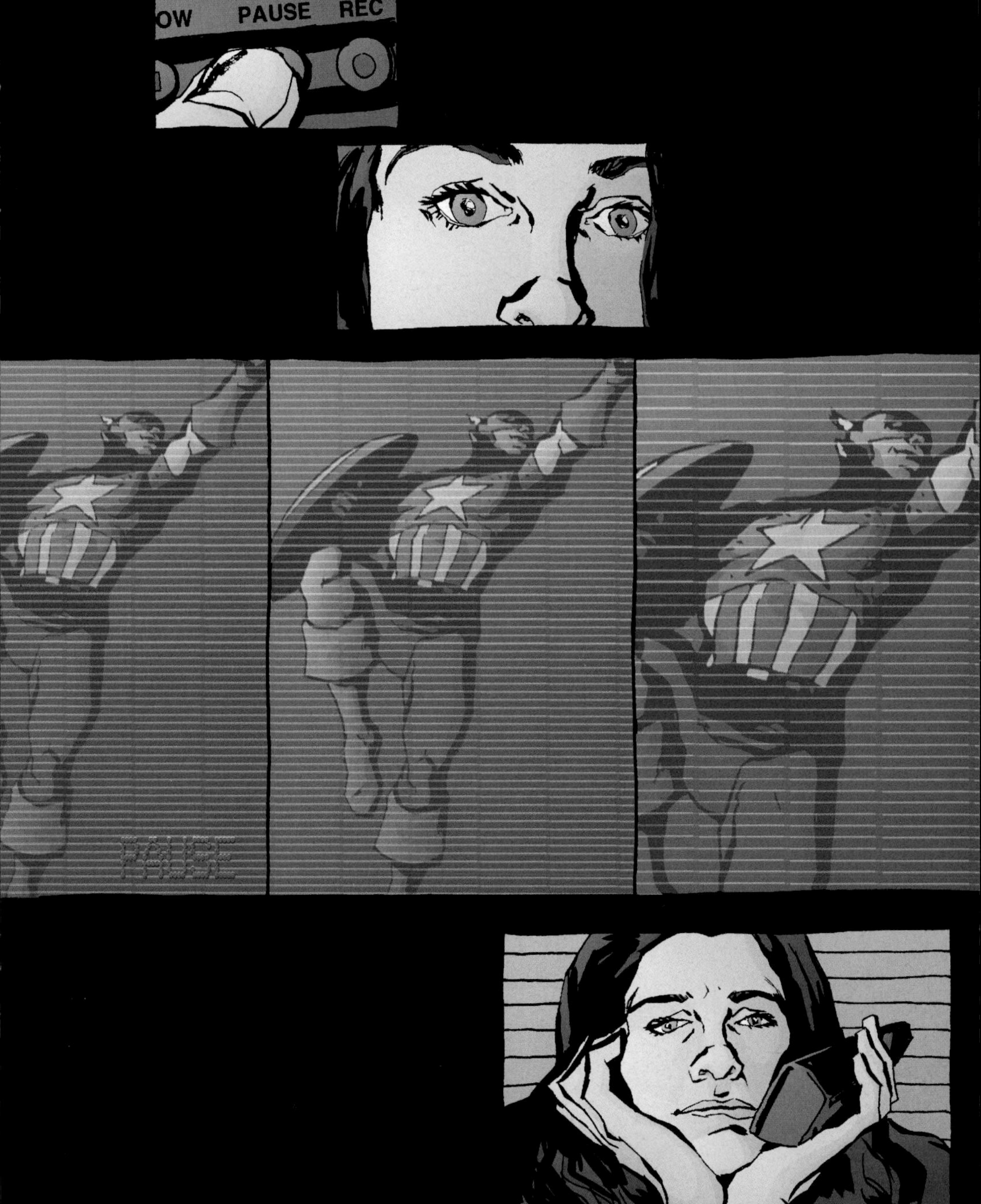

OW
PAUSE
REC
PAUSE

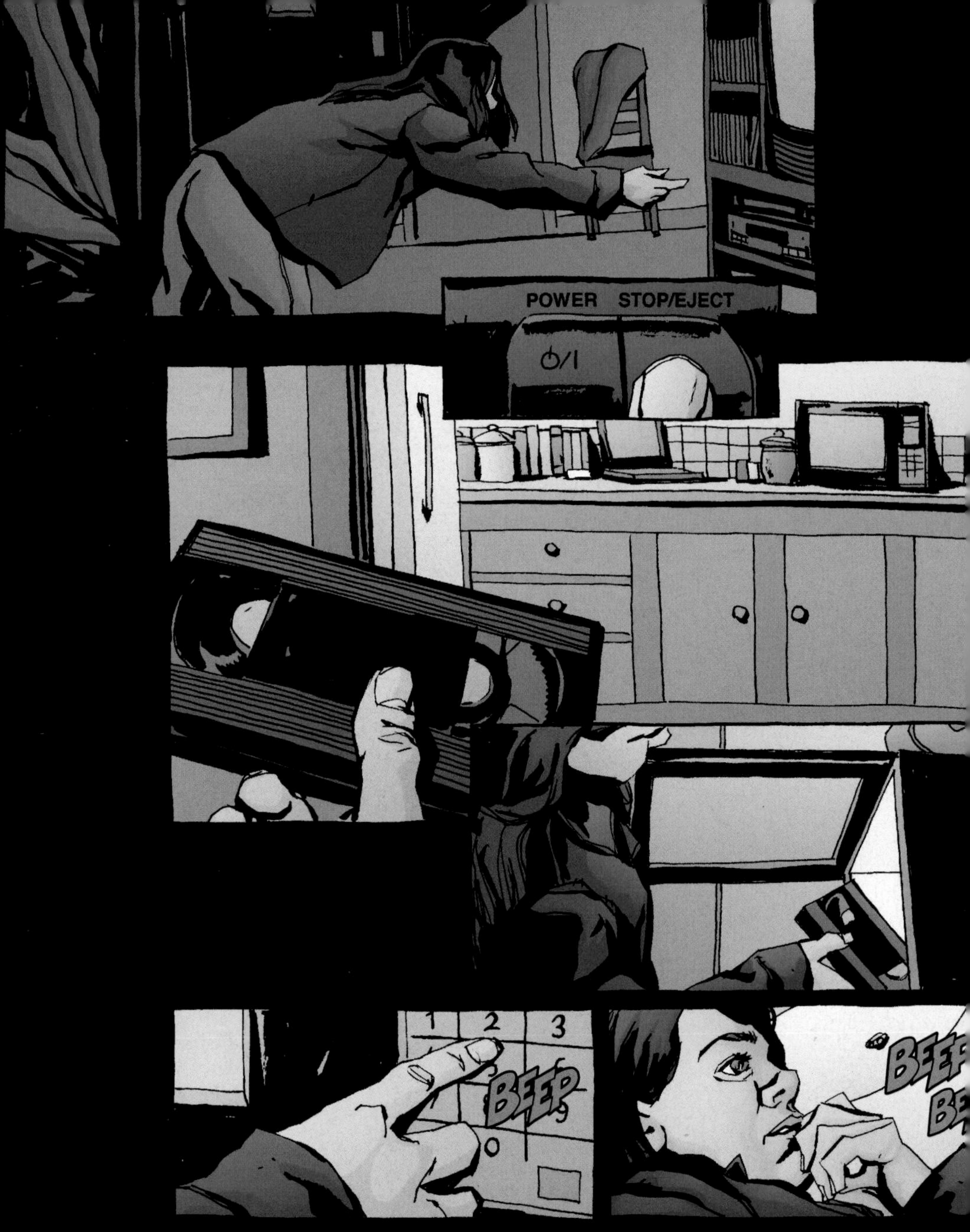

POWER STOP/EJECT
1 2 3
BEEP
BEEP

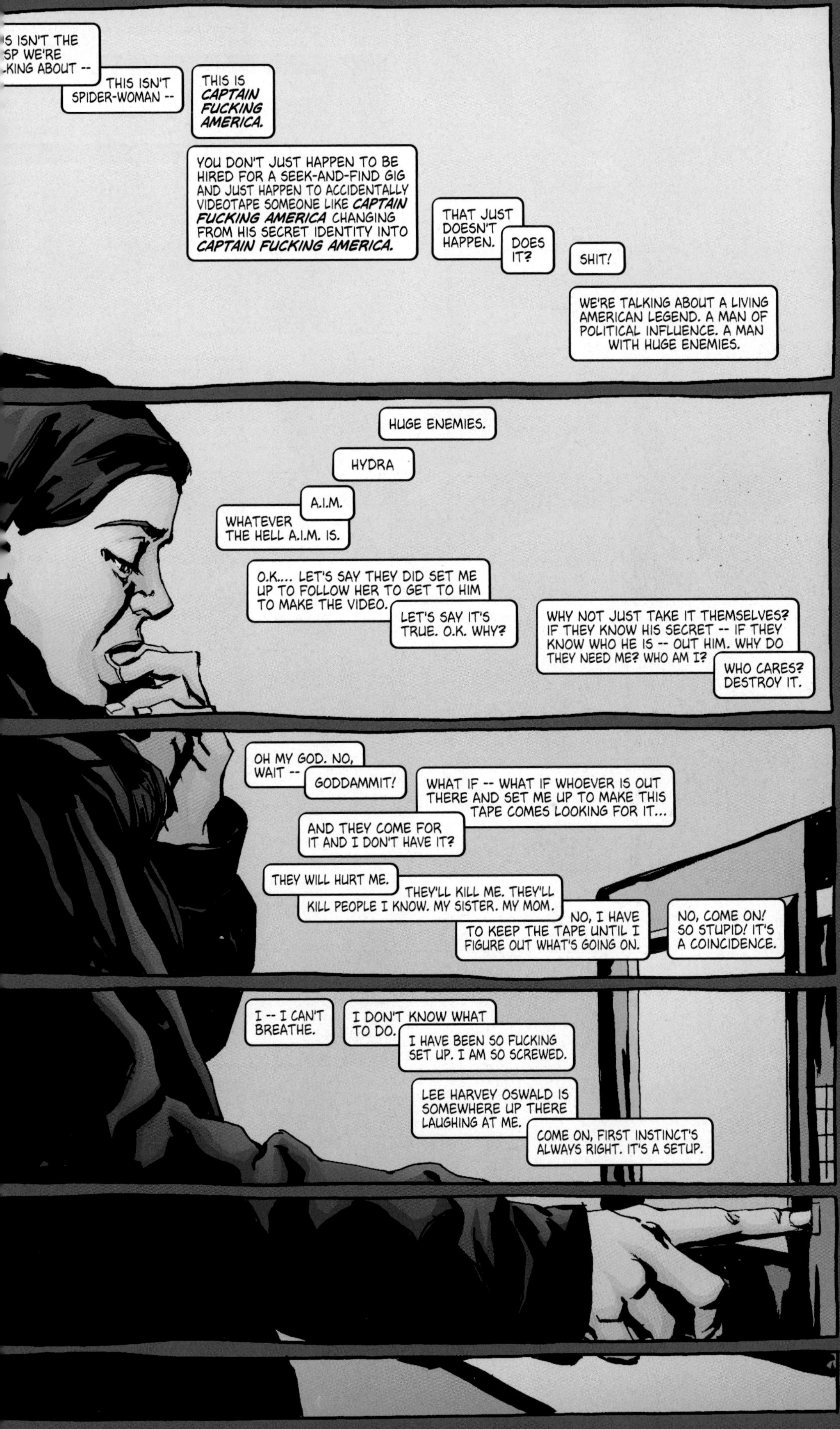
S ISN'T THE SP WE'RE KING ABOUT --
THIS ISN'T SPIDER-WOMAN --
THIS IS *CAPTAIN FUCKING AMERICA.*
YOU DON'T JUST HAPPEN TO BE HIRED FOR A SEEK-AND-FIND GIG AND JUST HAPPEN TO ACCIDENTALLY VIDEOTAPE SOMEONE LIKE *CAPTAIN FUCKING AMERICA* CHANGING FROM HIS SECRET IDENTITY INTO *CAPTAIN FUCKING AMERICA.*
THAT JUST DOESN'T HAPPEN.
DOES IT?
SHIT!
WE'RE TALKING ABOUT A LIVING AMERICAN LEGEND. A MAN OF POLITICAL INFLUENCE. A MAN WITH HUGE ENEMIES.
HUGE ENEMIES.
HYDRA
A.I.M.
WHATEVER THE HELL A.I.M. IS.
O.K.... LET'S SAY THEY DID SET ME UP TO FOLLOW HER TO GET TO HIM TO MAKE THE VIDEO.
LET'S SAY IT'S TRUE. O.K. WHY?
WHY NOT JUST TAKE IT THEMSELVES? IF THEY KNOW HIS SECRET -- IF THEY KNOW WHO HE IS -- OUT HIM. WHY DO THEY NEED ME? WHO AM I?
WHO CARES? DESTROY IT.
OH MY GOD. NO, WAIT --
GODDAMMIT!
WHAT IF -- WHAT IF WHOEVER IS OUT THERE AND SET ME UP TO MAKE THIS TAPE COMES LOOKING FOR IT...
AND THEY COME FOR IT AND I DON'T HAVE IT?
THEY WILL HURT ME.
THEY'LL KILL ME. THEY'LL KILL PEOPLE I KNOW. MY SISTER. MY MOM.
NO, I HAVE TO KEEP THE TAPE UNTIL I FIGURE OUT WHAT'S GOING ON.
NO, COME ON! SO STUPID! IT'S A COINCIDENCE.
I -- I CAN'T BREATHE.
I DON'T KNOW WHAT TO DO.
I HAVE BEEN SO FUCKING SET UP. I AM SO SCREWED.
LEE HARVEY OSWALD IS SOMEWHERE UP THERE LAUGHING AT ME.
COME ON, FIRST INSTINCT'S ALWAYS RIGHT. IT'S A SETUP.

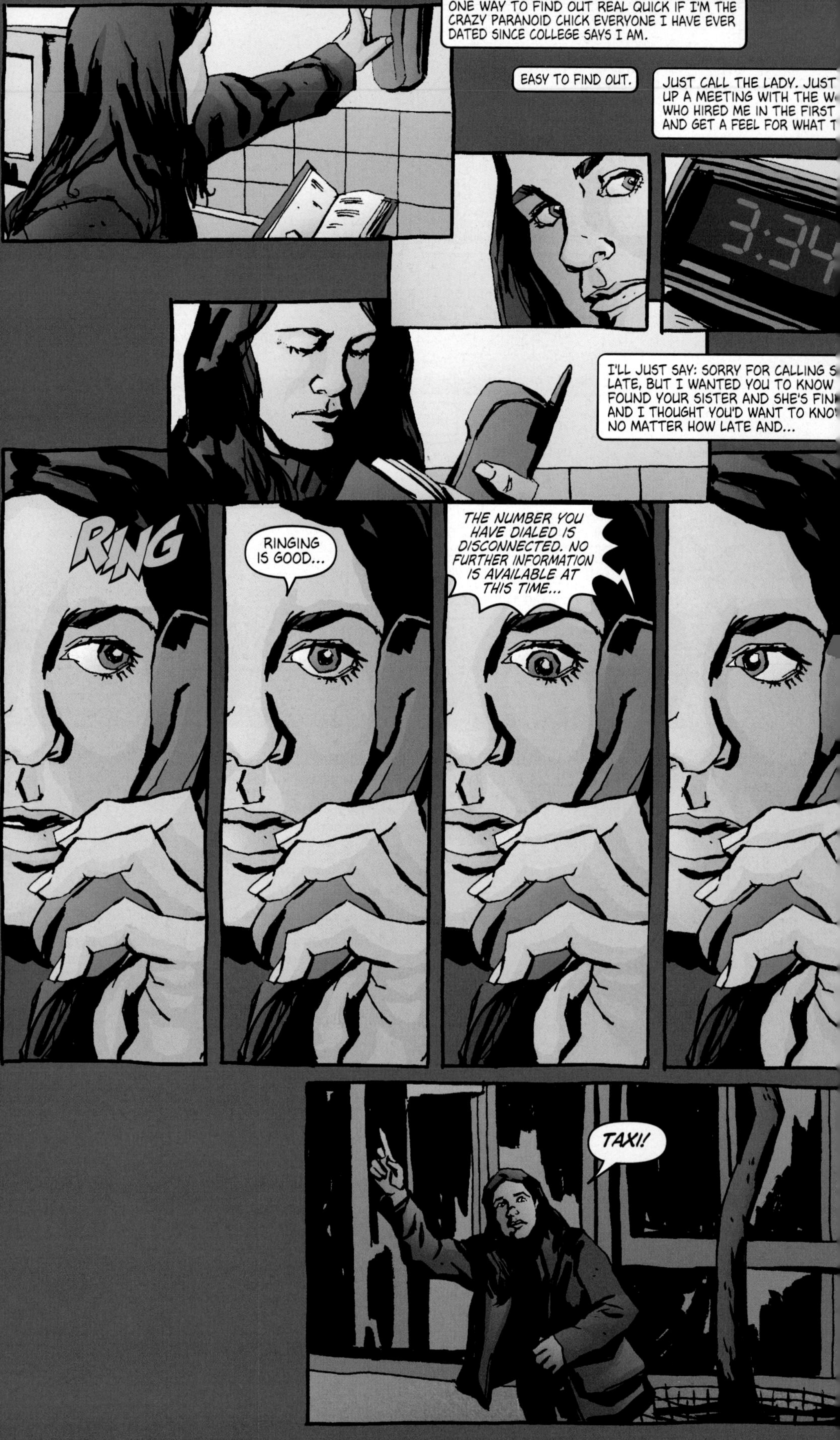
ONE WAY TO FIND OUT REAL QUICK IF I'M THE CRAZY PARANOID CHICK EVERYONE I HAVE EVER DATED SINCE COLLEGE SAYS I AM.
EASY TO FIND OUT.
JUST CALL THE LADY. JUST UP A MEETING WITH THE W WHO HIRED ME IN THE FIRST AND GET A FEEL FOR WHAT T
3:34
I'LL JUST SAY: SORRY FOR CALLING S LATE, BUT I WANTED YOU TO KNOW FOUND YOUR SISTER AND SHE'S FIN AND I THOUGHT YOU'D WANT TO KNO NO MATTER HOW LATE AND...
RING
RINGING IS GOOD...
THE NUMBER YOU HAVE DIALED IS DISCONNECTED. NO FURTHER INFORMATION IS AVAILABLE AT THIS TIME...
TAXI!

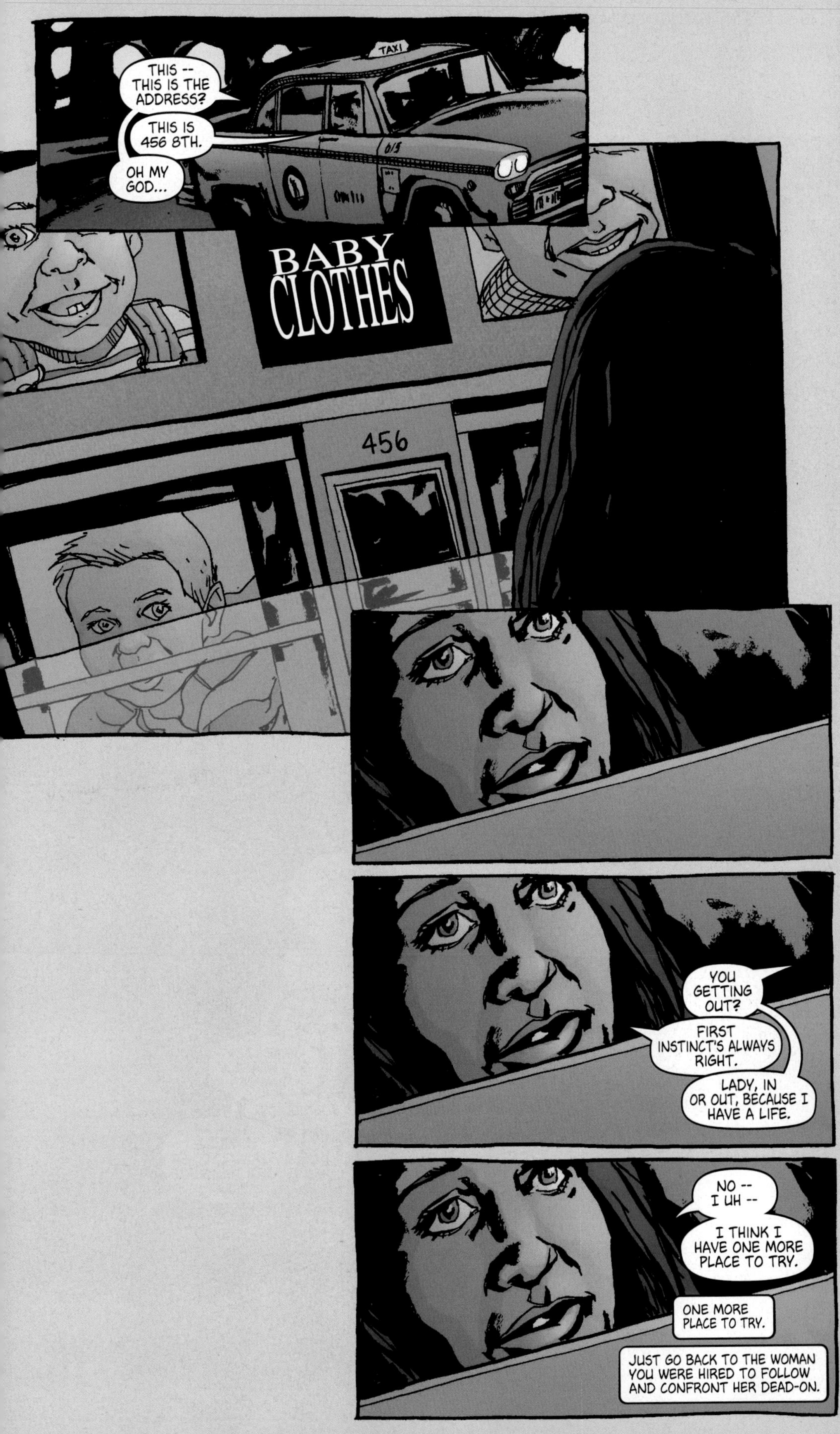
THIS -- THIS IS THE ADDRESS?
THIS IS 456 8TH.
OH MY GOD...
TAXI
BABY CLOTHES
456
YOU GETTING OUT?
FIRST INSTINCT'S ALWAYS RIGHT.
LADY, IN OR OUT, BECAUSE I HAVE A LIFE.
NO -- I UH --
I THINK I HAVE ONE MORE PLACE TO TRY.
ONE MORE PLACE TO TRY.
JUST GO BACK TO THE WOMAN YOU WERE HIRED TO FOLLOW AND CONFRONT HER DEAD-ON.

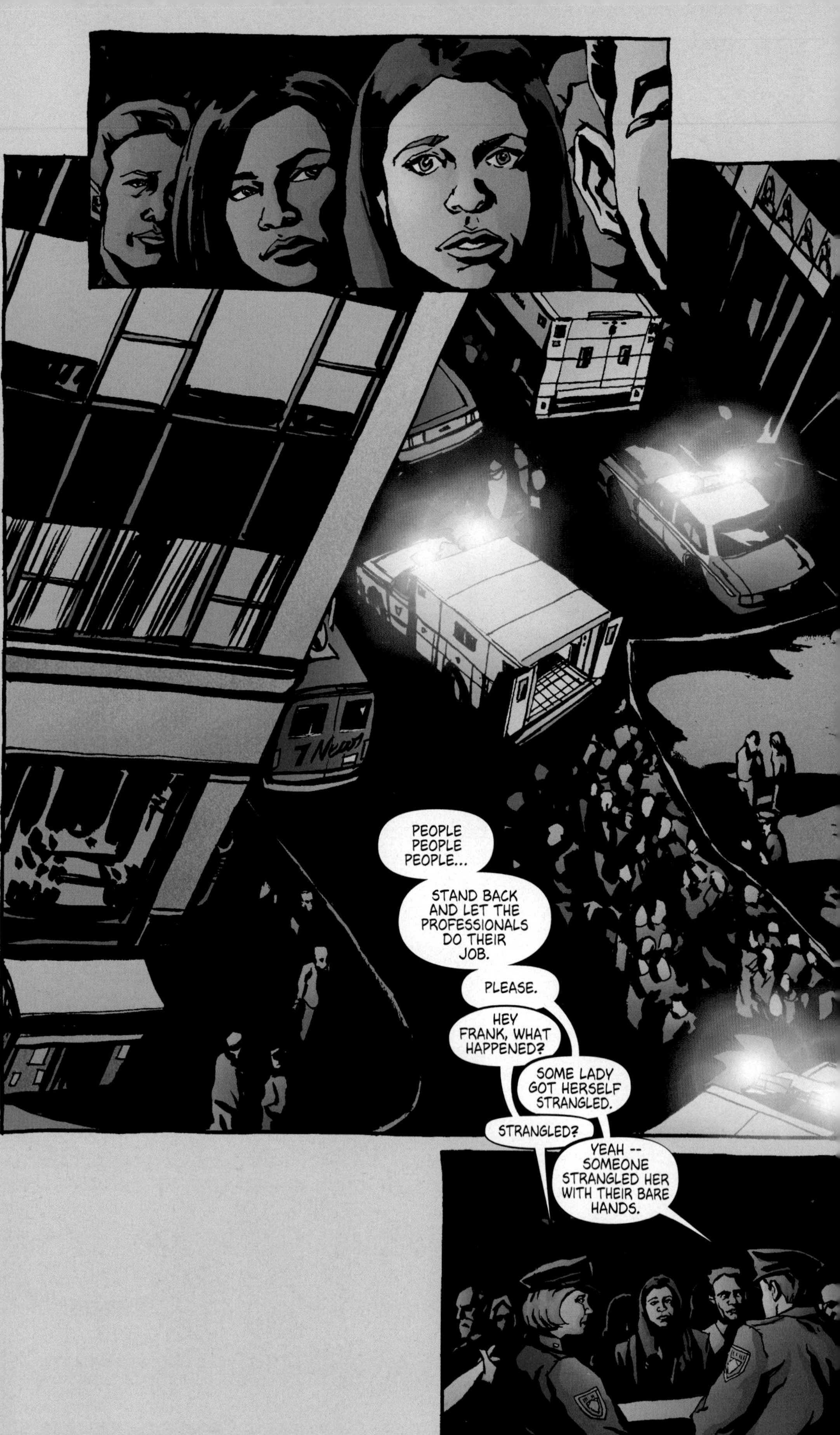
7 News
PEOPLE PEOPLE PEOPLE...
STAND BACK AND LET THE PROFESSIONALS DO THEIR JOB.
PLEASE.
HEY FRANK, WHAT HAPPENED?
SOME LADY GOT HERSELF STRANGLED.
STRANGLED?
YEAH -- SOMEONE STRANGLED HER WITH THEIR BARE HANDS.

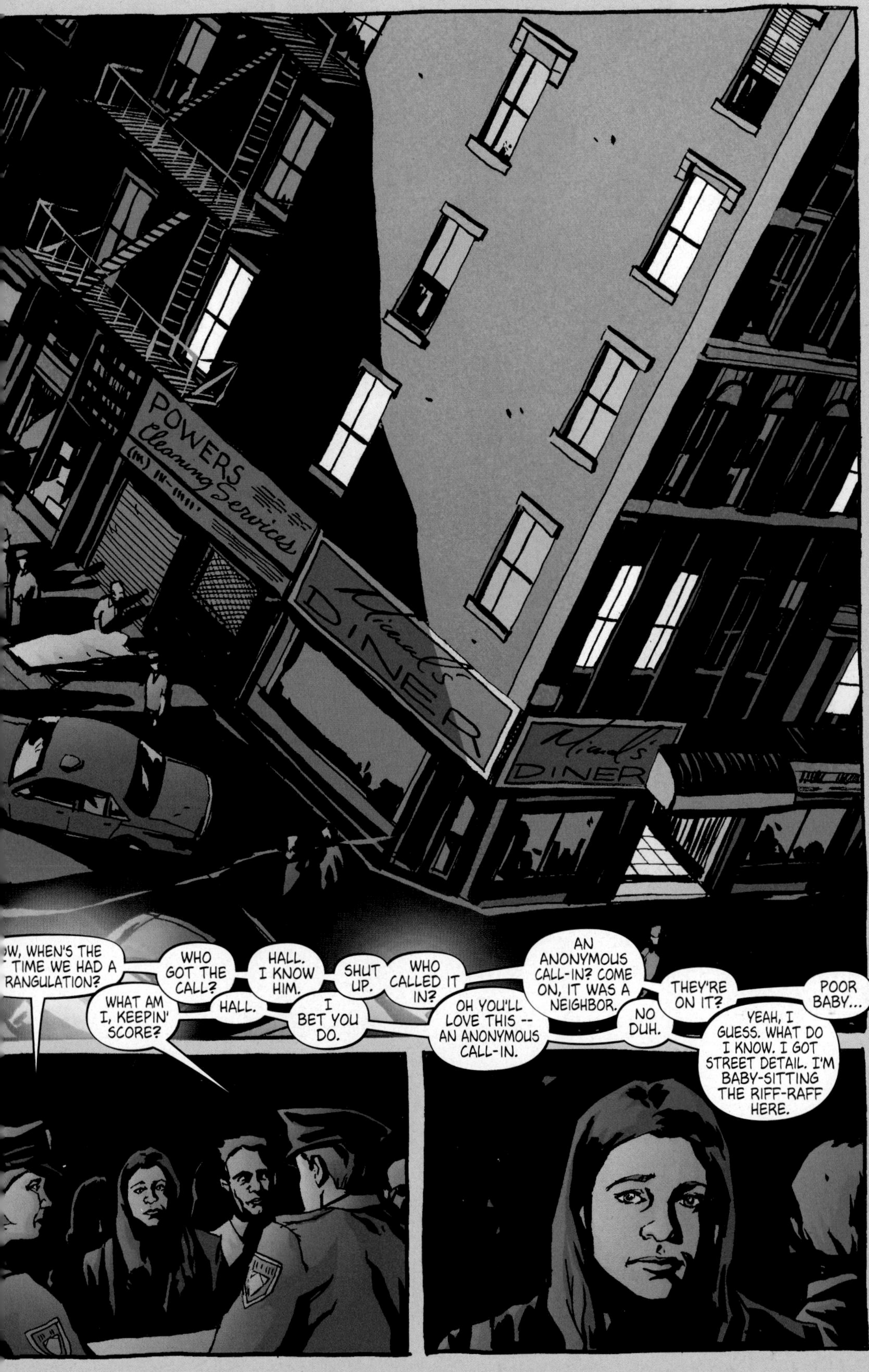
POWERS
Cleaning Services
Miami's DINER
Miami's DINER
OW, WHEN'S THE
TIME WE HAD A
RANGULATION?
WHAT AM I, KEEPIN' SCORE?
WHO GOT THE CALL?
HALL.
HALL. I KNOW HIM.
I BET YOU DO.
SHUT UP.
WHO CALLED IT IN?
OH YOU'LL LOVE THIS -- AN ANONYMOUS CALL-IN.
AN ANONYMOUS CALL-IN? COME ON, IT WAS A NEIGHBOR.
NO DUH.
THEY'RE ON IT?
YEAH, I GUESS. WHAT DO I KNOW. I GOT STREET DETAIL. I'M BABY-SITTING THE RIFF-RAFF HERE.
POOR BABY...

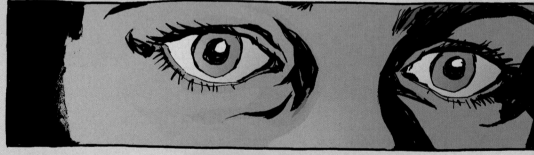

I CAN FEEL THE TAPE IN MY PURSE.

IT --

I SWEAR TO GOD I CAN FEEL IT MOVING.

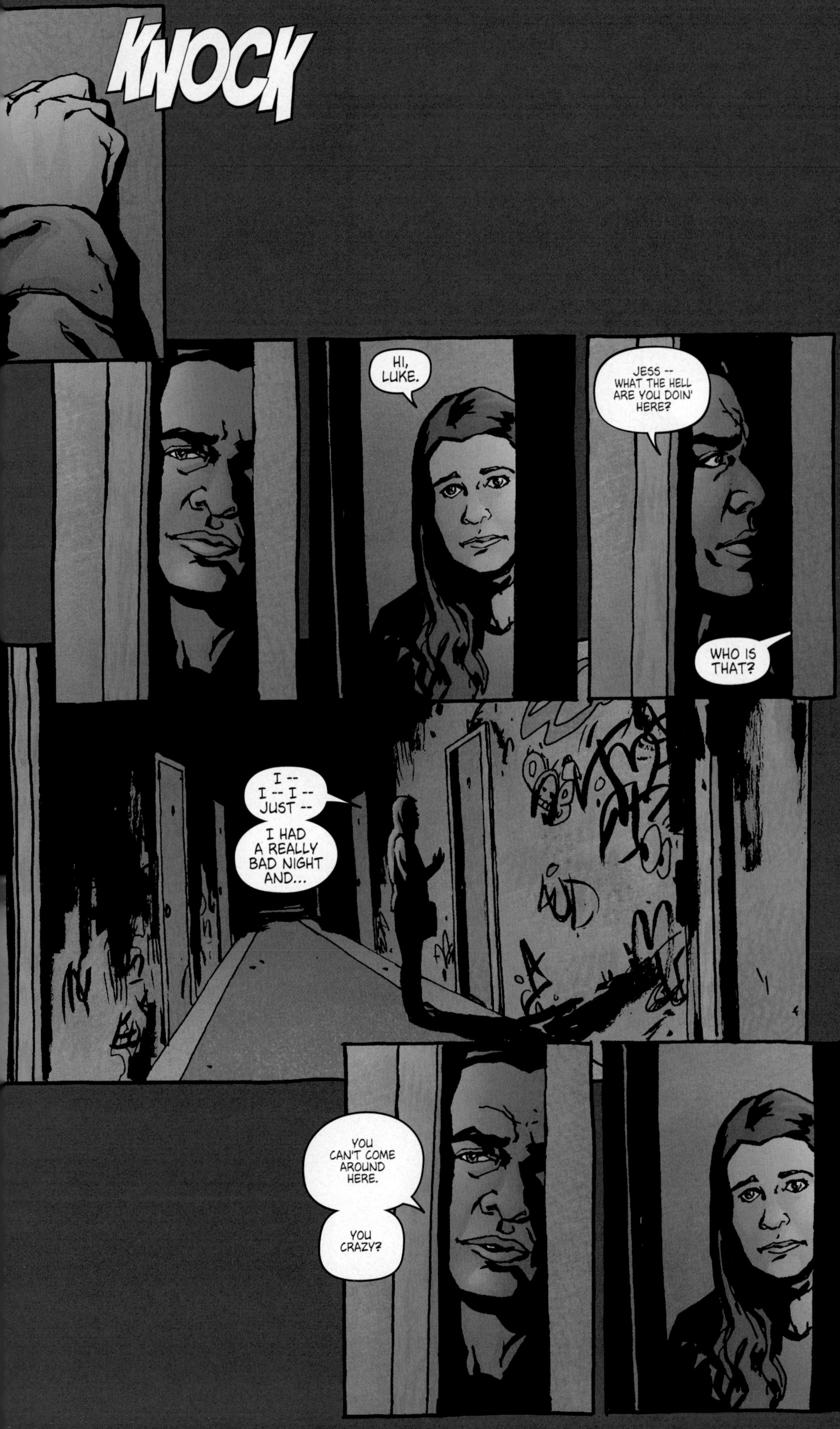
KNOCK
HI, LUKE.
JESS -- WHAT THE HELL ARE YOU DOIN' HERE?
WHO IS THAT?
I -- I -- I -- JUST --
I HAD A REALLY BAD NIGHT AND...
YOU CAN'T COME AROUND HERE.
YOU CRAZY?

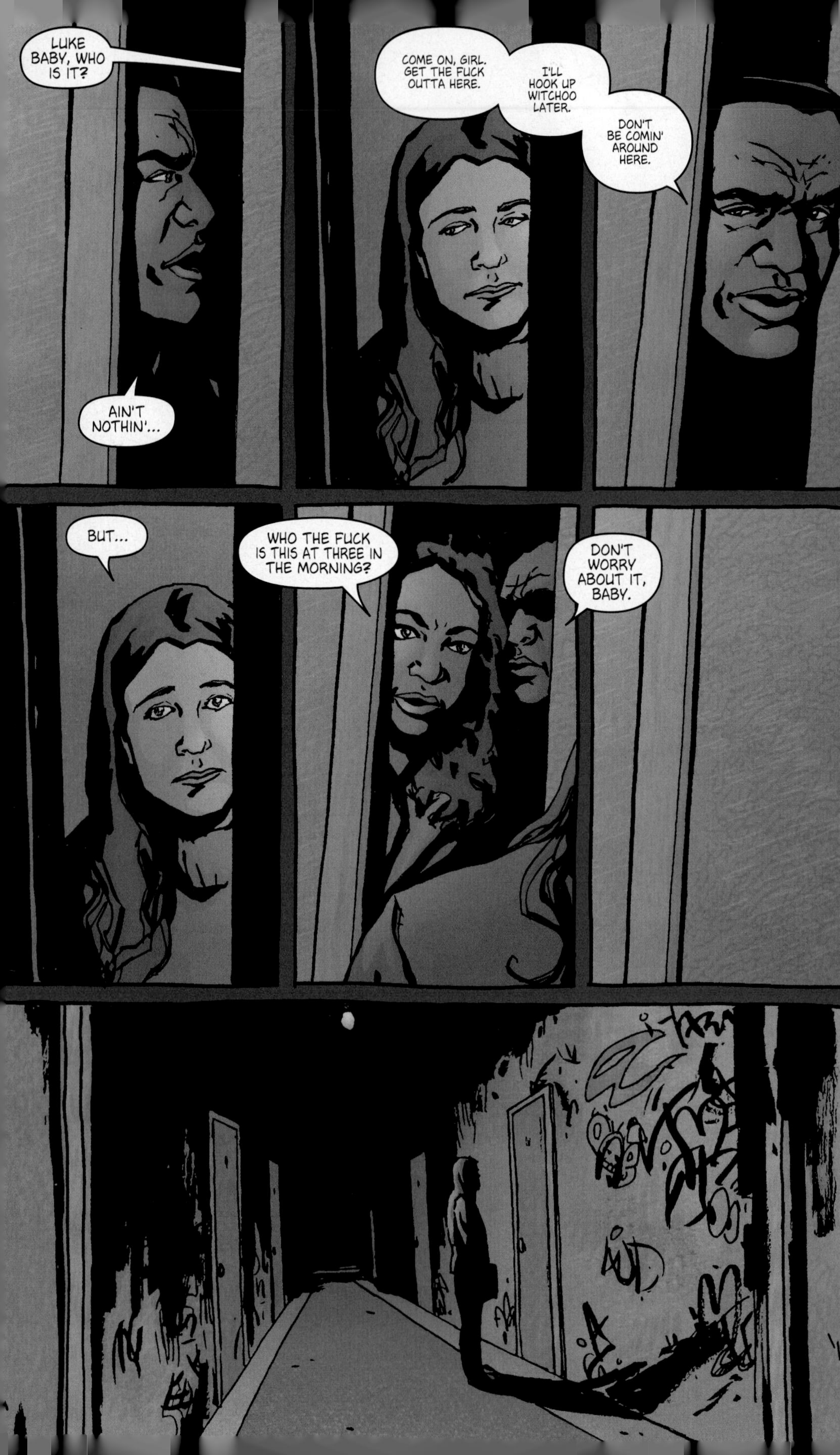
LUKE BABY, WHO IS IT?
AIN'T NOTHIN'...
COME ON, GIRL. GET THE FUCK OUTTA HERE.
I'LL HOOK UP WITCHOO LATER.
DON'T BE COMIN' AROUND HERE.
BUT...
WHO THE FUCK IS THIS AT THREE IN THE MORNING?
DON'T WORRY ABOUT IT, BABY.

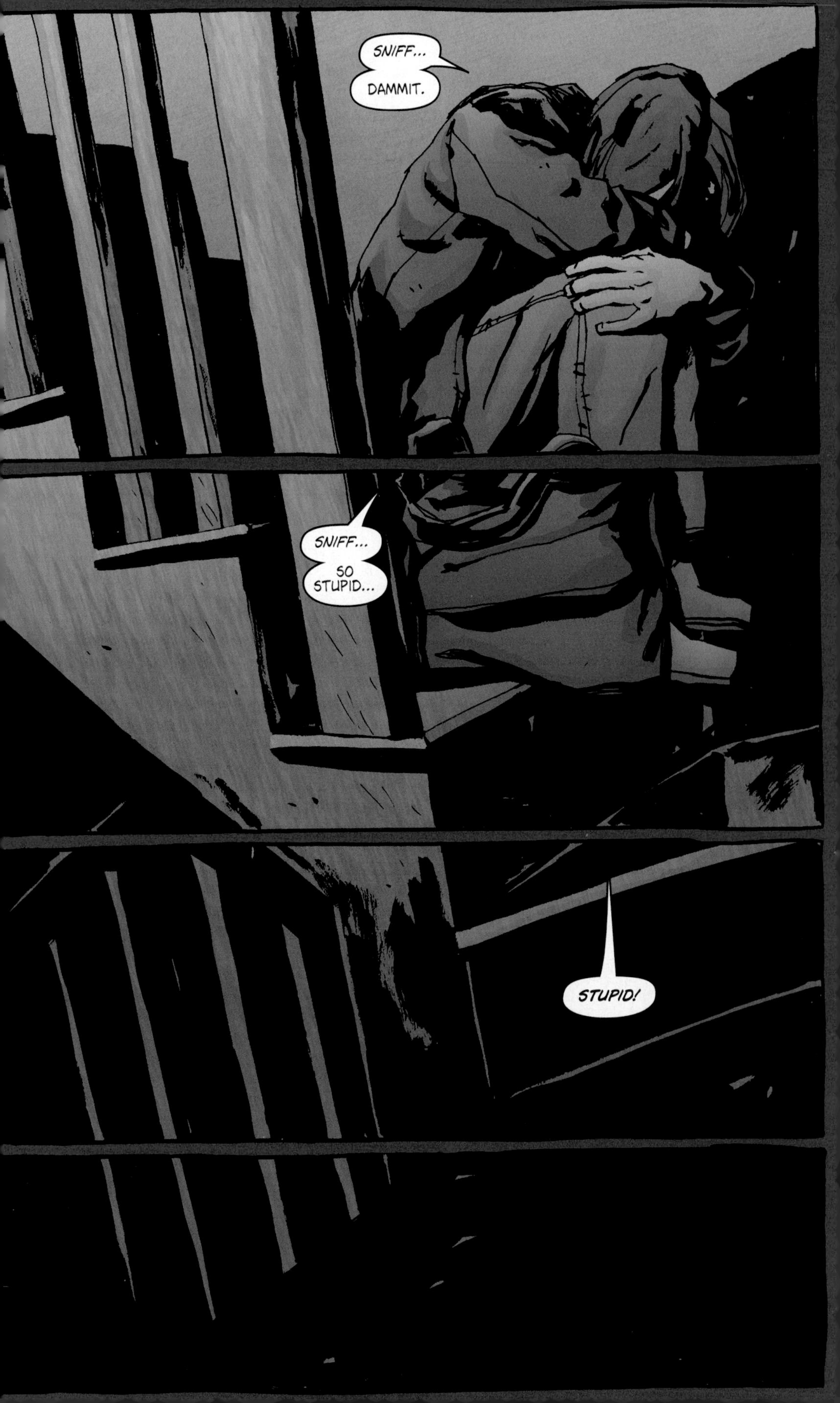
SNIFF...
DAMMIT.
SNIFF...
SO STUPID...
STUPID!

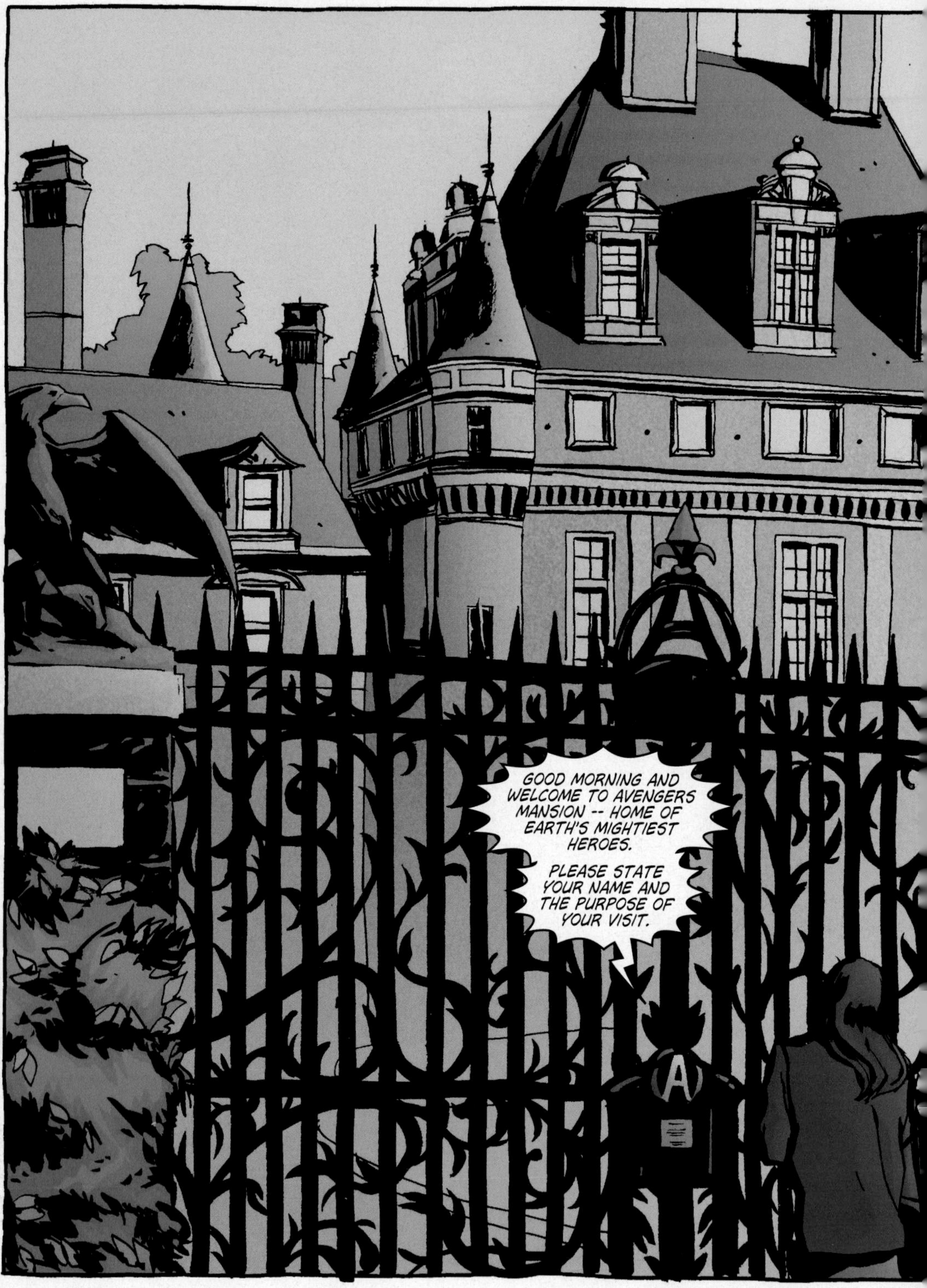
GOOD MORNING AND WELCOME TO AVENGERS MANSION -- HOME OF EARTH'S MIGHTIEST HEROES.
PLEASE STATE YOUR NAME AND THE PURPOSE OF YOUR VISIT.

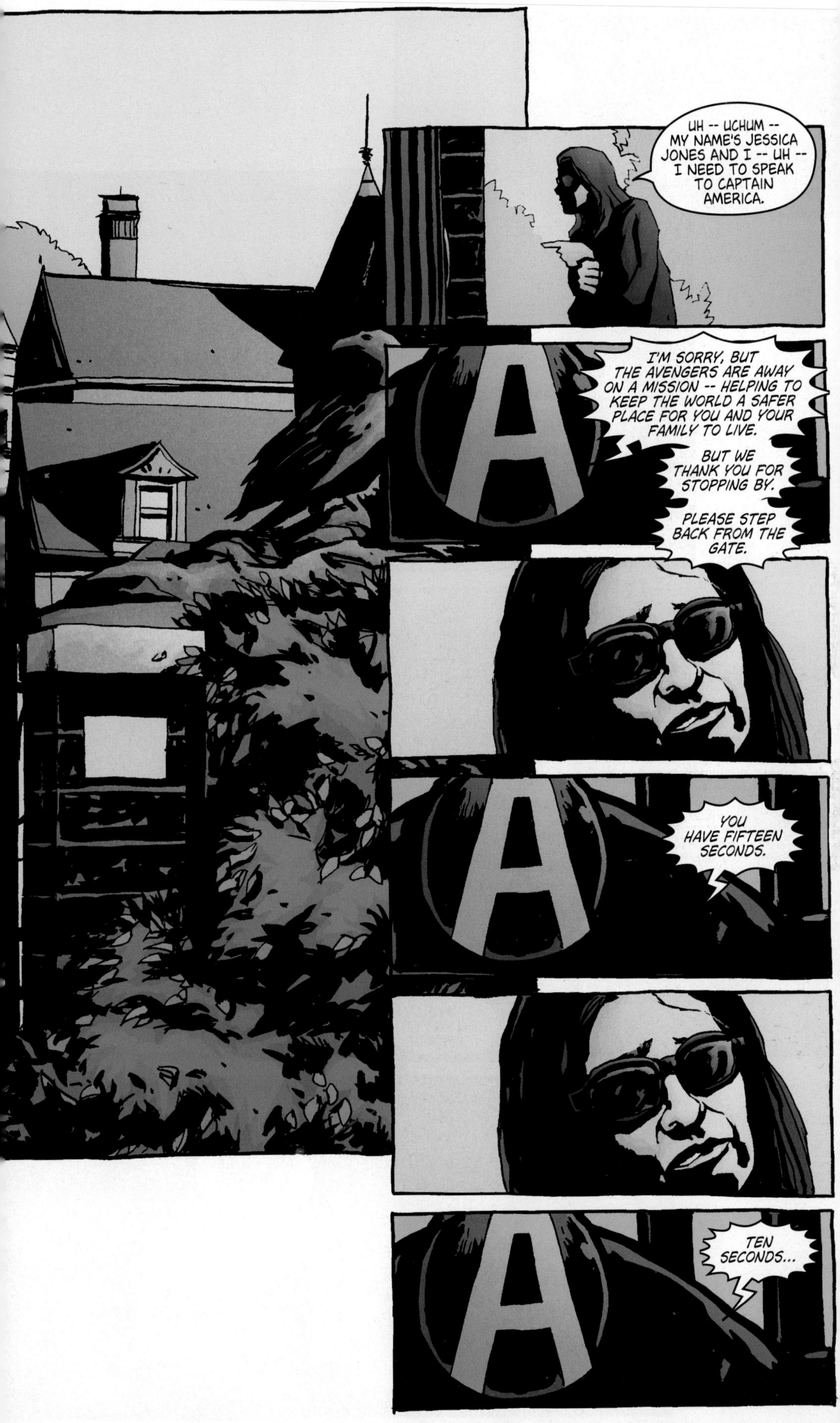
UH -- UCHUM -- MY NAME'S JESSICA JONES AND I -- UH -- I NEED TO SPEAK TO CAPTAIN AMERICA.
I'M SORRY, BUT THE AVENGERS ARE AWAY ON A MISSION -- HELPING TO KEEP THE WORLD A SAFER PLACE FOR YOU AND YOUR FAMILY TO LIVE.
BUT WE THANK YOU FOR STOPPING BY.
PLEASE STEP BACK FROM THE GATE.
YOU HAVE FIFTEEN SECONDS.
TEN SECONDS...

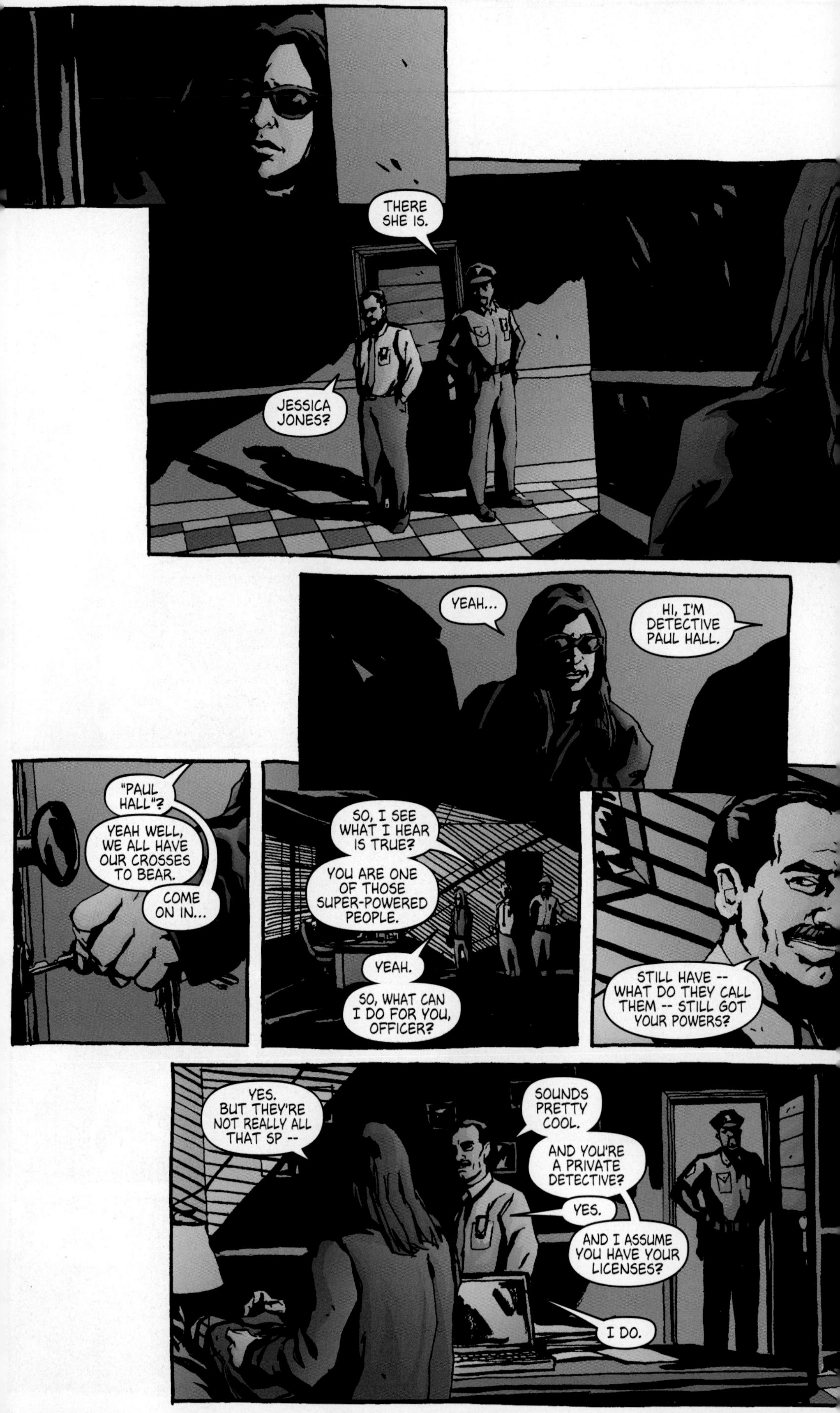
THERE SHE IS.
JESSICA JONES?
YEAH...
HI, I'M DETECTIVE PAUL HALL.
"PAUL HALL"?
YEAH WELL, WE ALL HAVE OUR CROSSES TO BEAR.
COME ON IN...
SO, I SEE WHAT I HEAR IS TRUE?
YOU ARE ONE OF THOSE SUPER-POWERED PEOPLE.
YEAH.
SO, WHAT CAN I DO FOR YOU, OFFICER?
STILL HAVE -- WHAT DO THEY CALL THEM -- STILL GOT YOUR POWERS?
YES. BUT THEY'RE NOT REALLY ALL THAT SP --
SOUNDS PRETTY COOL.
AND YOU'RE A PRIVATE DETECTIVE?
YES.
AND I ASSUME YOU HAVE YOUR LICENSES?
I DO.

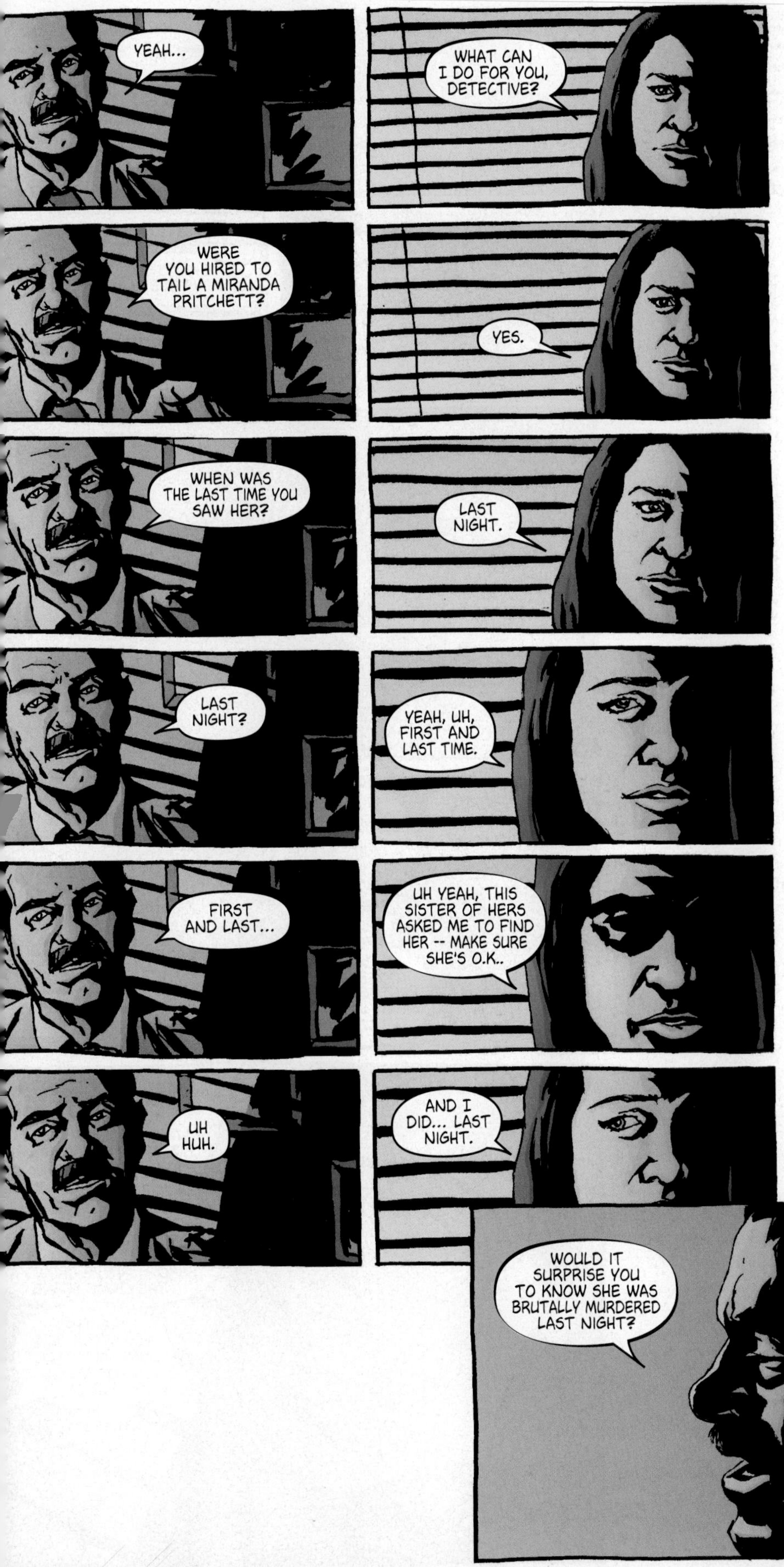
YEAH...
WHAT CAN I DO FOR YOU, DETECTIVE?
WERE YOU HIRED TO TAIL A MIRANDA PRITCHETT?
YES.
WHEN WAS THE LAST TIME YOU SAW HER?
LAST NIGHT.
LAST NIGHT?
YEAH, UH, FIRST AND LAST TIME.
FIRST AND LAST...
UH YEAH, THIS SISTER OF HERS ASKED ME TO FIND HER -- MAKE SURE SHE'S O.K..
UH HUH.
AND I DID... LAST NIGHT.
WOULD IT SURPRISE YOU TO KNOW SHE WAS BRUTALLY MURDERED LAST NIGHT?

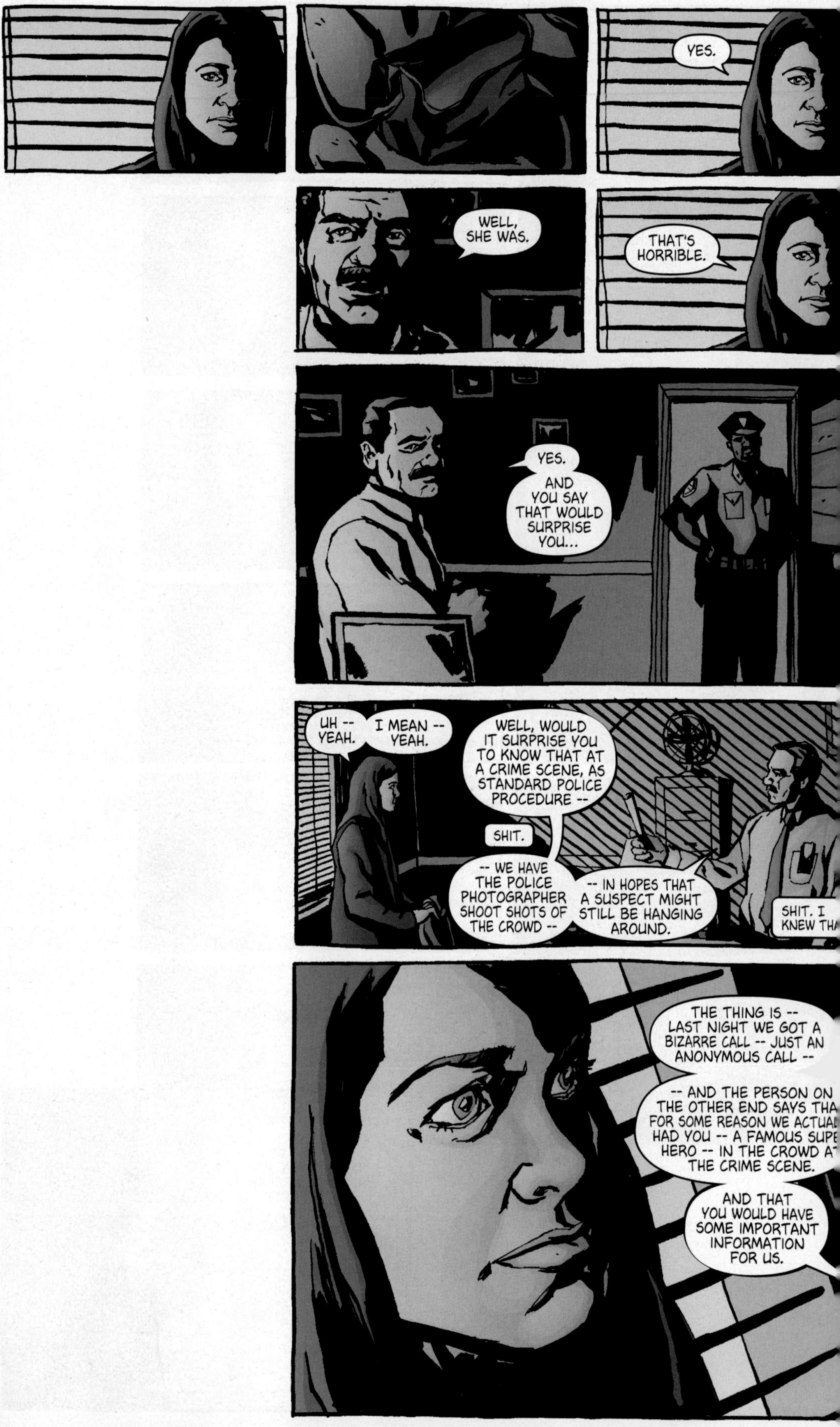
YES.
WELL, SHE WAS.
THAT'S HORRIBLE.
YES.
AND YOU SAY THAT WOULD SURPRISE YOU...
UH -- YEAH.
I MEAN -- YEAH.
WELL, WOULD IT SURPRISE YOU TO KNOW THAT AT A CRIME SCENE, AS STANDARD POLICE PROCEDURE --
SHIT.
-- WE HAVE THE POLICE PHOTOGRAPHER SHOOT SHOTS OF THE CROWD --
-- IN HOPES THAT A SUSPECT MIGHT STILL BE HANGING AROUND.
SHIT. I
THE THING IS -- LAST NIGHT WE GOT A BIZARRE CALL -- JUST AN ANONYMOUS CALL --
AND THAT YOU WOULD HAVE SOME IMPORTANT INFORMATION FOR US.

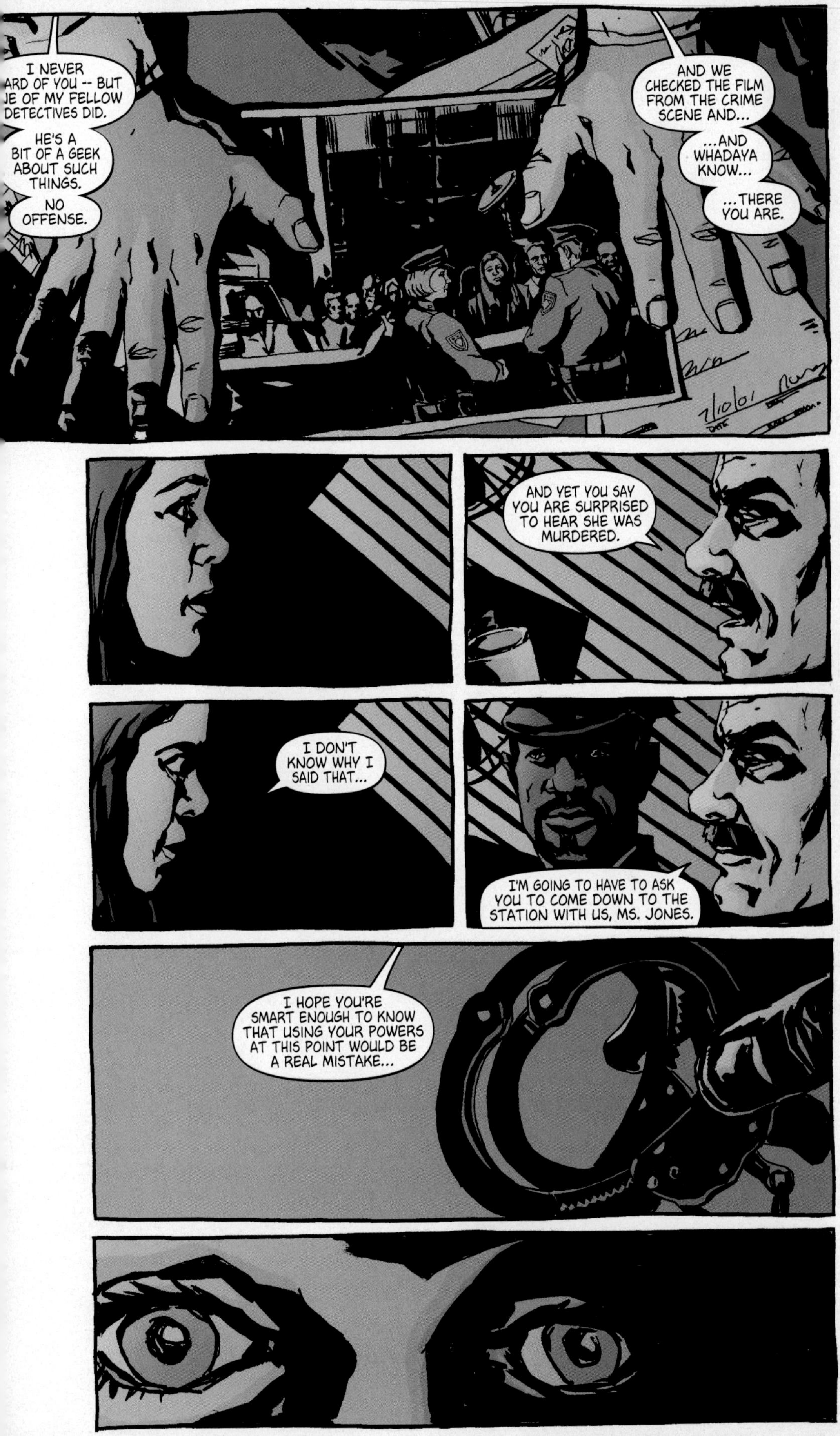
I NEVER
ARD OF YOU -- BUT
IE OF MY FELLOW
DETECTIVES DID.
HE'S A BIT OF A GEEK ABOUT SUCH THINGS.
NO OFFENSE.
AND WE CHECKED THE FILM FROM THE CRIME SCENE AND...
...AND WHADAYA KNOW...
...THERE YOU ARE.
AND YET YOU SAY YOU ARE SURPRISED TO HEAR SHE WAS MURDERED.
I DON'T KNOW WHY I SAID THAT...
I'M GOING TO HAVE TO ASK YOU TO COME DOWN TO THE STATION WITH US, MS. JONES.
I HOPE YOU'RE SMART ENOUGH TO KNOW THAT USING YOUR POWERS AT THIS POINT WOULD BE A REAL MISTAKE...

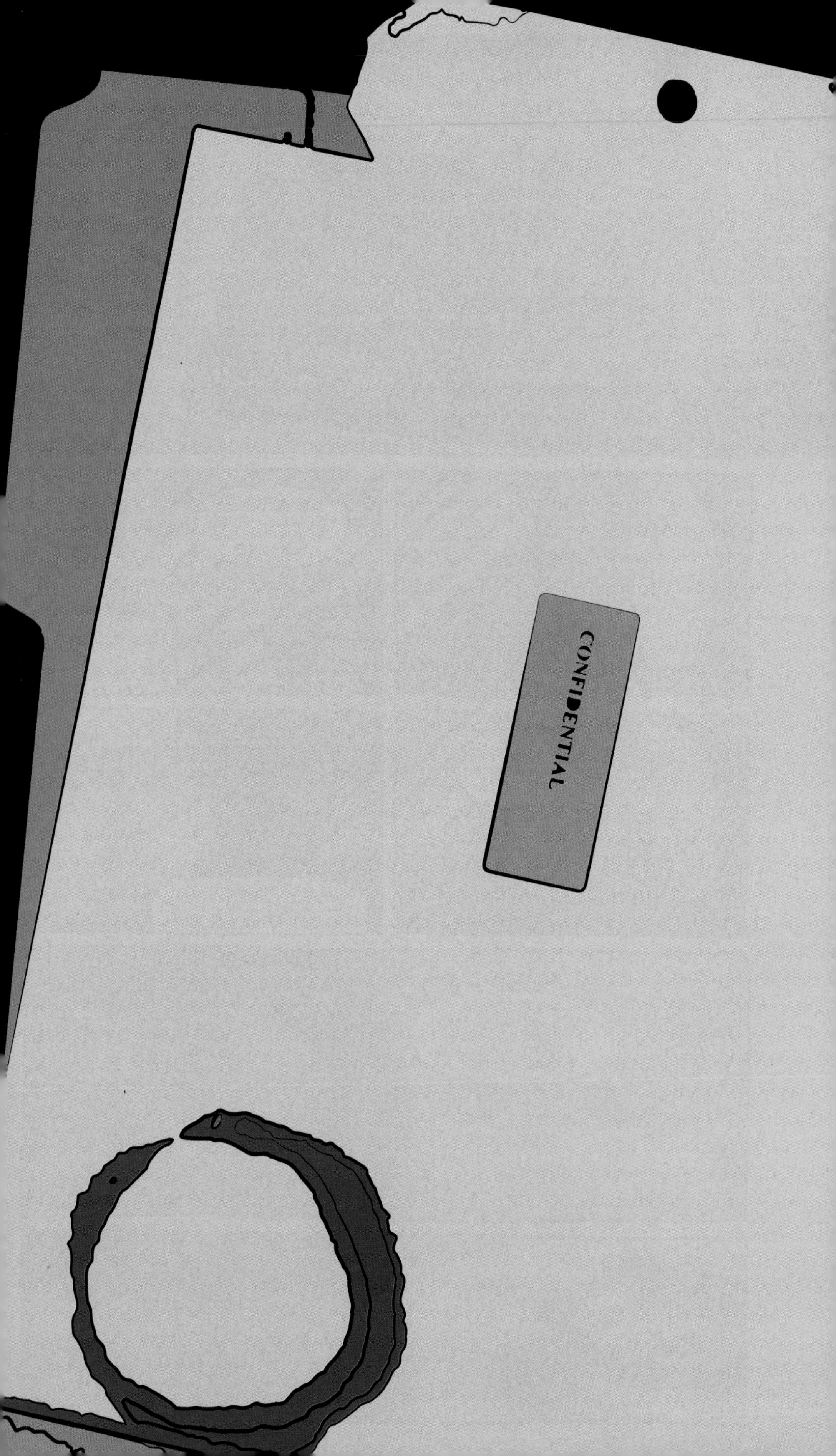
CONFIDENTIAL

[redacted]ap n[redacted]

ISSUE #3

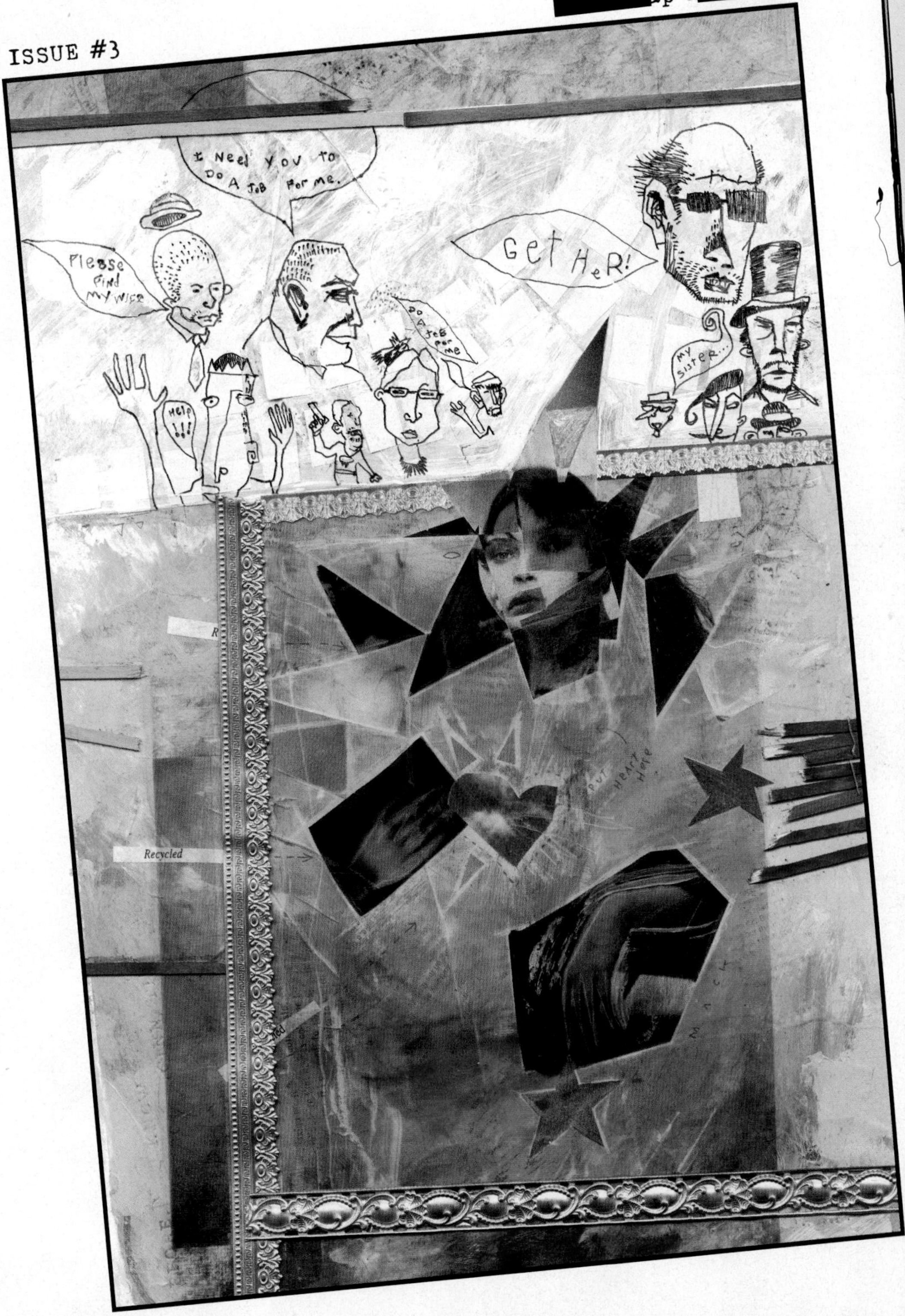

I Need You to Do A JoB For me.
Please Find MY Wife
Get HeR!
Do A JoB For me
my sister...
Help !!!
Recycled
Put Heart Here

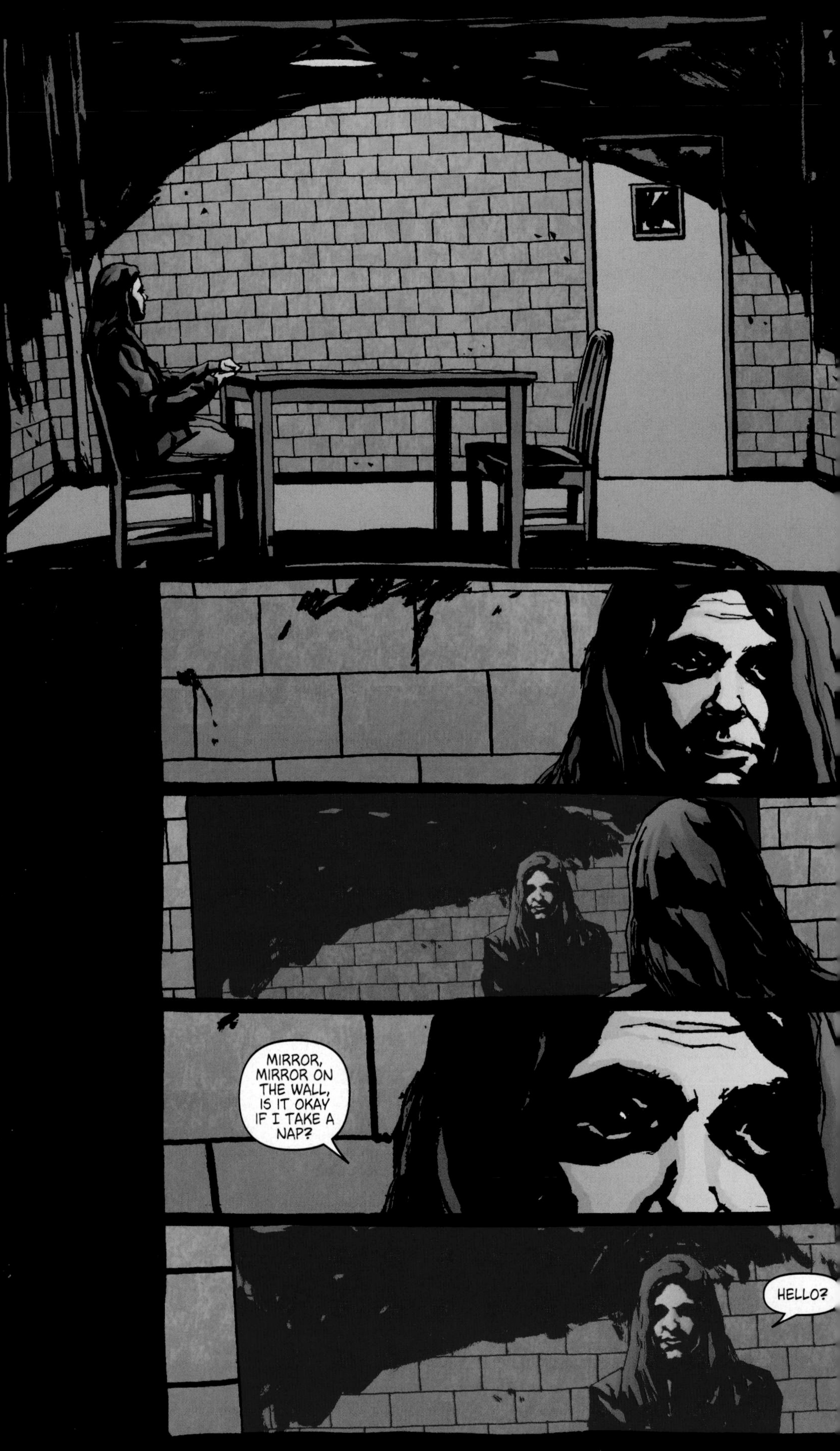
MIRROR, MIRROR ON THE WALL, IS IT OKAY IF I TAKE A NAP?
HELLO?

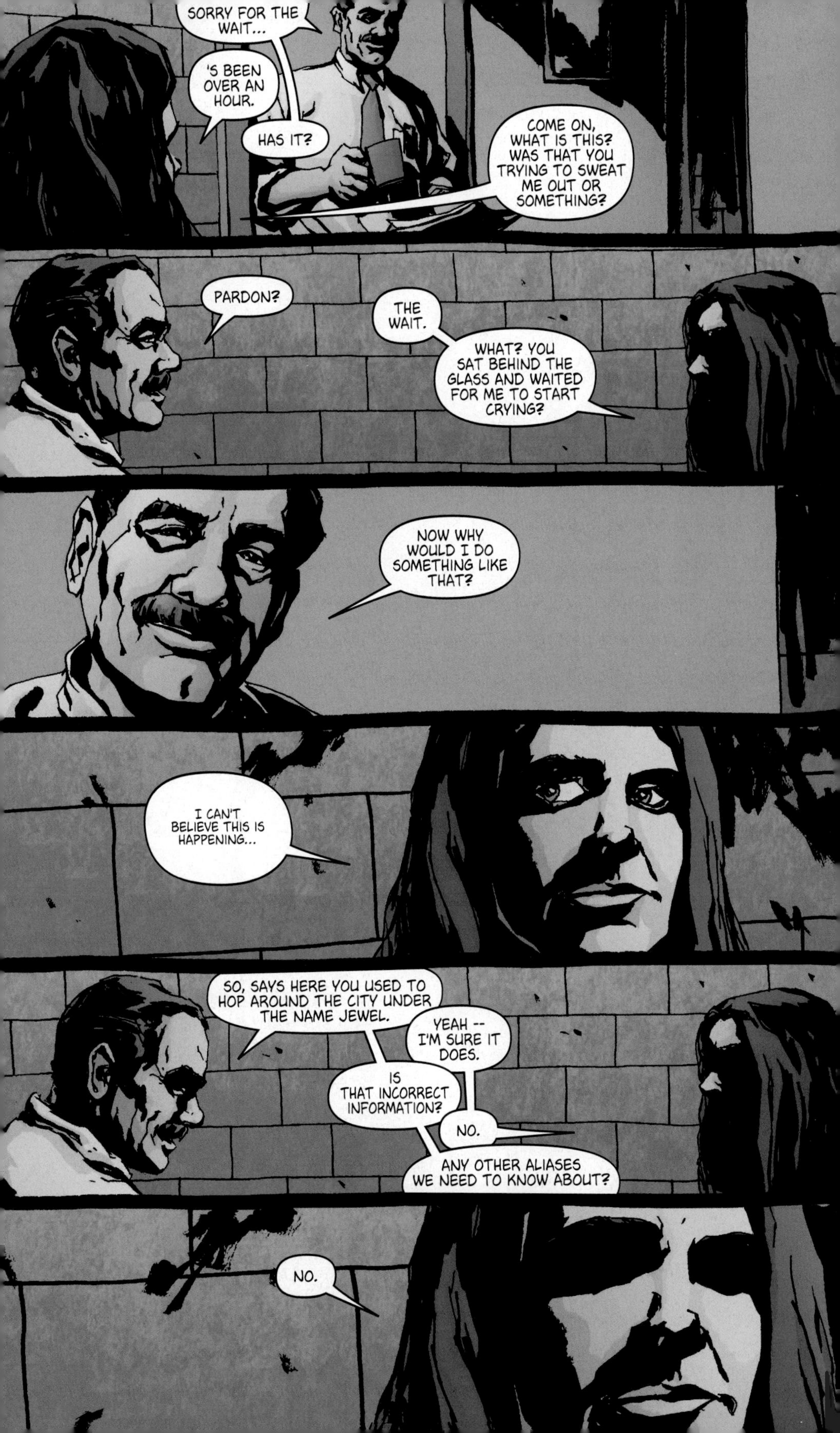
SORRY FOR THE WAIT...
'S BEEN OVER AN HOUR.
HAS IT?
COME ON, WHAT IS THIS? WAS THAT YOU TRYING TO SWEAT ME OUT OR SOMETHING?
PARDON?
THE WAIT.
WHAT? YOU SAT BEHIND THE GLASS AND WAITED FOR ME TO START CRYING?
NOW WHY WOULD I DO SOMETHING LIKE THAT?
I CAN'T BELIEVE THIS IS HAPPENING...
SO, SAYS HERE YOU USED TO HOP AROUND THE CITY UNDER THE NAME JEWEL.
YEAH -- I'M SURE IT DOES.
IS THAT INCORRECT INFORMATION?
NO.
ANY OTHER ALIASES WE NEED TO KNOW ABOUT?
NO.

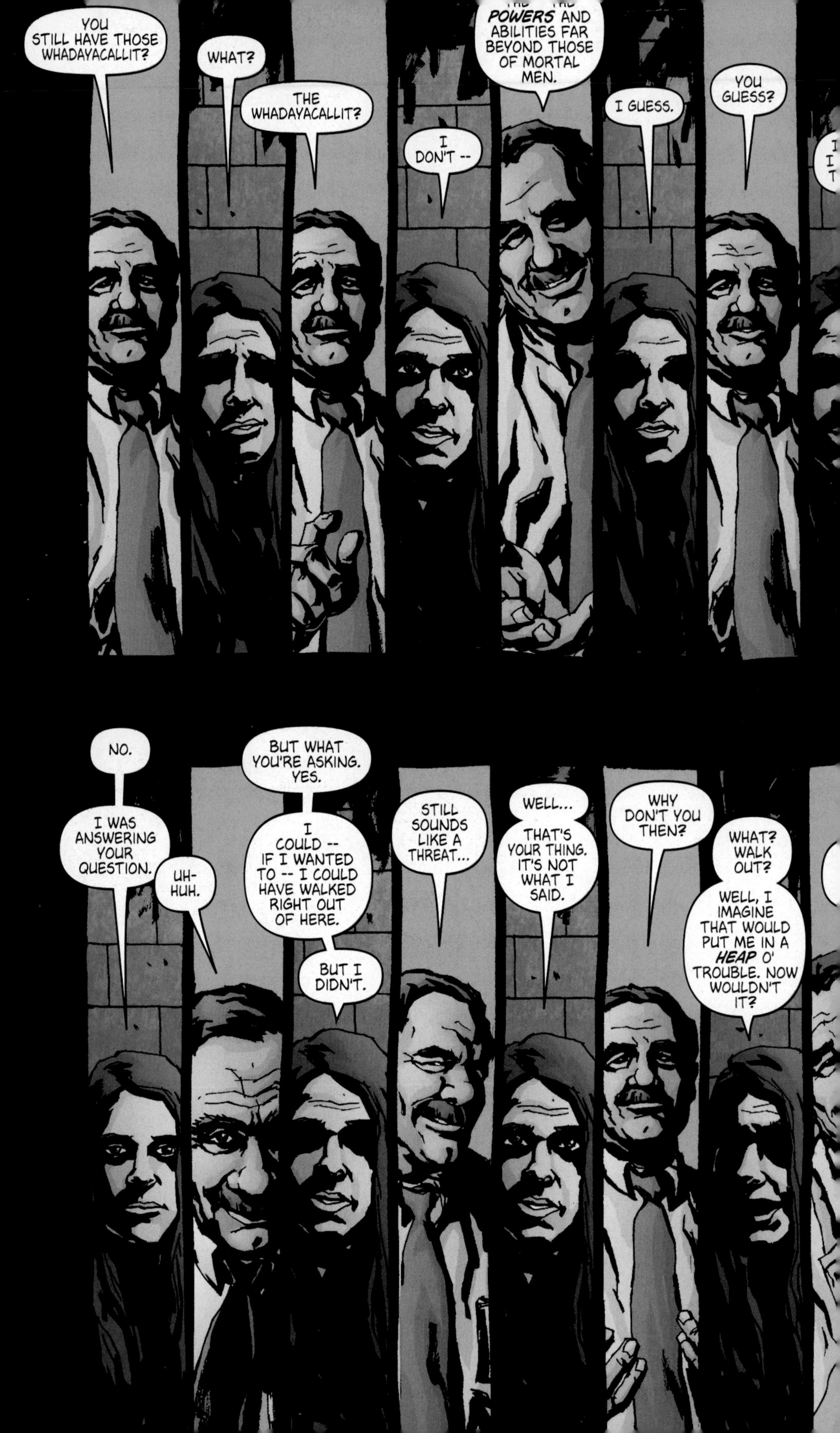
YOU STILL HAVE THOSE WHADAYACALLIT?
WHAT?
THE WHADAYACALLIT?
I DON'T --
POWERS AND ABILITIES FAR BEYOND THOSE OF MORTAL MEN.
I GUESS.
YOU GUESS?
NO.
I WAS ANSWERING YOUR QUESTION.
UH-HUH.
BUT WHAT YOU'RE ASKING. YES.
I COULD -- IF I WANTED TO -- I COULD HAVE WALKED RIGHT OUT OF HERE.
BUT I DIDN'T.
STILL SOUNDS LIKE A THREAT...
WELL...
THAT'S YOUR THING. IT'S NOT WHAT I SAID.
WHY DON'T YOU THEN?
WHAT? WALK OUT?
WELL, I IMAGINE THAT WOULD PUT ME IN A HEAP O' TROUBLE. NOW WOULDN'T IT?

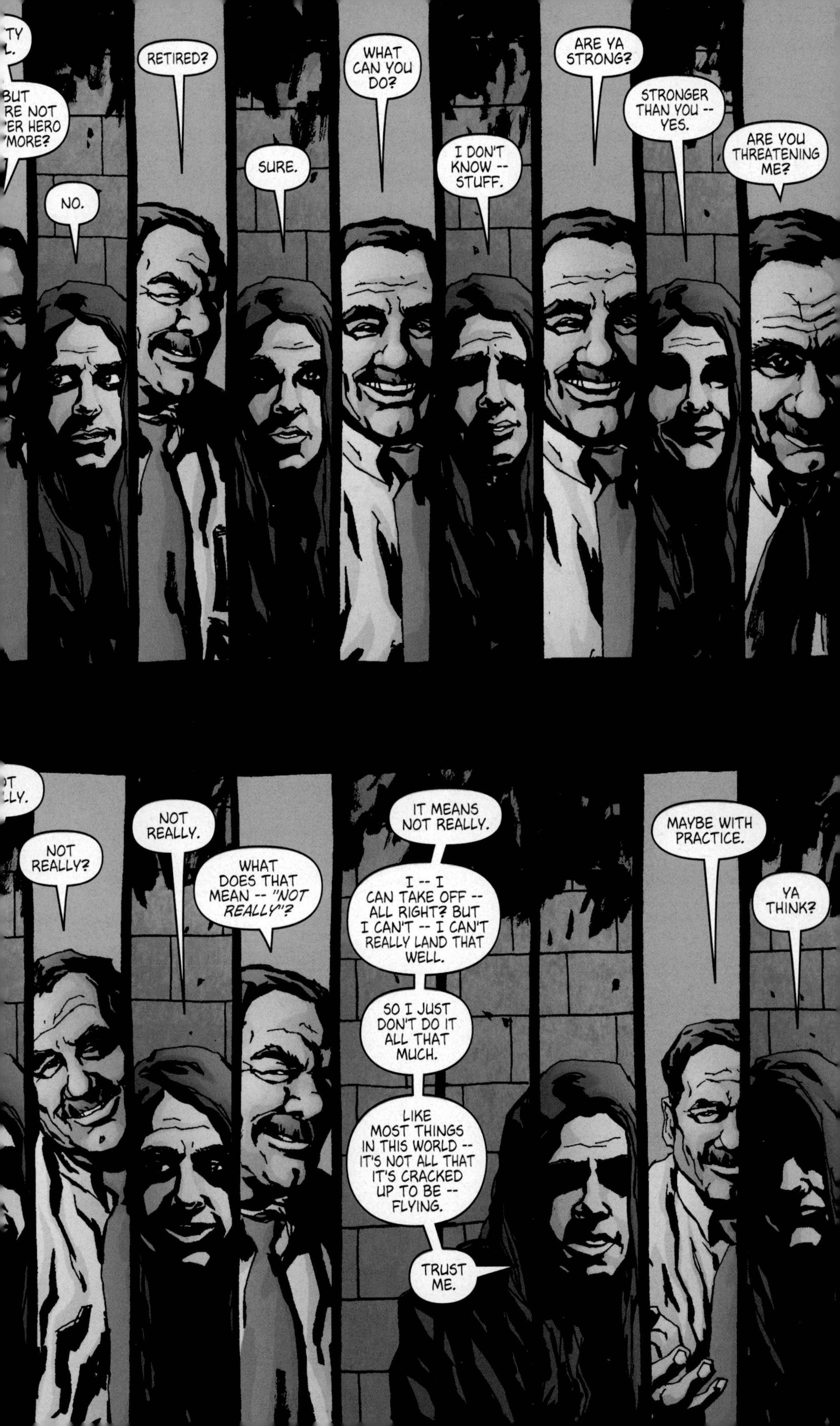
NO.
RETIRED?
SURE.
WHAT CAN YOU DO?
I DON'T KNOW -- STUFF.
ARE YA STRONG?
STRONGER THAN YOU -- YES.
ARE YOU THREATENING ME?
NOT REALLY?
NOT REALLY.
WHAT DOES THAT MEAN -- *"NOT REALLY"*?
IT MEANS NOT REALLY.
I -- I CAN TAKE OFF -- ALL RIGHT? BUT I CAN'T -- I CAN'T REALLY LAND THAT WELL.
SO I JUST DON'T DO IT ALL THAT MUCH.
LIKE MOST THINGS IN THIS WORLD -- IT'S NOT ALL THAT IT'S CRACKED UP TO BE -- FLYING.
TRUST ME.
MAYBE WITH PRACTICE.
YA THINK?

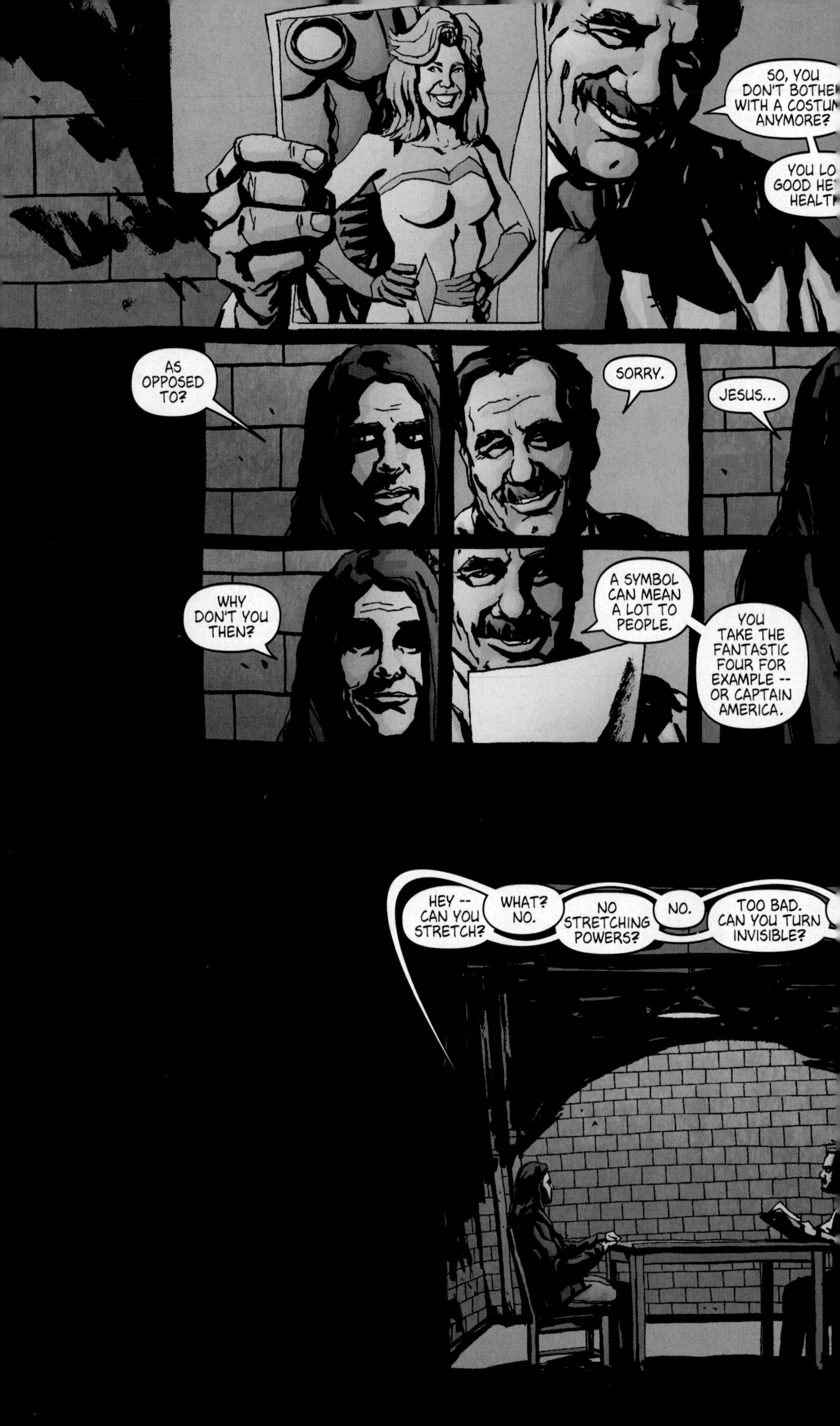
SO, YOU DON'T BOTHE WITH A COSTU ANYMORE?
YOU LO GOOD HE HEALT
AS OPPOSED TO?
SORRY.
JESUS...
WHY DON'T YOU THEN?
A SYMBOL CAN MEAN A LOT TO PEOPLE.
YOU TAKE THE FANTASTIC FOUR FOR EXAMPLE -- OR CAPTAIN AMERICA.
HEY -- CAN YOU STRETCH?
WHAT? NO.
NO STRETCHING POWERS?
NO.
TOO BAD. CAN YOU TURN INVISIBLE?

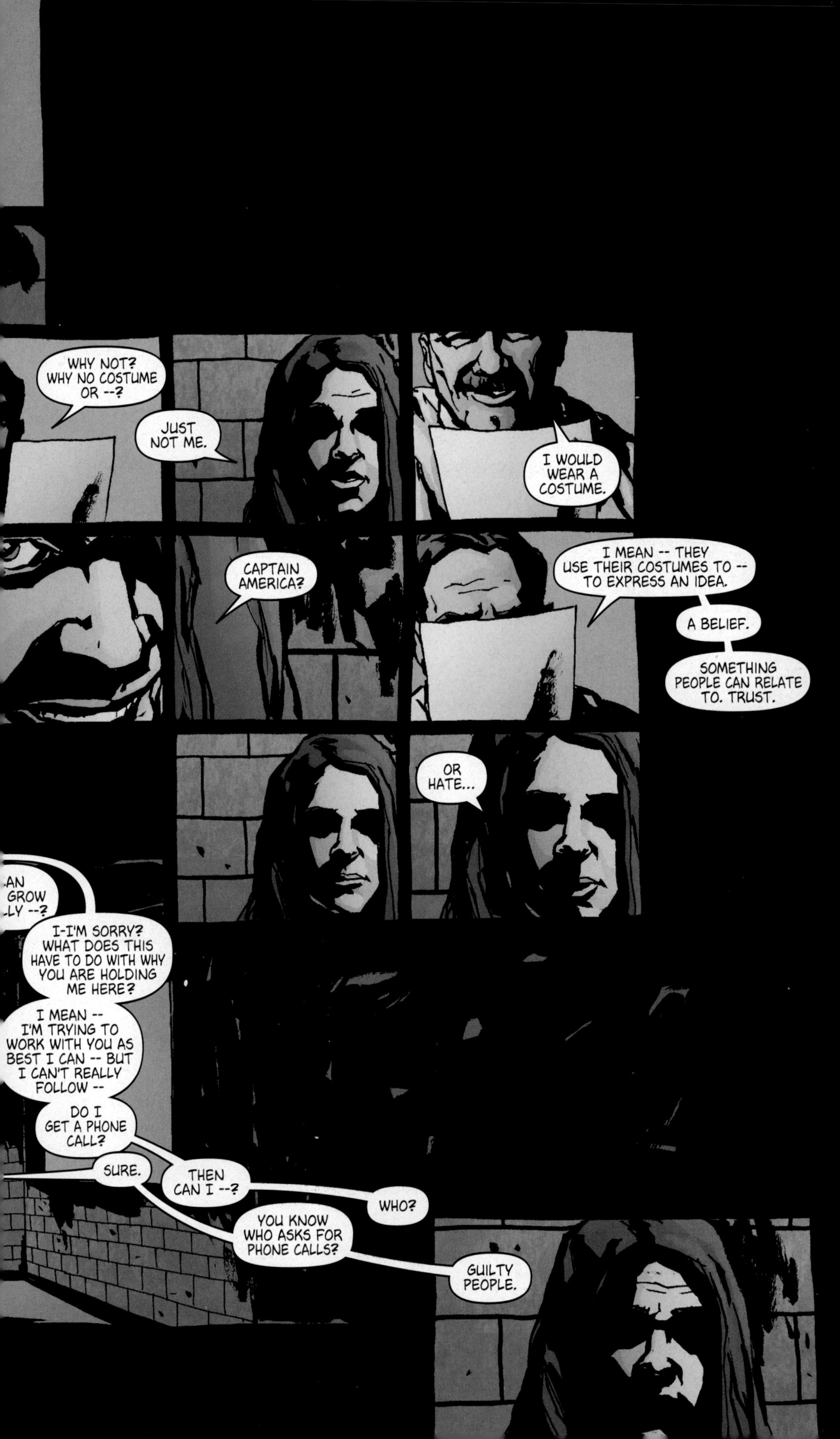

WHY NOT? WHY NO COSTUME OR --?
JUST NOT ME.
I WOULD WEAR A COSTUME.
CAPTAIN AMERICA?
I MEAN -- THEY USE THEIR COSTUMES TO -- TO EXPRESS AN IDEA.
A BELIEF.
SOMETHING PEOPLE CAN RELATE TO. TRUST.
OR HATE...
I-I'M SORRY? WHAT DOES THIS HAVE TO DO WITH WHY YOU ARE HOLDING ME HERE?
I MEAN -- I'M TRYING TO WORK WITH YOU AS BEST I CAN -- BUT I CAN'T REALLY FOLLOW --
DO I GET A PHONE CALL?
SURE.
THEN CAN I --?
WHO?
YOU KNOW WHO ASKS FOR PHONE CALLS?
GUILTY PEOPLE.

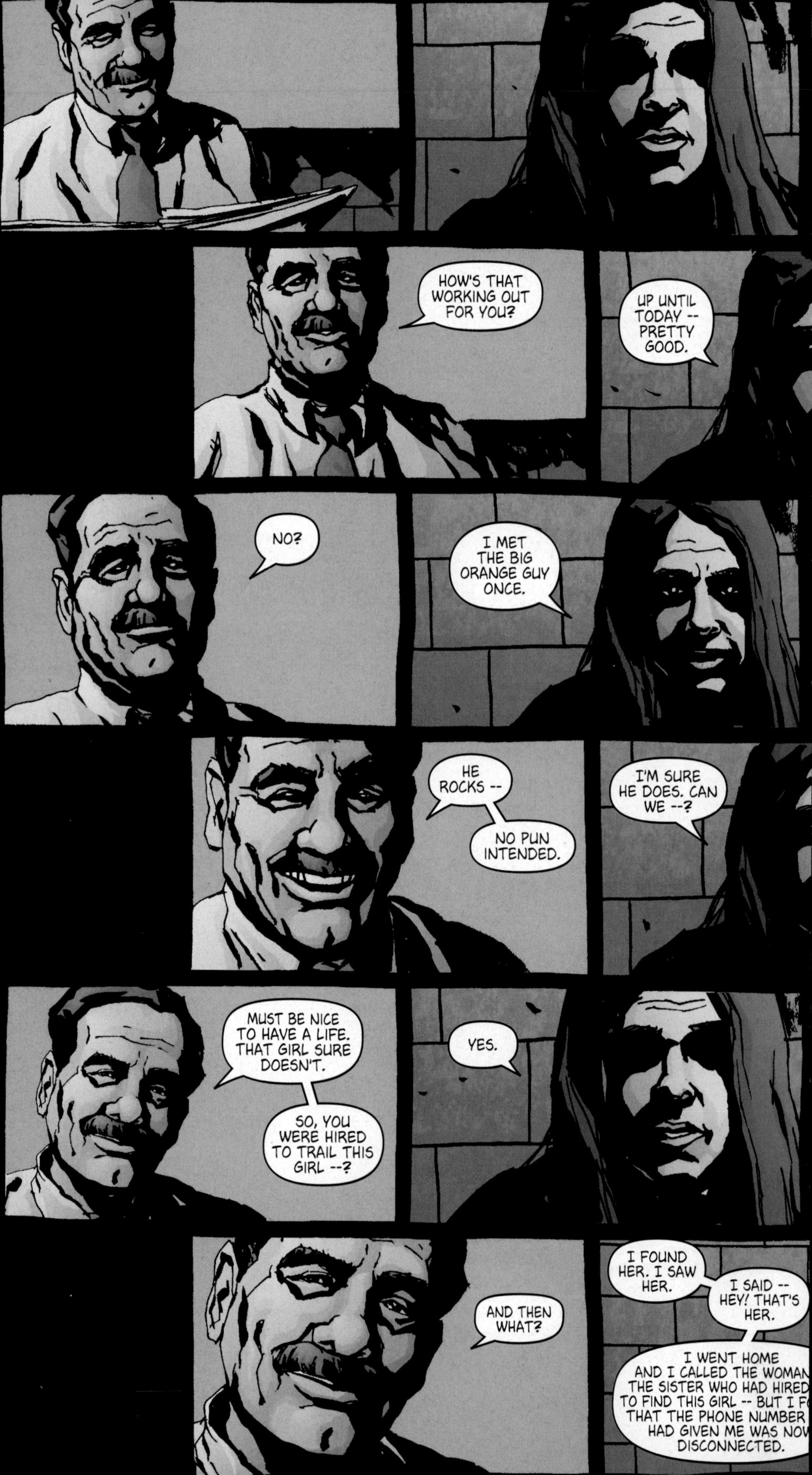
HOW'S THAT WORKING OUT FOR YOU?
UP UNTIL TODAY -- PRETTY GOOD.
NO?
I MET THE BIG ORANGE GUY ONCE.
HE ROCKS --
NO PUN INTENDED.
I'M SURE HE DOES. CAN WE --?
MUST BE NICE TO HAVE A LIFE. THAT GIRL SURE DOESN'T.
SO, YOU WERE HIRED TO TRAIL THIS GIRL --?
YES.
AND THEN WHAT?
I FOUND HER. I SAW HER.
I SAID -- HEY! THAT'S HER.

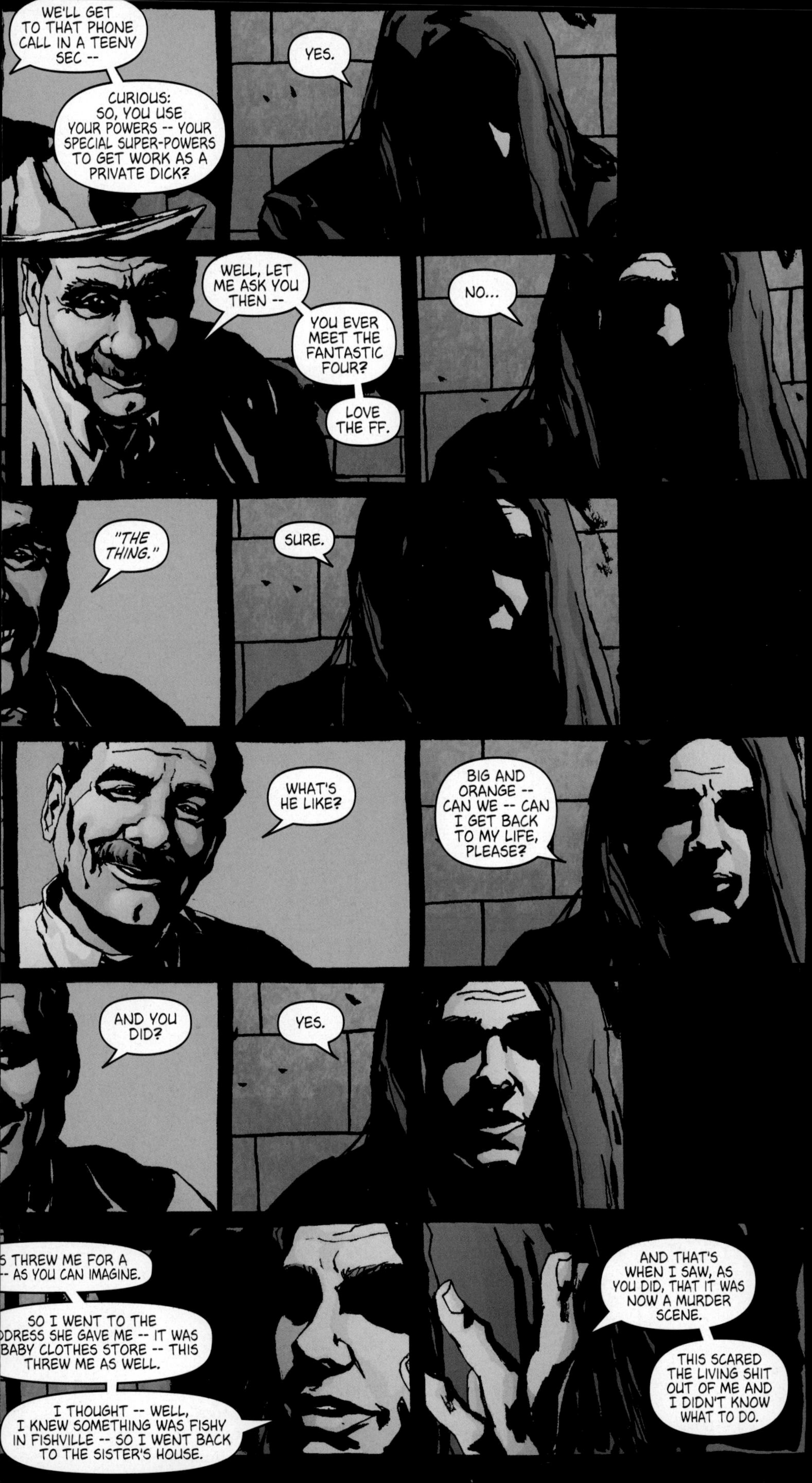
WE'LL GET TO THAT PHONE CALL IN A TEENY SEC --
CURIOUS: SO, YOU USE YOUR POWERS -- YOUR SPECIAL SUPER-POWERS TO GET WORK AS A PRIVATE DICK?
YES.
WELL, LET ME ASK YOU THEN --
YOU EVER MEET THE FANTASTIC FOUR?
LOVE THE FF.
NO...
"THE THING."
SURE.
WHAT'S HE LIKE?
BIG AND ORANGE -- CAN WE -- CAN I GET BACK TO MY LIFE, PLEASE?
AND YOU DID?
YES.
S THREW ME FOR A -- AS YOU CAN IMAGINE.
SO I WENT TO THE DDRESS SHE GAVE ME -- IT WAS BABY CLOTHES STORE -- THIS THREW ME AS WELL.
I THOUGHT -- WELL, I KNEW SOMETHING WAS FISHY IN FISHVILLE -- SO I WENT BACK TO THE SISTER'S HOUSE.
AND THAT'S WHEN I SAW, AS YOU DID, THAT IT WAS NOW A MURDER SCENE.
THIS SCARED THE LIVING SHIT OUT OF ME AND I DIDN'T KNOW WHAT TO DO.

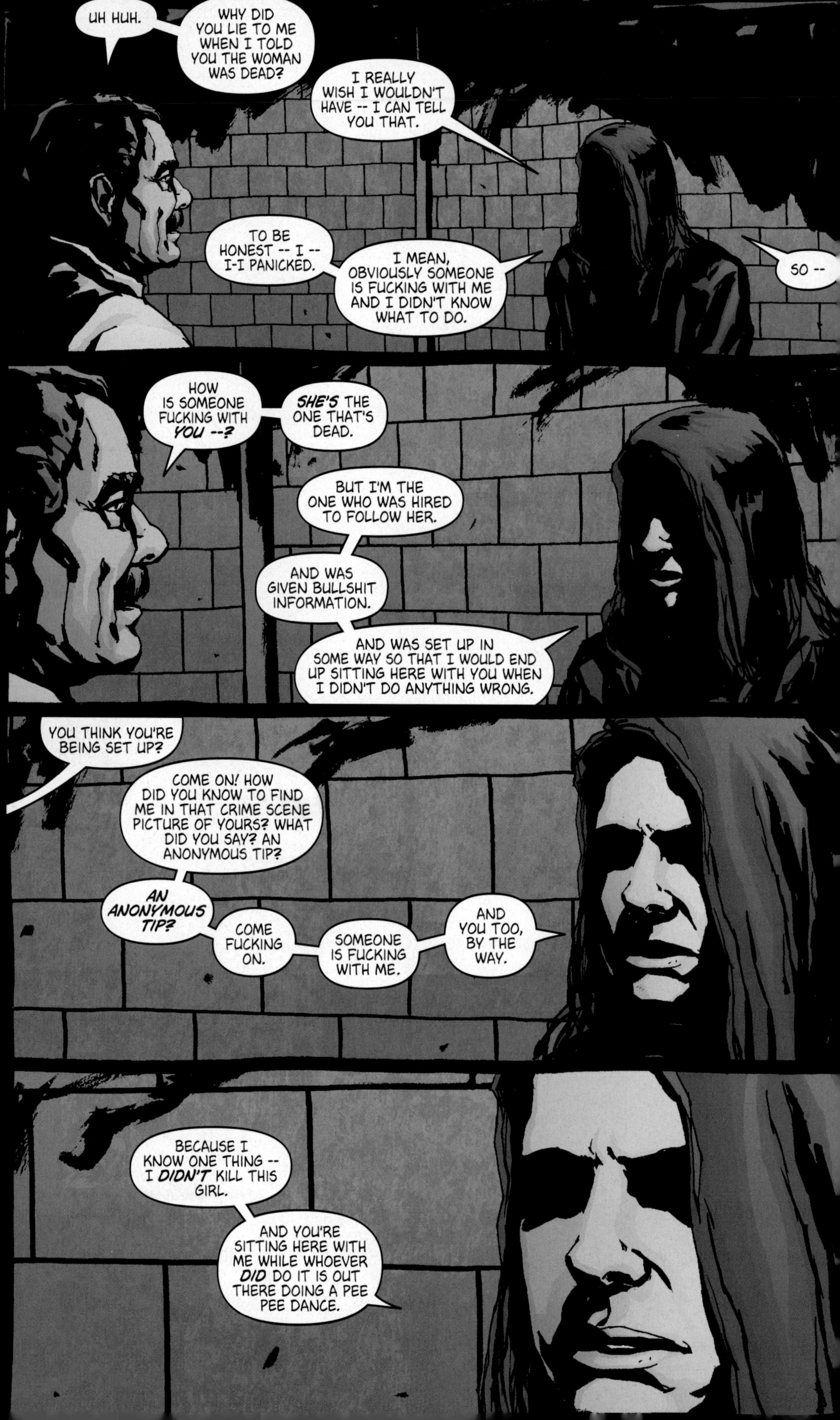
UH HUH.
WHY DID YOU LIE TO ME WHEN I TOLD YOU THE WOMAN WAS DEAD?
I REALLY WISH I WOULDN'T HAVE -- I CAN TELL YOU THAT.
TO BE HONEST -- I -- I-I PANICKED.
I MEAN, OBVIOUSLY SOMEONE IS FUCKING WITH ME AND I DIDN'T KNOW WHAT TO DO.
SO --
HOW IS SOMEONE FUCKING WITH *YOU* --?
SHE'S THE ONE THAT'S DEAD.
BUT I'M THE ONE WHO WAS HIRED TO FOLLOW HER.
AND WAS GIVEN BULLSHIT INFORMATION.
AND WAS SET UP IN SOME WAY SO THAT I WOULD END UP SITTING HERE WITH YOU WHEN I DIDN'T DO ANYTHING WRONG.
YOU THINK YOU'RE BEING SET UP?
COME ON! HOW DID YOU KNOW TO FIND ME IN THAT CRIME SCENE PICTURE OF YOURS? WHAT DID YOU SAY? AN ANONYMOUS TIP?
AN ANONYMOUS TIP?
COME FUCKING ON.
SOMEONE IS FUCKING WITH ME.
AND YOU TOO, BY THE WAY.
BECAUSE I KNOW ONE THING -- I *DIDN'T* KILL THIS GIRL.
AND YOU'RE SITTING HERE WITH ME WHILE WHOEVER *DID* DO IT IS OUT THERE DOING A PEE PEE DANCE.

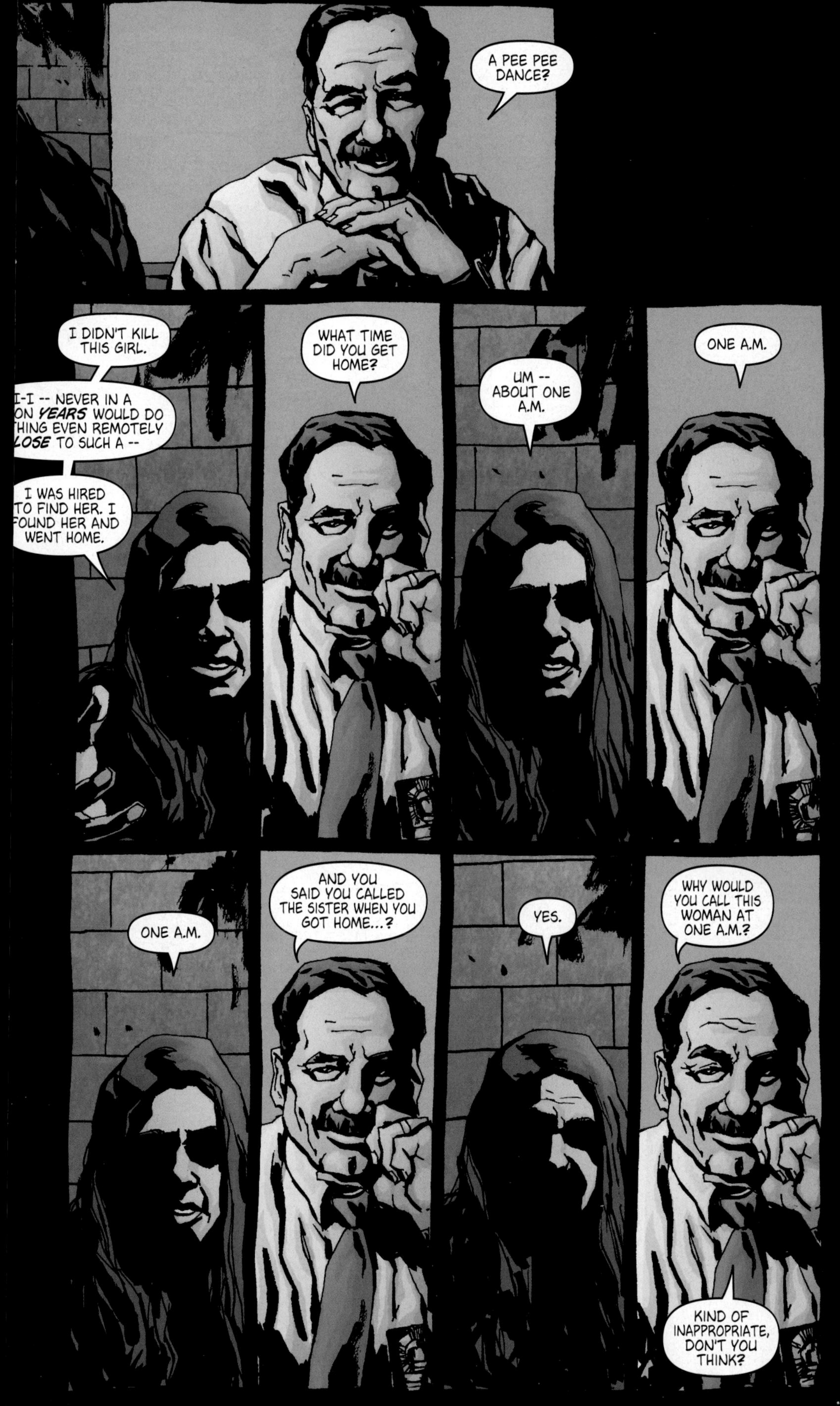
A PEE PEE DANCE?
I DIDN'T KILL THIS GIRL.
I-I -- NEVER IN A ON YEARS WOULD DO THING EVEN REMOTELY LOSE TO SUCH A --
I WAS HIRED TO FIND HER. I FOUND HER AND WENT HOME.
WHAT TIME DID YOU GET HOME?
UM -- ABOUT ONE A.M.
ONE A.M.
ONE A.M.
AND YOU SAID YOU CALLED THE SISTER WHEN YOU GOT HOME...?
YES.
WHY WOULD YOU CALL THIS WOMAN AT ONE A.M.?
KIND OF INAPPROPRIATE, DON'T YOU THINK?

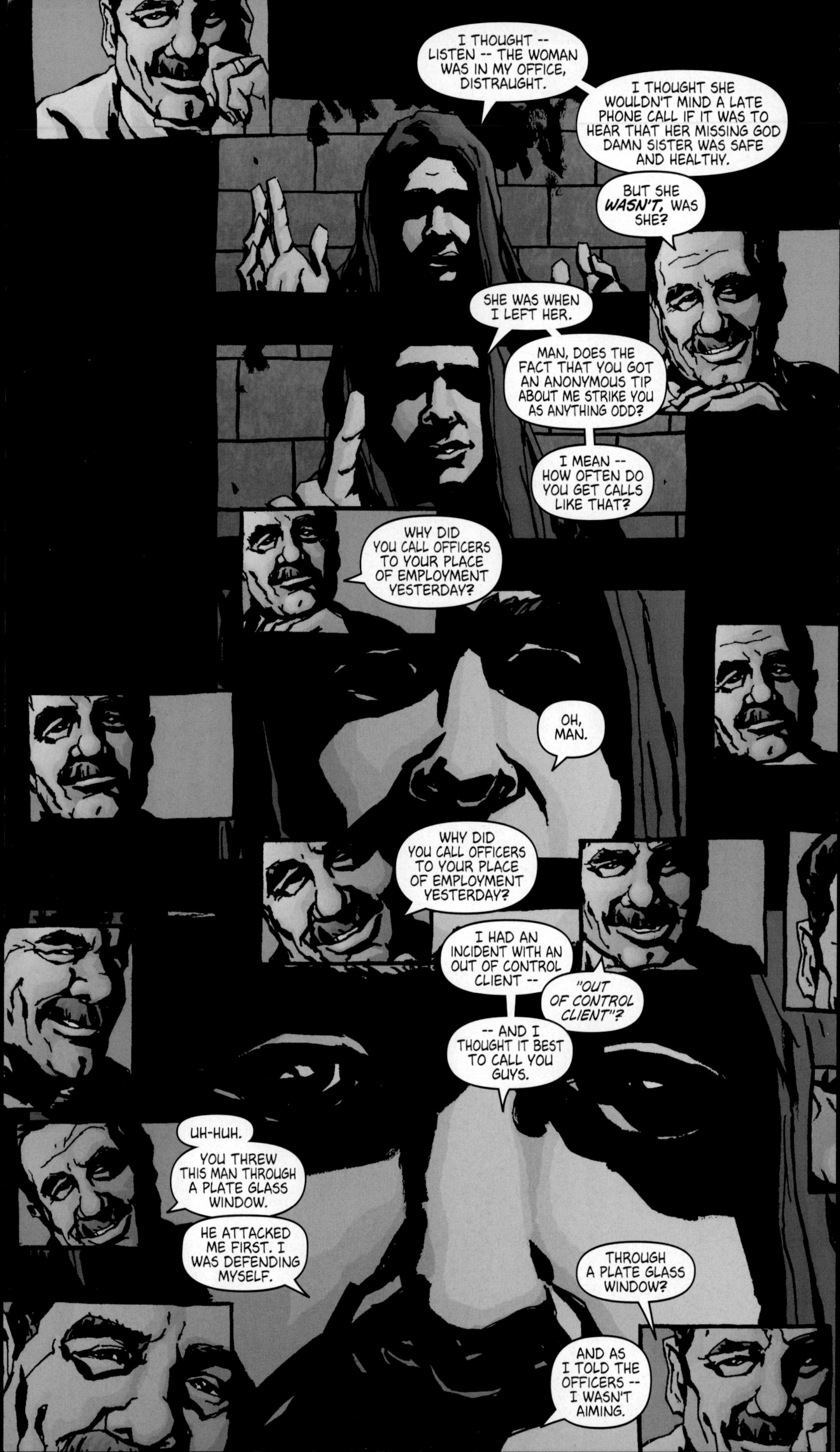
I THOUGHT -- LISTEN -- THE WOMAN WAS IN MY OFFICE, DISTRAUGHT.
I THOUGHT SHE WOULDN'T MIND A LATE PHONE CALL IF IT WAS TO HEAR THAT HER MISSING GOD DAMN SISTER WAS SAFE AND HEALTHY.
BUT SHE *WASN'T*, WAS SHE?
SHE WAS WHEN I LEFT HER.
MAN, DOES THE FACT THAT YOU GOT AN ANONYMOUS TIP ABOUT ME STRIKE YOU AS ANYTHING ODD?
I MEAN -- HOW OFTEN DO YOU GET CALLS LIKE THAT?
WHY DID YOU CALL OFFICERS TO YOUR PLACE OF EMPLOYMENT YESTERDAY?
OH, MAN.
WHY DID YOU CALL OFFICERS TO YOUR PLACE OF EMPLOYMENT YESTERDAY?
I HAD AN INCIDENT WITH AN OUT OF CONTROL CLIENT --
"OUT OF CONTROL CLIENT"?
-- AND I THOUGHT IT BEST TO CALL YOU GUYS.
UH-HUH.
YOU THREW THIS MAN THROUGH A PLATE GLASS WINDOW.
HE ATTACKED ME FIRST. I WAS DEFENDING MYSELF.
THROUGH A PLATE GLASS WINDOW?
AND AS I TOLD THE OFFICERS -- I WASN'T AIMING.

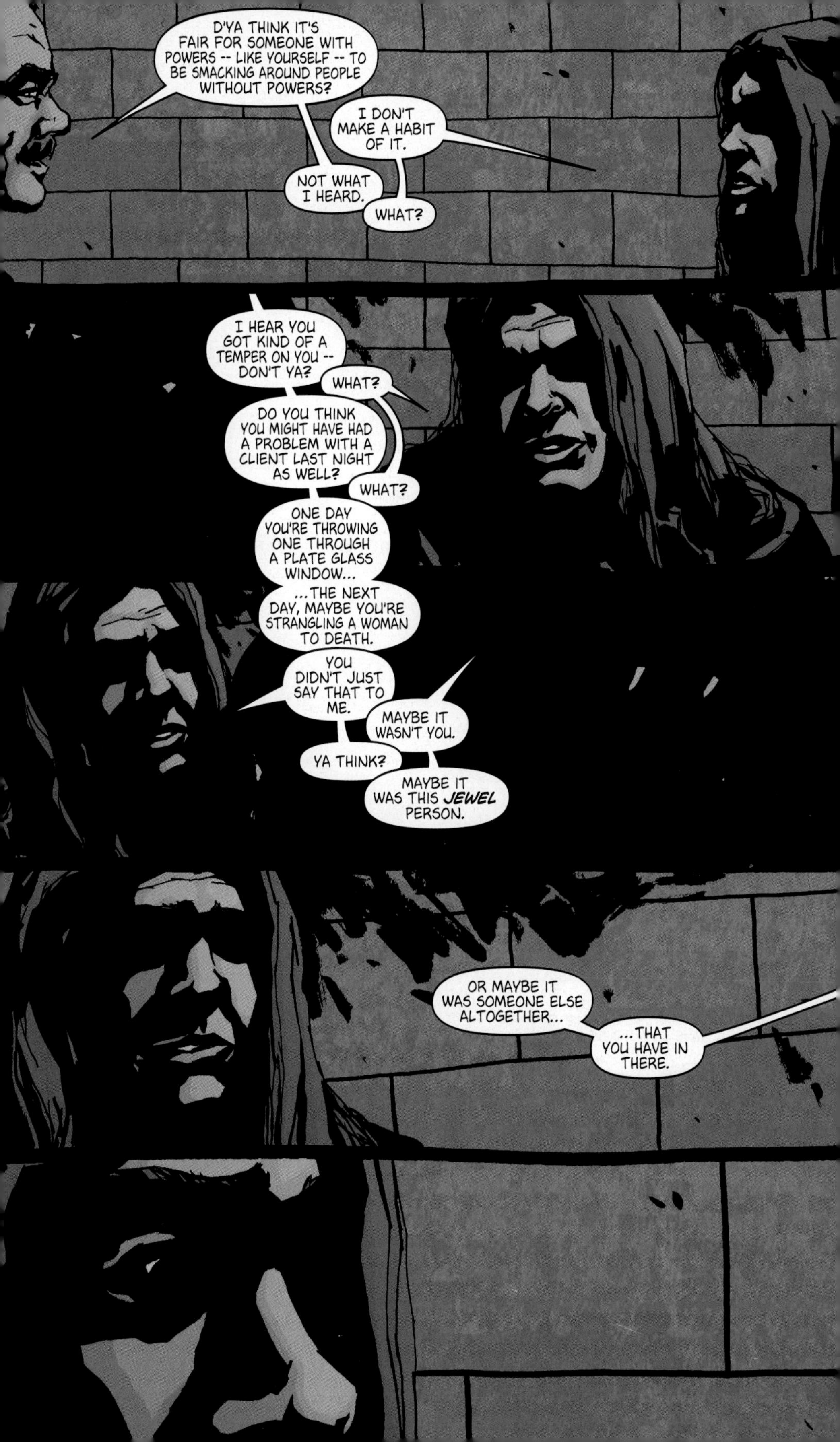
D'YA THINK IT'S FAIR FOR SOMEONE WITH POWERS -- LIKE YOURSELF -- TO BE SMACKING AROUND PEOPLE WITHOUT POWERS?
I DON'T MAKE A HABIT OF IT.
NOT WHAT I HEARD.
WHAT?
I HEAR YOU GOT KIND OF A TEMPER ON YOU -- DON'T YA?
WHAT?
DO YOU THINK YOU MIGHT HAVE HAD A PROBLEM WITH A CLIENT LAST NIGHT AS WELL?
WHAT?
ONE DAY YOU'RE THROWING ONE THROUGH A PLATE GLASS WINDOW...
...THE NEXT DAY, MAYBE YOU'RE STRANGLING A WOMAN TO DEATH.
YOU DIDN'T JUST SAY THAT TO ME.
MAYBE IT WASN'T YOU.
YA THINK?
MAYBE IT WAS THIS *JEWEL* PERSON.
OR MAYBE IT WAS SOMEONE ELSE ALTOGETHER...
...THAT YOU HAVE IN THERE.

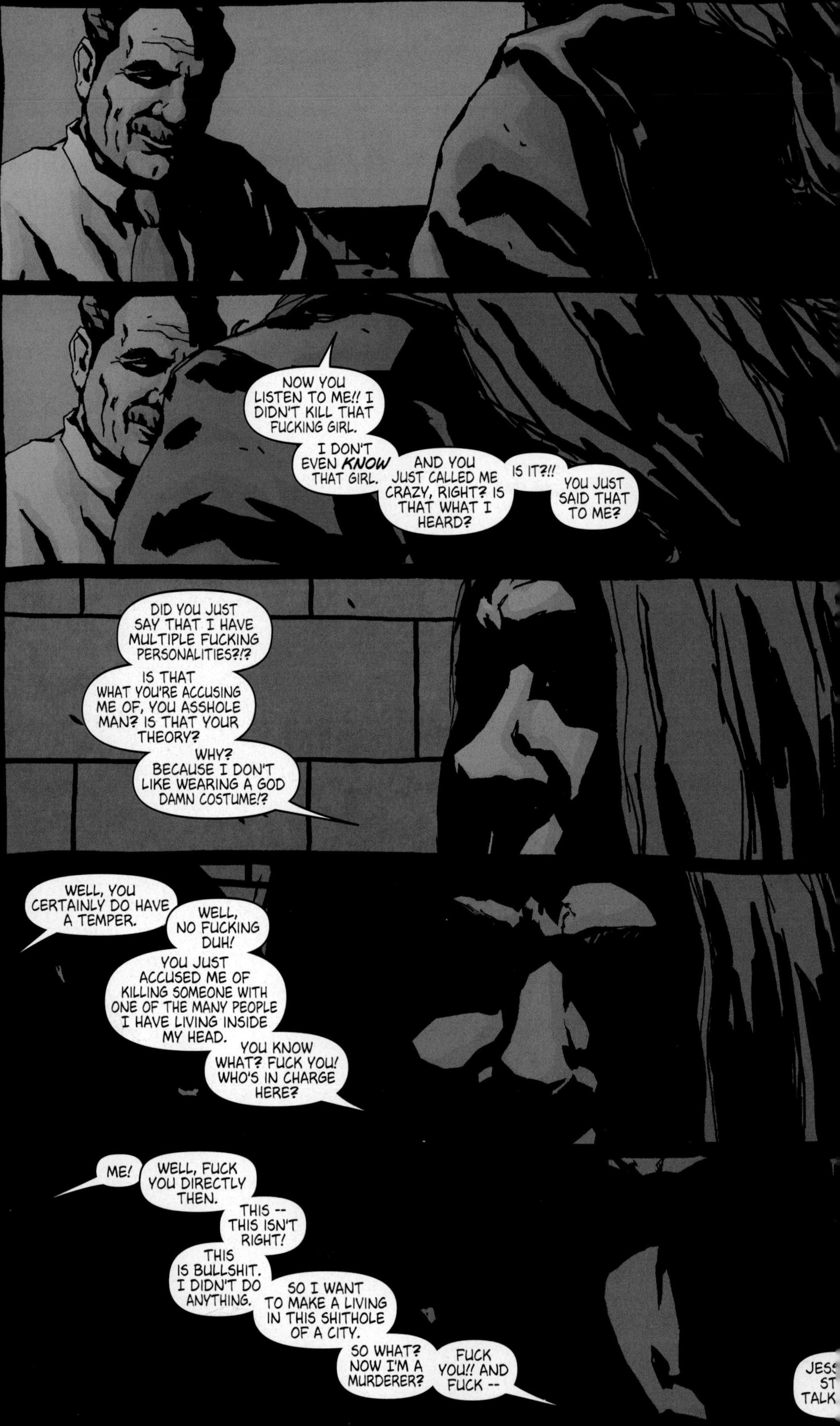

NOW YOU LISTEN TO ME!! I DIDN'T KILL THAT FUCKING GIRL.
I DON'T EVEN *KNOW* THAT GIRL.
AND YOU JUST CALLED ME CRAZY, RIGHT? IS THAT WHAT I HEARD?
IS IT?!!
YOU JUST SAID THAT TO ME?
DID YOU JUST SAY THAT I HAVE MULTIPLE FUCKING PERSONALITIES?!?
IS THAT WHAT YOU'RE ACCUSING ME OF, YOU ASSHOLE MAN? IS THAT YOUR THEORY?
WHY? BECAUSE I DON'T LIKE WEARING A GOD DAMN COSTUME!?
WELL, YOU CERTAINLY DO HAVE A TEMPER.
WELL, NO FUCKING DUH!
YOU JUST ACCUSED ME OF KILLING SOMEONE WITH ONE OF THE MANY PEOPLE I HAVE LIVING INSIDE MY HEAD.
YOU KNOW WHAT? FUCK YOU! WHO'S IN CHARGE HERE?
ME!
WELL, FUCK YOU DIRECTLY THEN.
THIS -- THIS ISN'T RIGHT!
THIS IS BULLSHIT. I DIDN'T DO ANYTHING.
SO I WANT TO MAKE A LIVING IN THIS SHITHOLE OF A CITY.
SO WHAT? NOW I'M A MURDERER?
FUCK YOU!! AND FUCK --

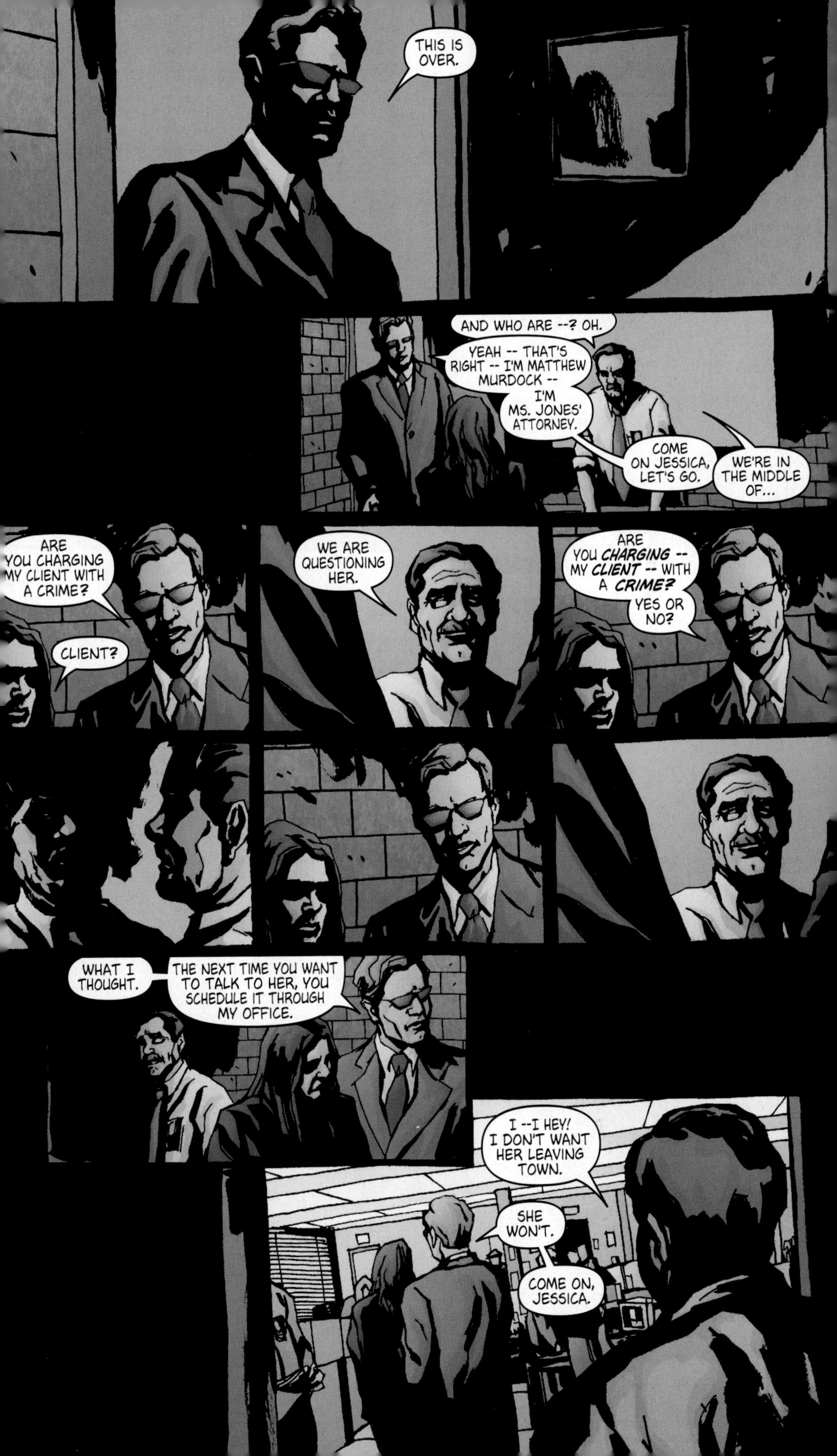
THIS IS OVER.
AND WHO ARE --? OH.
YEAH -- THAT'S RIGHT -- I'M MATTHEW MURDOCK --
I'M MS. JONES' ATTORNEY.
COME ON JESSICA, LET'S GO.
WE'RE IN THE MIDDLE OF...
ARE YOU CHARGING MY CLIENT WITH A CRIME?
CLIENT?
WE ARE QUESTIONING HER.
ARE YOU CHARGING -- MY CLIENT -- WITH A CRIME?
YES OR NO?
WHAT I THOUGHT.
THE NEXT TIME YOU WANT TO TALK TO HER, YOU SCHEDULE IT THROUGH MY OFFICE.
I --I HEY! I DON'T WANT HER LEAVING TOWN.
SHE WON'T.
COME ON, JESSICA.

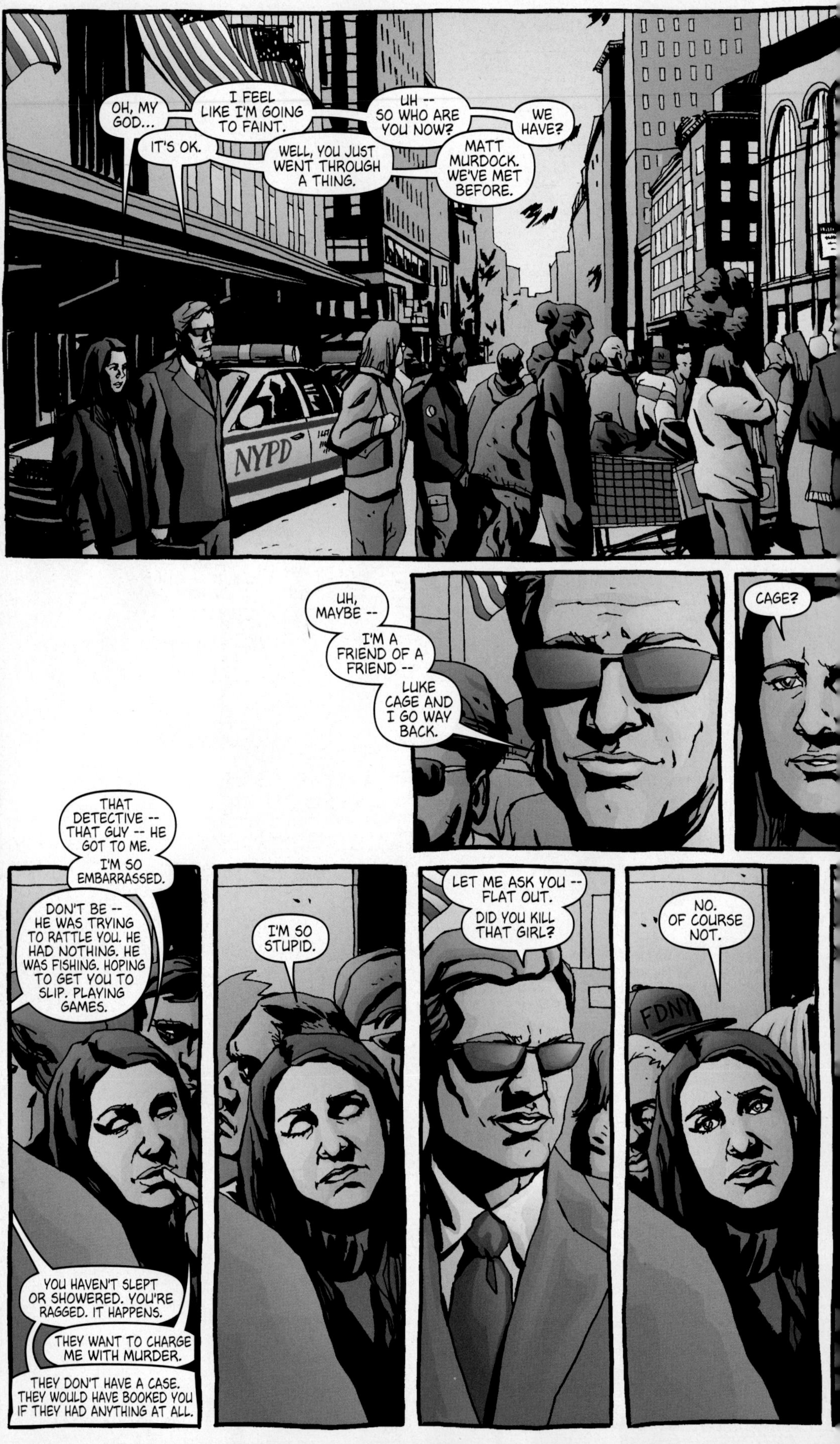
OH, MY GOD...
I FEEL LIKE I'M GOING TO FAINT.
IT'S OK.
WELL, YOU JUST WENT THROUGH A THING.
UH -- SO WHO ARE YOU NOW?
WE HAVE?
MATT MURDOCK. WE'VE MET BEFORE.
NYPD
UH, MAYBE --
I'M A FRIEND OF A FRIEND --
LUKE CAGE AND I GO WAY BACK.
CAGE?
THAT DETECTIVE -- THAT GUY -- HE GOT TO ME.
I'M SO EMBARRASSED.
DON'T BE -- HE WAS TRYING TO RATTLE YOU. HE HAD NOTHING. HE WAS FISHING. HOPING TO GET YOU TO SLIP. PLAYING GAMES.
YOU HAVEN'T SLEPT OR SHOWERED. YOU'RE RAGGED. IT HAPPENS.
THEY WANT TO CHARGE ME WITH MURDER.
THEY DON'T HAVE A CASE. THEY WOULD HAVE BOOKED YOU IF THEY HAD ANYTHING AT ALL.
I'M SO STUPID.
LET ME ASK YOU -- FLAT OUT.
DID YOU KILL THAT GIRL?
FDNY
NO. OF COURSE NOT.

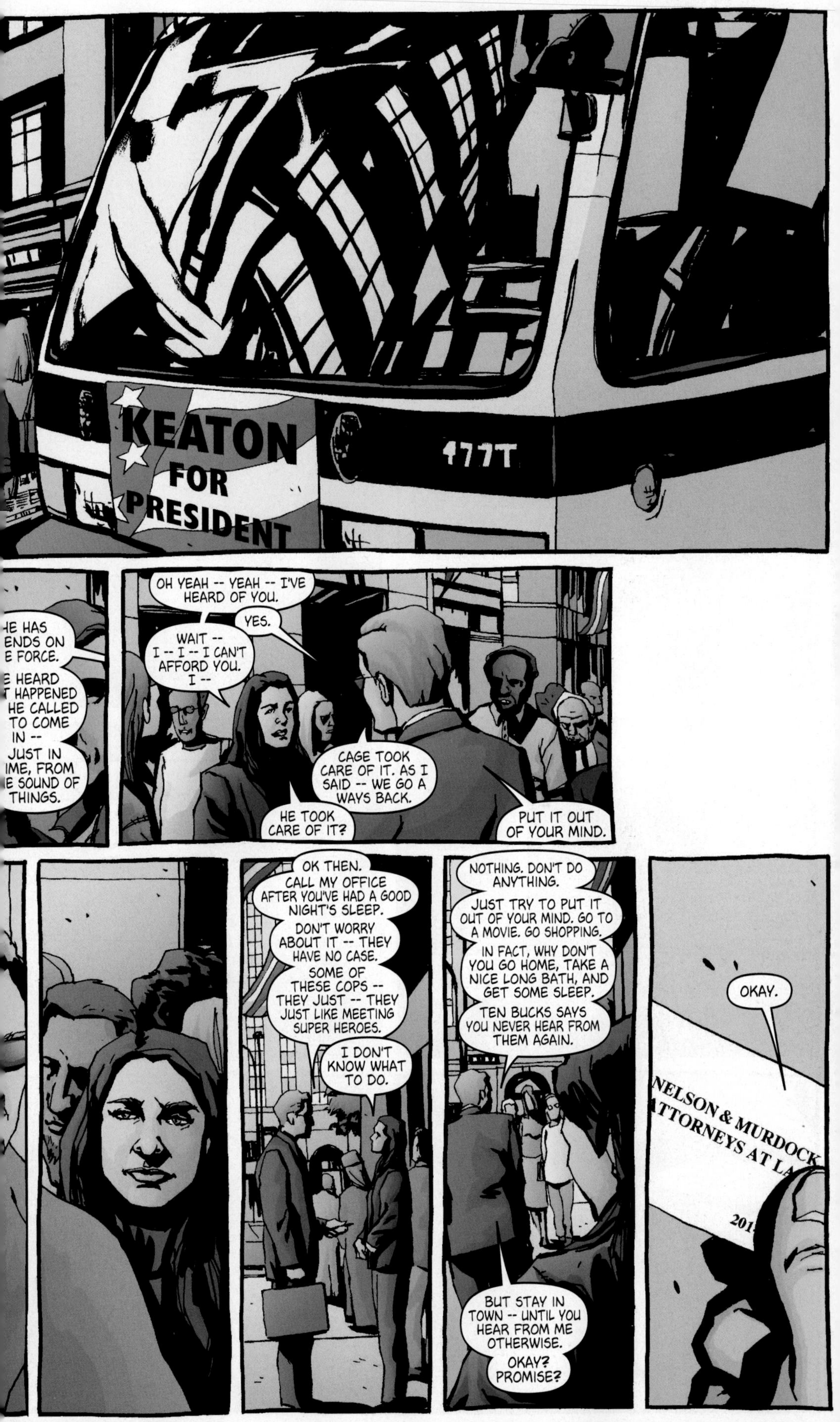
KEATON FOR PRESIDENT
477T
HE HAS ENDS ON E FORCE.
E HEARD T HAPPENED HE CALLED TO COME IN -- JUST IN IME, FROM E SOUND OF THINGS.
OH YEAH -- YEAH -- I'VE HEARD OF YOU.
YES.
WAIT -- I -- I -- I CAN'T AFFORD YOU. I --
CAGE TOOK CARE OF IT. AS I SAID -- WE GO A WAYS BACK.
HE TOOK CARE OF IT?
PUT IT OUT OF YOUR MIND.
OK THEN. CALL MY OFFICE AFTER YOU'VE HAD A GOOD NIGHT'S SLEEP.
DON'T WORRY ABOUT IT -- THEY HAVE NO CASE.
SOME OF THESE COPS -- THEY JUST -- THEY JUST LIKE MEETING SUPER HEROES.
I DON'T KNOW WHAT TO DO.
NOTHING. DON'T DO ANYTHING.
JUST TRY TO PUT IT OUT OF YOUR MIND. GO TO A MOVIE. GO SHOPPING.
IN FACT, WHY DON'T YOU GO HOME, TAKE A NICE LONG BATH, AND GET SOME SLEEP.
TEN BUCKS SAYS YOU NEVER HEAR FROM THEM AGAIN.
BUT STAY IN TOWN -- UNTIL YOU HEAR FROM ME OTHERWISE.
OKAY? PROMISE?
OKAY.
NELSON & MURDOCK
ATTORNEYS AT LA

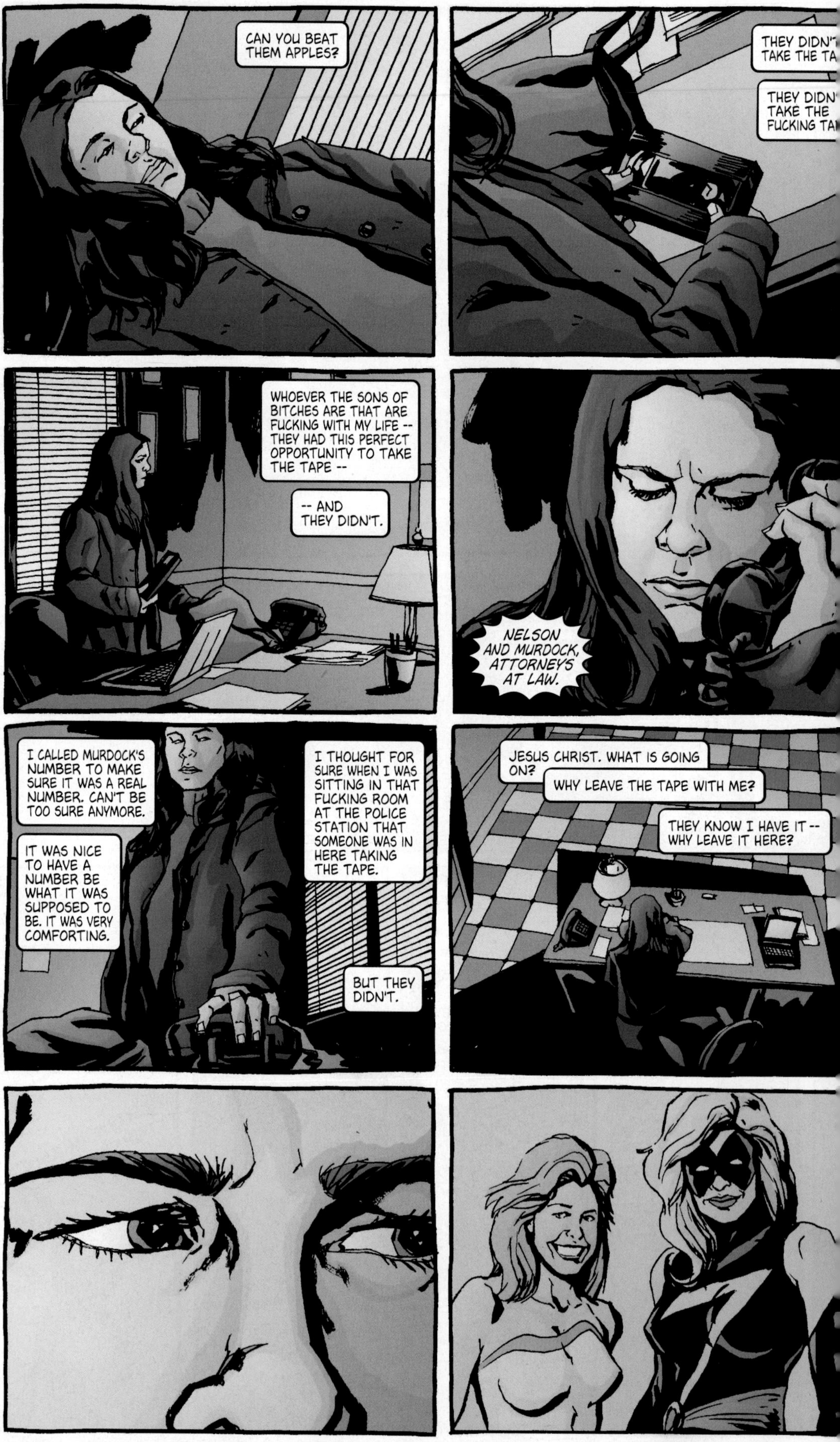
CAN YOU BEAT THEM APPLES?
THEY DIDN'T TAKE THE TA
THEY DIDN TAKE THE FUCKING TA
WHOEVER THE SONS OF BITCHES ARE THAT ARE FUCKING WITH MY LIFE -- THEY HAD THIS PERFECT OPPORTUNITY TO TAKE THE TAPE --
-- AND THEY DIDN'T.
NELSON AND MURDOCK, ATTORNEYS AT LAW.
I CALLED MURDOCK'S NUMBER TO MAKE SURE IT WAS A REAL NUMBER. CAN'T BE TOO SURE ANYMORE.
IT WAS NICE TO HAVE A NUMBER BE WHAT IT WAS SUPPOSED TO BE. IT WAS VERY COMFORTING.
I THOUGHT FOR SURE WHEN I WAS SITTING IN THAT FUCKING ROOM AT THE POLICE STATION THAT SOMEONE WAS IN HERE TAKING THE TAPE.
BUT THEY DIDN'T.
JESUS CHRIST. WHAT IS GOING ON?
WHY LEAVE THE TAPE WITH ME?
THEY KNOW I HAVE IT -- WHY LEAVE IT HERE?

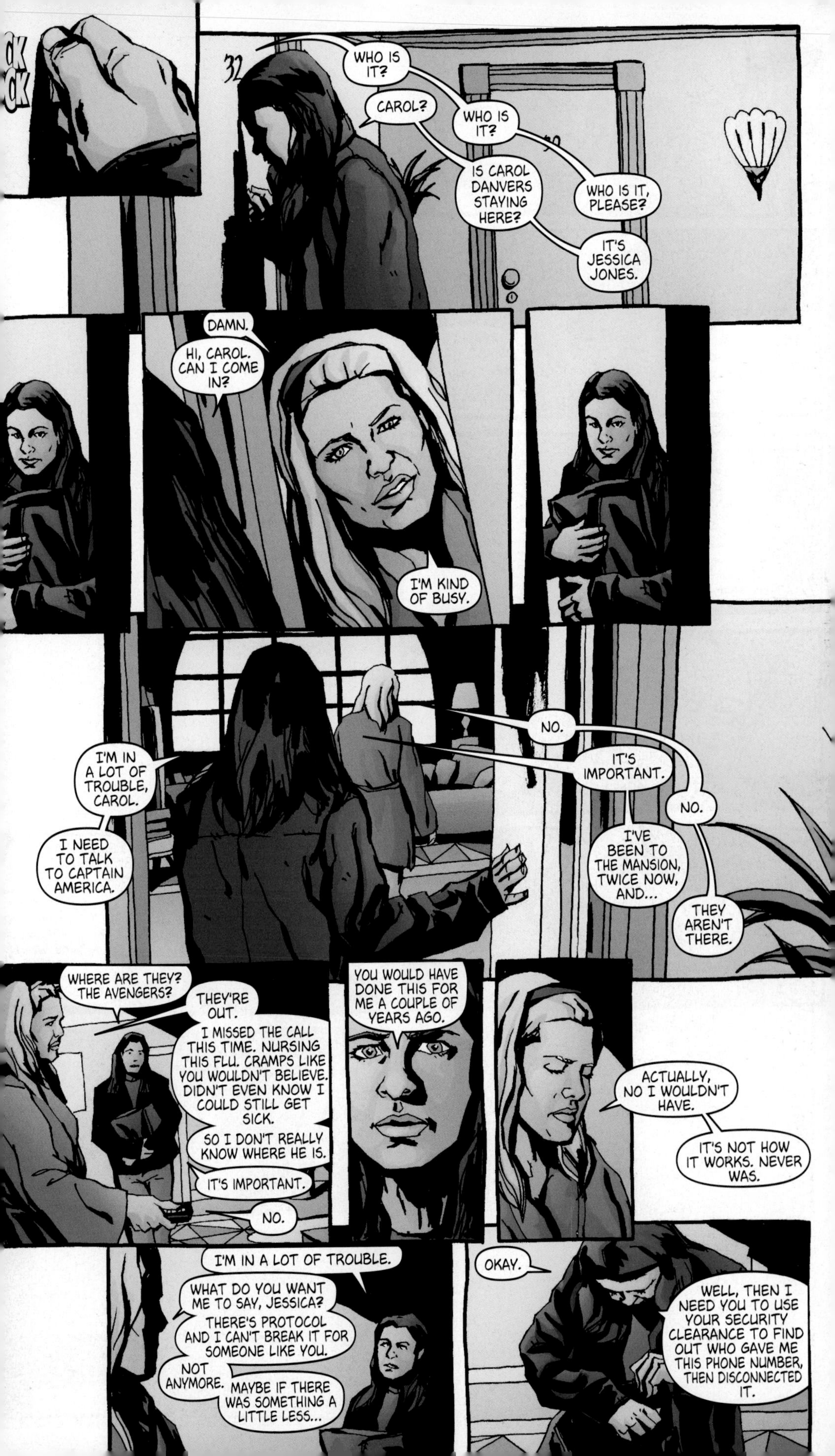
CK
CK
32
WHO IS IT?
CAROL?
WHO IS IT?
IS CAROL DANVERS STAYING HERE?
WHO IS IT, PLEASE?
IT'S JESSICA JONES.
DAMN.
HI, CAROL. CAN I COME IN?
I'M KIND OF BUSY.
I'M IN A LOT OF TROUBLE, CAROL.
I NEED TO TALK TO CAPTAIN AMERICA.
NO.
IT'S IMPORTANT.
I'VE BEEN TO THE MANSION, TWICE NOW, AND...
NO.
THEY AREN'T THERE.
WHERE ARE THEY? THE AVENGERS?
THEY'RE OUT.
I MISSED THE CALL THIS TIME. NURSING THIS FLU. CRAMPS LIKE YOU WOULDN'T BELIEVE. DIDN'T EVEN KNOW I COULD STILL GET SICK.
SO I DON'T REALLY KNOW WHERE HE IS.
IT'S IMPORTANT.
NO.
YOU WOULD HAVE DONE THIS FOR ME A COUPLE OF YEARS AGO.
ACTUALLY, NO I WOULDN'T HAVE.
IT'S NOT HOW IT WORKS. NEVER WAS.
I'M IN A LOT OF TROUBLE.
WHAT DO YOU WANT ME TO SAY, JESSICA?
THERE'S PROTOCOL AND I CAN'T BREAK IT FOR SOMEONE LIKE YOU.
NOT ANYMORE.
MAYBE IF THERE WAS SOMETHING A LITTLE LESS...
OKAY.
WELL, THEN I NEED YOU TO USE YOUR SECURITY CLEARANCE TO FIND OUT WHO GAVE ME THIS PHONE NUMBER, THEN DISCONNECTED IT.

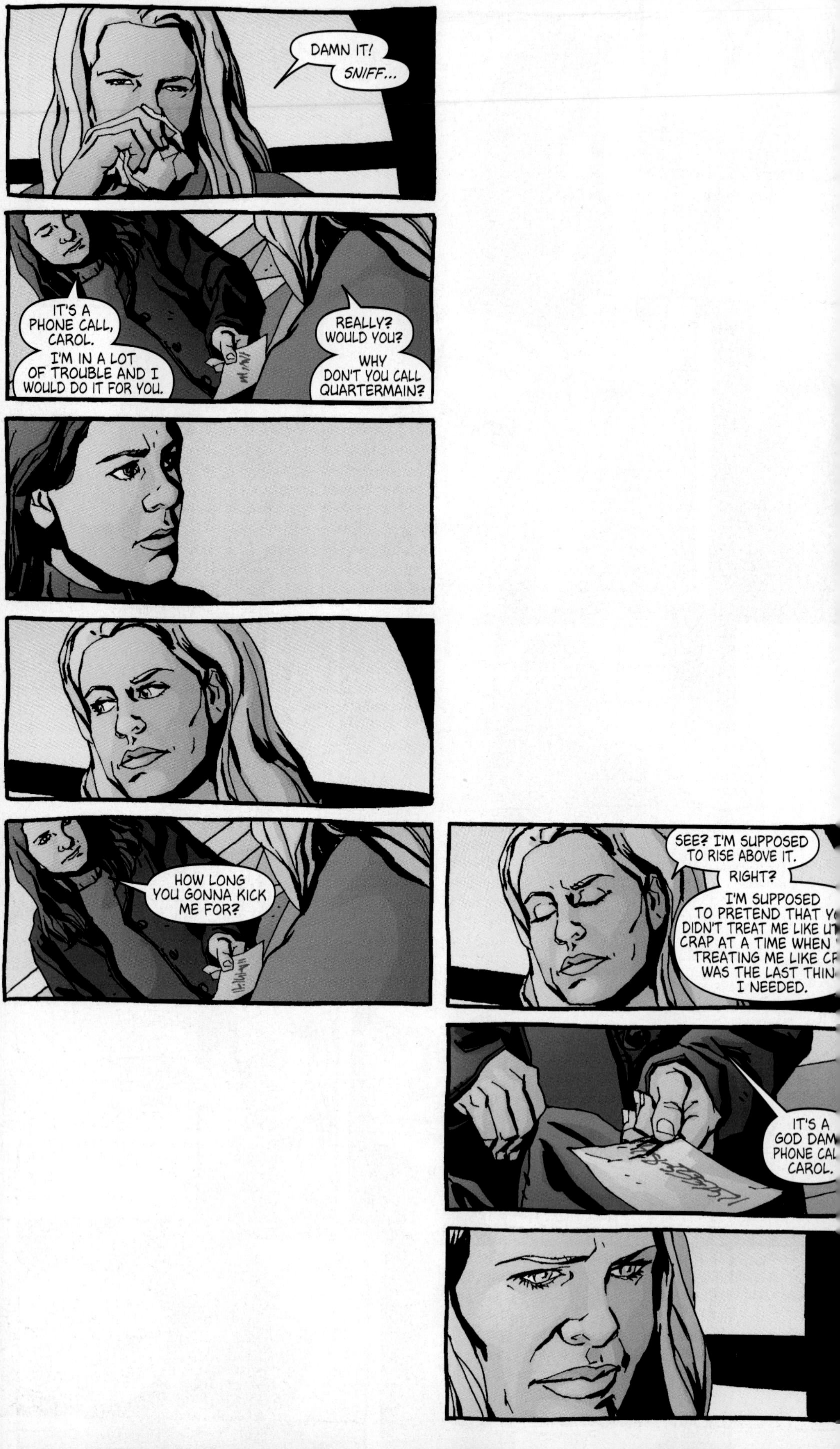
DAMN IT!
SNIFF...
IT'S A PHONE CALL, CAROL.
I'M IN A LOT OF TROUBLE AND I WOULD DO IT FOR YOU.
REALLY? WOULD YOU?
WHY DON'T YOU CALL QUARTERMAIN?
HOW LONG YOU GONNA KICK ME FOR?
SEE? I'M SUPPOSED TO RISE ABOVE IT.
RIGHT?
I'M SUPPOSED TO PRETEND THAT Y DIDN'T TREAT ME LIKE U CRAP AT A TIME WHEN TREATING ME LIKE C WAS THE LAST THIN I NEEDED.
IT'S A GOD DAM PHONE CA CAROL.

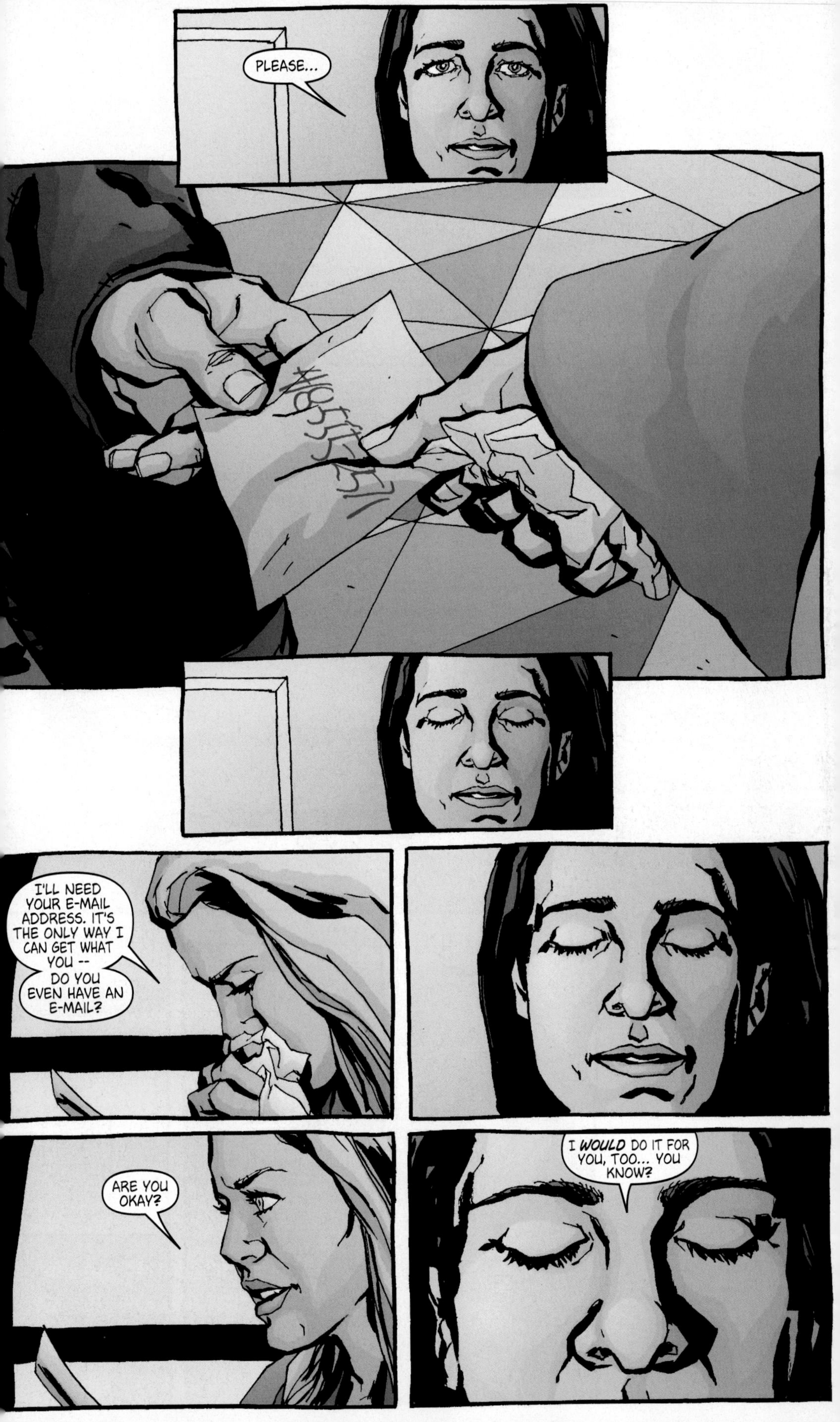
PLEASE...
I'LL NEED YOUR E-MAIL ADDRESS. IT'S THE ONLY WAY I CAN GET WHAT YOU -- DO YOU EVEN HAVE AN E-MAIL?
ARE YOU OKAY?
I WOULD DO IT FOR YOU, TOO... YOU KNOW?

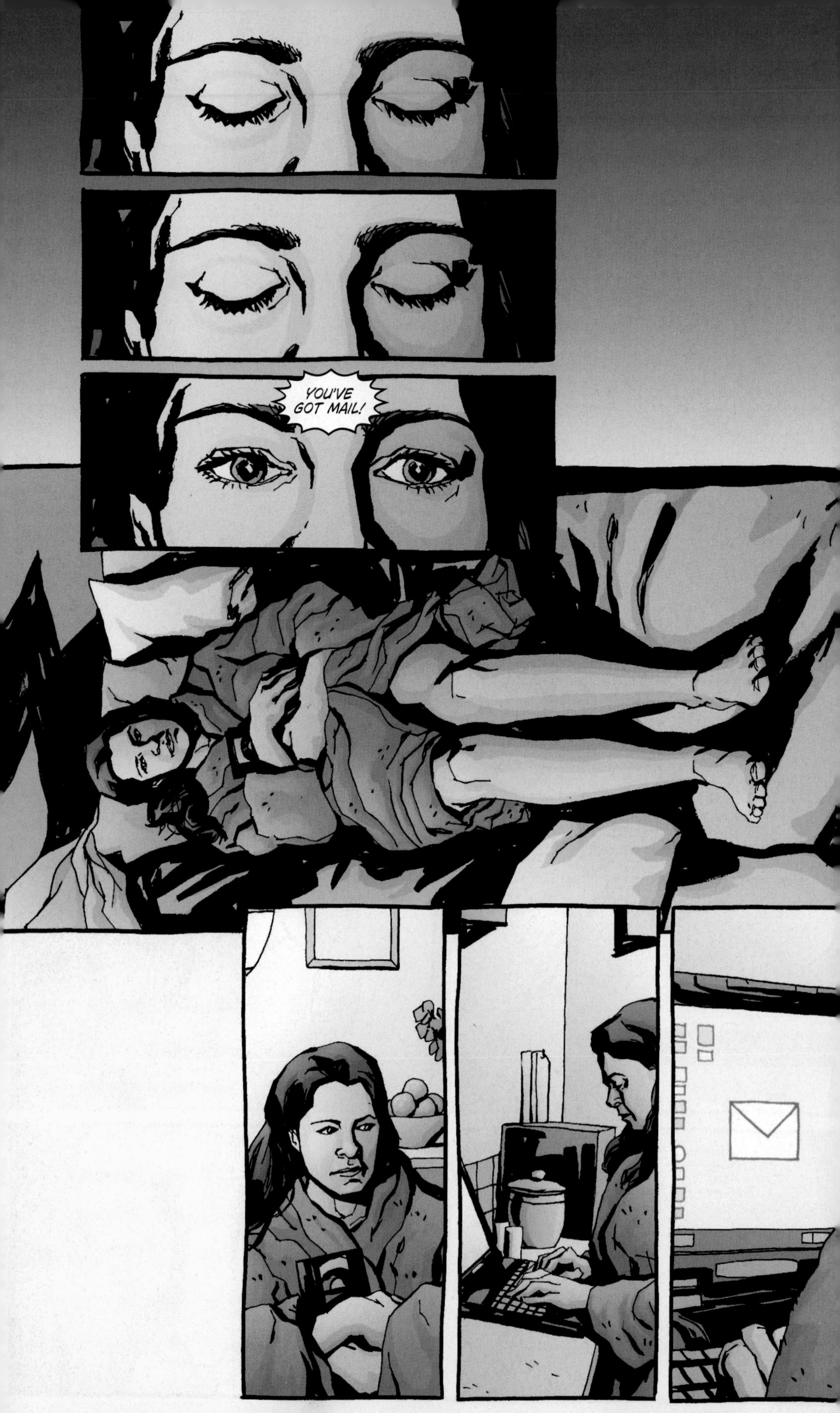
YOU'VE GOT MAIL!

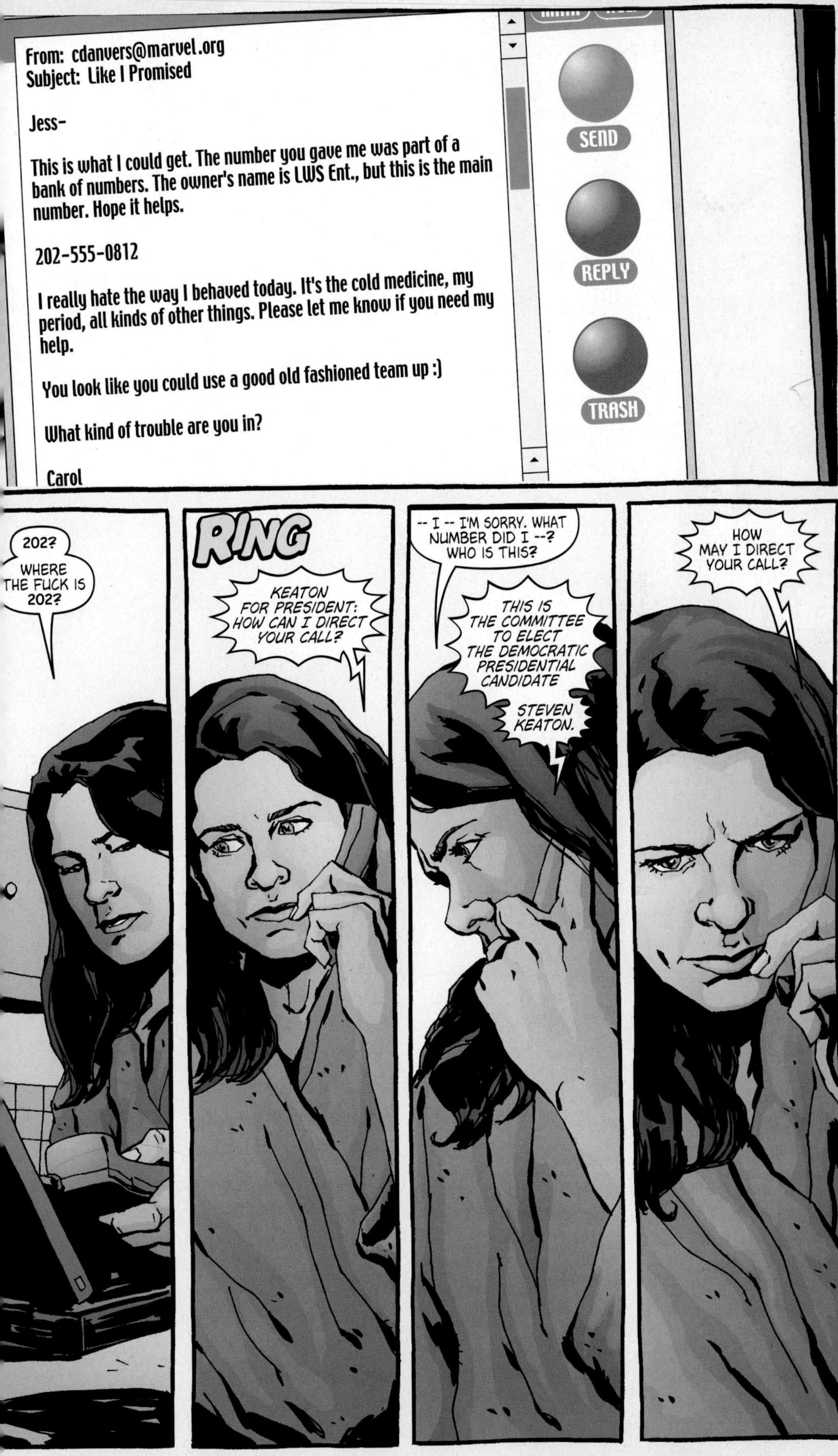
From: cdanvers@marvel.org
Subject: Like I Promised
Jess-
This is what I could get. The number you gave me was part of a bank of numbers. The owner's name is LWS Ent., but this is the main number. Hope it helps.
202-555-0812
I really hate the way I behaved today. It's the cold medicine, my period, all kinds of other things. Please let me know if you need my help.
You look like you could use a good old fashioned team up :)
What kind of trouble are you in?
Carol
SEND
REPLY
TRASH
202?
WHERE THE FUCK IS 202?
RING
KEATON FOR PRESIDENT: HOW CAN I DIRECT YOUR CALL?
-- I -- I'M SORRY. WHAT NUMBER DID I --? WHO IS THIS?
THIS IS THE COMMITTEE TO ELECT THE DEMOCRATIC PRESIDENTIAL CANDIDATE
STEVEN KEATON.
HOW MAY I DIRECT YOUR CALL?

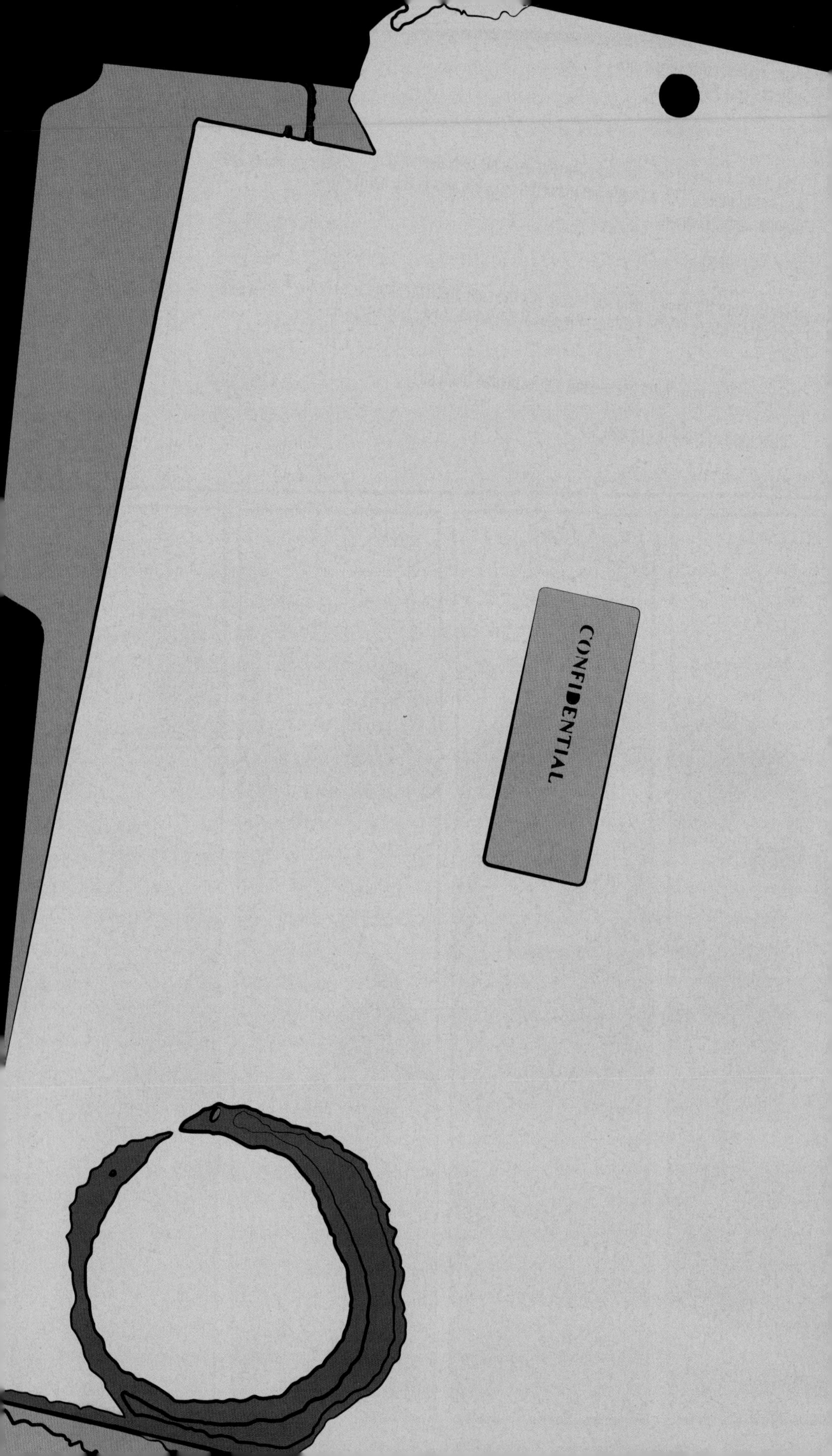
CONFIDENTIAL

ISSUE #4 BE[redacted]

[redacted]2

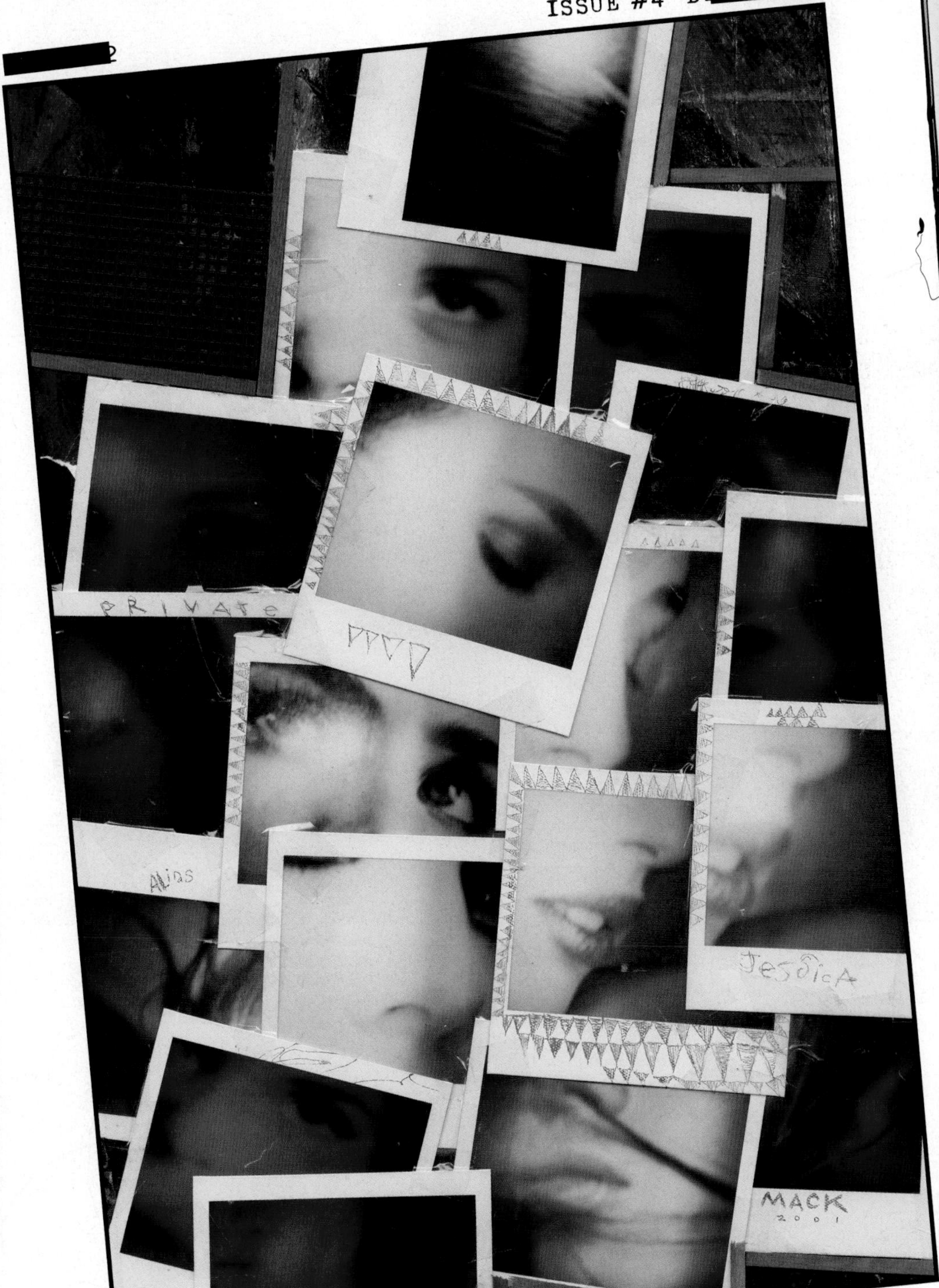

PRIVATE
ALias
Jessica
MACK
2001

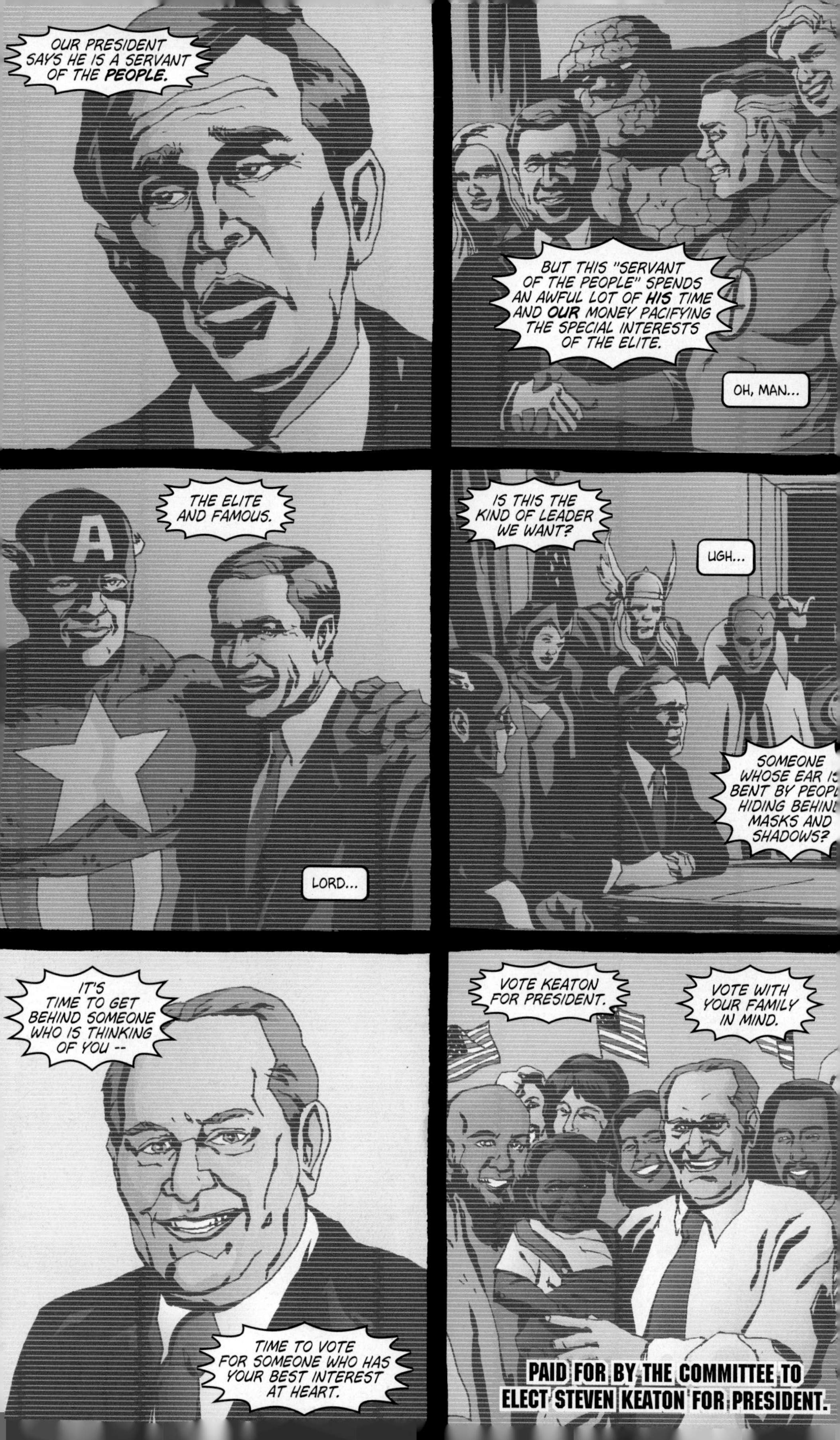
OUR PRESIDENT SAYS HE IS A SERVANT OF THE PEOPLE.
BUT THIS "SERVANT OF THE PEOPLE" SPENDS AN AWFUL LOT OF HIS TIME AND OUR MONEY PACIFYING THE SPECIAL INTERESTS OF THE ELITE.
OH, MAN...
THE ELITE AND FAMOUS.
LORD...
IS THIS THE KIND OF LEADER WE WANT?
UGH...
SOMEONE WHOSE EAR IS BENT BY PEOPLE HIDING BEHIND MASKS AND SHADOWS?
IT'S TIME TO GET BEHIND SOMEONE WHO IS THINKING OF YOU --
TIME TO VOTE FOR SOMEONE WHO HAS YOUR BEST INTEREST AT HEART.
VOTE KEATON FOR PRESIDENT.
VOTE WITH YOUR FAMILY IN MIND.
PAID FOR BY THE COMMITTEE TO ELECT STEVEN KEATON FOR PRESIDENT.

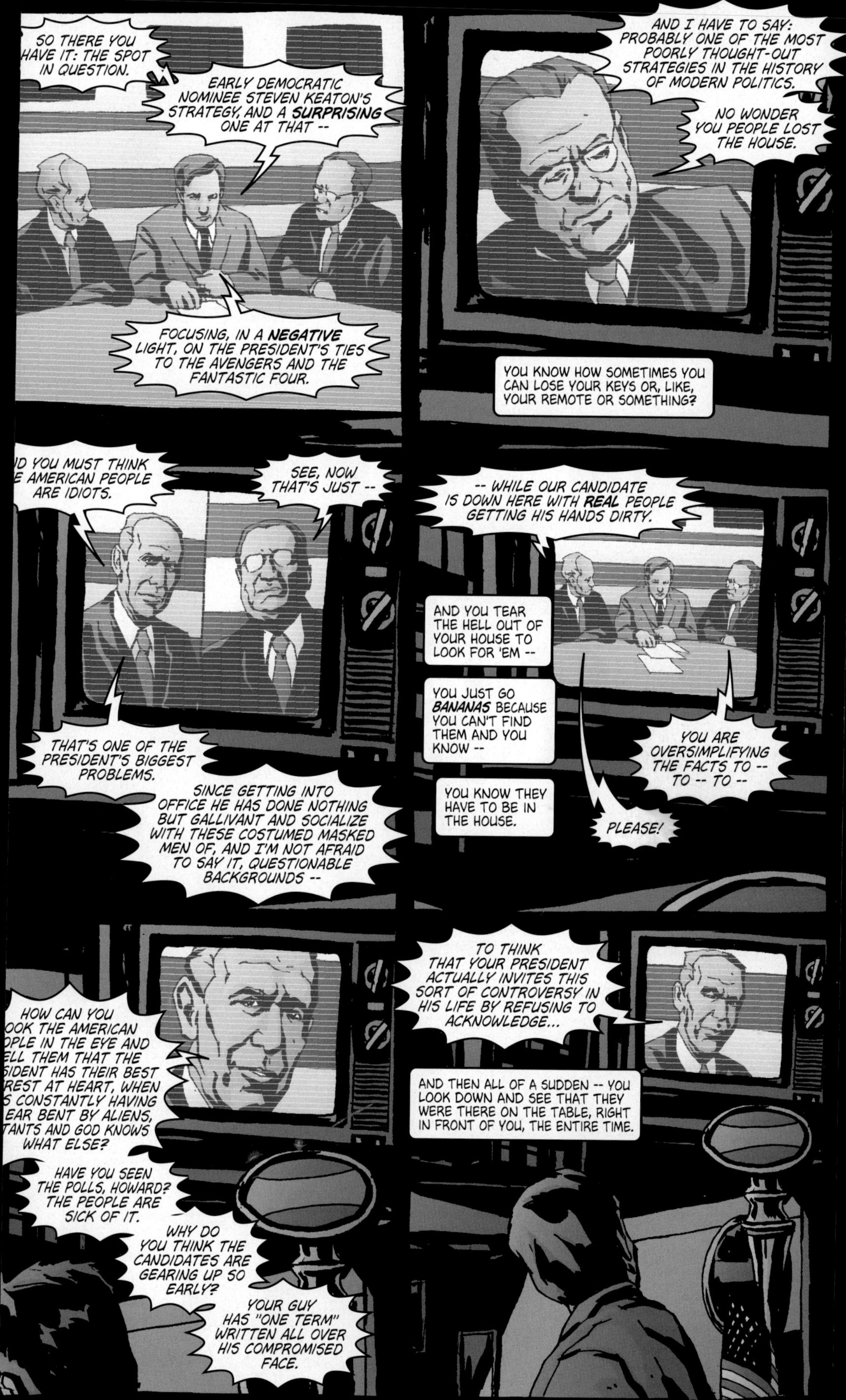
SO THERE YOU HAVE IT: THE SPOT IN QUESTION.
EARLY DEMOCRATIC NOMINEE STEVEN KEATON'S STRATEGY, AND A **SURPRISING** ONE AT THAT --
FOCUSING, IN A **NEGATIVE** LIGHT, ON THE PRESIDENT'S TIES TO THE AVENGERS AND THE FANTASTIC FOUR.
AND I HAVE TO SAY: PROBABLY ONE OF THE MOST POORLY THOUGHT-OUT STRATEGIES IN THE HISTORY OF MODERN POLITICS.
NO WONDER YOU PEOPLE LOST THE HOUSE.
YOU KNOW HOW SOMETIMES YOU CAN LOSE YOUR KEYS OR, LIKE, YOUR REMOTE OR SOMETHING?
YOU MUST THINK AMERICAN PEOPLE ARE IDIOTS.
SEE, NOW THAT'S JUST --
THAT'S ONE OF THE PRESIDENT'S BIGGEST PROBLEMS.
SINCE GETTING INTO OFFICE HE HAS DONE NOTHING BUT GALLIVANT AND SOCIALIZE WITH THESE COSTUMED MASKED MEN OF, AND I'M NOT AFRAID TO SAY IT, QUESTIONABLE BACKGROUNDS --
-- WHILE OUR CANDIDATE IS DOWN HERE WITH **REAL** PEOPLE GETTING HIS HANDS DIRTY.
AND YOU TEAR THE HELL OUT OF YOUR HOUSE TO LOOK FOR 'EM --
YOU JUST GO ***BANANAS*** BECAUSE YOU CAN'T FIND THEM AND YOU KNOW --
YOU KNOW THEY HAVE TO BE IN THE HOUSE.
YOU ARE OVERSIMPLIFYING THE FACTS TO -- TO -- TO --
PLEASE!
HOW CAN YOU LOOK THE AMERICAN PLE IN THE EYE AND TELL THEM THAT THE SIDENT HAS THEIR BEST REST AT HEART, WHEN CONSTANTLY HAVING EAR BENT BY ALIENS, TANTS AND GOD KNOWS WHAT ELSE?
HAVE YOU SEEN THE POLLS, HOWARD? THE PEOPLE ARE SICK OF IT.
WHY DO YOU THINK THE CANDIDATES ARE GEARING UP SO EARLY?
YOUR GUY HAS "ONE TERM" WRITTEN ALL OVER HIS COMPROMISED FACE.
TO THINK THAT YOUR PRESIDENT ACTUALLY INVITES THIS SORT OF CONTROVERSY IN HIS LIFE BY REFUSING TO ACKNOWLEDGE...
AND THEN ALL OF A SUDDEN -- YOU LOOK DOWN AND SEE THAT THEY WERE THERE ON THE TABLE, RIGHT IN FRONT OF YOU, THE ENTIRE TIME.

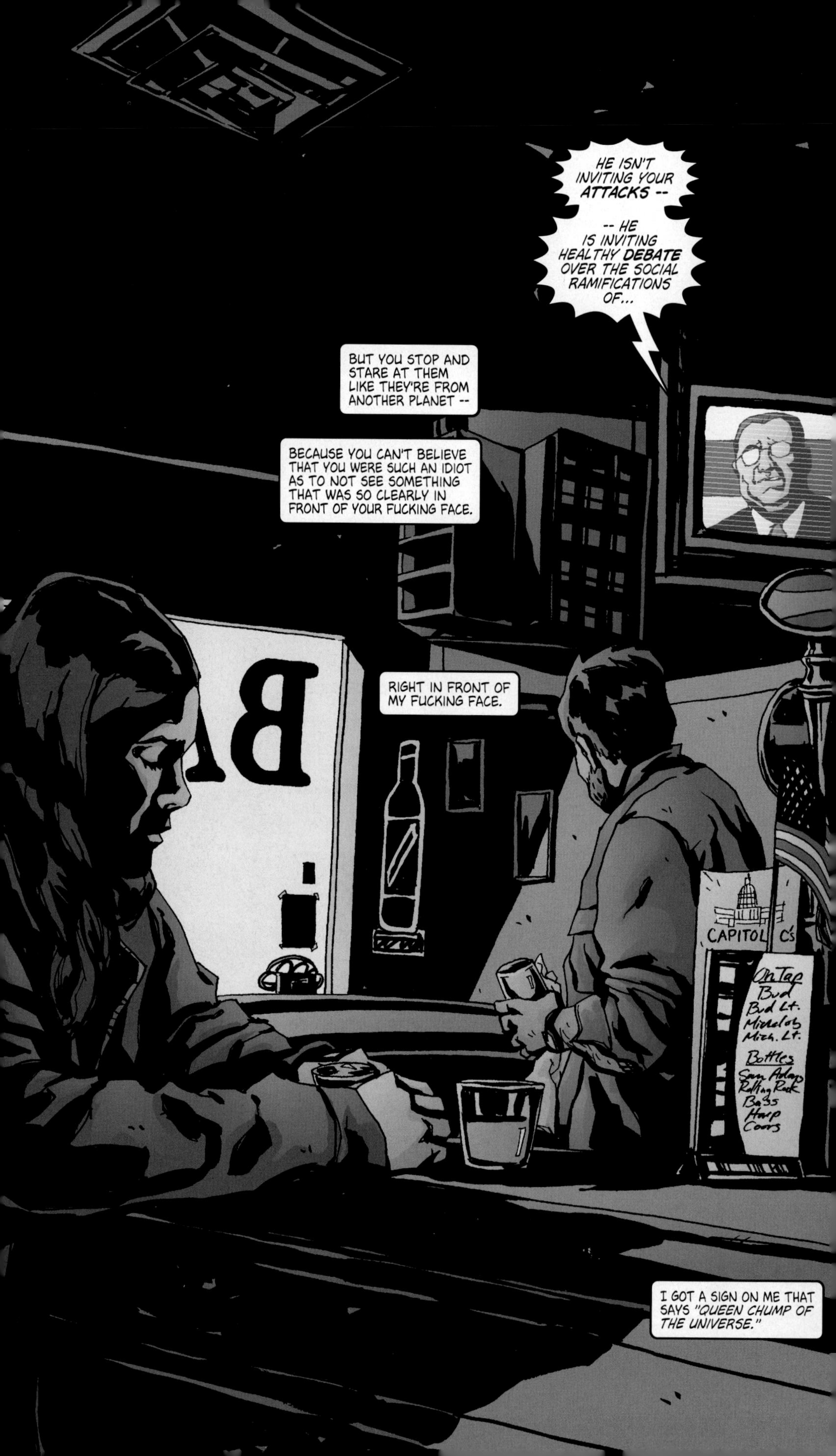
HE ISN'T INVITING YOUR ATTACKS -- -- HE IS INVITING HEALTHY DEBATE OVER THE SOCIAL RAMIFICATIONS OF...
BUT YOU STOP AND STARE AT THEM LIKE THEY'RE FROM ANOTHER PLANET --
BECAUSE YOU CAN'T BELIEVE THAT YOU WERE SUCH AN IDIOT AS TO NOT SEE SOMETHING THAT WAS SO CLEARLY IN FRONT OF YOUR FUCKING FACE.
RIGHT IN FRONT OF MY FUCKING FACE.
CAPITOL C's
On Tap Bud Bud Lt. Michelob Mich. Lt.
Bottles Sam Adams Rolling Rock Bass Harp Coors
I GOT A SIGN ON ME THAT SAYS "QUEEN CHUMP OF THE UNIVERSE."

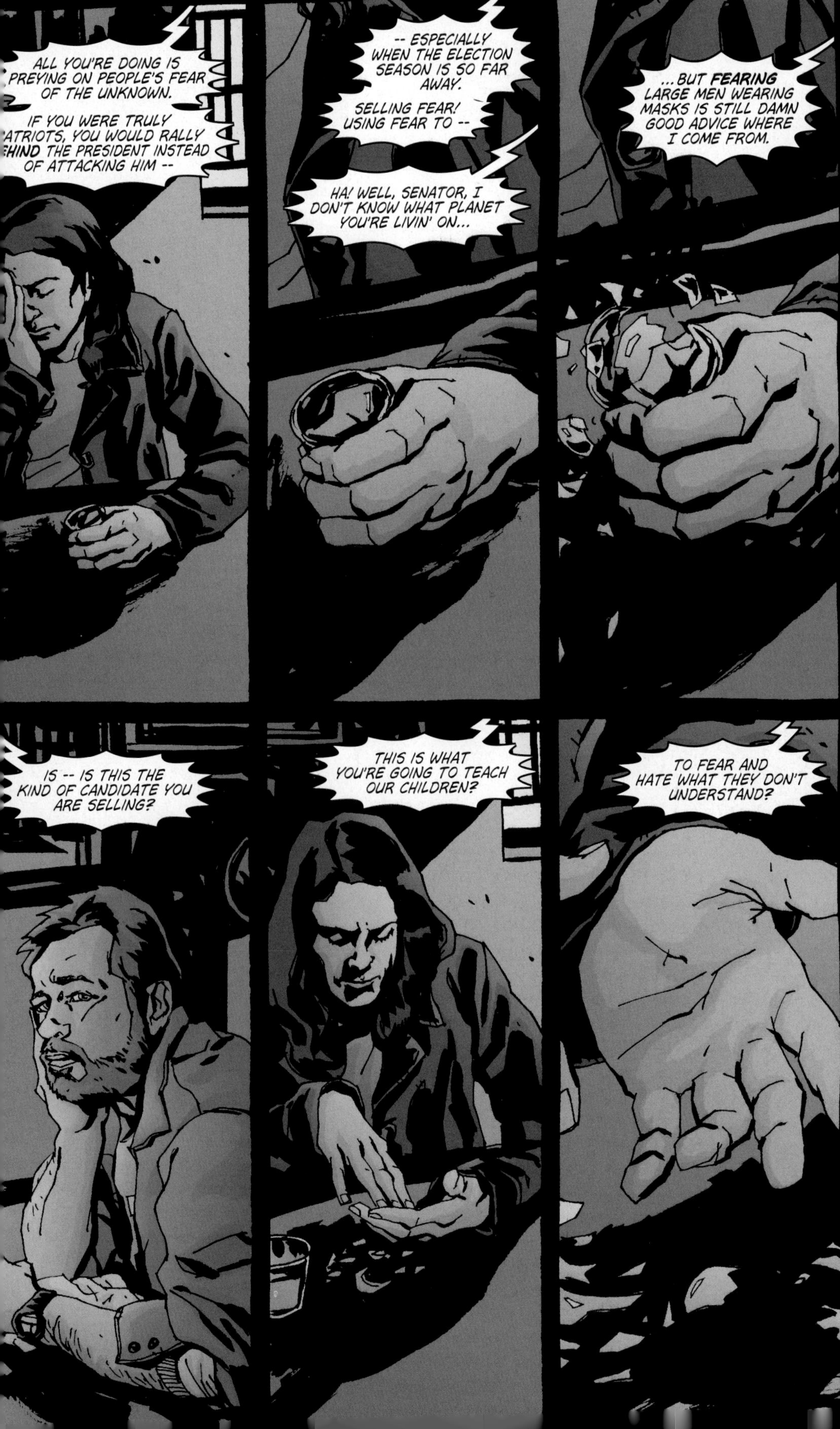
ALL YOU'RE DOING IS PREYING ON PEOPLE'S FEAR OF THE UNKNOWN.
IF YOU WERE TRULY PATRIOTS, YOU WOULD RALLY BEHIND THE PRESIDENT INSTEAD OF ATTACKING HIM --
-- ESPECIALLY WHEN THE ELECTION SEASON IS SO FAR AWAY.
SELLING FEAR! USING FEAR TO --
HA! WELL, SENATOR, I DON'T KNOW WHAT PLANET YOU'RE LIVIN' ON...
...BUT FEARING LARGE MEN WEARING MASKS IS STILL DAMN GOOD ADVICE WHERE I COME FROM.
IS -- IS THIS THE KIND OF CANDIDATE YOU ARE SELLING?
THIS IS WHAT YOU'RE GOING TO TEACH OUR CHILDREN?
TO FEAR AND HATE WHAT THEY DON'T UNDERSTAND?

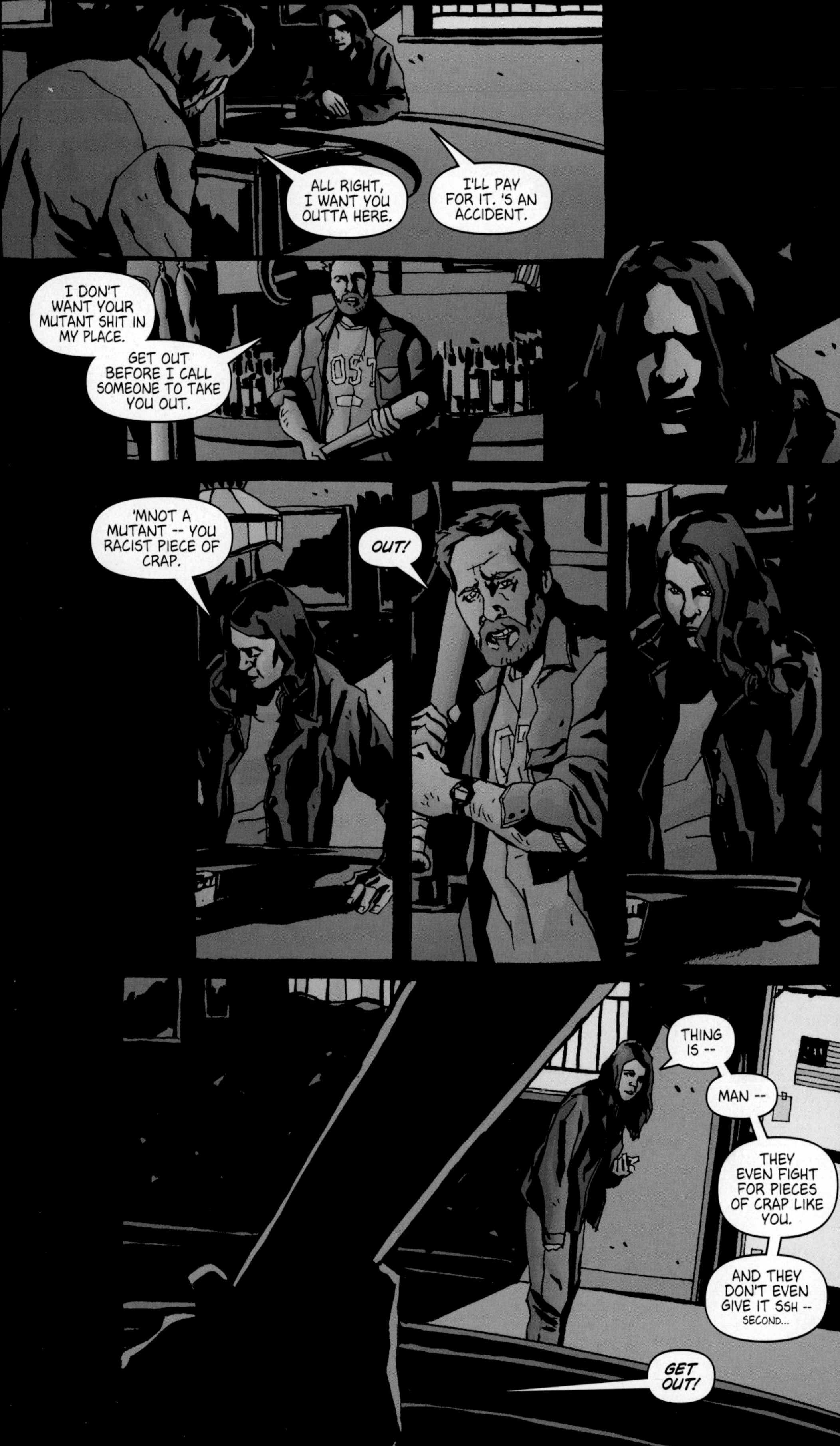
ALL RIGHT, I WANT YOU OUTTA HERE.
I'LL PAY FOR IT. 'S AN ACCIDENT.
I DON'T WANT YOUR MUTANT SHIT IN MY PLACE.
GET OUT BEFORE I CALL SOMEONE TO TAKE YOU OUT.
'MNOT A MUTANT -- YOU RACIST PIECE OF CRAP.
OUT!
THING IS --
MAN --
THEY EVEN FIGHT FOR PIECES OF CRAP LIKE YOU.
AND THEY DON'T EVEN GIVE IT SSH -- SECOND...
GET OUT!

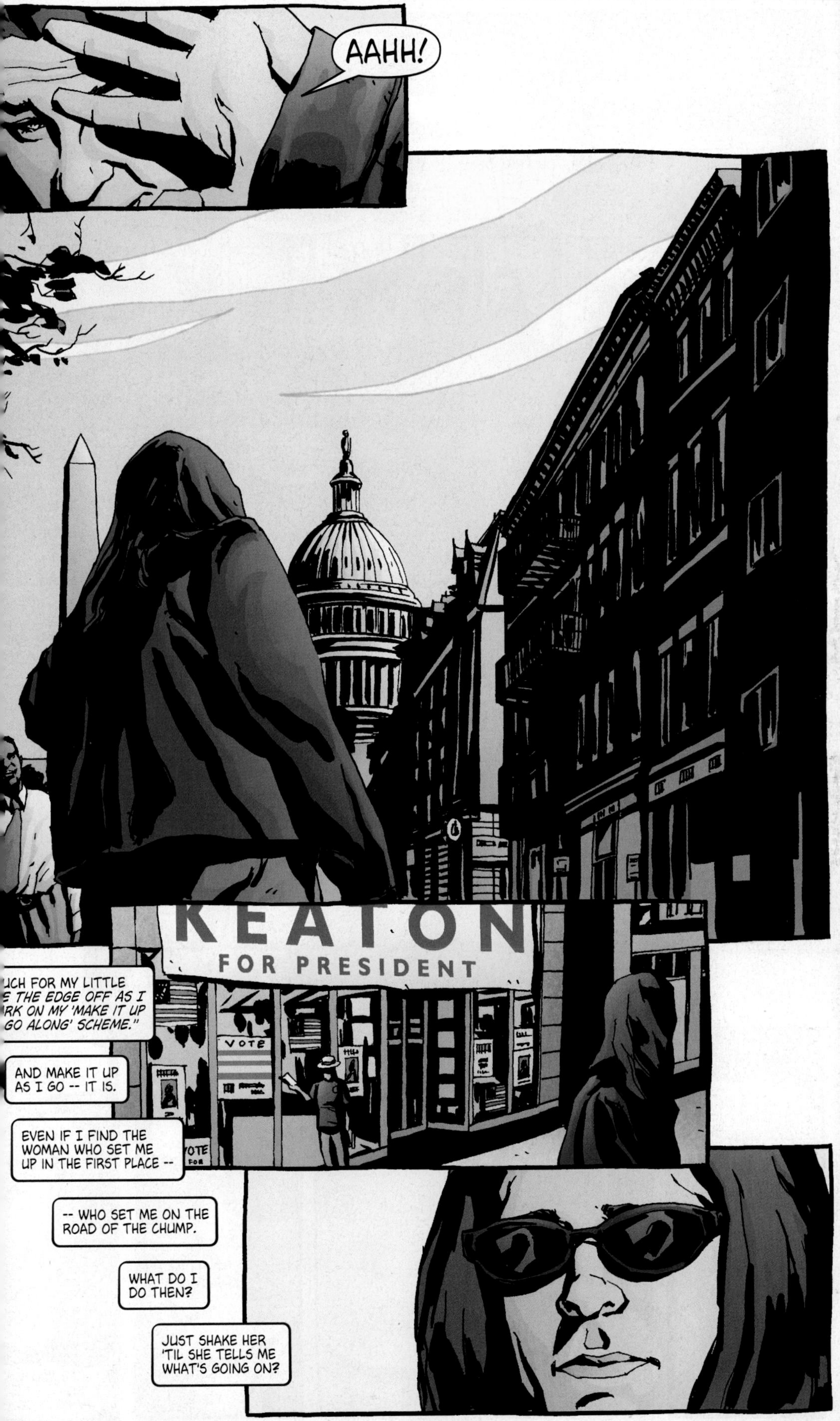
AAHH!
KEATON
FOR PRESIDENT
VOTE
VOTE FOR
...UCH FOR MY LITTLE ...E THE EDGE OFF AS I ...RK ON MY 'MAKE IT UP ...GO ALONG' SCHEME."
AND MAKE IT UP AS I GO -- IT IS.
EVEN IF I FIND THE WOMAN WHO SET ME UP IN THE FIRST PLACE --
-- WHO SET ME ON THE ROAD OF THE CHUMP.
WHAT DO I DO THEN?
JUST SHAKE HER 'TIL SHE TELLS ME WHAT'S GOING ON?

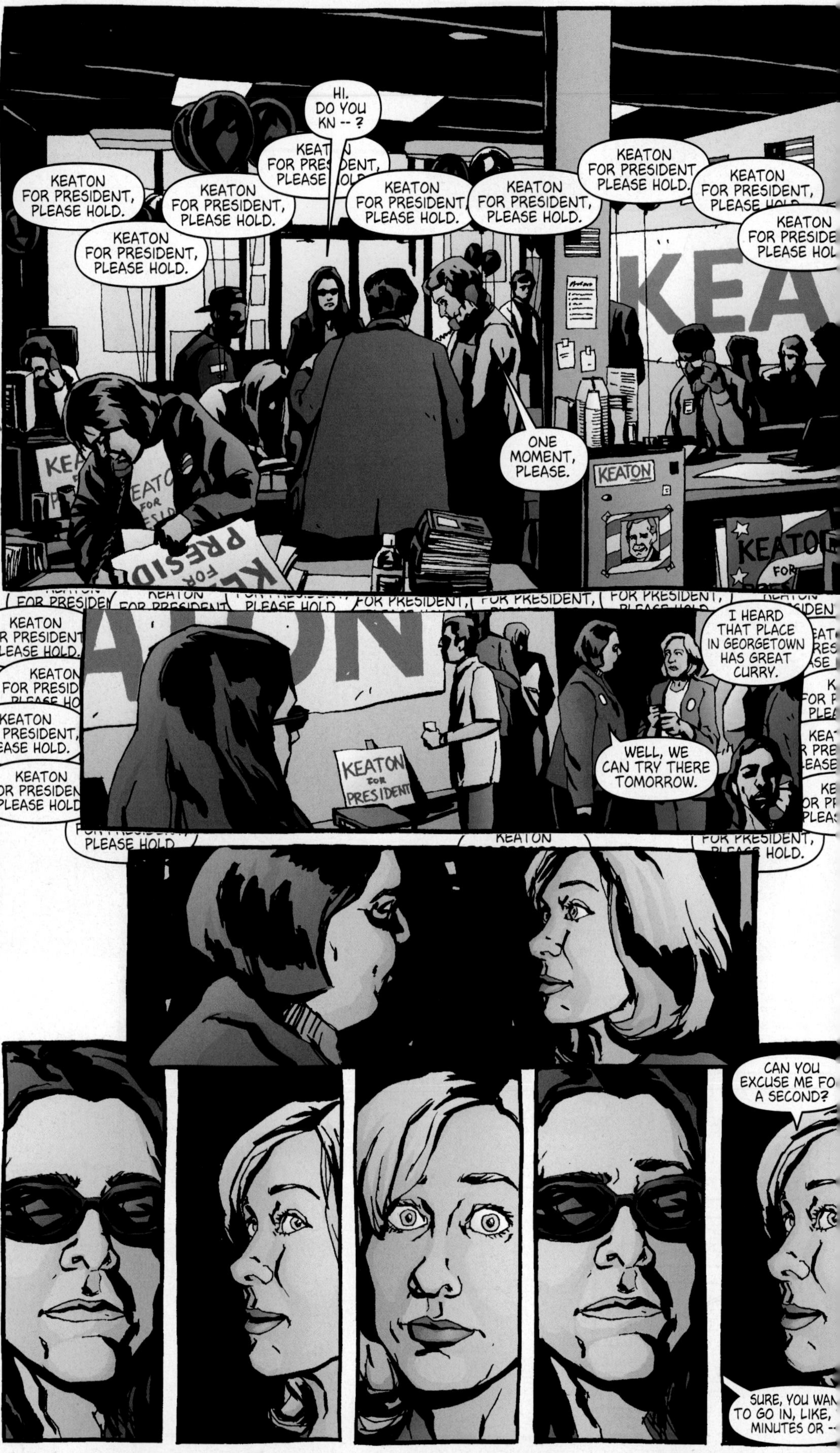
KEATON FOR PRESIDENT, PLEASE HOLD.
KEATON FOR PRESIDENT, PLEASE HOLD.
KEATON FOR PRESIDENT, PLEASE HOLD.
HI. DO YOU KN -- ?
KEATON FOR PRESIDENT, PLEASE HOLD.
KEATON FOR PRESIDENT, PLEASE HOLD.
KEATON FOR PRESIDENT, PLEASE HOLD.
ONE MOMENT, PLEASE.
KEATON
KEATON FOR PRESIDENT, PLEASE HOLD.
KEATON FOR PRESIDENT, PLEASE HOLD.
I HEARD THAT PLACE IN GEORGETOWN HAS GREAT CURRY.
WELL, WE CAN TRY THERE TOMORROW.
KEATON FOR PRESIDENT
CAN YOU EXCUSE ME FO A SECOND?
SURE, YOU WAN TO GO IN, LIKE, MINUTES OR --

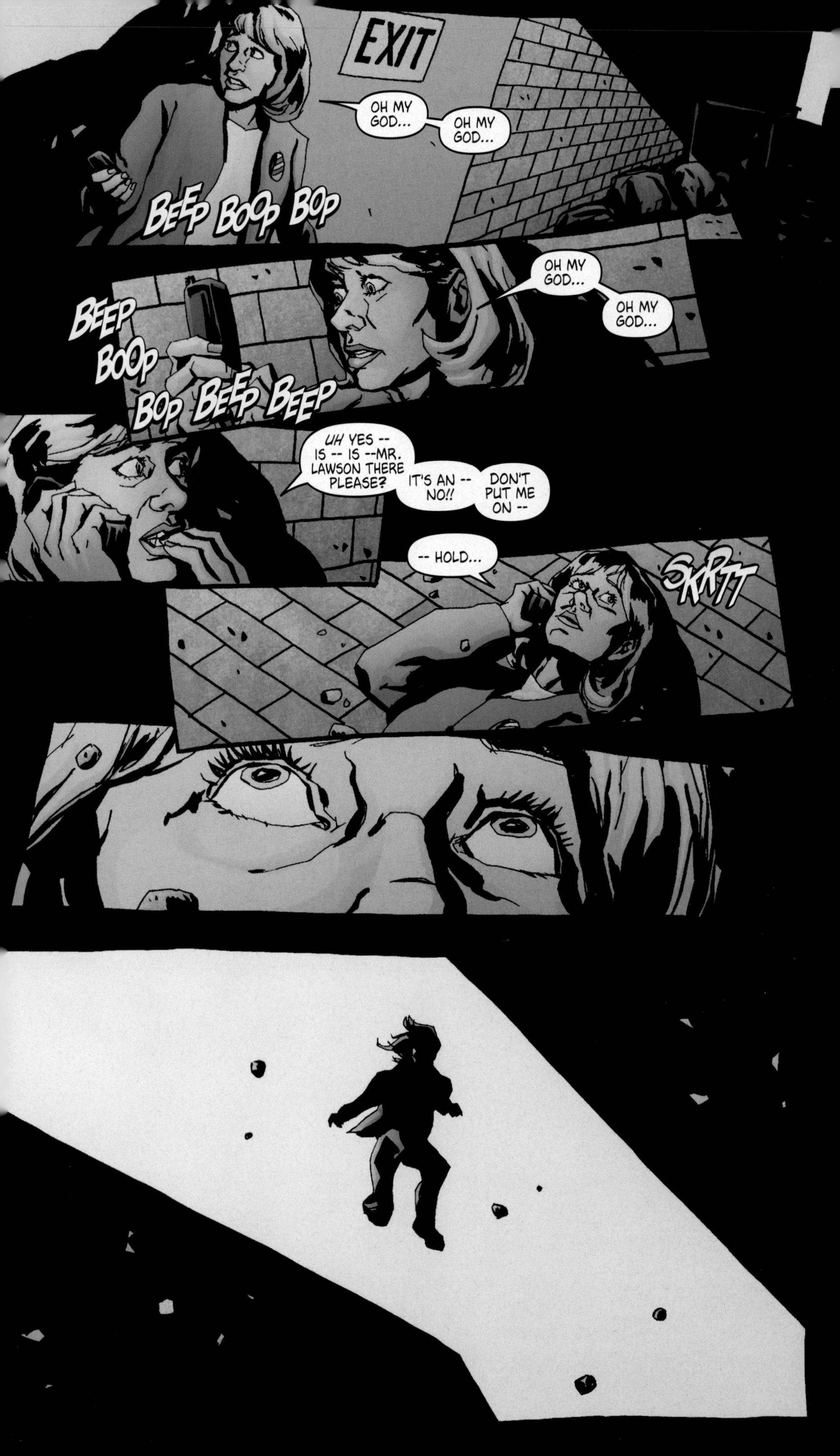
EXIT
OH MY GOD...
OH MY GOD...
BEEP BOOP BOP
OH MY GOD...
OH MY GOD...
BEEP BOOP BOP BEEP BEEP
UH YES -- IS -- IS --MR. LAWSON THERE PLEASE?
IT'S AN -- NO!!
DON'T PUT ME ON --
-- HOLD...
SKRTT

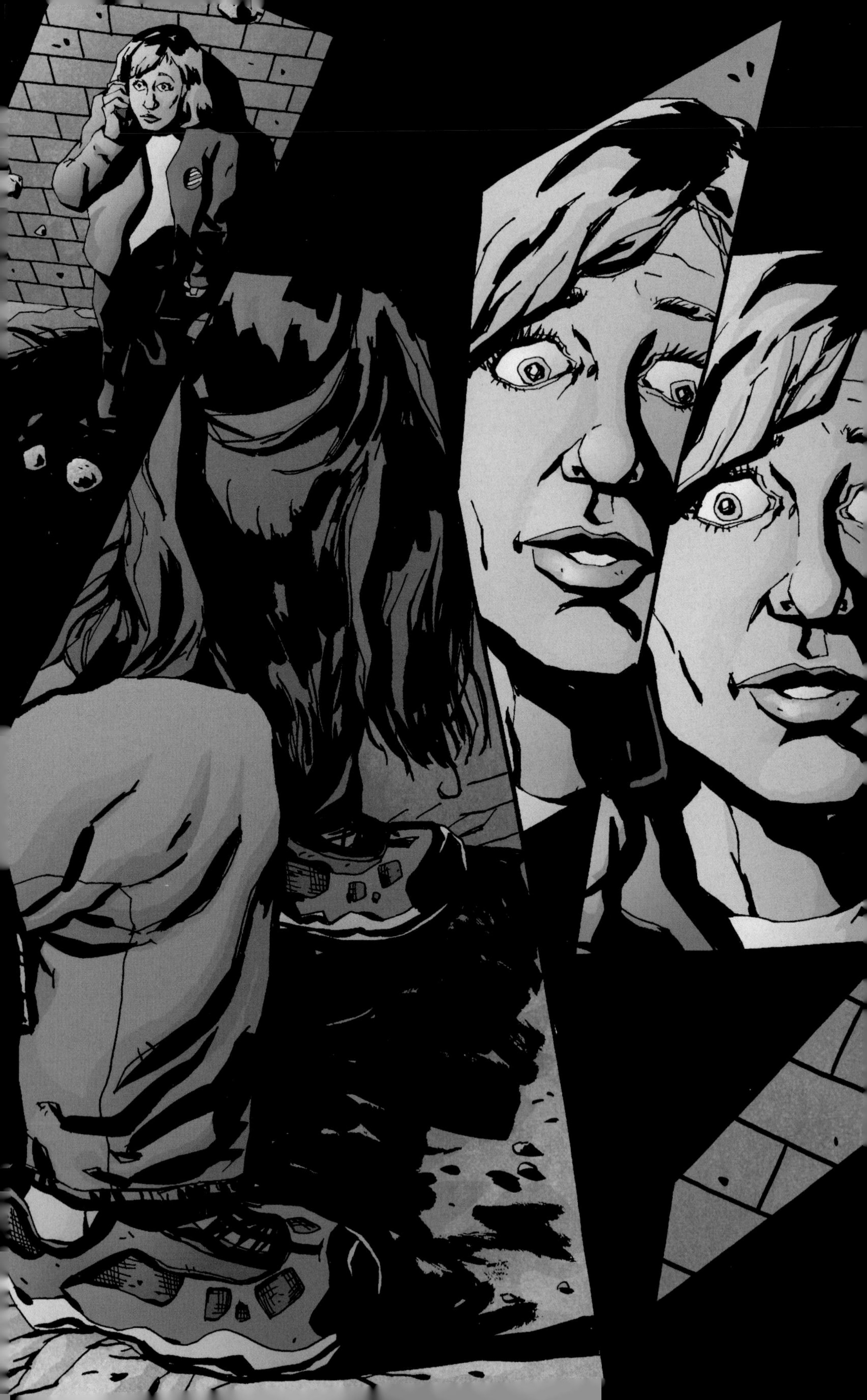

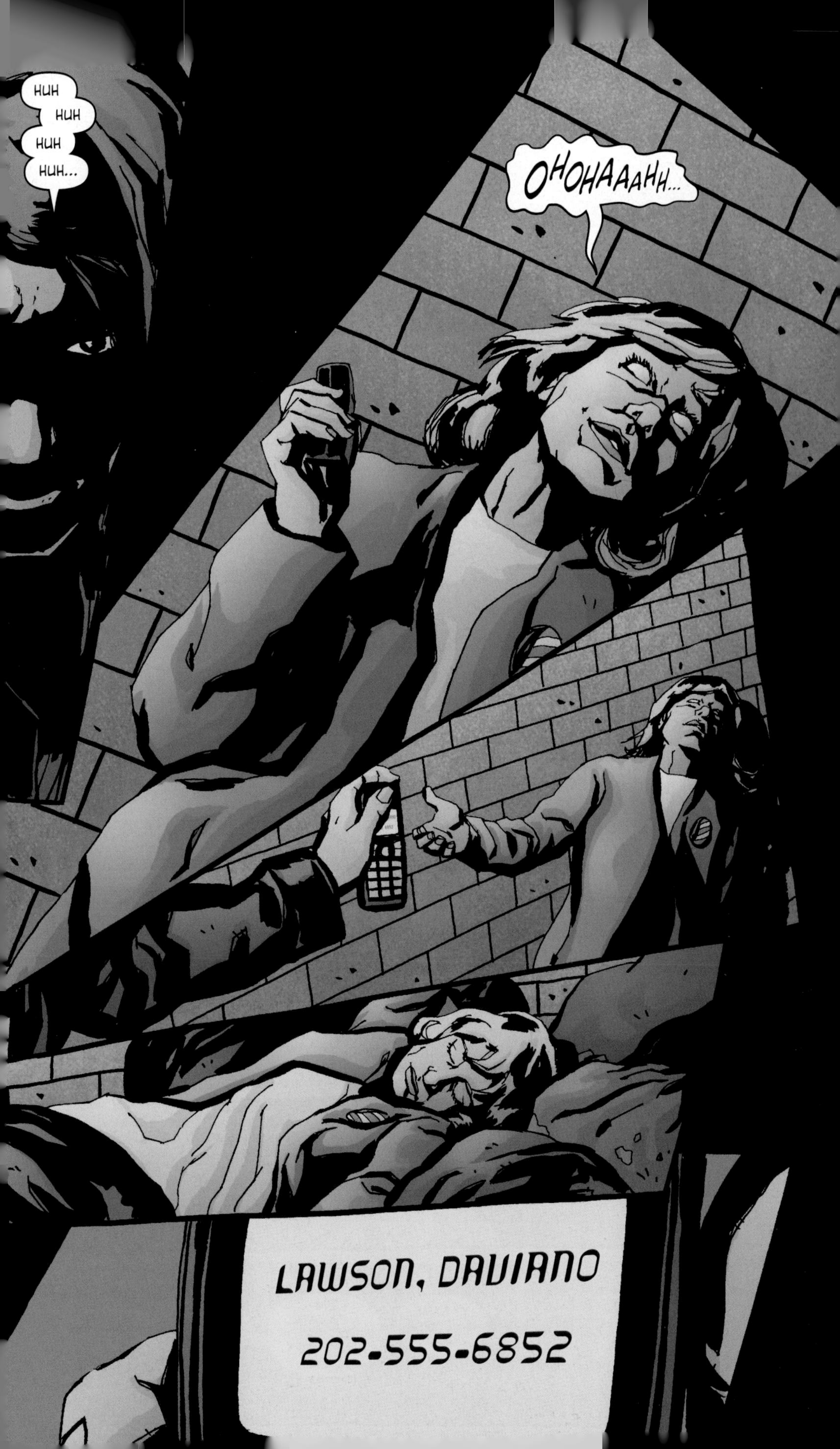
HUH
HUH
HUH
HUH...
OHOHAAAAHH...
LAWSON, DAVIANO
202-555-6852

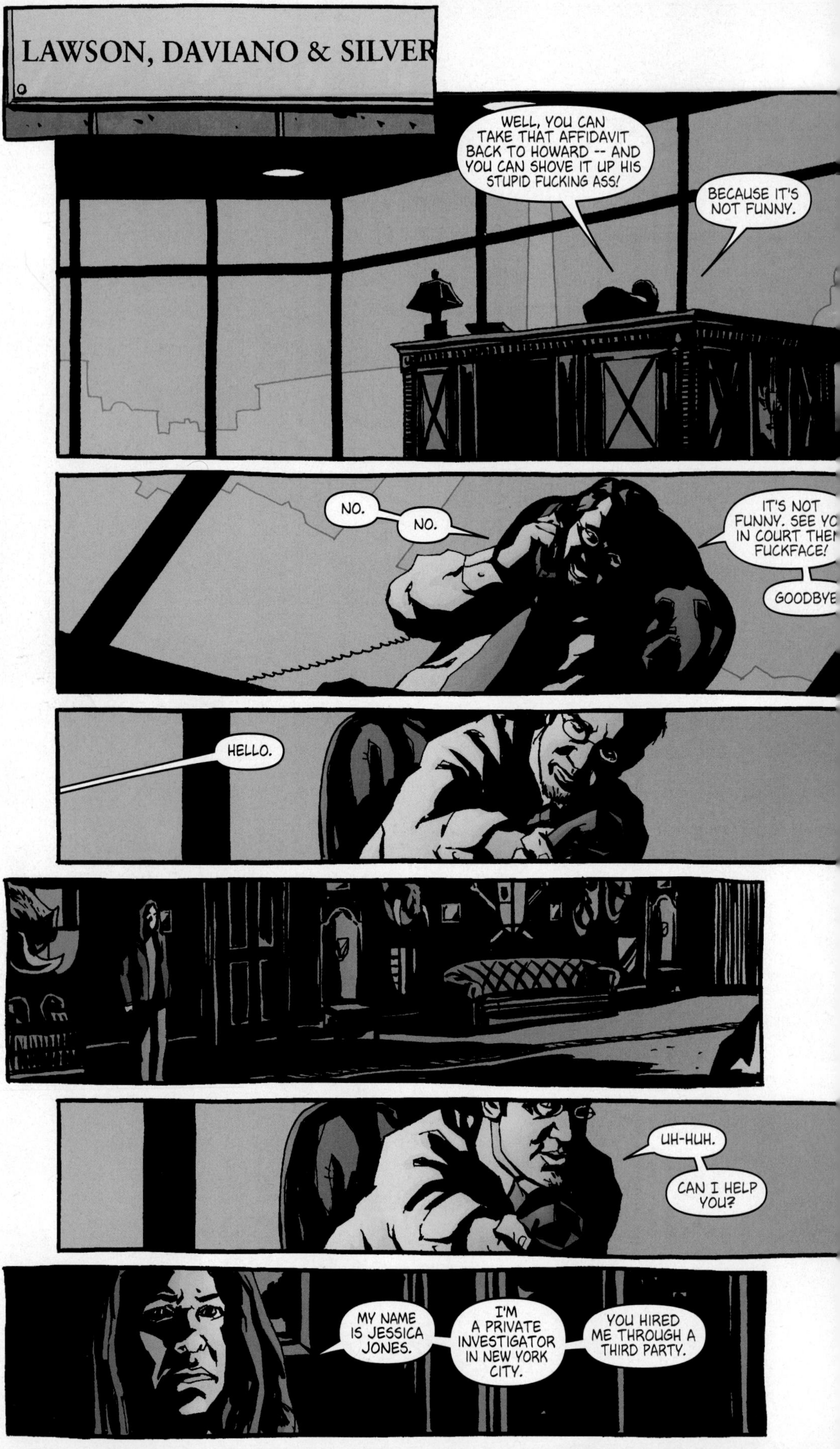
LAWSON, DAVIANO & SILVER
WELL, YOU CAN TAKE THAT AFFIDAVIT BACK TO HOWARD -- AND YOU CAN SHOVE IT UP HIS STUPID FUCKING ASS!
BECAUSE IT'S NOT FUNNY.
NO.
NO.
IT'S NOT FUNNY. SEE YO IN COURT THEN FUCKFACE!
GOODBYE
HELLO.
UH-HUH.
CAN I HELP YOU?
MY NAME IS JESSICA JONES.
I'M A PRIVATE INVESTIGATOR IN NEW YORK CITY.
YOU HIRED ME THROUGH A THIRD PARTY.

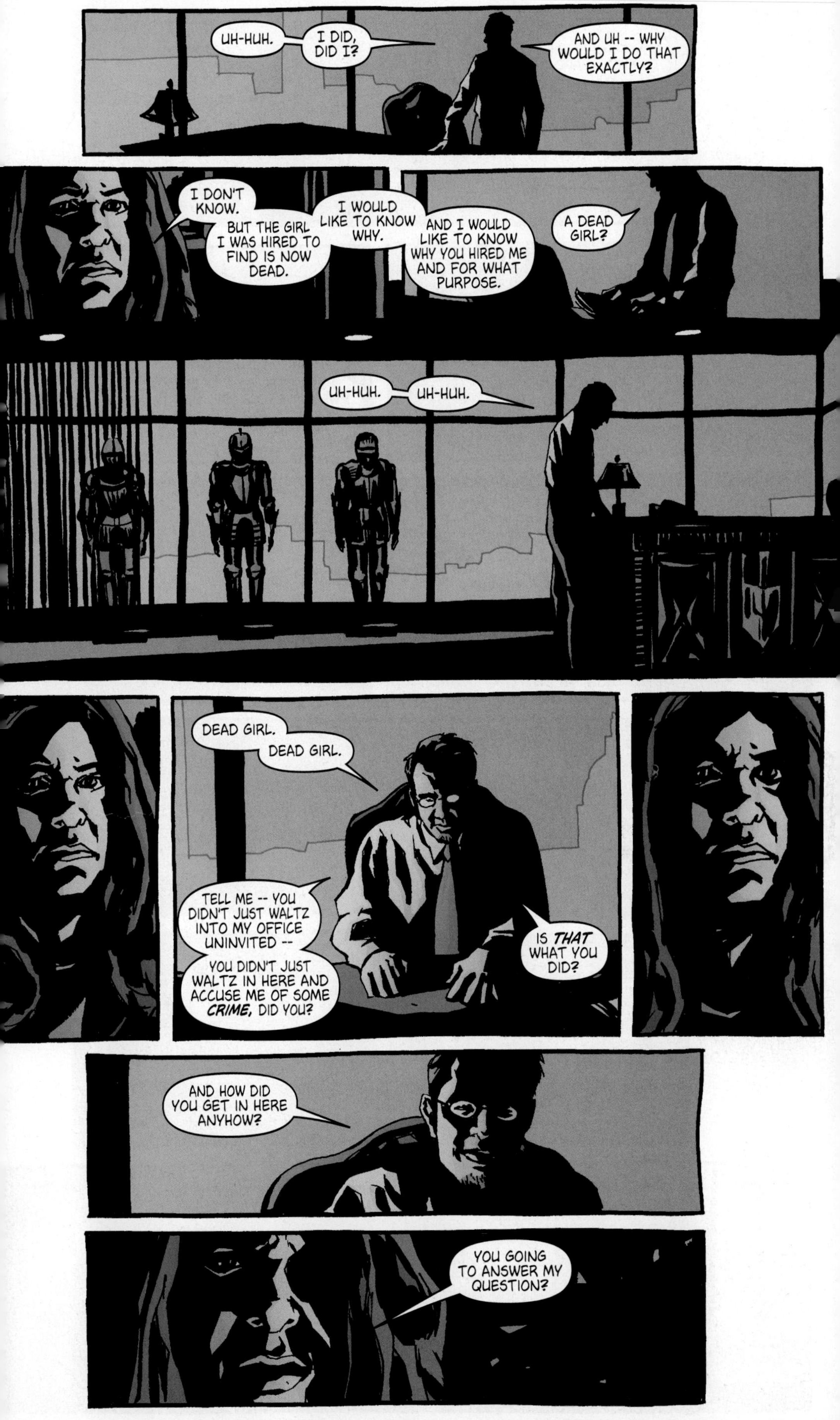
UH-HUH.
I DID, DID I?
AND UH -- WHY WOULD I DO THAT EXACTLY?
I DON'T KNOW.
BUT THE GIRL I WAS HIRED TO FIND IS NOW DEAD.
I WOULD LIKE TO KNOW WHY.
AND I WOULD LIKE TO KNOW WHY YOU HIRED ME AND FOR WHAT PURPOSE.
A DEAD GIRL?
UH-HUH.
UH-HUH.
DEAD GIRL.
DEAD GIRL.
TELL ME -- YOU DIDN'T JUST WALTZ INTO MY OFFICE UNINVITED --
YOU DIDN'T JUST WALTZ IN HERE AND ACCUSE ME OF SOME *CRIME,* DID YOU?
IS *THAT* WHAT YOU DID?
AND HOW DID YOU GET IN HERE ANYHOW?
YOU GOING TO ANSWER MY QUESTION?

LADY, I DON'T KNOW YOU... I NEVER HEARD OF YOU...

AND I DO *NOT* KNOW WHAT YOU ARE TALKING ABOUT OR *WHAT* YOU ARE REFERRING TO --

BUT YOU *CANNOT* COME IN HERE AND MAKE VEILED ACCUSATIONS.

AND YOU KNOW WHAT? I THINK I'M GOING TO HAVE TO ASK YOU TO *LEAVE.*

ALL RIGHT, THEN I'LL CALL SECURITY AND HAVE YOUR BONY ASS *TOSSED* OUT OF HERE --

NO! BETTER YET, I WILL HAVE YOUR ASS THROWN IN *JAIL* FOR *TRESPASSING.*

CALL TH COPS RIG FUCKIN NOW!

YEAH? AND WHAT WILL YOU *TELL* THE COPS?

YOU KNOW?

BECAUSE I KNOW WHAT I'LL SAY.

THEY WOULD LOVE TO HEAR WHAT I HAVE TO SAY.

CALLED *THAT* BLUFF.

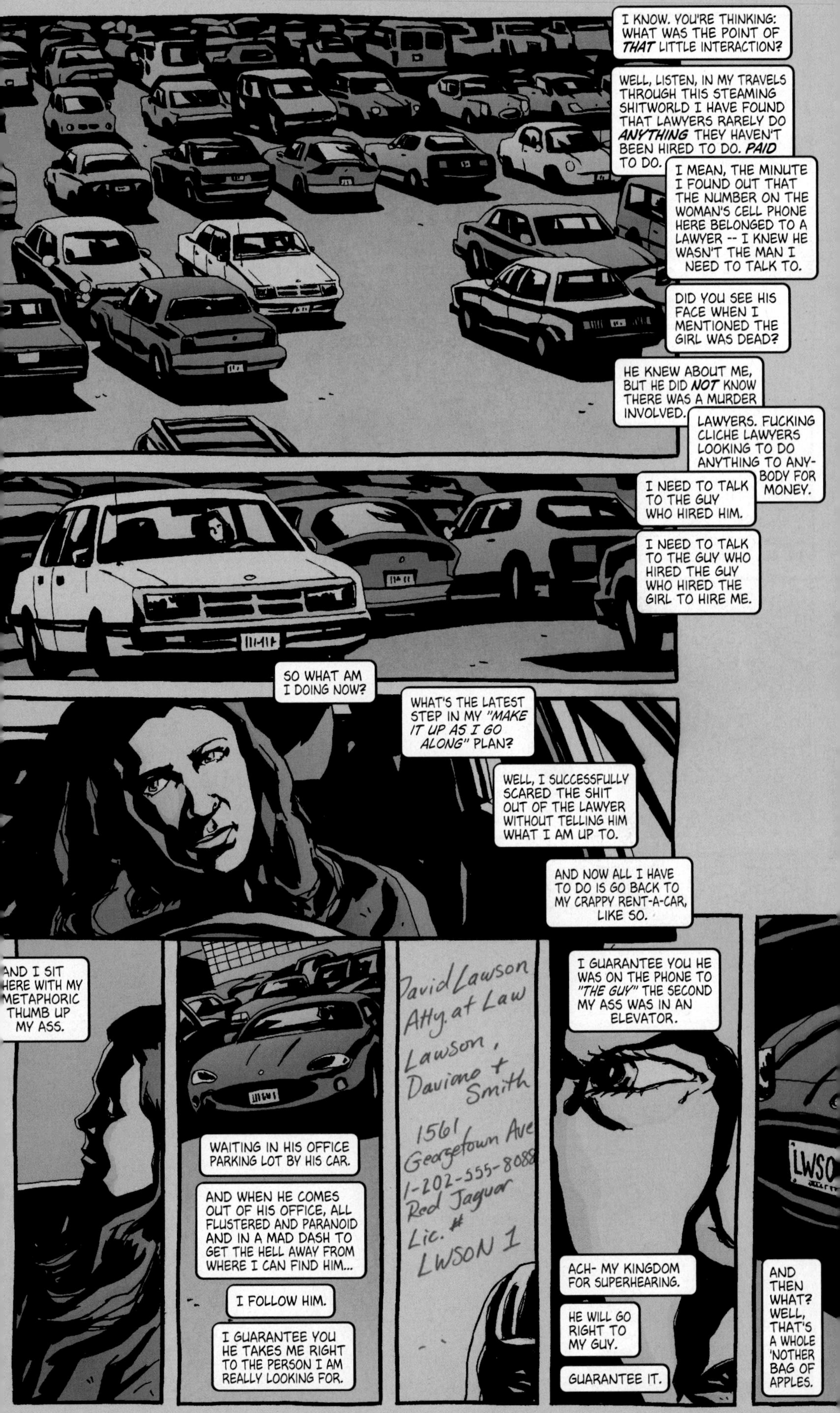
I KNOW. YOU'RE THINKING: WHAT WAS THE POINT OF *THAT* LITTLE INTERACTION?
WELL, LISTEN, IN MY TRAVELS THROUGH THIS STEAMING SHITWORLD I HAVE FOUND THAT LAWYERS RARELY DO *ANYTHING* THEY HAVEN'T BEEN HIRED TO DO. *PAID* TO DO.
I MEAN, THE MINUTE I FOUND OUT THAT THE NUMBER ON THE WOMAN'S CELL PHONE HERE BELONGED TO A LAWYER -- I KNEW HE WASN'T THE MAN I NEED TO TALK TO.
DID YOU SEE HIS FACE WHEN I MENTIONED THE GIRL WAS DEAD?
HE KNEW ABOUT ME, BUT HE DID *NOT* KNOW THERE WAS A MURDER INVOLVED.
LAWYERS. FUCKING CLICHE LAWYERS LOOKING TO DO ANYTHING TO ANYBODY FOR MONEY.
I NEED TO TALK TO THE GUY WHO HIRED HIM.
I NEED TO TALK TO THE GUY WHO HIRED THE GUY WHO HIRED THE GIRL TO HIRE ME.
SO WHAT AM I DOING NOW?
WHAT'S THE LATEST STEP IN MY *"MAKE IT UP AS I GO ALONG"* PLAN?
WELL, I SUCCESSFULLY SCARED THE SHIT OUT OF THE LAWYER WITHOUT TELLING HIM WHAT I AM UP TO.
AND NOW ALL I HAVE TO DO IS GO BACK TO MY CRAPPY RENT-A-CAR, LIKE SO.
AND I SIT HERE WITH MY METAPHORIC THUMB UP MY ASS.
WAITING IN HIS OFFICE PARKING LOT BY HIS CAR.
AND WHEN HE COMES OUT OF HIS OFFICE, ALL FLUSTERED AND PARANOID AND IN A MAD DASH TO GET THE HELL AWAY FROM WHERE I CAN FIND HIM...
I FOLLOW HIM.
I GUARANTEE YOU HE TAKES ME RIGHT TO THE PERSON I AM REALLY LOOKING FOR.
David Lawson
Atty. at Law
Lawson, Daviano + Smith
1561 Georgetown Ave
1-202-555-8088
Red Jaguar
Lic. #
LWSON 1
I GUARANTEE YOU HE WAS ON THE PHONE TO *"THE GUY"* THE SECOND MY ASS WAS IN AN ELEVATOR.
ACH- MY KINGDOM FOR SUPERHEARING.
HE WILL GO RIGHT TO MY GUY.
GUARANTEE IT.
AND THEN WHAT? WELL, THAT'S A WHOLE 'NOTHER BAG OF APPLES.

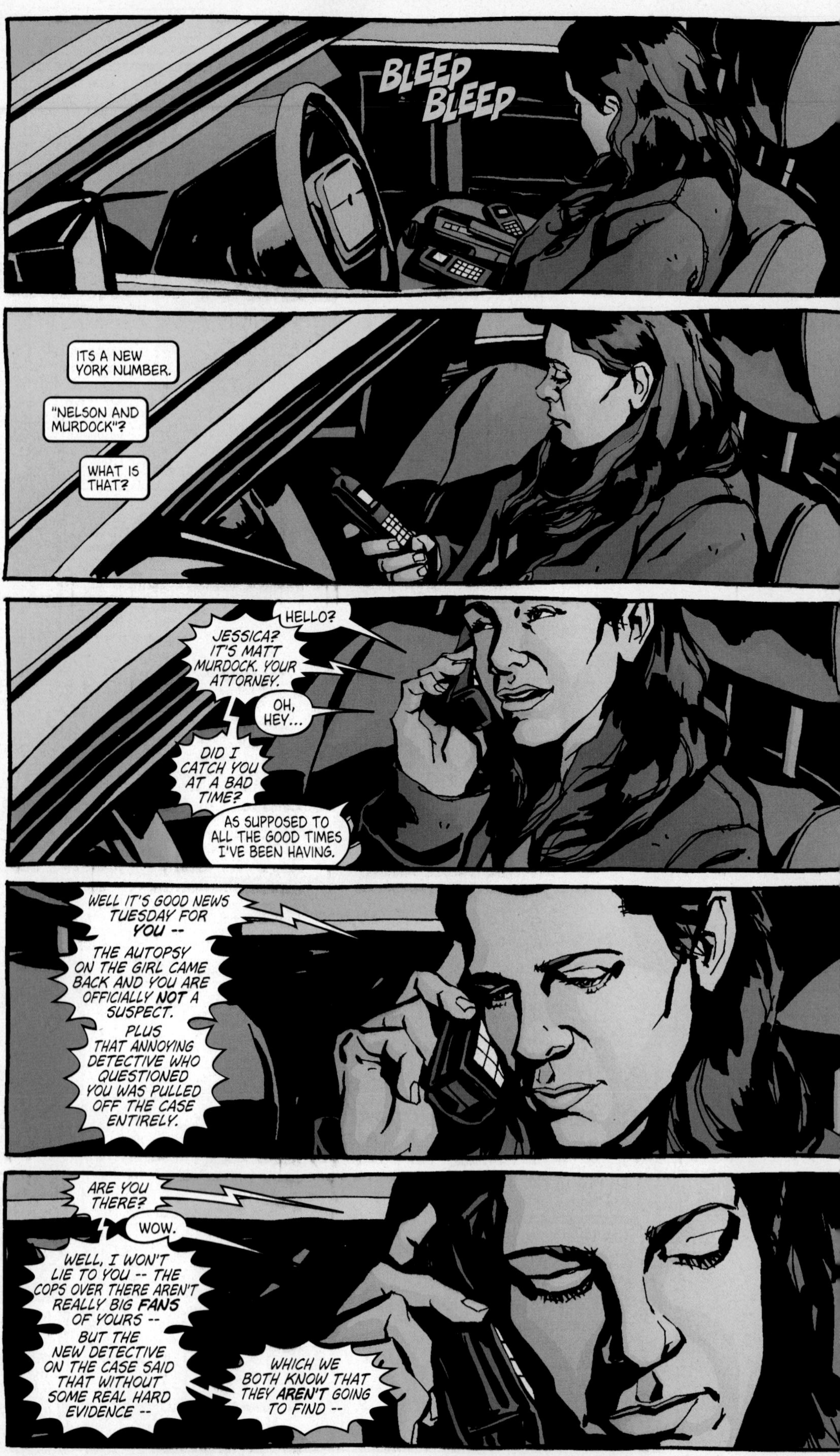
BLEEP BLEEP
ITS A NEW YORK NUMBER.
"NELSON AND MURDOCK"?
WHAT IS THAT?
HELLO?
JESSICA? IT'S MATT MURDOCK. YOUR ATTORNEY.
OH, HEY...
DID I CATCH YOU AT A BAD TIME?
AS SUPPOSED TO ALL THE GOOD TIMES I'VE BEEN HAVING.
WELL IT'S GOOD NEWS TUESDAY FOR YOU --
THE AUTOPSY ON THE GIRL CAME BACK AND YOU ARE OFFICIALLY NOT A SUSPECT.
PLUS THAT ANNOYING DETECTIVE WHO QUESTIONED YOU WAS PULLED OFF THE CASE ENTIRELY.
ARE YOU THERE?
WOW.
WELL, I WON'T LIE TO YOU -- THE COPS OVER THERE AREN'T REALLY BIG FANS OF YOURS --
BUT THE NEW DETECTIVE ON THE CASE SAID THAT WITHOUT SOME REAL HARD EVIDENCE --
WHICH WE BOTH KNOW THAT THEY AREN'T GOING TO FIND --

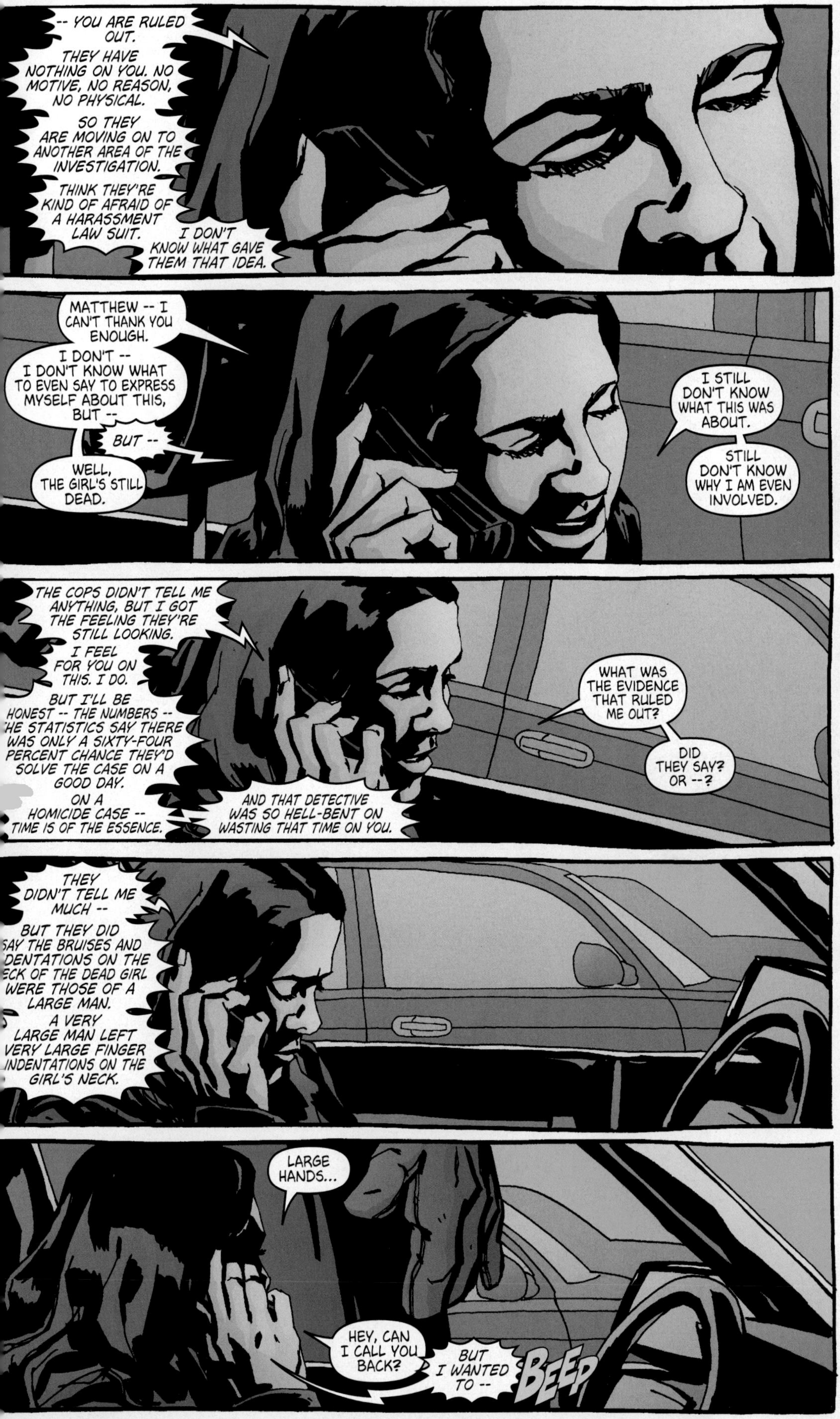
-- YOU ARE RULED OUT.
THEY HAVE NOTHING ON YOU. NO MOTIVE, NO REASON, NO PHYSICAL.
SO THEY ARE MOVING ON TO ANOTHER AREA OF THE INVESTIGATION.
THINK THEY'RE KIND OF AFRAID OF A HARASSMENT LAW SUIT.
I DON'T KNOW WHAT GAVE THEM THAT IDEA.
MATTHEW -- I CAN'T THANK YOU ENOUGH.
I DON'T -- I DON'T KNOW WHAT TO EVEN SAY TO EXPRESS MYSELF ABOUT THIS, BUT --
BUT --
WELL, THE GIRL'S STILL DEAD.
I STILL DON'T KNOW WHAT THIS WAS ABOUT.
STILL DON'T KNOW WHY I AM EVEN INVOLVED.
THE COPS DIDN'T TELL ME ANYTHING, BUT I GOT THE FEELING THEY'RE STILL LOOKING.
I FEEL FOR YOU ON THIS. I DO.
BUT I'LL BE HONEST -- THE NUMBERS -- THE STATISTICS SAY THERE WAS ONLY A SIXTY-FOUR PERCENT CHANCE THEY'D SOLVE THE CASE ON A GOOD DAY.
ON A HOMICIDE CASE -- TIME IS OF THE ESSENCE.
AND THAT DETECTIVE WAS SO HELL-BENT ON WASTING THAT TIME ON YOU.
WHAT WAS THE EVIDENCE THAT RULED ME OUT?
DID THEY SAY? OR --?
THEY DIDN'T TELL ME MUCH --
BUT THEY DID SAY THE BRUISES AND INDENTATIONS ON THE NECK OF THE DEAD GIRL WERE THOSE OF A LARGE MAN.
A VERY LARGE MAN LEFT VERY LARGE FINGER INDENTATIONS ON THE GIRL'S NECK.
LARGE HANDS...
HEY, CAN I CALL YOU BACK?
BUT I WANTED TO --
BEEP

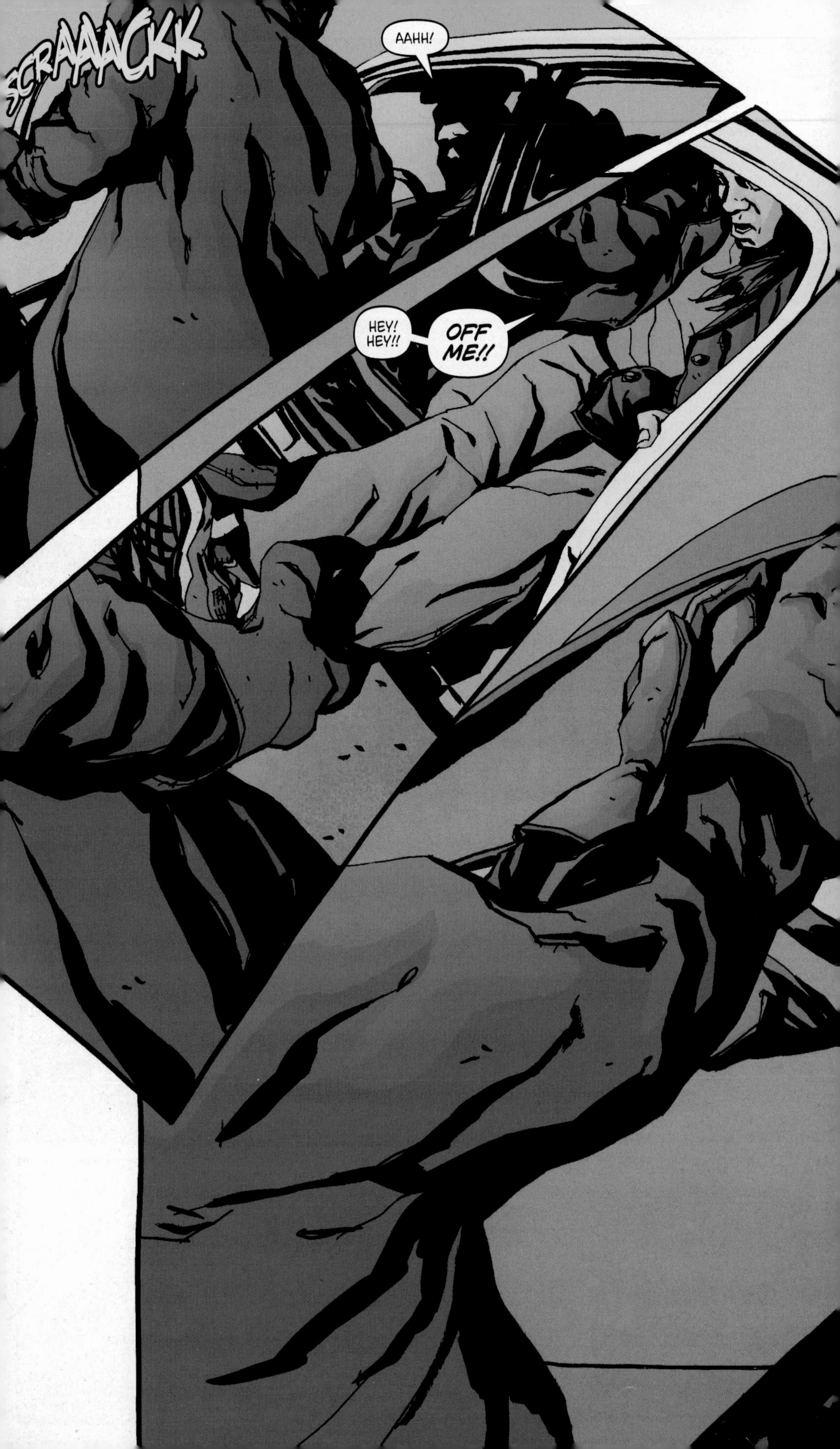
SCRAAACKK
AAHH!
HEY! HEY!!
OFF ME!!

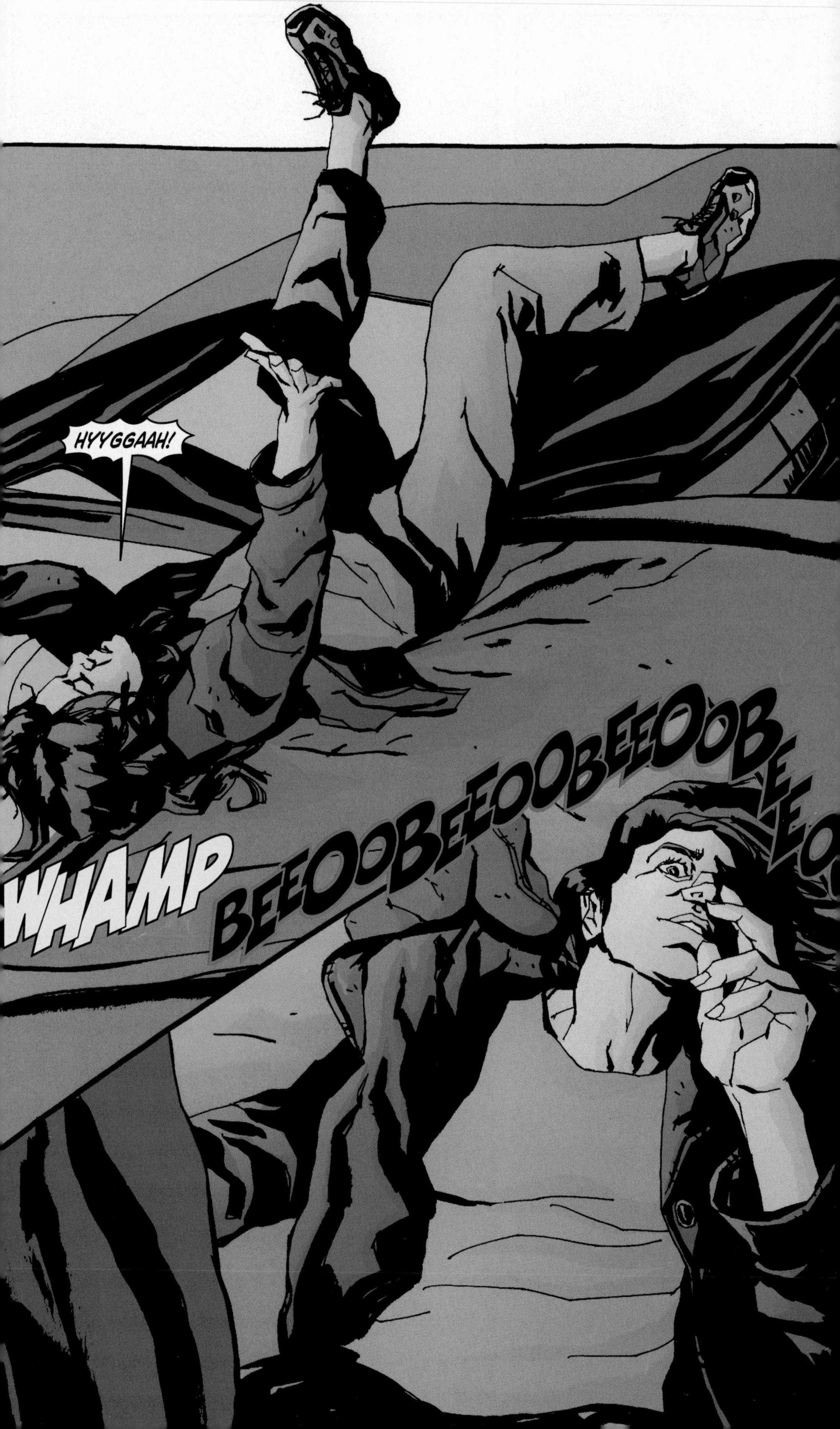
HYYGGAAH!
WHAMP
BEEOOBEEOOBEEOOBEEO

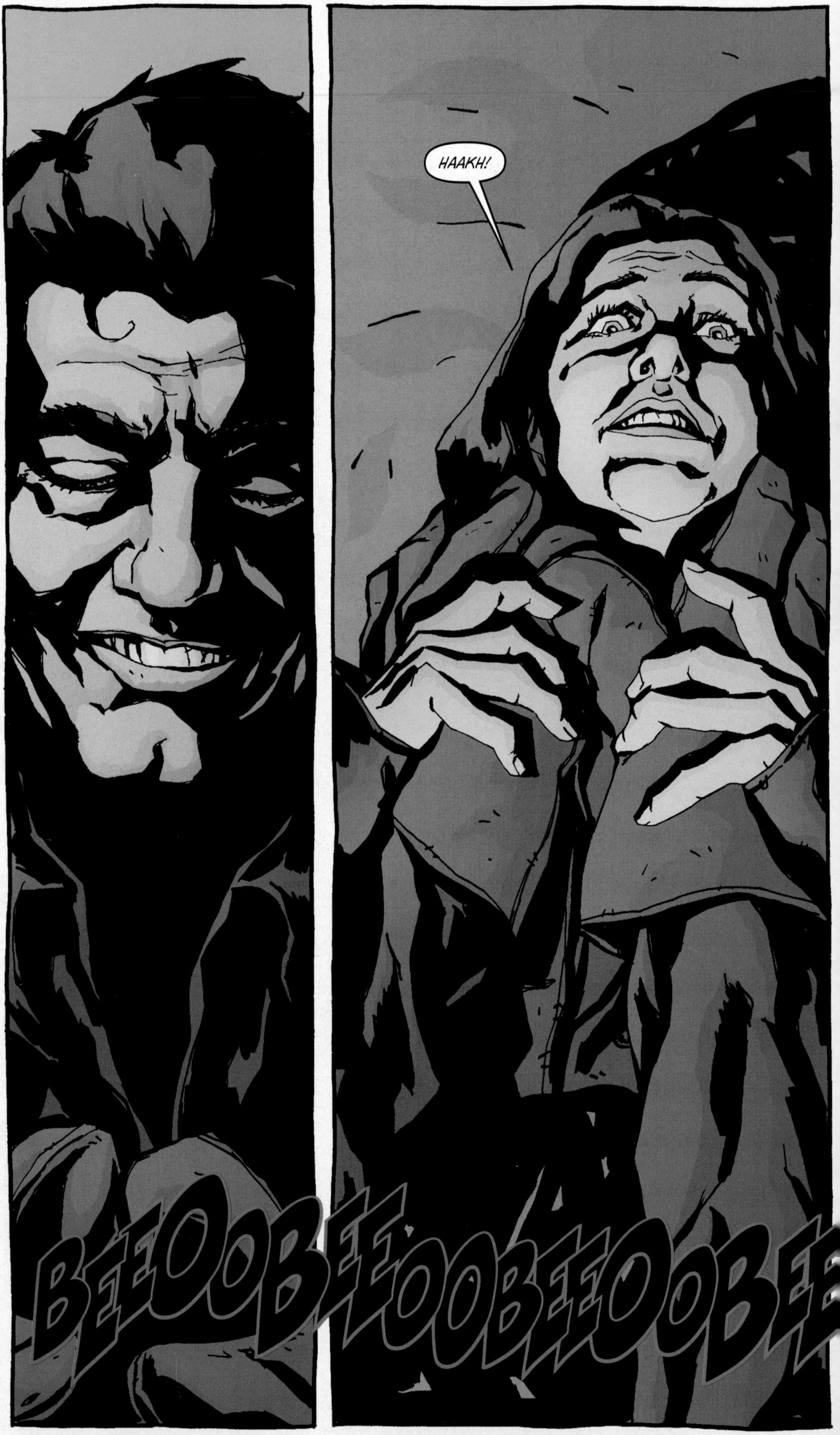
HAAKH!
BEEOOBEEOOBEEOOBEE

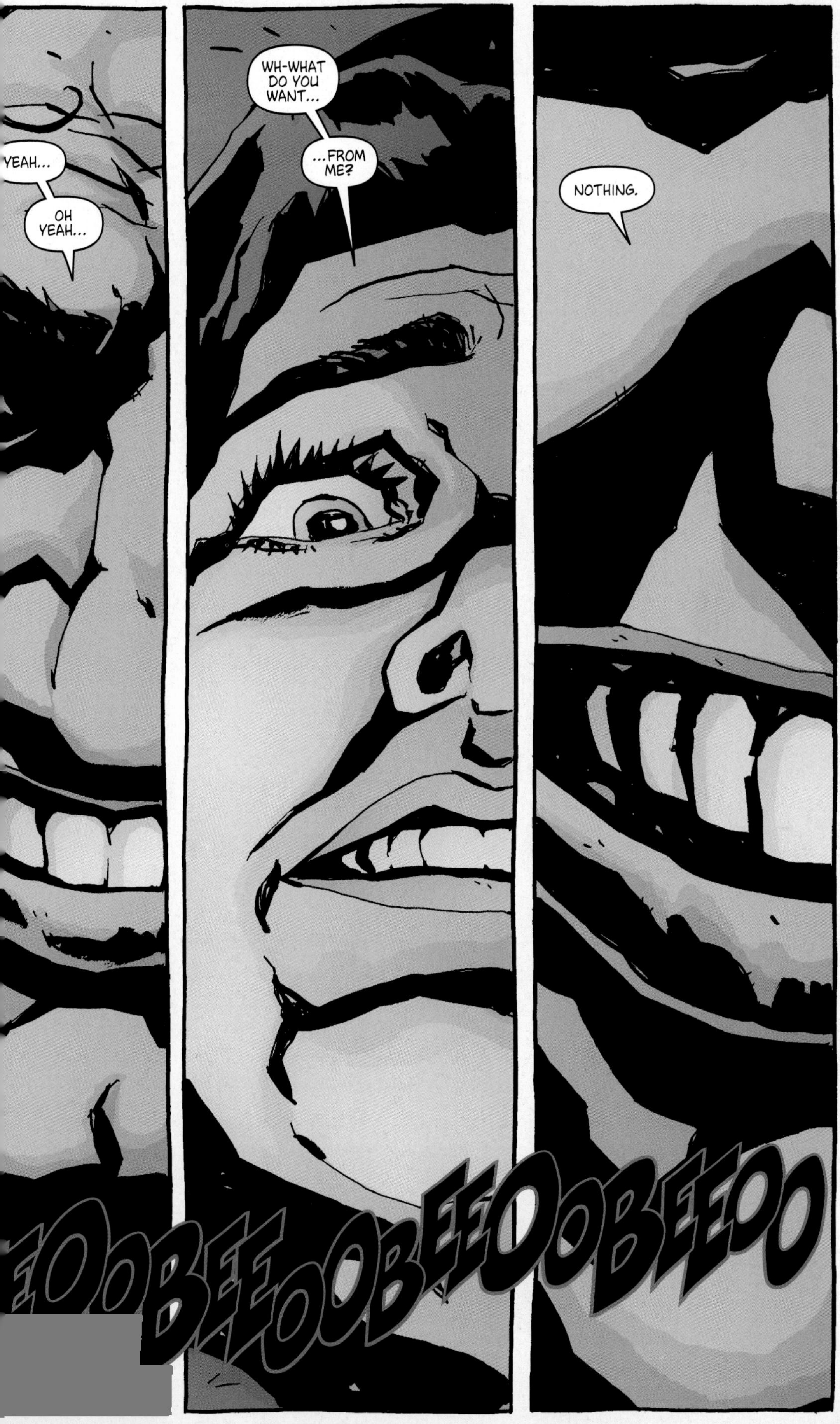
YEAH...
OH YEAH...
WH-WHAT DO YOU WANT...
...FROM ME?
NOTHING.
EOOBEEOOBEEOOBEEOO

PO[redacted]PART[redacted]

ISSUE #5

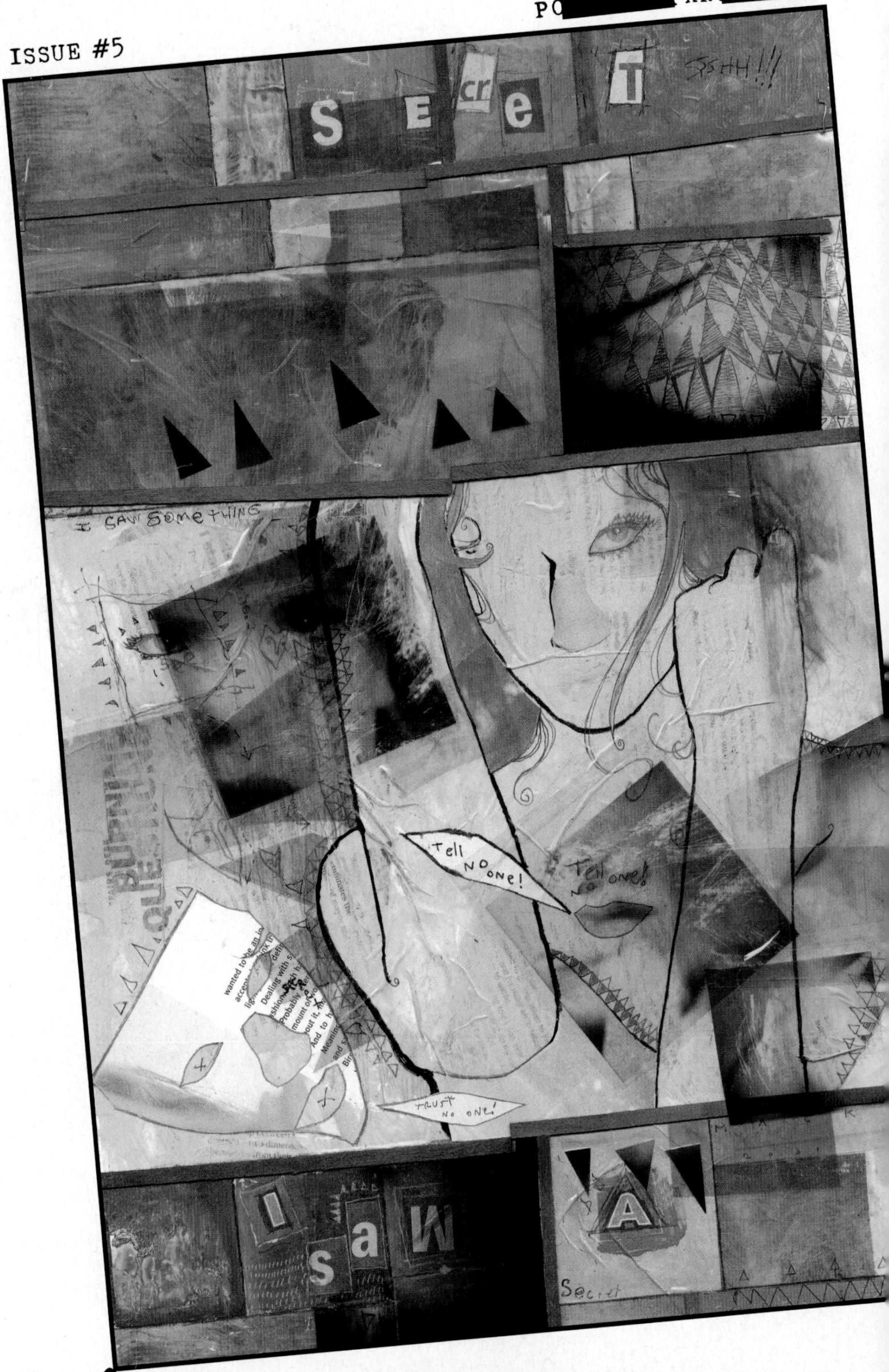

SEcreT
SSHH!!!
I SAW SOmeTHING
Tell NO one!
Tell NO one!
TRUST NO ONE!
I saw A
Secret

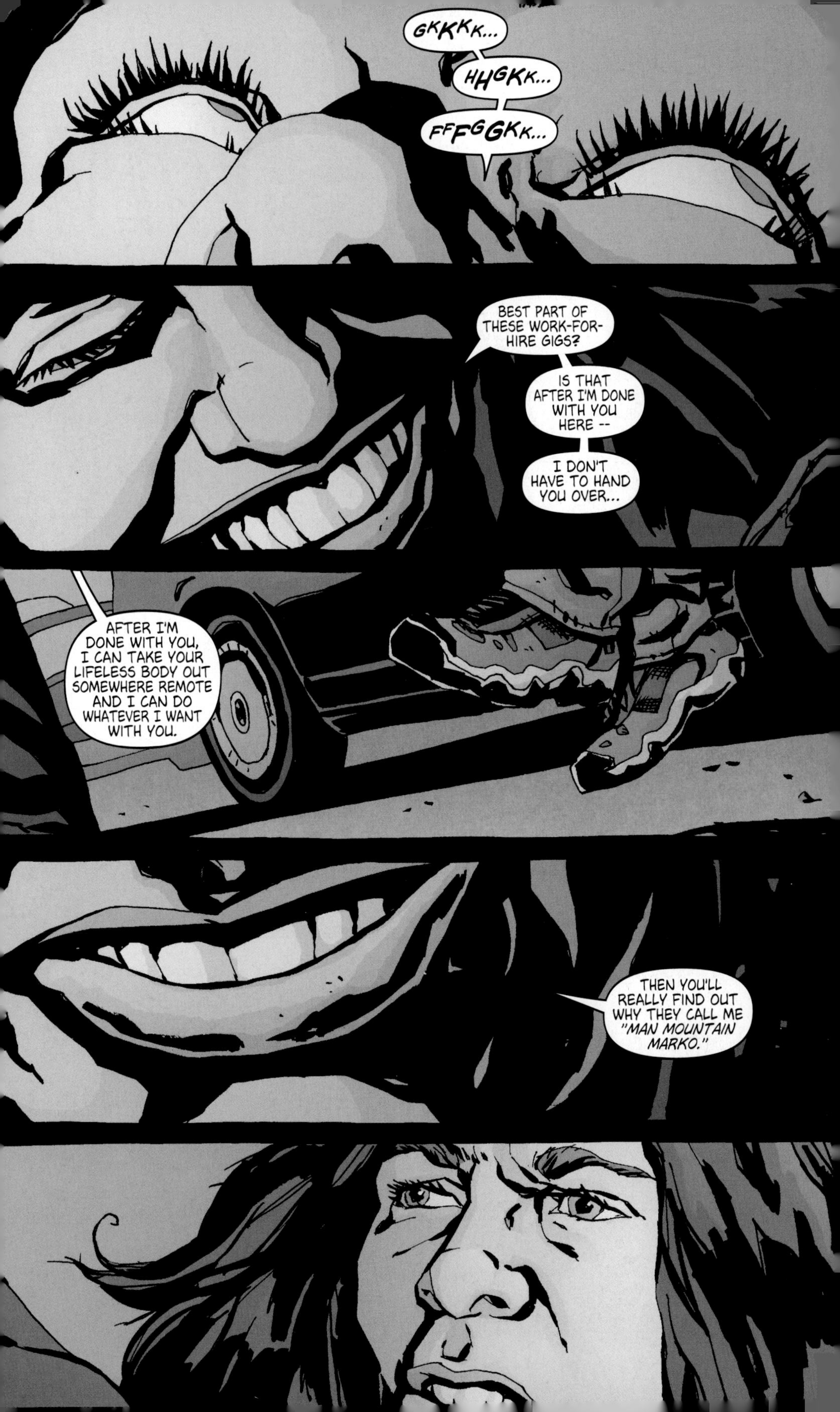

GKKKK...
HHGKK...
FFFGGKK...
BEST PART OF THESE WORK-FOR-HIRE GIGS?
IS THAT AFTER I'M DONE WITH YOU HERE --
I DON'T HAVE TO HAND YOU OVER...
AFTER I'M DONE WITH YOU, I CAN TAKE YOUR LIFELESS BODY OUT SOMEWHERE REMOTE AND I CAN DO WHATEVER I WANT WITH YOU.
THEN YOU'LL REALLY FIND OUT WHY THEY CALL ME *"MAN MOUNTAIN MARKO."*

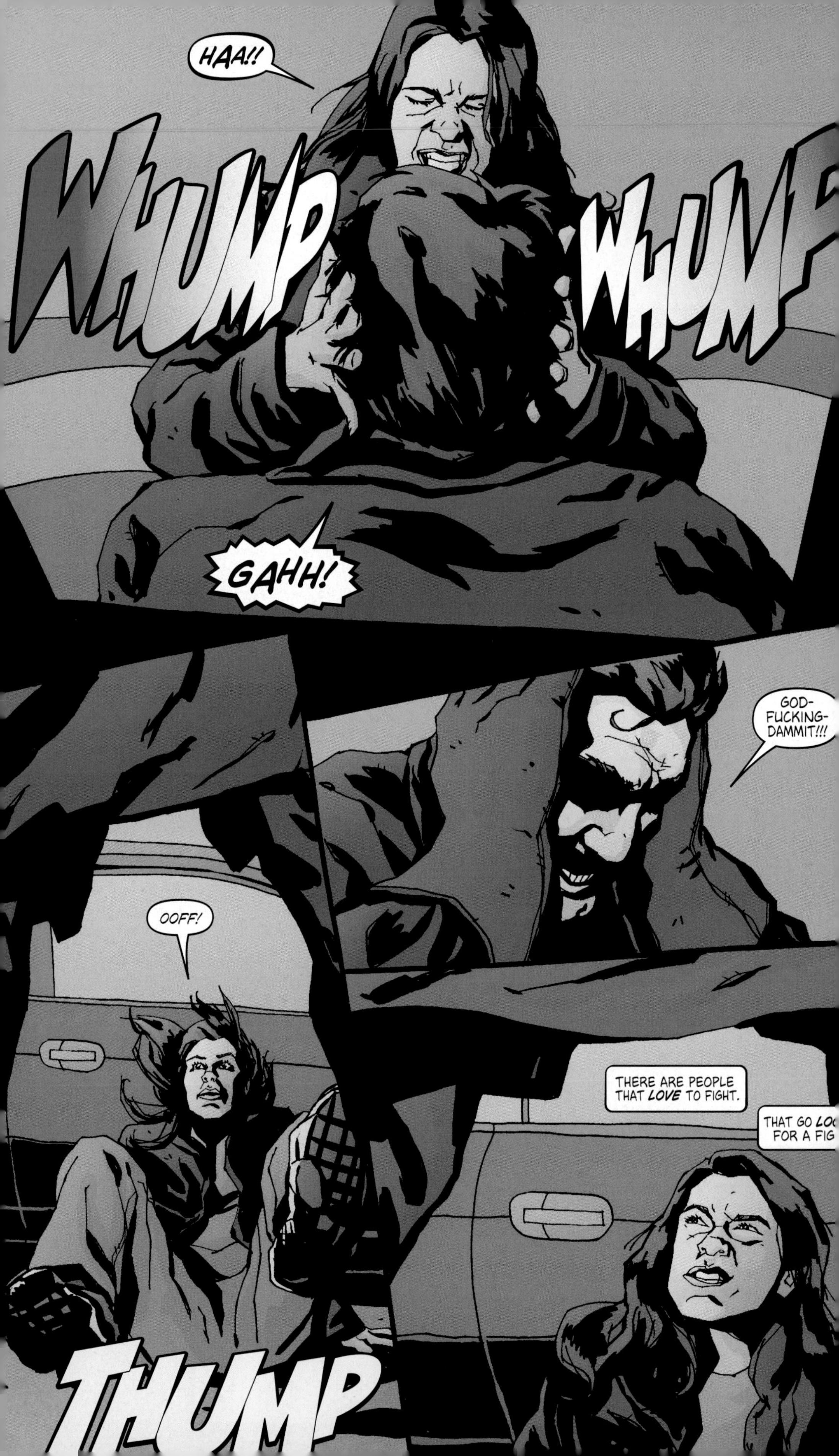
HAA!!
WHUMP
WHUMF
GAHH!
GOD-FUCKING-DAMMIT!!!
OOFF!
THERE ARE PEOPLE THAT *LOVE* TO FIGHT.
THAT GO
FOR A FIG
THUMP

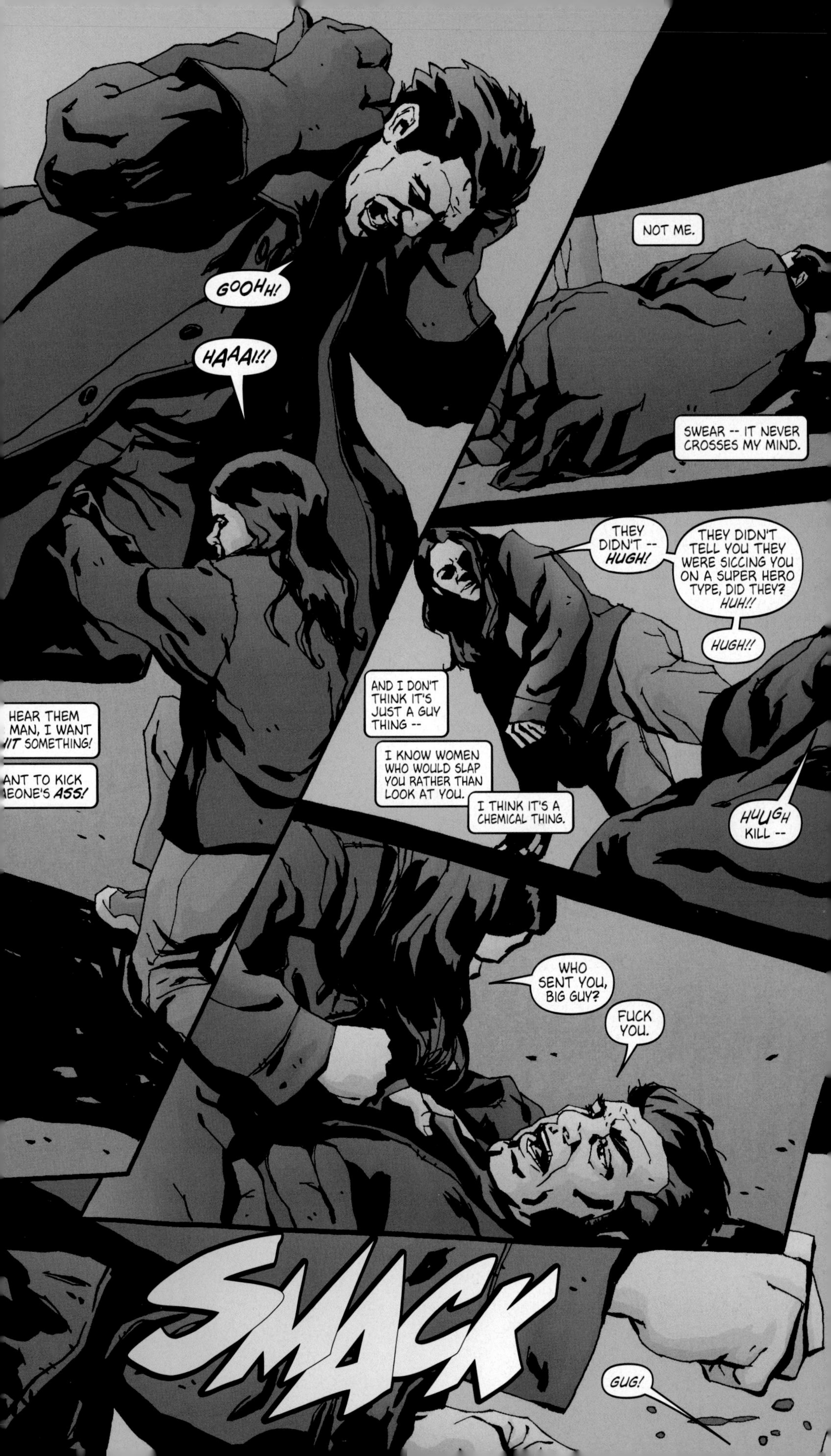
GOOHH!
HAAAI!!
NOT ME.
SWEAR -- IT NEVER CROSSES MY MIND.
HEAR THEM MAN, I WANT IT SOMETHING!
ANT TO KICK EONE'S ASS!
AND I DON'T THINK IT'S JUST A GUY THING --
I KNOW WOMEN WHO WOULD SLAP YOU RATHER THAN LOOK AT YOU.
I THINK IT'S A CHEMICAL THING.
THEY DIDN'T -- HUGH!
THEY DIDN'T TELL YOU THEY WERE SICCING YOU ON A SUPER HERO TYPE, DID THEY? HUH!!
HUGH!!
HUUGH KILL --
WHO SENT YOU, BIG GUY?
FUCK YOU.
SMACK
GUG!

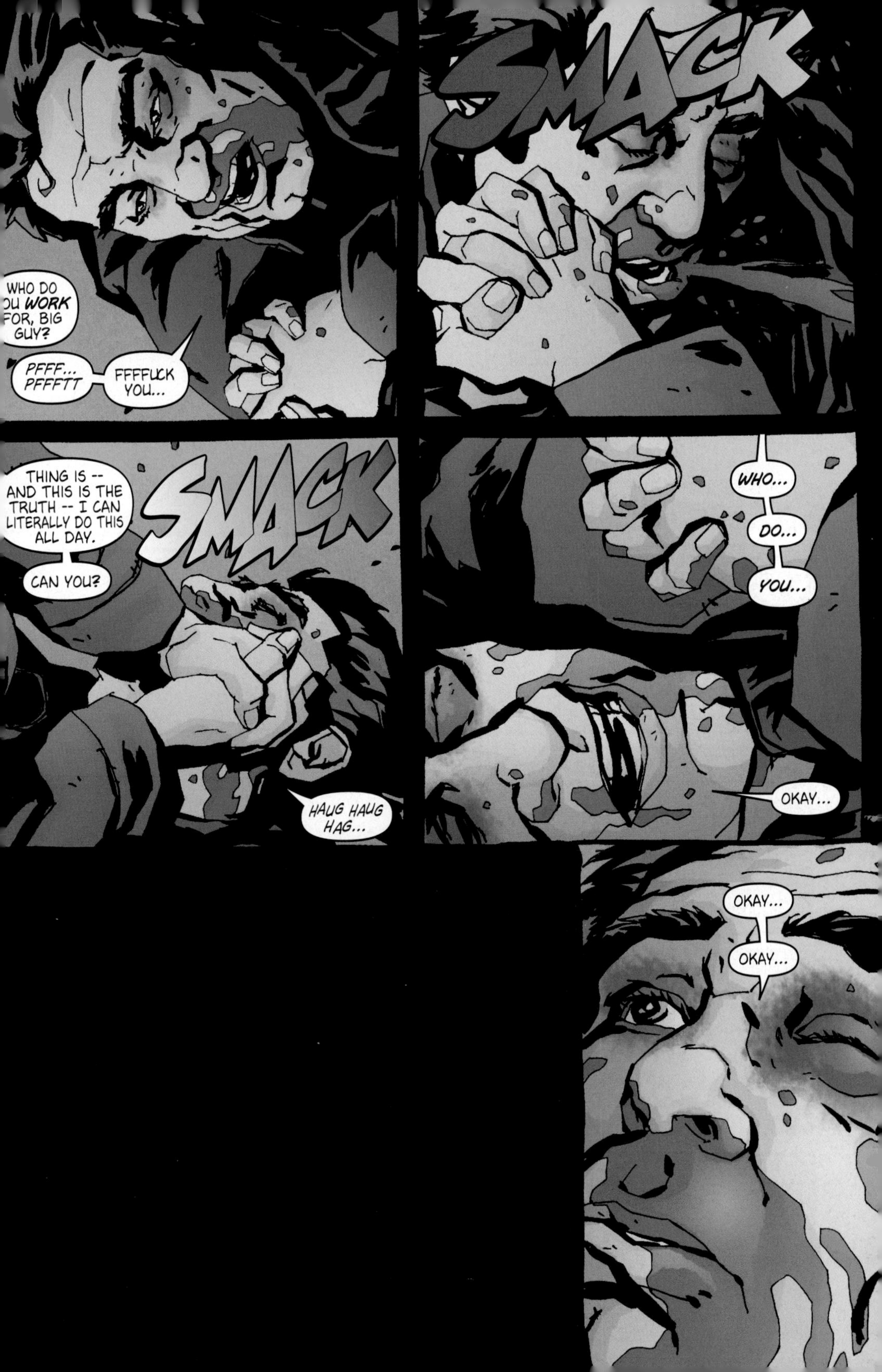

SMACK
WHO DO
OU WORK
FOR, BIG
GUY?
PFFF... PFFFTT
FFFFUCK YOU...
THING IS -- AND THIS IS THE TRUTH -- I CAN LITERALLY DO THIS ALL DAY.
CAN YOU?
SMACK
HAUG HAUG HAG...
WHO...
DO...
YOU...
OKAY...
OKAY...
OKAY...

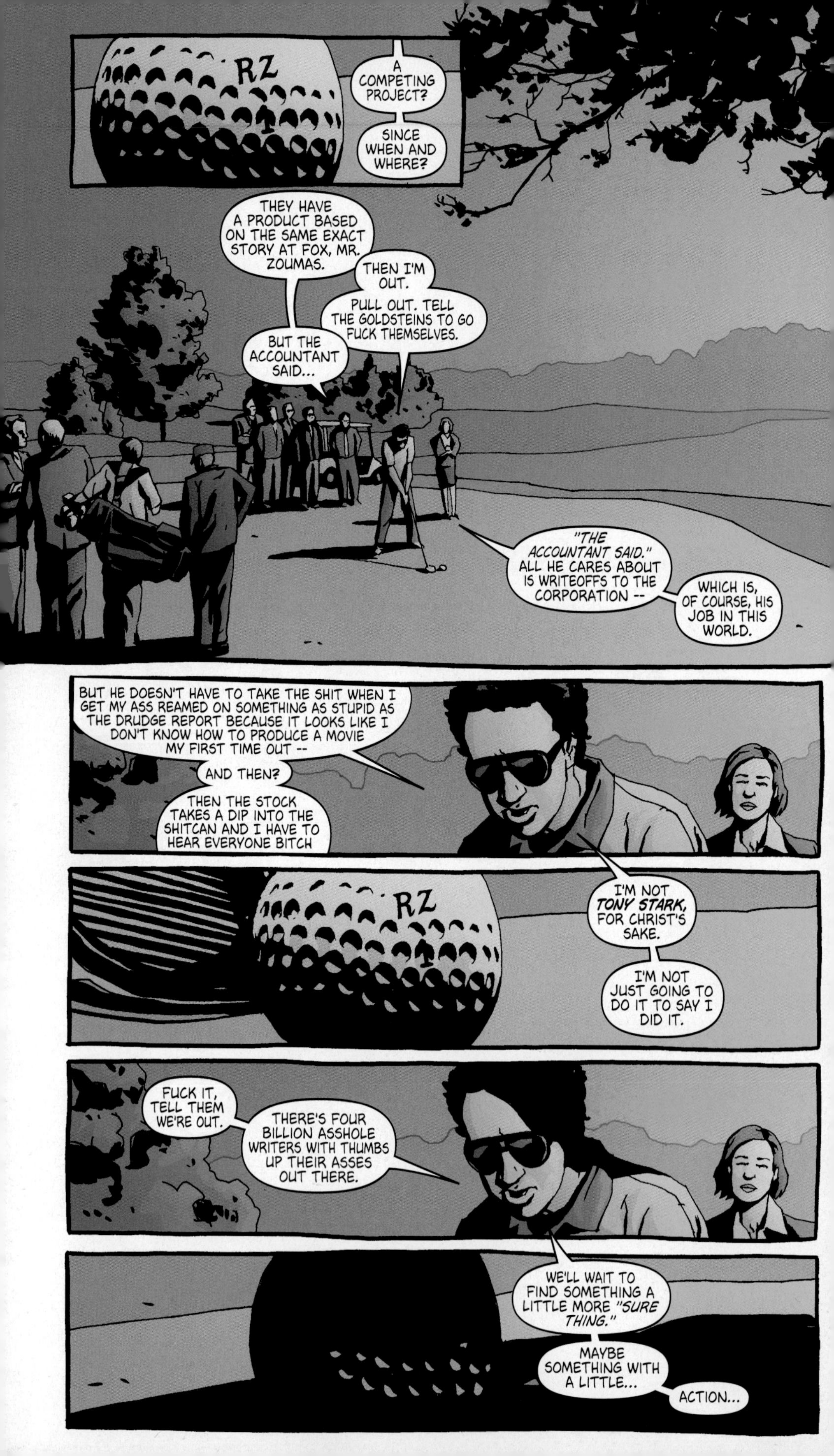
RZ
A COMPETING PROJECT?
SINCE WHEN AND WHERE?
THEY HAVE A PRODUCT BASED ON THE SAME EXACT STORY AT FOX, MR. ZOUMAS.
THEN I'M OUT.
PULL OUT. TELL THE GOLDSTEINS TO GO FUCK THEMSELVES.
BUT THE ACCOUNTANT SAID...
"THE ACCOUNTANT SAID." ALL HE CARES ABOUT IS WRITEOFFS TO THE CORPORATION --
WHICH IS, OF COURSE, HIS JOB IN THIS WORLD.
BUT HE DOESN'T HAVE TO TAKE THE SHIT WHEN I GET MY ASS REAMED ON SOMETHING AS STUPID AS THE DRUDGE REPORT BECAUSE IT LOOKS LIKE I DON'T KNOW HOW TO PRODUCE A MOVIE MY FIRST TIME OUT --
AND THEN?
THEN THE STOCK TAKES A DIP INTO THE SHITCAN AND I HAVE TO HEAR EVERYONE BITCH
RZ
I'M NOT *TONY STARK,* FOR CHRIST'S SAKE.
I'M NOT JUST GOING TO DO IT TO SAY I DID IT.
FUCK IT, TELL THEM WE'RE OUT.
THERE'S FOUR BILLION ASSHOLE WRITERS WITH THUMBS UP THEIR ASSES OUT THERE.
WE'LL WAIT TO FIND SOMETHING A LITTLE MORE *"SURE THING."*
MAYBE SOMETHING WITH A LITTLE...
ACTION...

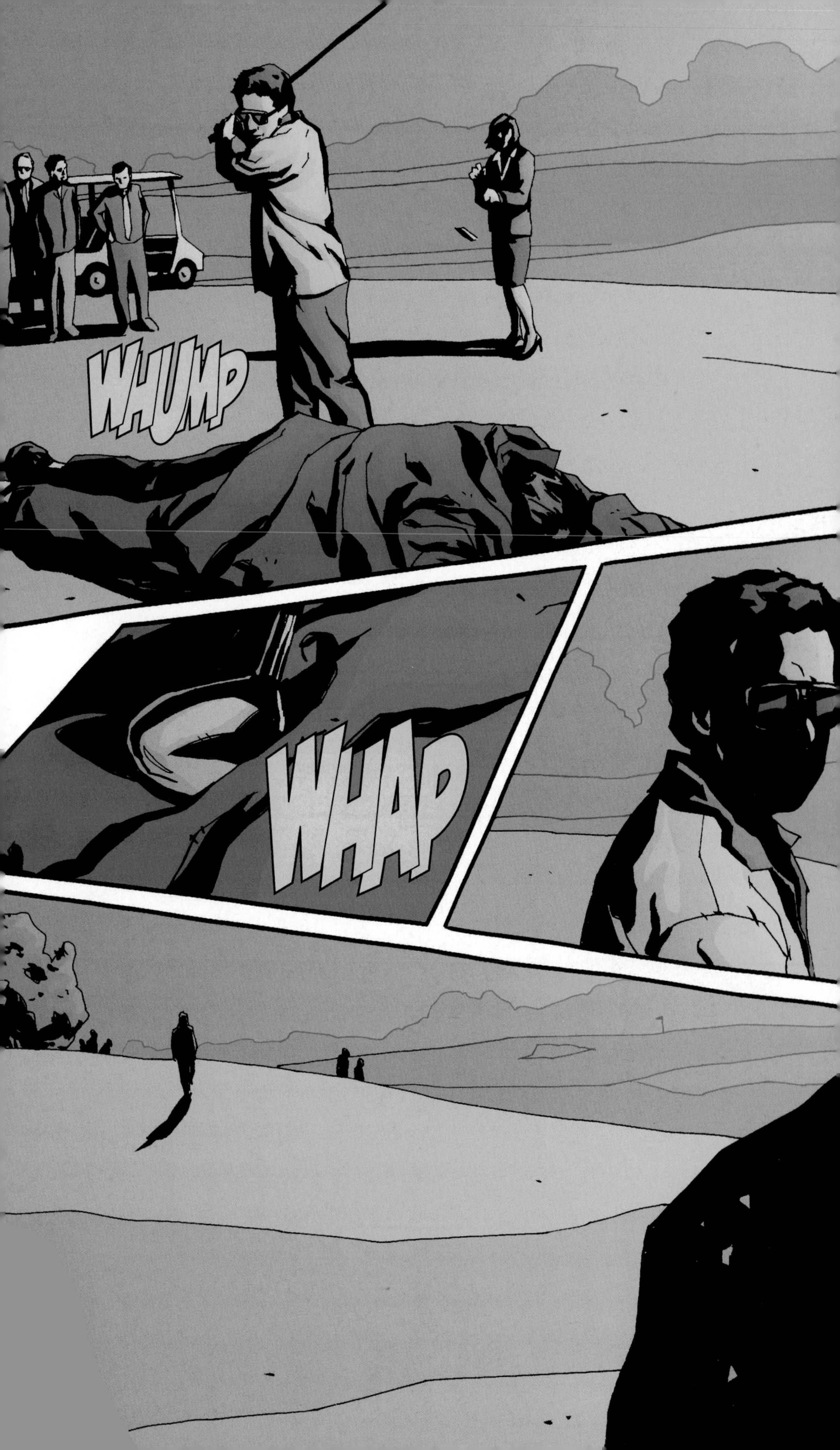
WHUMP
WHAP

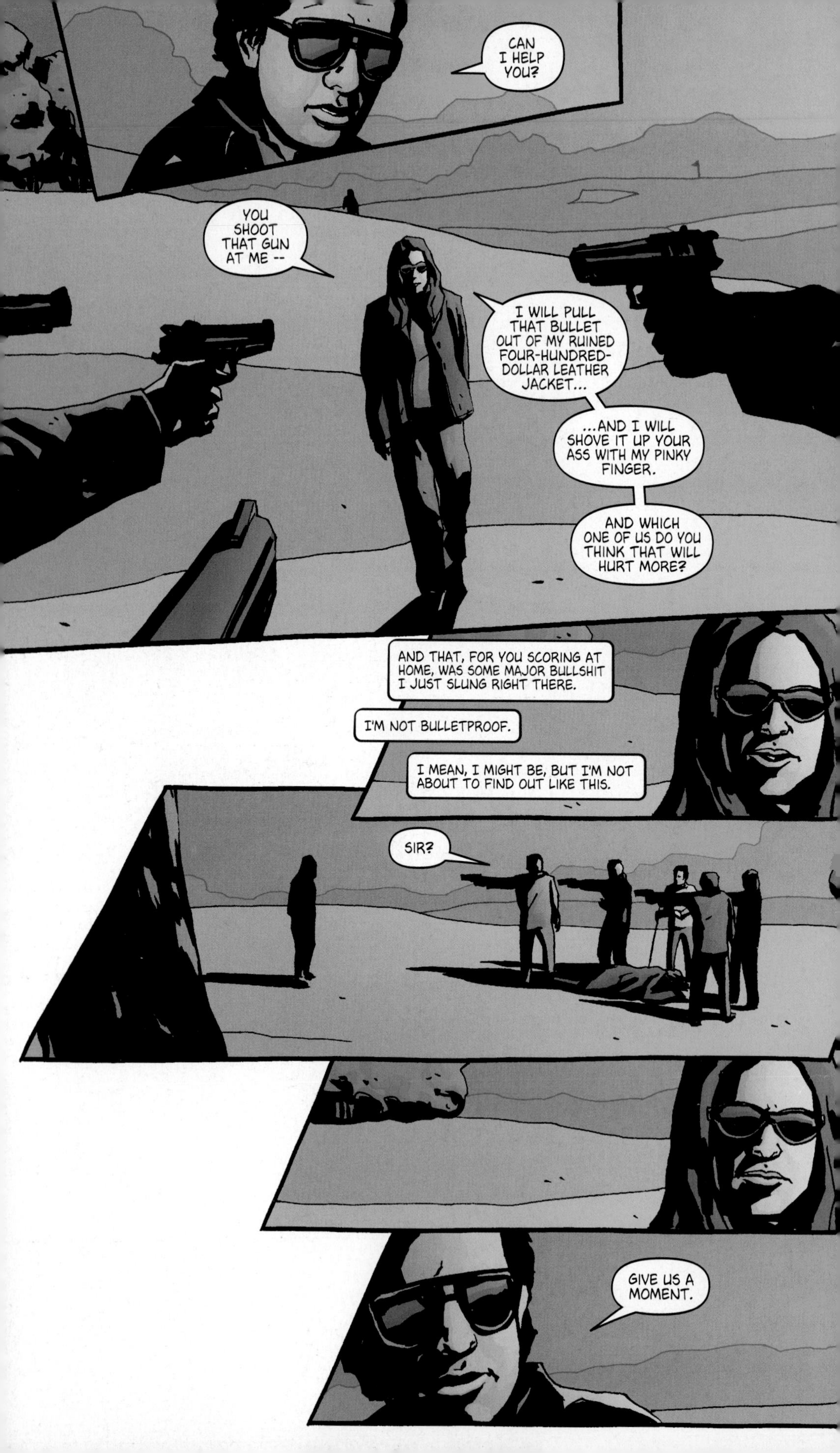
CAN I HELP YOU?
YOU SHOOT THAT GUN AT ME --
I WILL PULL THAT BULLET OUT OF MY RUINED FOUR-HUNDRED-DOLLAR LEATHER JACKET...
...AND I WILL SHOVE IT UP YOUR ASS WITH MY PINKY FINGER.
AND WHICH ONE OF US DO YOU THINK THAT WILL HURT MORE?
AND THAT, FOR YOU SCORING AT HOME, WAS SOME MAJOR BULLSHIT I JUST SLUNG RIGHT THERE.
I'M NOT BULLETPROOF.
I MEAN, I MIGHT BE, BUT I'M NOT ABOUT TO FIND OUT LIKE THIS.
SIR?
GIVE US A MOMENT.

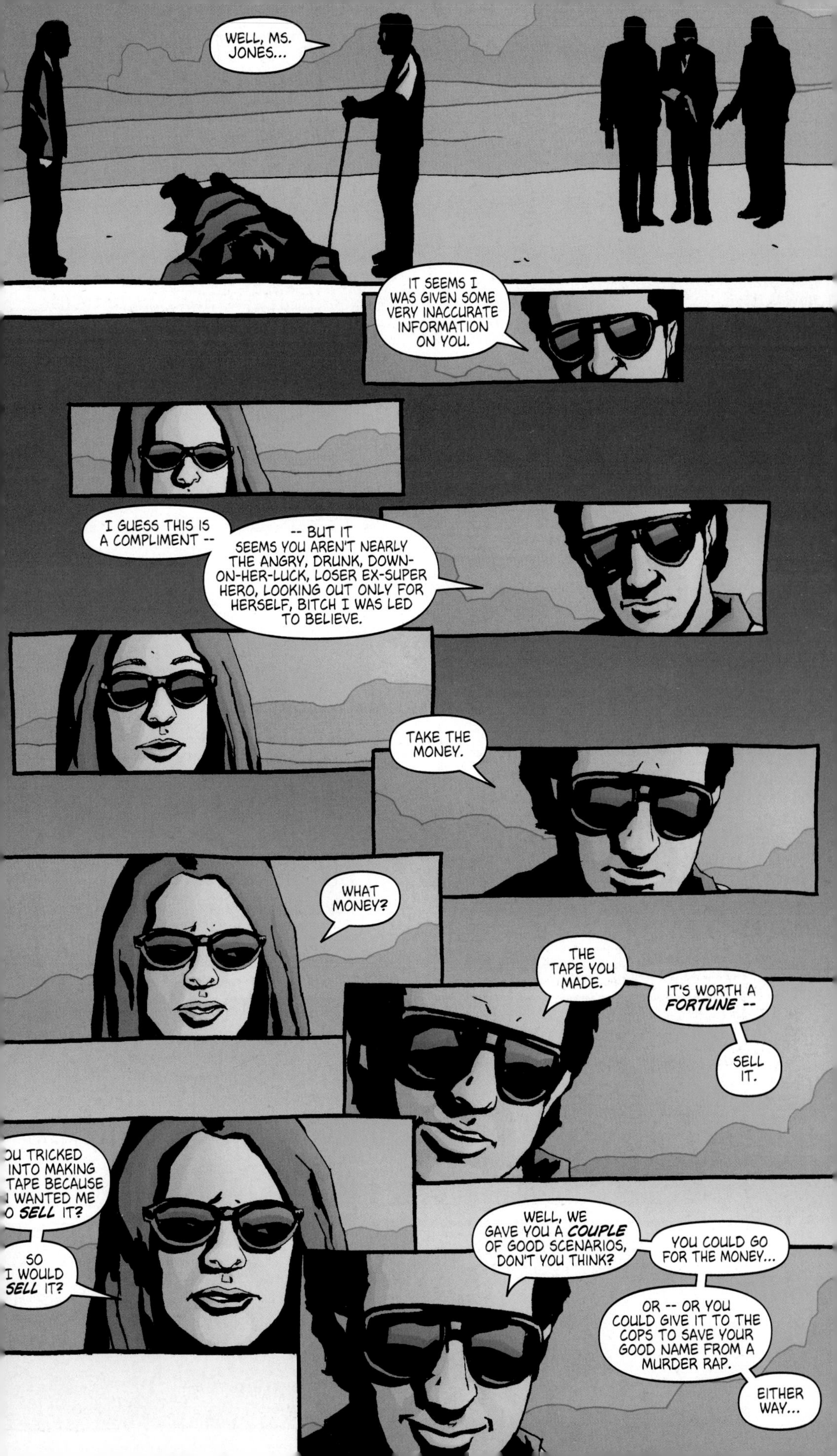
WELL, MS. JONES...
IT SEEMS I WAS GIVEN SOME VERY INACCURATE INFORMATION ON YOU.
I GUESS THIS IS A COMPLIMENT --
-- BUT IT SEEMS YOU AREN'T NEARLY THE ANGRY, DRUNK, DOWN-ON-HER-LUCK, LOSER EX-SUPER HERO, LOOKING OUT ONLY FOR HERSELF, BITCH I WAS LED TO BELIEVE.
TAKE THE MONEY.
WHAT MONEY?
THE TAPE YOU MADE.
IT'S WORTH A *FORTUNE* --
SELL IT.
OU TRICKED INTO MAKING TAPE BECAUSE WANTED ME O *SELL* IT?
SO I WOULD *SELL* IT?
WELL, WE GAVE YOU A *COUPLE* OF GOOD SCENARIOS, DON'T YOU THINK?
YOU COULD GO FOR THE MONEY...
OR -- OR YOU COULD GIVE IT TO THE COPS TO SAVE YOUR GOOD NAME FROM A MURDER RAP.
EITHER WAY...

YOU -- YOU *MURDERED* A GIRL BECAUSE YOU WANTED ME TO *GIVE* THE TAPE AWAY...?

IT'S OKAY, GEORGE.

IT'S OKAY.

NOTHING -- NOTHING TO WORRY ABOUT. GO BACK.

WHAT DID YOU COME HERE FOR?

WHAT DO YOU *WANT*?

I WANTED THE TRUTH.

I JUST --

YOU'VE DONE SOMETHING TERRIBLE, AND I WANT YOU TO CONFESS.

YOU WOULD LIKE ME TO CONFESS TO WHAT? TO WHOM?

TO THE POLICE? TO HIRING YOU? I DIDN'T HIRE YOU.

TRICKING YOU INTO MAKING A TAPE OF CAPTAIN AMERICA AND HIS SECRET IDENTITY?

I DID THAT? DID I DO THAT?

CONFESS TO A *MURDER? WHAT* MURDER?

DON'T YOU THINK IF ALLEGATIONS LIKE THIS WERE MADE, THAT THE AUTHORITIES WOULD NEED TO SEE THIS CONTROVERSIAL TAPE YOU ARE REFERRING TO?

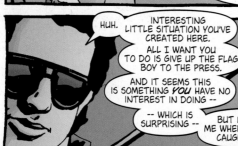

HUH.

INTERESTING LITTLE SITUATION YOU'VE CREATED HERE.

ALL I WANT YOU TO DO IS GIVE UP THE FLAG BOY TO THE PRESS.

AND IT SEEMS THIS IS SOMETHING *YOU* HAVE NO INTEREST IN DOING --

-- WHICH IS SURPRISING --

BUT NOW YOU'VE GOT ME WHERE YOU WANT ME -- CAUGHT RED-HANDED.

BUT TO DO ANYTHING ABOUT IT, YOU HAVE TO GIVE UP THE FLAG BOY.

THEY CALL IT A STALEMATE, GIRL.

WHY HIM?

BECAUSE HE'S THE PRESIDENT'S LITTLE BUDDY.

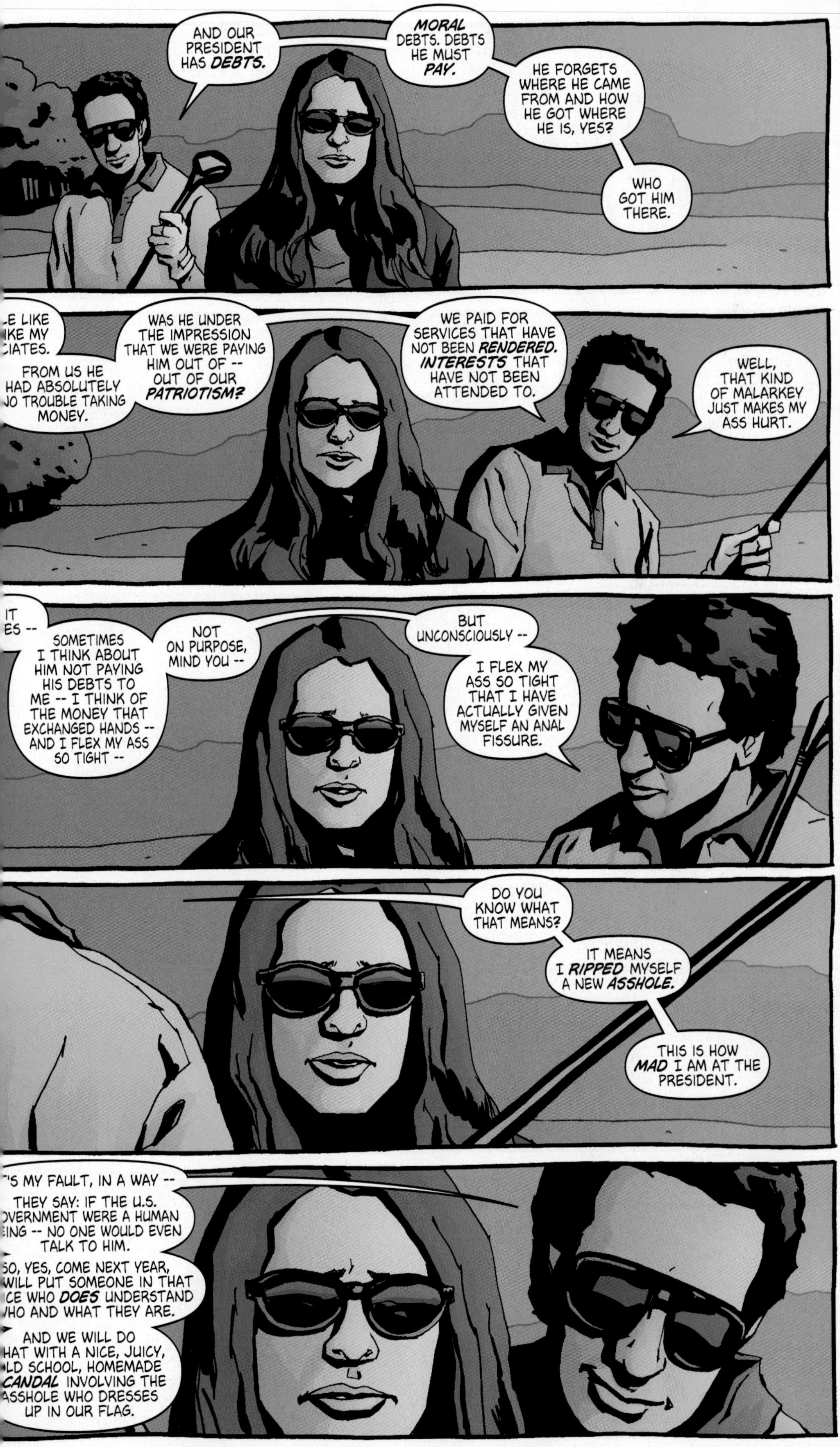

AND OUR PRESIDENT HAS DEBTS.
MORAL DEBTS. DEBTS HE MUST PAY.
HE FORGETS WHERE HE CAME FROM AND HOW HE GOT WHERE HE IS, YES?
WHO GOT HIM THERE.
E LIKE IKE MY CIATES.
FROM US HE HAD ABSOLUTELY JO TROUBLE TAKING MONEY.
WAS HE UNDER THE IMPRESSION THAT WE WERE PAYING HIM OUT OF -- OUT OF OUR PATRIOTISM?
WE PAID FOR SERVICES THAT HAVE NOT BEEN RENDERED. INTERESTS THAT HAVE NOT BEEN ATTENDED TO.
WELL, THAT KIND OF MALARKEY JUST MAKES MY ASS HURT.
IT ES --
SOMETIMES I THINK ABOUT HIM NOT PAYING HIS DEBTS TO ME -- I THINK OF THE MONEY THAT EXCHANGED HANDS -- AND I FLEX MY ASS SO TIGHT --
NOT ON PURPOSE, MIND YOU --
BUT UNCONSCIOUSLY --
I FLEX MY ASS SO TIGHT THAT I HAVE ACTUALLY GIVEN MYSELF AN ANAL FISSURE.
DO YOU KNOW WHAT THAT MEANS?
IT MEANS I RIPPED MYSELF A NEW ASSHOLE.
THIS IS HOW MAD I AM AT THE PRESIDENT.
'S MY FAULT, IN A WAY --
THEY SAY: IF THE U.S. OVERNMENT WERE A HUMAN EING -- NO ONE WOULD EVEN TALK TO HIM.
SO, YES, COME NEXT YEAR, WILL PUT SOMEONE IN THAT CE WHO DOES UNDERSTAND WHO AND WHAT THEY ARE.
AND WE WILL DO HAT WITH A NICE, JUICY, LD SCHOOL, HOMEMADE CANDAL INVOLVING THE ASSHOLE WHO DRESSES UP IN OUR FLAG.

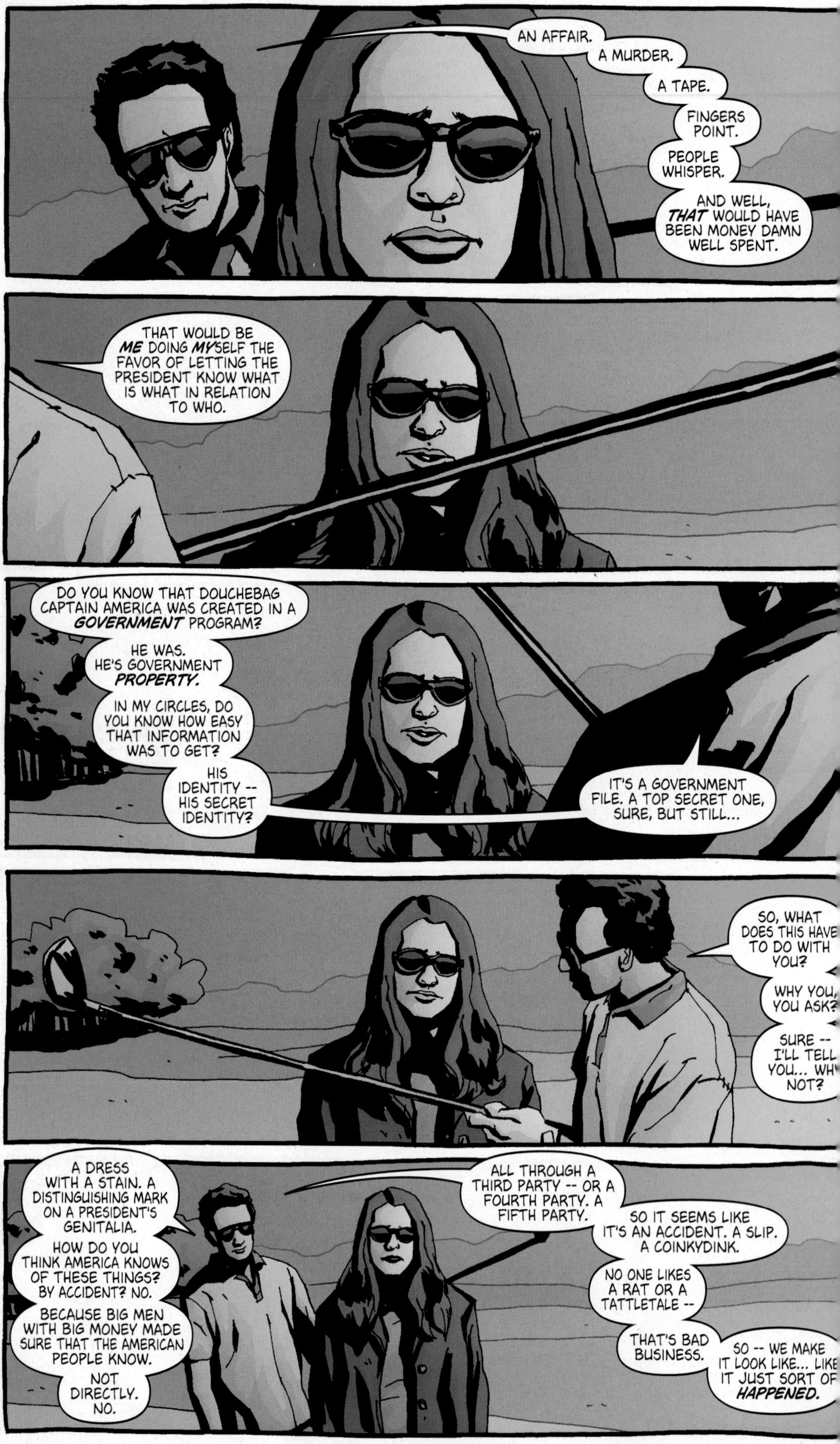

AN AFFAIR.
A MURDER.
A TAPE.
FINGERS POINT.
PEOPLE WHISPER.
AND WELL, *THAT* WOULD HAVE BEEN MONEY DAMN WELL SPENT.
THAT WOULD BE *ME* DOING *MY*SELF THE FAVOR OF LETTING THE PRESIDENT KNOW WHAT IS WHAT IN RELATION TO WHO.
DO YOU KNOW THAT DOUCHEBAG CAPTAIN AMERICA WAS CREATED IN A *GOVERNMENT* PROGRAM?
HE WAS. HE'S GOVERNMENT *PROPERTY.*
IN MY CIRCLES, DO YOU KNOW HOW EASY THAT INFORMATION WAS TO GET?
HIS IDENTITY -- HIS SECRET IDENTITY?
IT'S A GOVERNMENT FILE. A TOP SECRET ONE, SURE, BUT STILL...
SO, WHAT DOES THIS HAVE TO DO WITH YOU?
WHY YOU, YOU ASK?
SURE -- I'LL TELL YOU... WH NOT?
A DRESS WITH A STAIN. A DISTINGUISHING MARK ON A PRESIDENT'S GENITALIA.
HOW DO YOU THINK AMERICA KNOWS OF THESE THINGS? BY ACCIDENT? NO.
BECAUSE BIG MEN WITH BIG MONEY MADE SURE THAT THE AMERICAN PEOPLE KNOW.
NOT DIRECTLY. NO.
ALL THROUGH A THIRD PARTY -- OR A FOURTH PARTY. A FIFTH PARTY.
SO IT SEEMS LIKE IT'S AN ACCIDENT. A SLIP. A COINKYDINK.
NO ONE LIKES A RAT OR A TATTLETALE --
THAT'S BAD BUSINESS.
SO -- WE MAKE IT LOOK LIKE... LIKE IT JUST SORT OF *HAPPENED.*

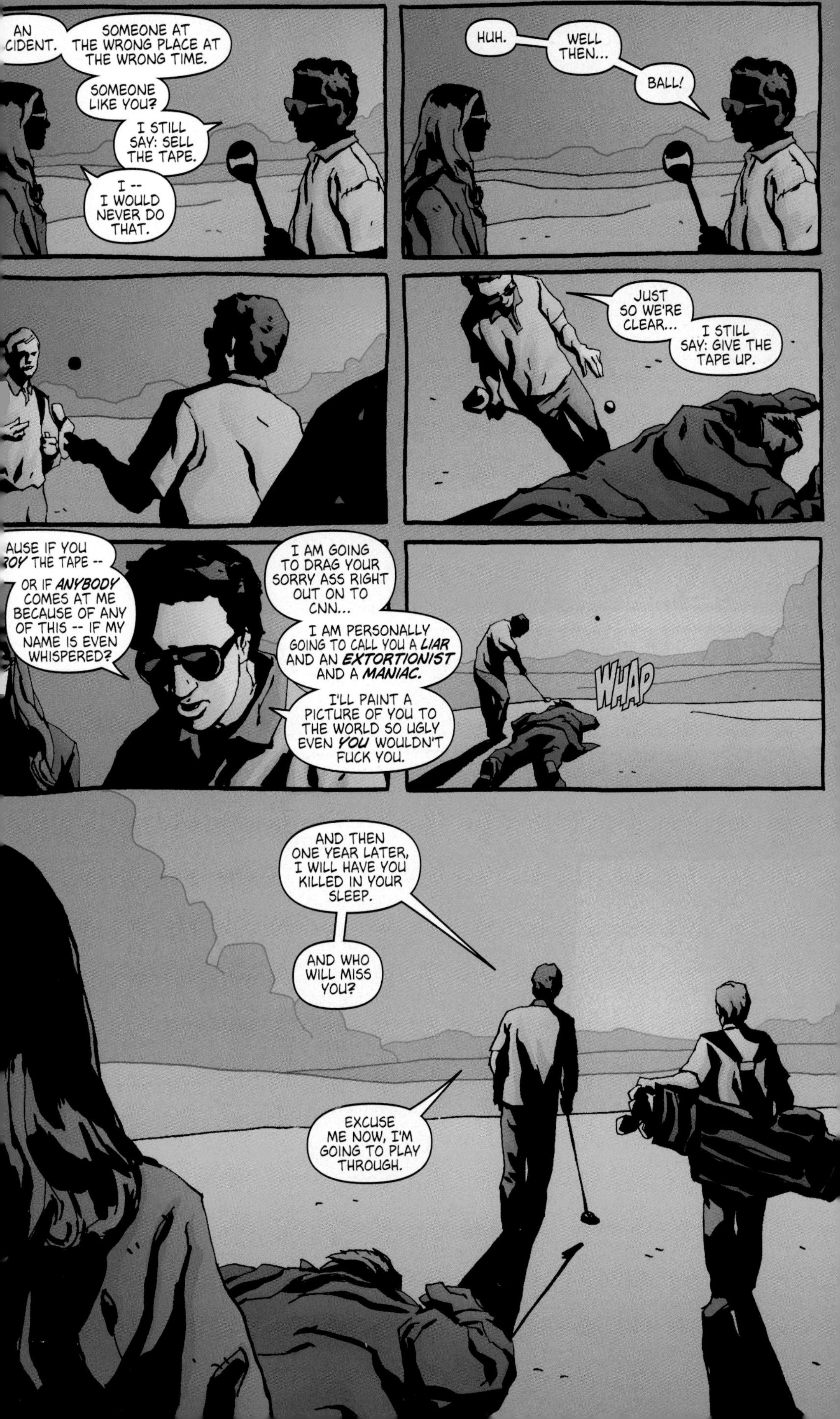

AN
CIDENT.
SOMEONE AT THE WRONG PLACE AT THE WRONG TIME.
SOMEONE LIKE YOU?
I STILL SAY: SELL THE TAPE.
I -- I WOULD NEVER DO THAT.
HUH.
WELL THEN...
BALL!
JUST SO WE'RE CLEAR...
I STILL SAY: GIVE THE TAPE UP.
AUSE IF YOU
ROY THE TAPE --
OR IF ANYBODY COMES AT ME BECAUSE OF ANY OF THIS -- IF MY NAME IS EVEN WHISPERED?
I AM GOING TO DRAG YOUR SORRY ASS RIGHT OUT ON TO CNN...
I AM PERSONALLY GOING TO CALL YOU A LIAR AND AN EXTORTIONIST AND A MANIAC.
I'LL PAINT A PICTURE OF YOU TO THE WORLD SO UGLY EVEN YOU WOULDN'T FUCK YOU.
WHAP
AND THEN ONE YEAR LATER, I WILL HAVE YOU KILLED IN YOUR SLEEP.
AND WHO WILL MISS YOU?
EXCUSE ME NOW, I'M GOING TO PLAY THROUGH.

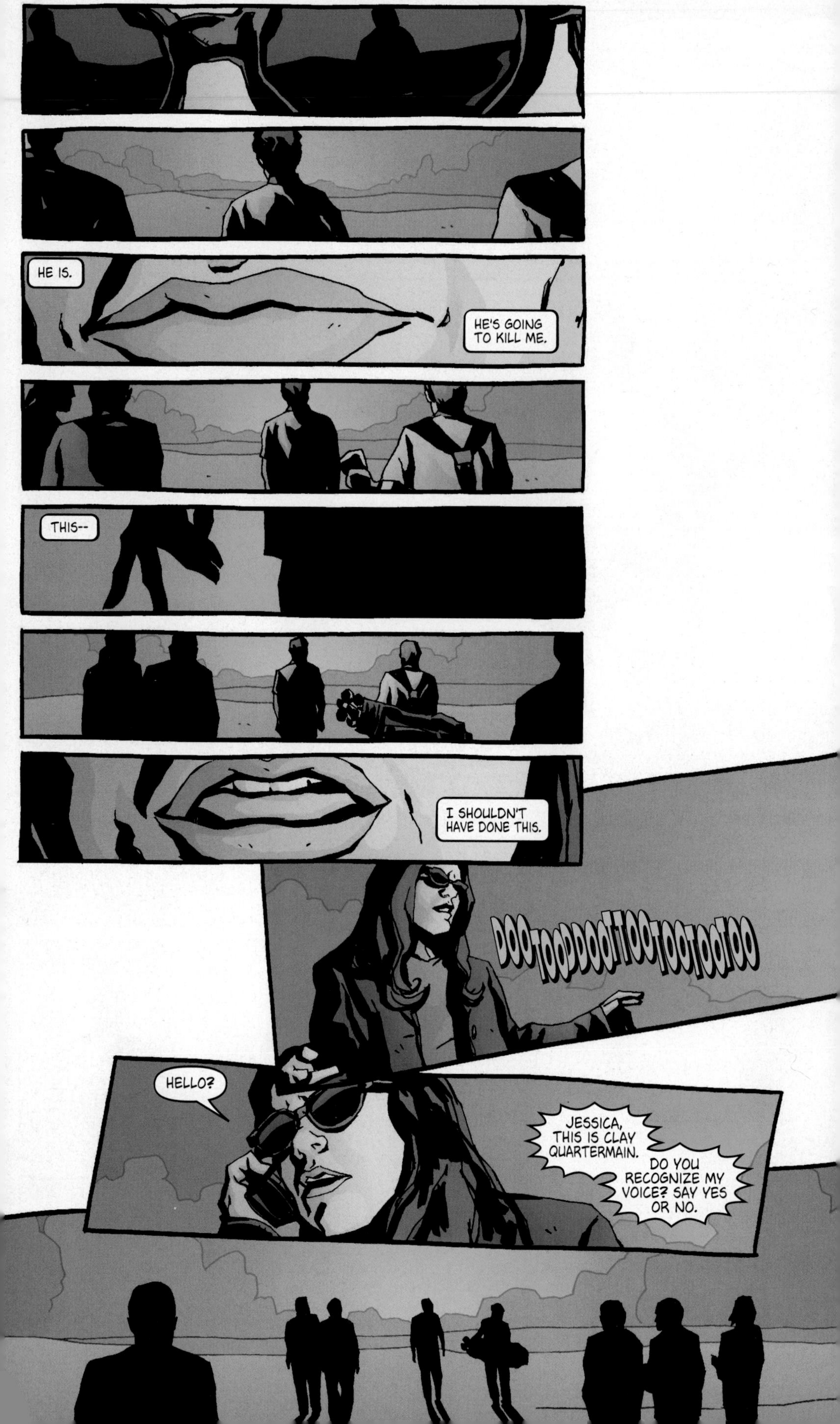
HE IS.
HE'S GOING TO KILL ME.
THIS--
I SHOULDN'T HAVE DONE THIS.
DOOTOODDOOTTOOTOOTOOTOO
HELLO?
JESSICA, THIS IS CLAY QUARTERMAIN.
DO YOU RECOGNIZE MY VOICE? SAY YES OR NO.

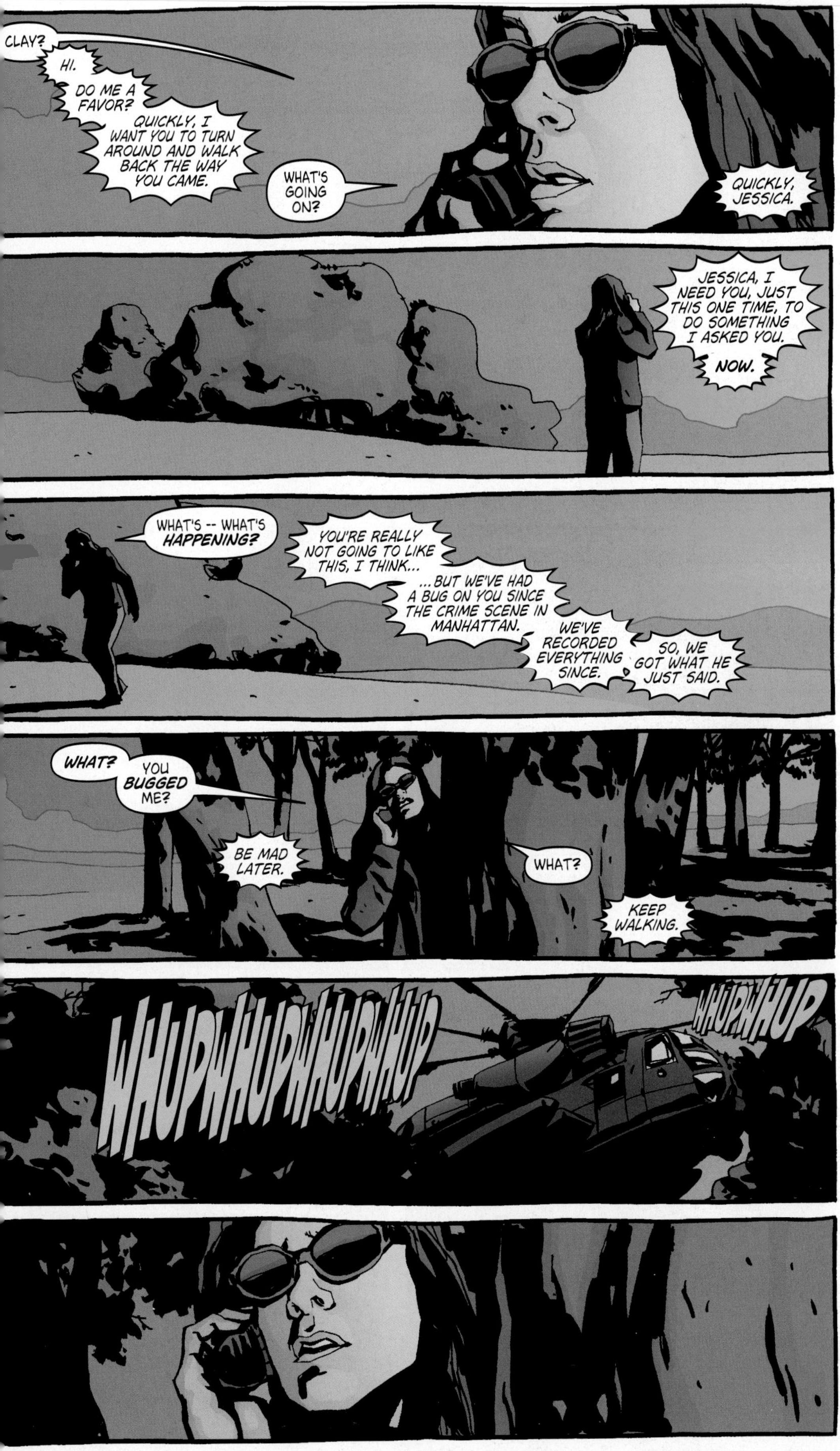

CLAY?
HI.
DO ME A FAVOR?
QUICKLY, I WANT YOU TO TURN AROUND AND WALK BACK THE WAY YOU CAME.
WHAT'S GOING ON?
QUICKLY, JESSICA.
JESSICA, I NEED YOU, JUST THIS ONE TIME, TO DO SOMETHING I ASKED YOU.
NOW.
WHAT'S -- WHAT'S HAPPENING?
YOU'RE REALLY NOT GOING TO LIKE THIS, I THINK...
...BUT WE'VE HAD A BUG ON YOU SINCE THE CRIME SCENE IN MANHATTAN.
WE'VE RECORDED EVERYTHING SINCE.
SO, WE GOT WHAT HE JUST SAID.
WHAT?
YOU BUGGED ME?
BE MAD LATER.
WHAT?
KEEP WALKING.
WHUPWHUPWHUPWHUPWHUP
WHUPWHUP

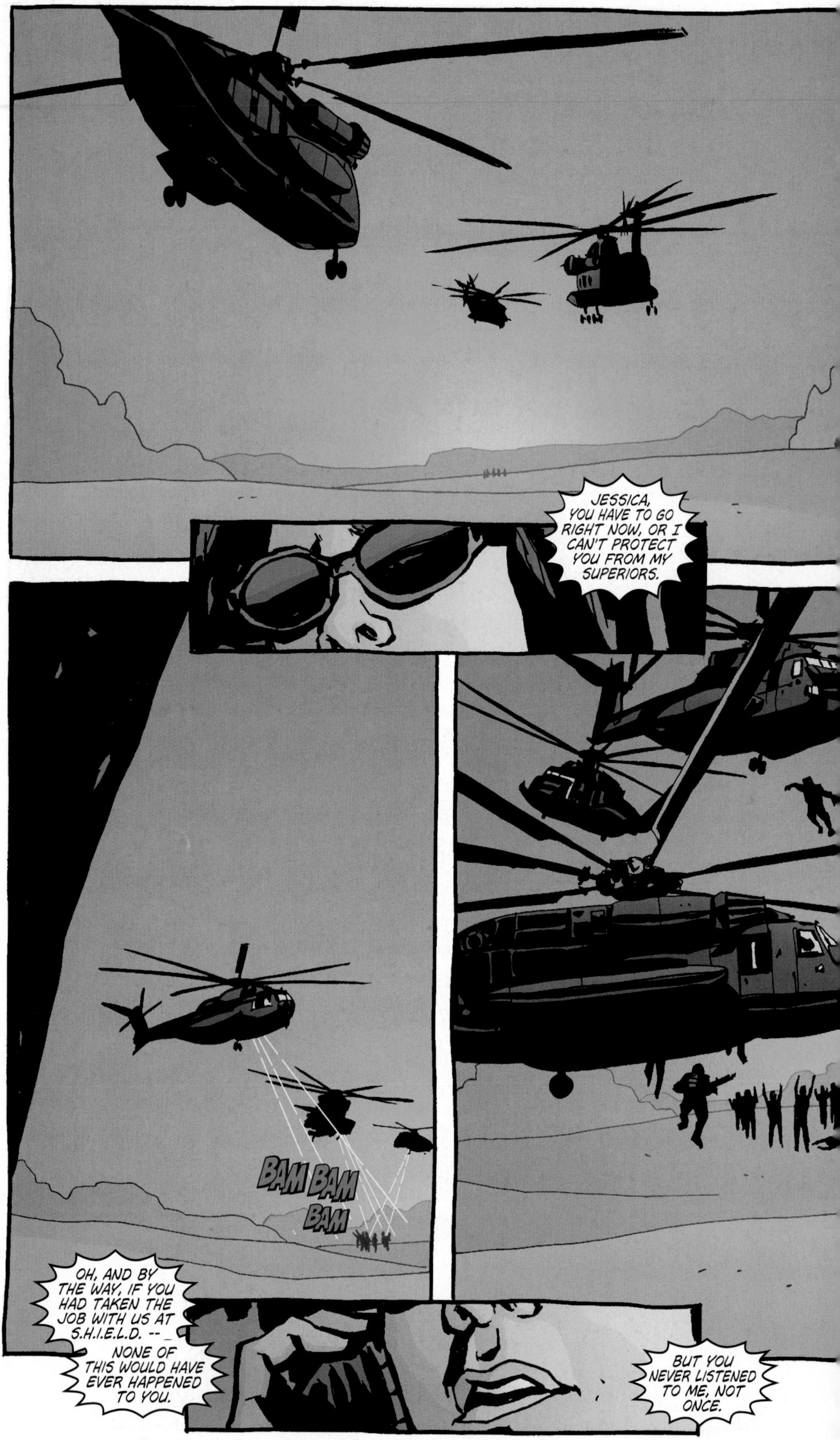
JESSICA, YOU HAVE TO GO RIGHT NOW, OR I CAN'T PROTECT YOU FROM MY SUPERIORS.
BAM BAM BAM
OH, AND BY THE WAY, IF YOU HAD TAKEN THE JOB WITH US AT S.H.I.E.L.D. --
NONE OF THIS WOULD HAVE EVER HAPPENED TO YOU.
BUT YOU NEVER LISTENED TO ME, NOT ONCE.

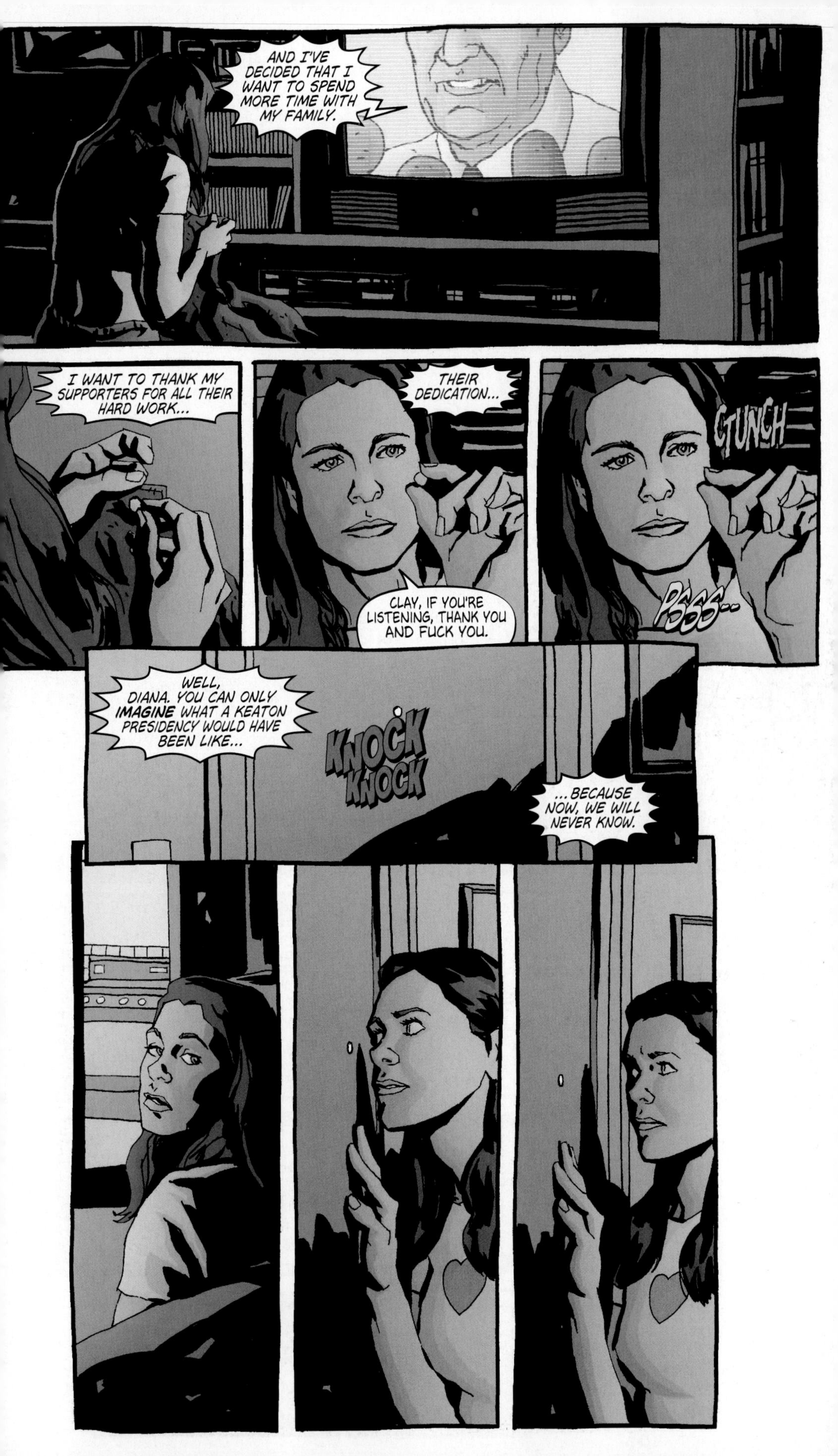

AND I'VE DECIDED THAT I WANT TO SPEND MORE TIME WITH MY FAMILY.
I WANT TO THANK MY SUPPORTERS FOR ALL THEIR HARD WORK...
THEIR DEDICATION...
CLAY, IF YOU'RE LISTENING, THANK YOU AND FUCK YOU.
CTUNCH
PSSS..
WELL, DIANA. YOU CAN ONLY IMAGINE WHAT A KEATON PRESIDENCY WOULD HAVE BEEN LIKE...
KNOCK KNOCK
...BECAUSE NOW, WE WILL NEVER KNOW.

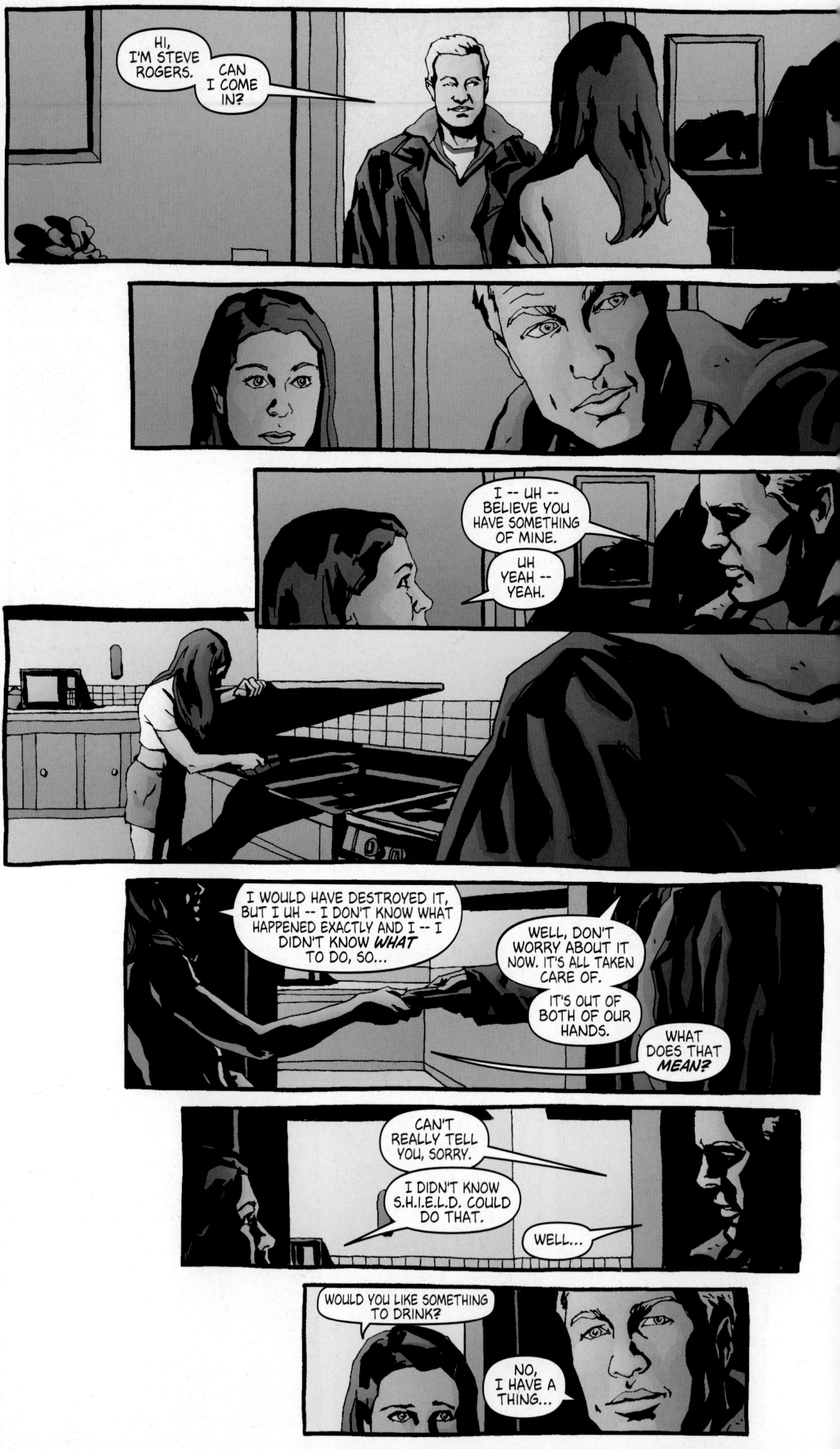
HI, I'M STEVE ROGERS.
CAN I COME IN?
I -- UH -- BELIEVE YOU HAVE SOMETHING OF MINE.
UH YEAH -- YEAH.
I WOULD HAVE DESTROYED IT, BUT I UH -- I DON'T KNOW WHAT HAPPENED EXACTLY AND I -- I DIDN'T KNOW *WHAT* TO DO, SO...
WELL, DON'T WORRY ABOUT IT NOW. IT'S ALL TAKEN CARE OF.
IT'S OUT OF BOTH OF OUR HANDS.
WHAT DOES THAT *MEAN?*
CAN'T REALLY TELL YOU, SORRY.
I DIDN'T KNOW S.H.I.E.L.D. COULD DO THAT.
WELL...
WOULD YOU LIKE SOMETHING TO DRINK?
NO, I HAVE A THING...

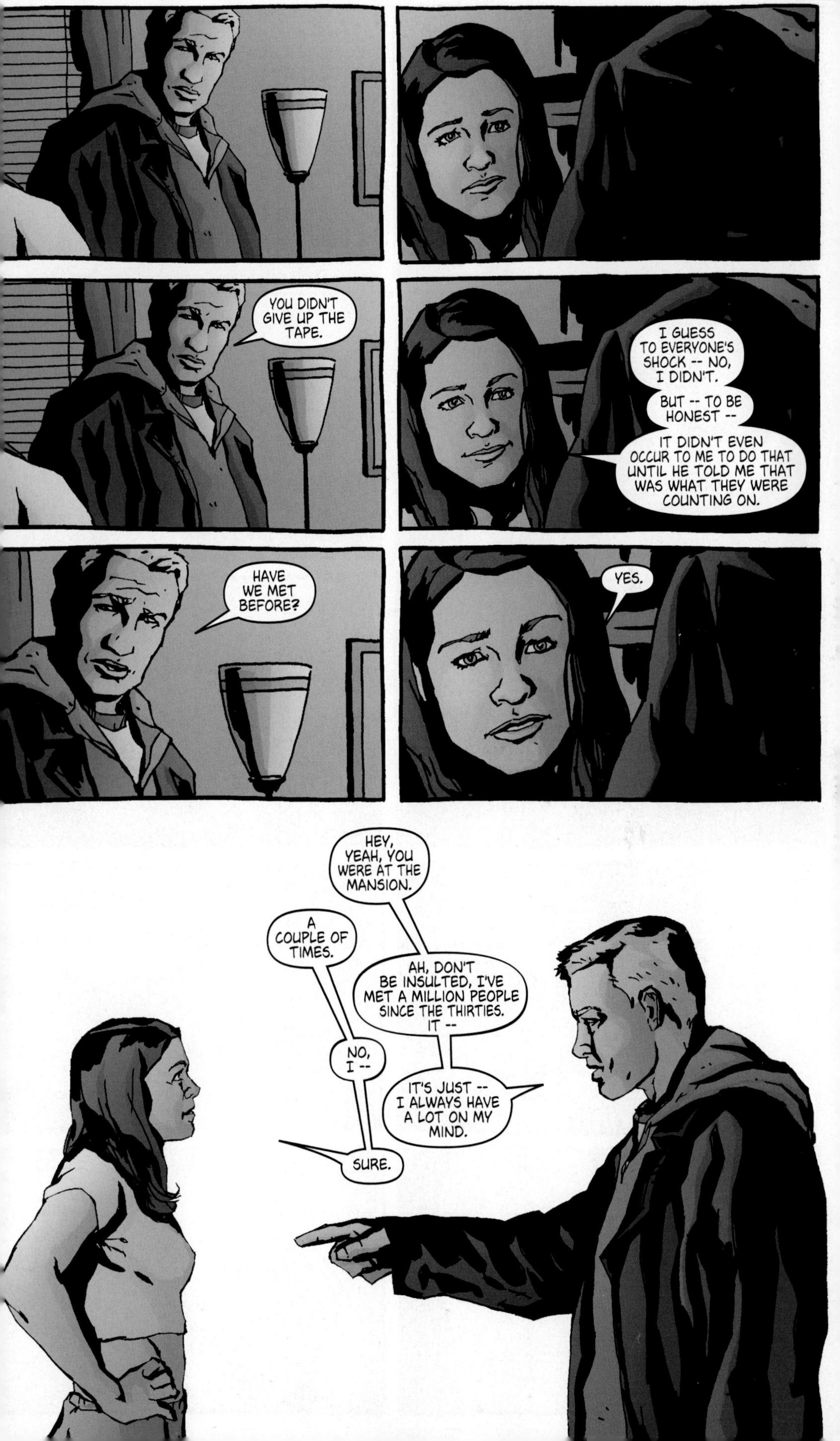
YOU DIDN'T GIVE UP THE TAPE.
I GUESS TO EVERYONE'S SHOCK -- NO, I DIDN'T.
BUT -- TO BE HONEST --
IT DIDN'T EVEN OCCUR TO ME TO DO THAT UNTIL HE TOLD ME THAT WAS WHAT THEY WERE COUNTING ON.
HAVE WE MET BEFORE?
YES.
HEY, YEAH, YOU WERE AT THE MANSION.
A COUPLE OF TIMES.
AH, DON'T BE INSULTED, I'VE MET A MILLION PEOPLE SINCE THE THIRTIES. IT --
NO, I --
IT'S JUST -- I ALWAYS HAVE A LOT ON MY MIND.
SURE.

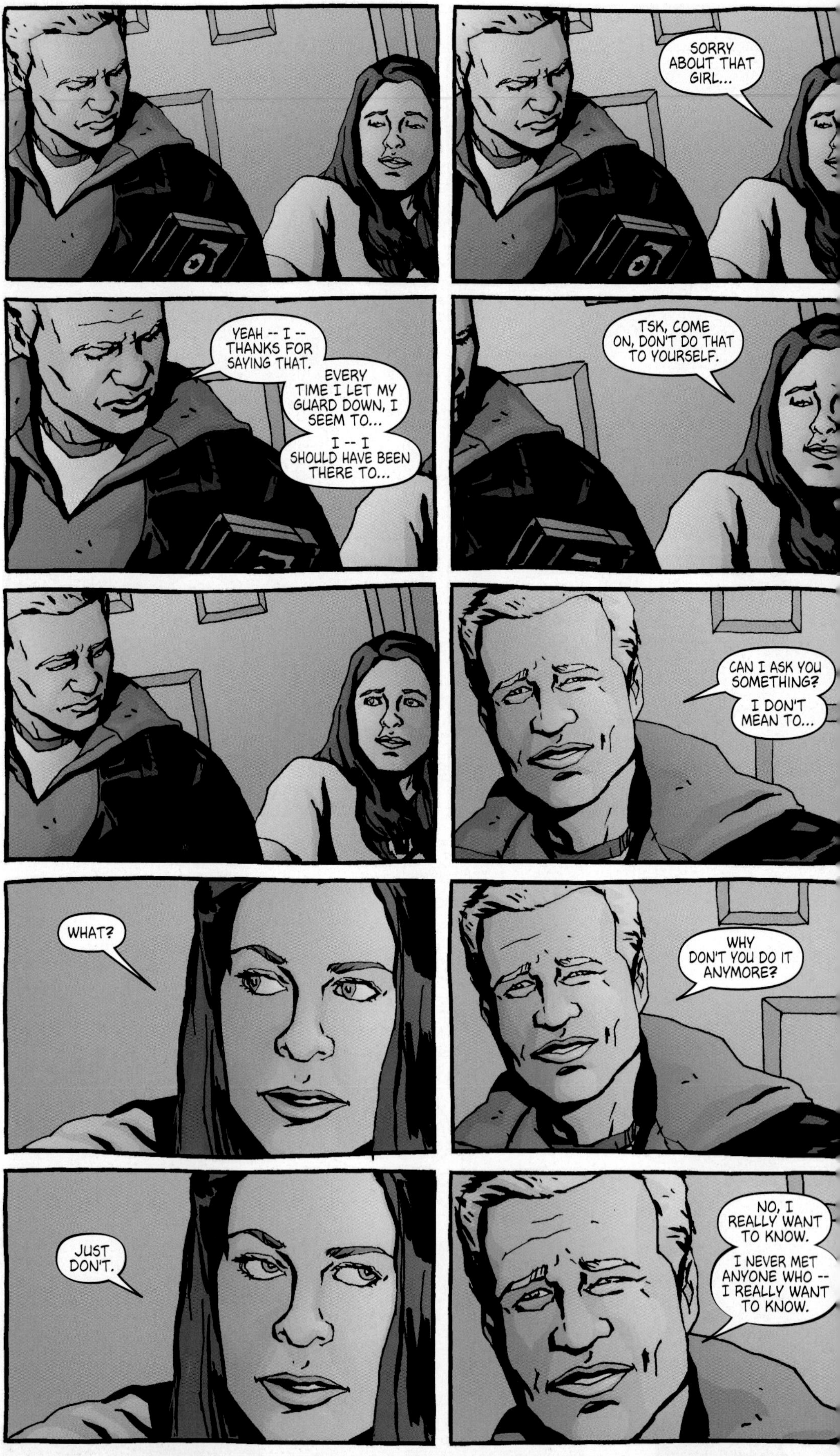
SORRY ABOUT THAT GIRL...
YEAH -- I -- THANKS FOR SAYING THAT.
EVERY TIME I LET MY GUARD DOWN, I SEEM TO...
I -- I SHOULD HAVE BEEN THERE TO...
TSK, COME ON, DON'T DO THAT TO YOURSELF.
CAN I ASK YOU SOMETHING?
I DON'T MEAN TO...
WHAT?
WHY DON'T YOU DO IT ANYMORE?
JUST DON'T.
NO, I REALLY WANT TO KNOW.
I NEVER MET ANYONE WHO -- I REALLY WANT TO KNOW.

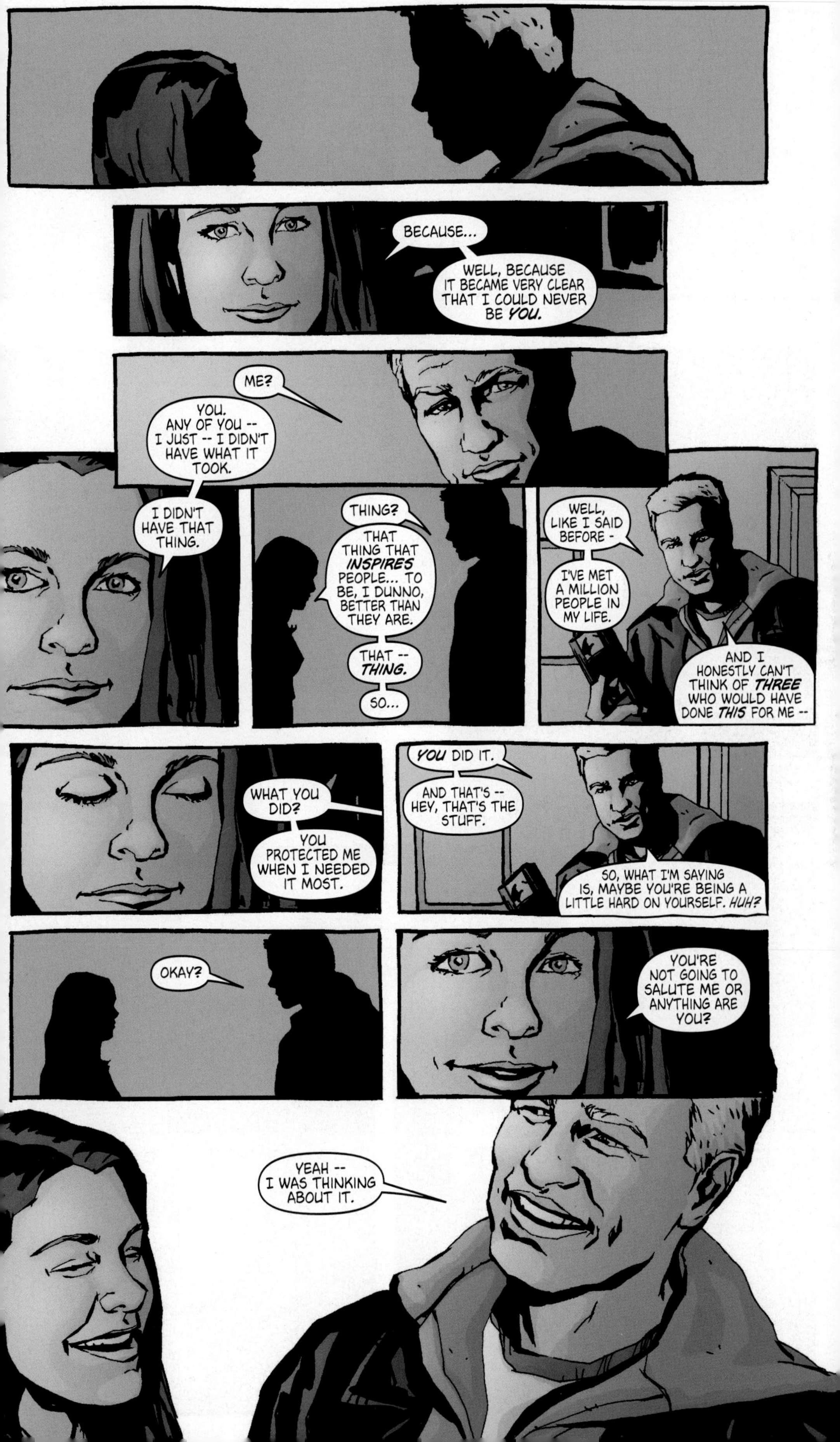
BECAUSE...
WELL, BECAUSE IT BECAME VERY CLEAR THAT I COULD NEVER BE *YOU.*
ME?
YOU. ANY OF YOU -- I JUST -- I DIDN'T HAVE WHAT IT TOOK.
I DIDN'T HAVE THAT THING.
THING?
THAT THING THAT *INSPIRES* PEOPLE... TO BE, I DUNNO, BETTER THAN THEY ARE.
THAT -- *THING.*
SO...
WELL, LIKE I SAID BEFORE -
I'VE MET A MILLION PEOPLE IN MY LIFE.
AND I HONESTLY CAN'T THINK OF *THREE* WHO WOULD HAVE DONE *THIS* FOR ME --
WHAT YOU DID?
YOU PROTECTED ME WHEN I NEEDED IT MOST.
YOU DID IT.
AND THAT'S -- HEY, THAT'S THE STUFF.
SO, WHAT I'M SAYING IS, MAYBE YOU'RE BEING A LITTLE HARD ON YOURSELF. *HUH?*
OKAY?
YOU'RE NOT GOING TO SALUTE ME OR ANYTHING ARE YOU?
YEAH -- I WAS THINKING ABOUT IT.

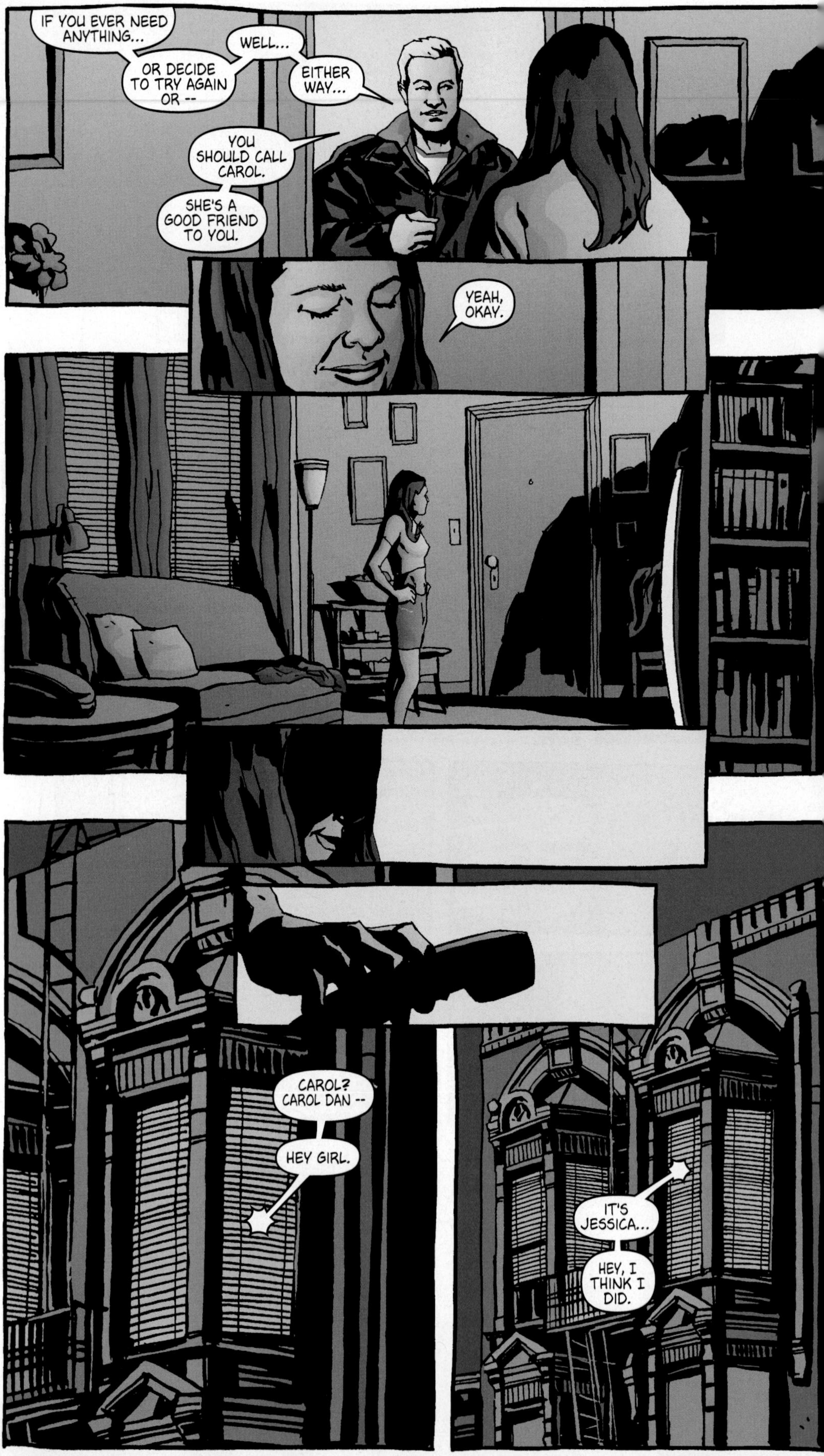
IF YOU EVER NEED ANYTHING...
OR DECIDE TO TRY AGAIN OR --
WELL...
EITHER WAY...
YOU SHOULD CALL CAROL.
SHE'S A GOOD FRIEND TO YOU.
YEAH, OKAY.
CAROL? CAROL DAN --
HEY GIRL.
IT'S JESSICA...
HEY, I THINK I DID.

[redacted]ISSUE #6 J[redacted]

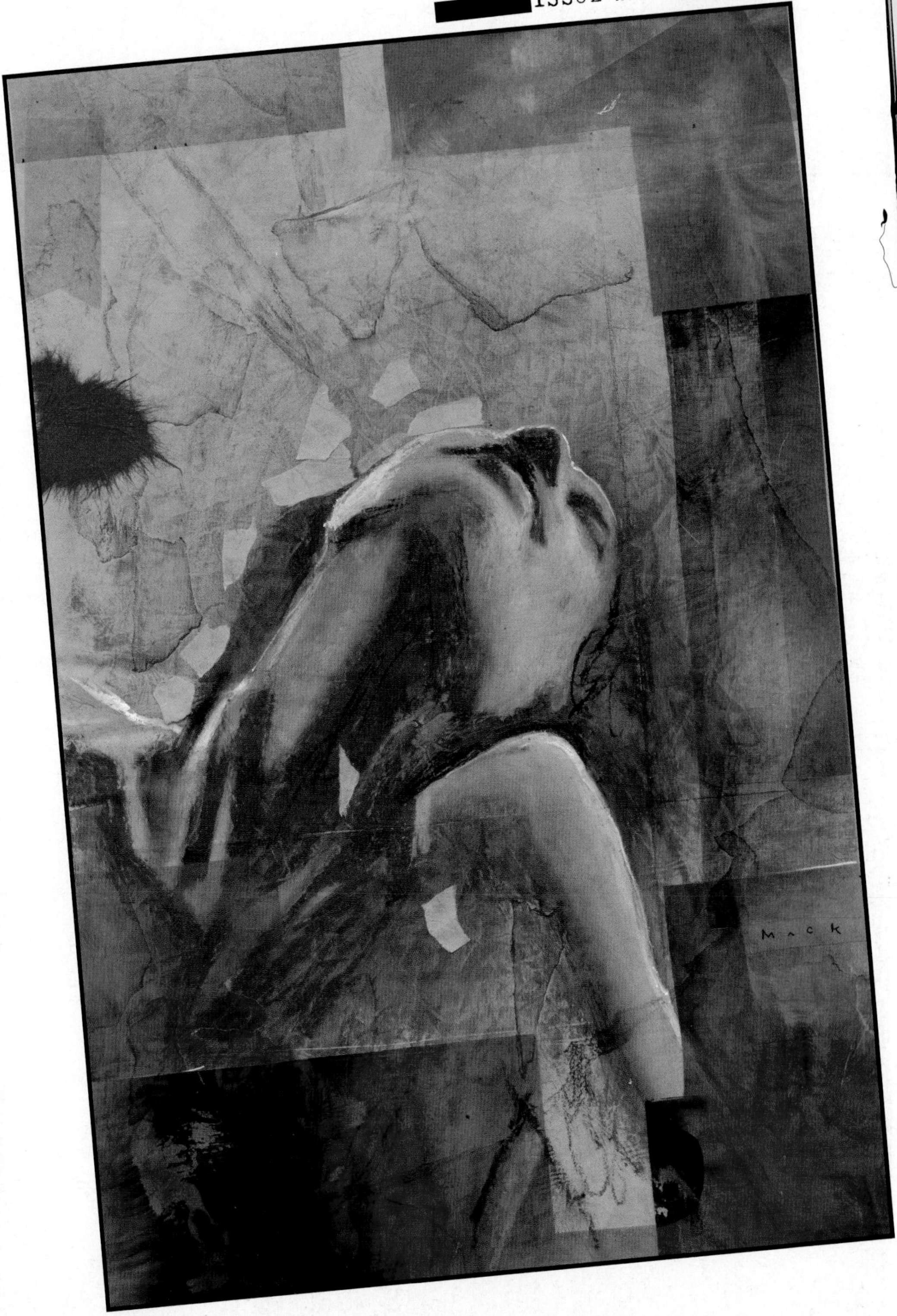
MACK

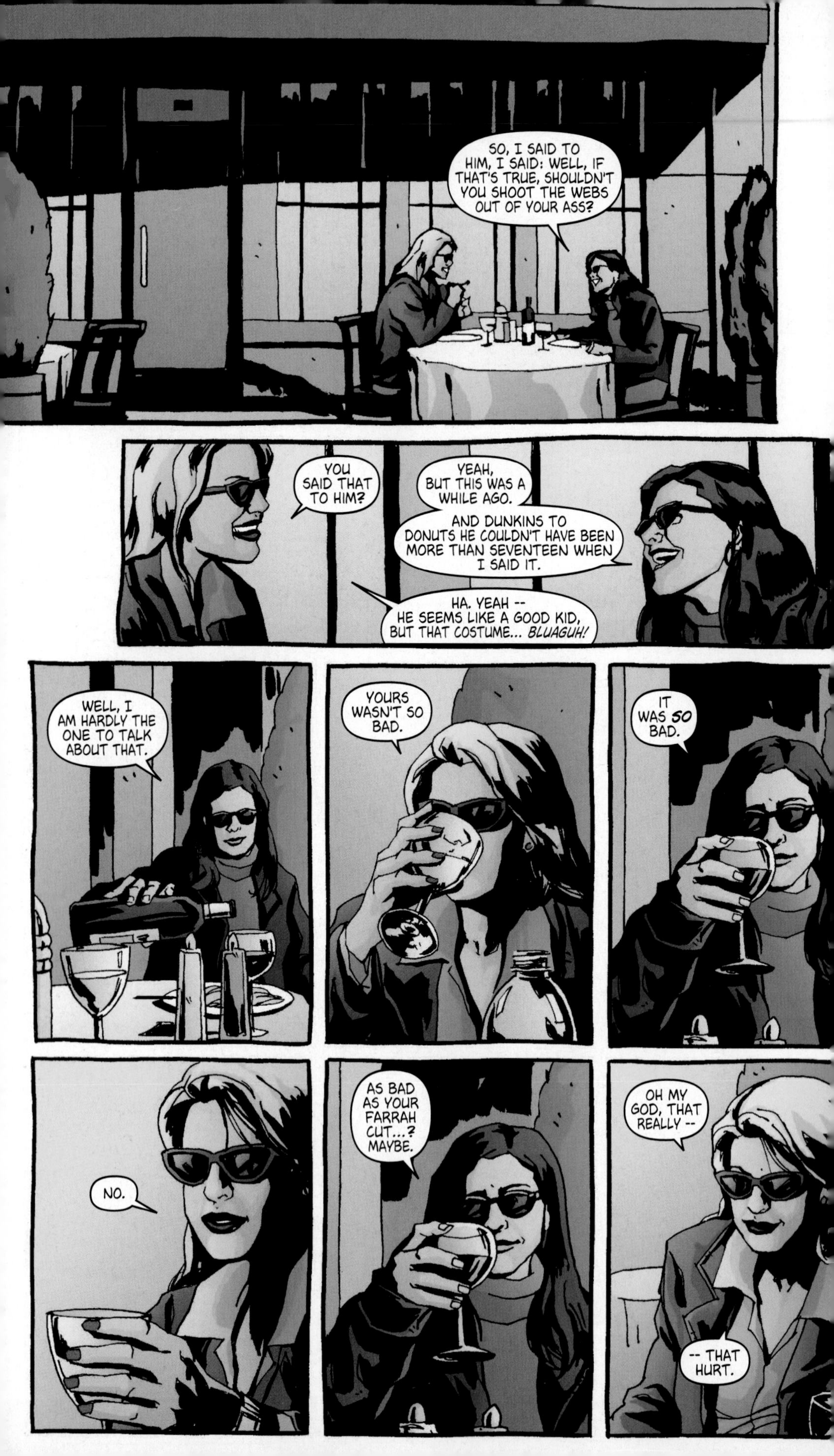
SO, I SAID TO HIM, I SAID: WELL, IF THAT'S TRUE, SHOULDN'T YOU SHOOT THE WEBS OUT OF YOUR ASS?
YOU SAID THAT TO HIM?
YEAH, BUT THIS WAS A WHILE AGO.
AND DUNKINS TO DONUTS HE COULDN'T HAVE BEEN MORE THAN SEVENTEEN WHEN I SAID IT.
HA. YEAH -- HE SEEMS LIKE A GOOD KID, BUT THAT COSTUME... *BLUAGUH!*
WELL, I AM HARDLY THE ONE TO TALK ABOUT THAT.
YOURS WASN'T SO BAD.
IT WAS *SO* BAD.
NO.
AS BAD AS YOUR FARRAH CUT...? MAYBE.
OH MY GOD, THAT REALLY --
-- THAT HURT.

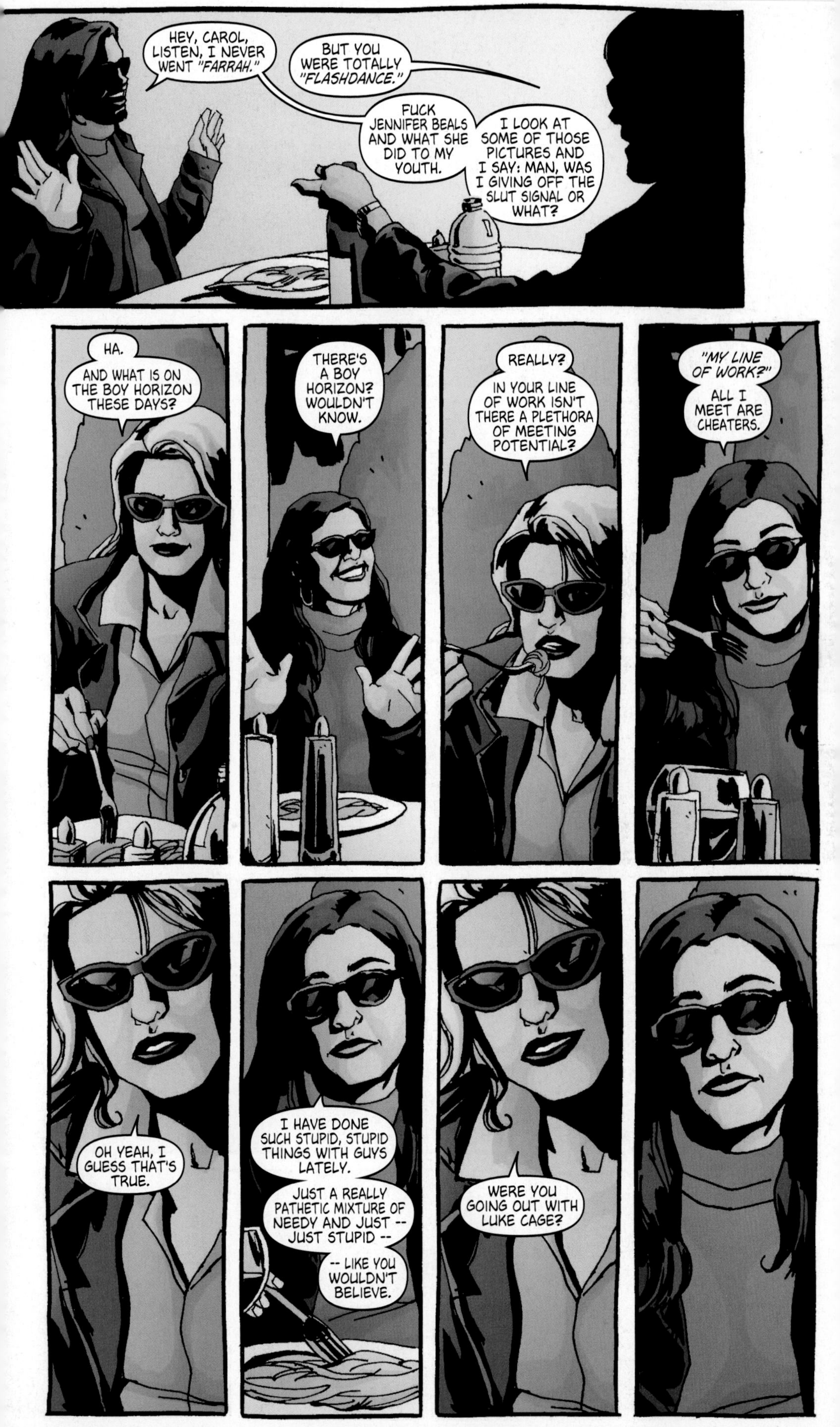
HEY, CAROL, LISTEN, I NEVER WENT "FARRAH."
BUT YOU WERE TOTALLY "FLASHDANCE."
FUCK JENNIFER BEALS AND WHAT SHE DID TO MY YOUTH.
I LOOK AT SOME OF THOSE PICTURES AND I SAY: MAN, WAS I GIVING OFF THE SLUT SIGNAL OR WHAT?
HA.
AND WHAT IS ON THE BOY HORIZON THESE DAYS?
THERE'S A BOY HORIZON? WOULDN'T KNOW.
REALLY?
IN YOUR LINE OF WORK ISN'T THERE A PLETHORA OF MEETING POTENTIAL?
"MY LINE OF WORK?"
ALL I MEET ARE CHEATERS.
OH YEAH, I GUESS THAT'S TRUE.
I HAVE DONE SUCH STUPID, STUPID THINGS WITH GUYS LATELY.
JUST A REALLY PATHETIC MIXTURE OF NEEDY AND JUST -- JUST STUPID --
-- LIKE YOU WOULDN'T BELIEVE.
WERE YOU GOING OUT WITH LUKE CAGE?

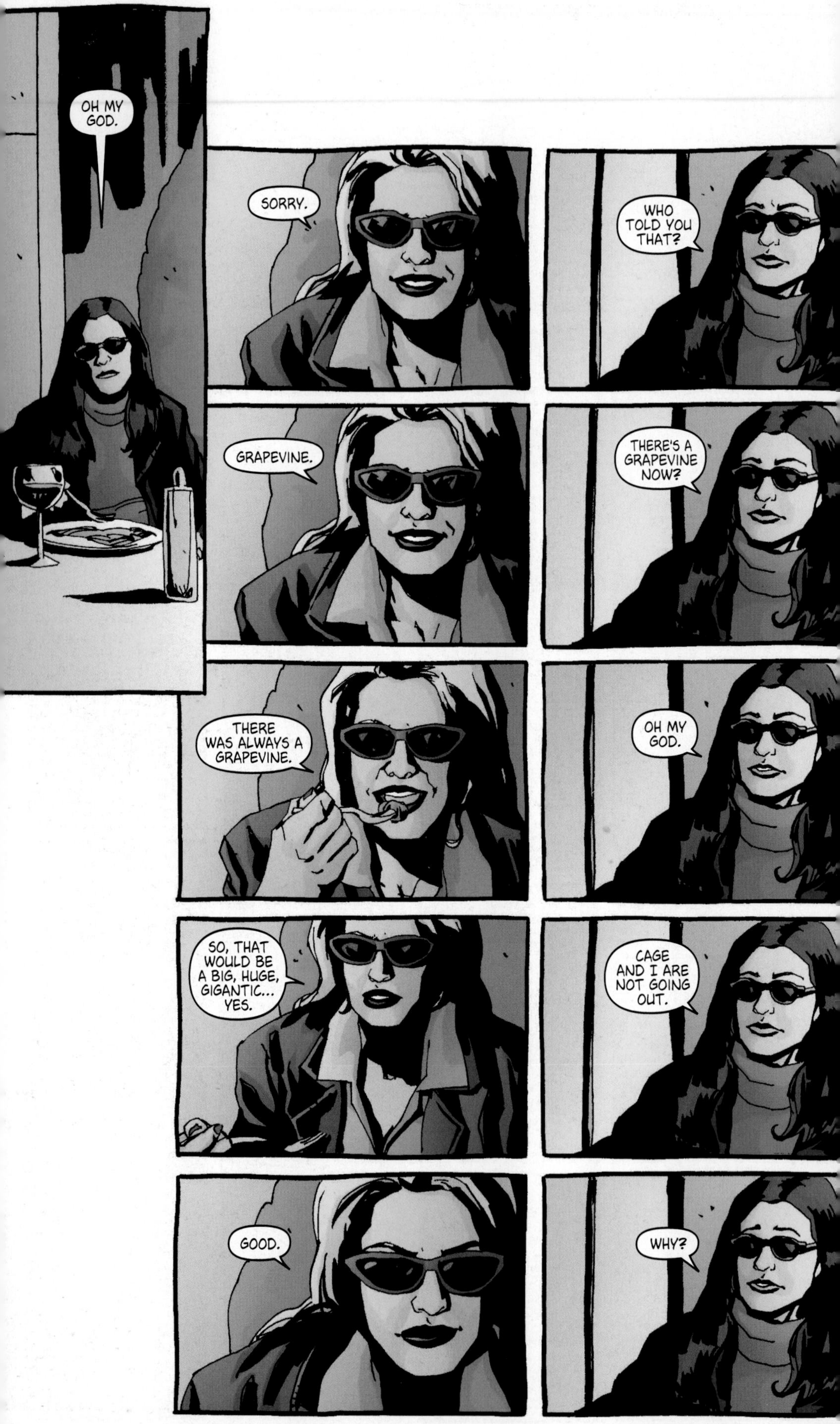
OH MY GOD.
SORRY.
WHO TOLD YOU THAT?
GRAPEVINE.
THERE'S A GRAPEVINE NOW?
THERE WAS ALWAYS A GRAPEVINE.
OH MY GOD.
SO, THAT WOULD BE A BIG, HUGE, GIGANTIC... YES.
CAGE AND I ARE NOT GOING OUT.
GOOD.
WHY?

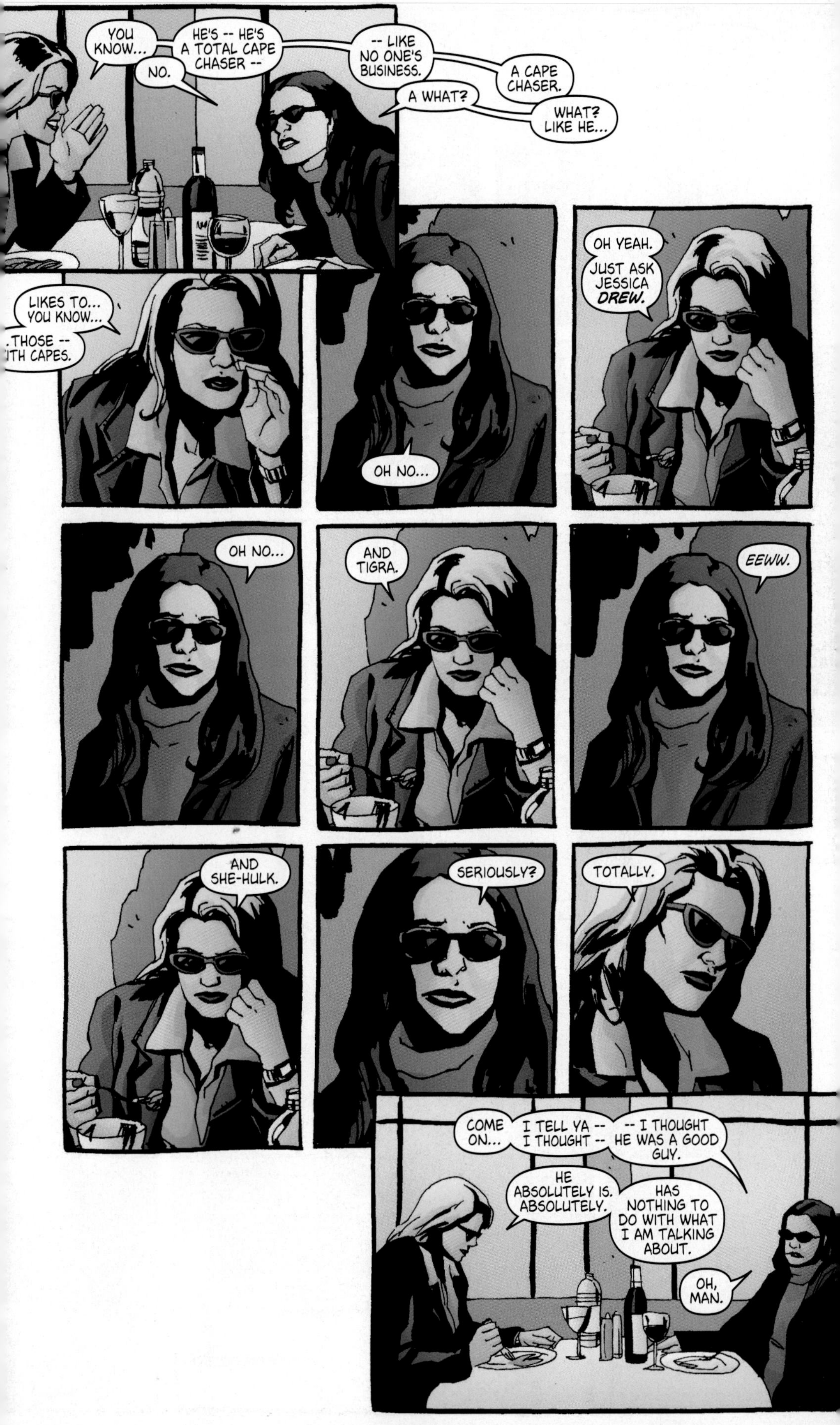
YOU KNOW...
HE'S -- HE'S A TOTAL CAPE CHASER --
NO.
-- LIKE NO ONE'S BUSINESS.
A CAPE CHASER.
A WHAT?
WHAT? LIKE HE...
LIKES TO... YOU KNOW...
.THOSE -- ITH CAPES.
OH NO...
OH YEAH.
JUST ASK JESSICA *DREW.*
OH NO...
AND TIGRA.
EEWW.
AND SHE-HULK.
SERIOUSLY?
TOTALLY.
COME ON...
I TELL YA -- I THOUGHT --
-- I THOUGHT HE WAS A GOOD GUY.
HE ABSOLUTELY IS. ABSOLUTELY.
HAS NOTHING TO DO WITH WHAT I AM TALKING ABOUT.
OH, MAN.

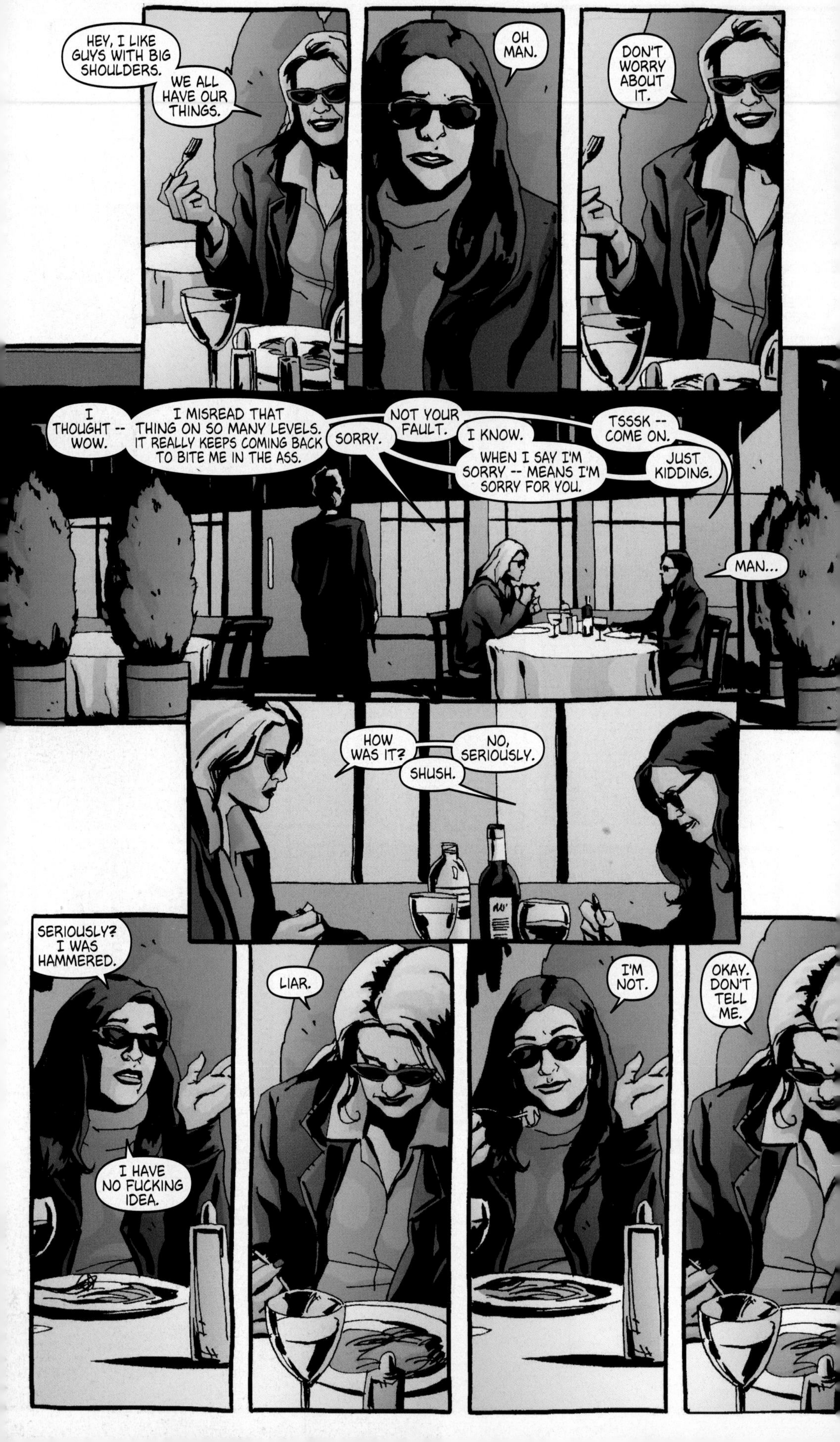
HEY, I LIKE GUYS WITH BIG SHOULDERS.
WE ALL HAVE OUR THINGS.
OH MAN.
DON'T WORRY ABOUT IT.
I THOUGHT -- WOW.
I MISREAD THAT THING ON SO MANY LEVELS. IT REALLY KEEPS COMING BACK TO BITE ME IN THE ASS.
SORRY.
NOT YOUR FAULT.
I KNOW.
WHEN I SAY I'M SORRY -- MEANS I'M SORRY FOR YOU.
TSSSK -- COME ON.
JUST KIDDING.
MAN...
HOW WAS IT?
NO, SERIOUSLY.
SHUSH.
SERIOUSLY? I WAS HAMMERED.
I HAVE NO FUCKING IDEA.
LIAR.
I'M NOT.
OKAY. DON'T TELL ME.

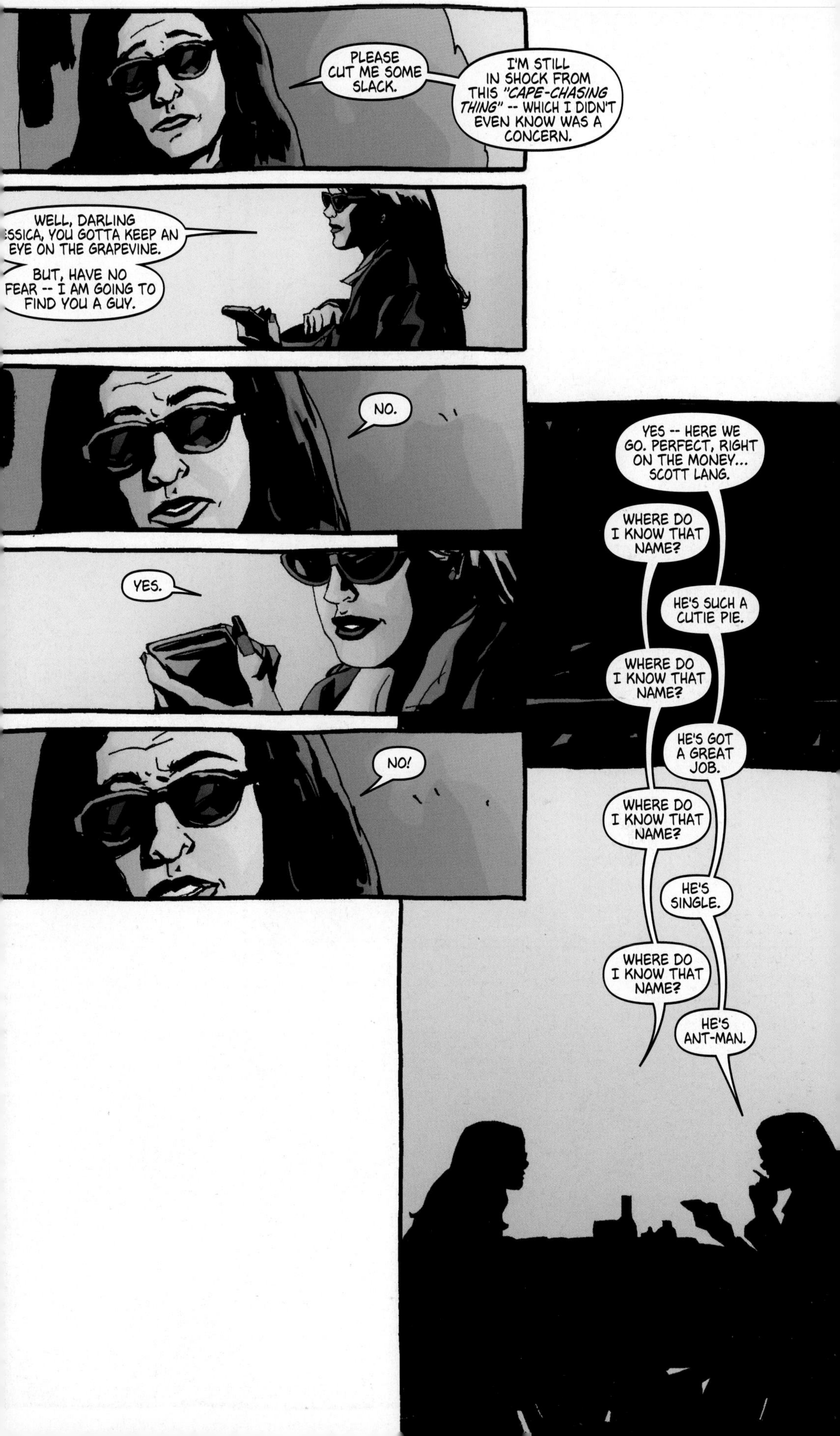
PLEASE CUT ME SOME SLACK.
I'M STILL IN SHOCK FROM THIS "CAPE-CHASING THING" -- WHICH I DIDN'T EVEN KNOW WAS A CONCERN.
WELL, DARLING ESSICA, YOU GOTTA KEEP AN EYE ON THE GRAPEVINE.
BUT, HAVE NO FEAR -- I AM GOING TO FIND YOU A GUY.
NO.
YES.
NO!
YES -- HERE WE GO. PERFECT, RIGHT ON THE MONEY... SCOTT LANG.
WHERE DO I KNOW THAT NAME?
HE'S SUCH A CUTIE PIE.
WHERE DO I KNOW THAT NAME?
HE'S GOT A GREAT JOB.
WHERE DO I KNOW THAT NAME?
HE'S SINGLE.
WHERE DO I KNOW THAT NAME?
HE'S ANT-MAN.

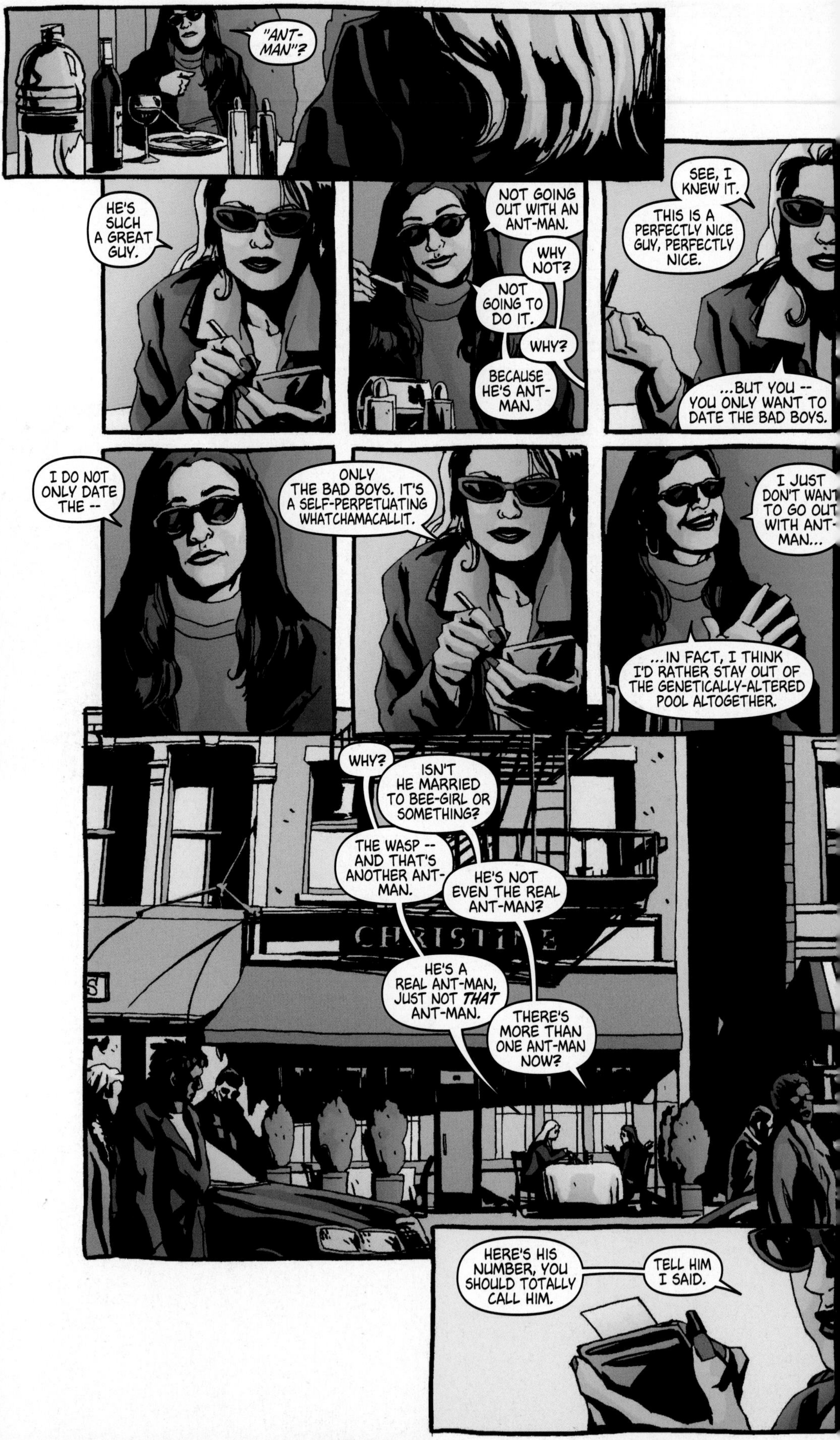
"ANT-MAN"?
HE'S SUCH A GREAT GUY.
NOT GOING OUT WITH AN ANT-MAN.
WHY NOT?
NOT GOING TO DO IT.
WHY?
BECAUSE HE'S ANT-MAN.
SEE, I KNEW IT.
THIS IS A PERFECTLY NICE GUY, PERFECTLY NICE.
...BUT YOU -- YOU ONLY WANT TO DATE THE BAD BOYS.
I DO NOT ONLY DATE THE --
ONLY THE BAD BOYS. IT'S A SELF-PERPETUATING WHATCHAMACALLIT.
I JUST DON'T WANT TO GO OUT WITH ANT-MAN...
...IN FACT, I THINK I'D RATHER STAY OUT OF THE GENETICALLY-ALTERED POOL ALTOGETHER.
WHY?
ISN'T HE MARRIED TO BEE-GIRL OR SOMETHING?
THE WASP -- AND THAT'S ANOTHER ANT-MAN.
HE'S NOT EVEN THE REAL ANT-MAN?
HE'S A REAL ANT-MAN, JUST NOT *THAT* ANT-MAN.
THERE'S MORE THAN ONE ANT-MAN NOW?
CHRISTINE
HERE'S HIS NUMBER, YOU SHOULD TOTALLY CALL HIM.
TELL HIM I SAID.

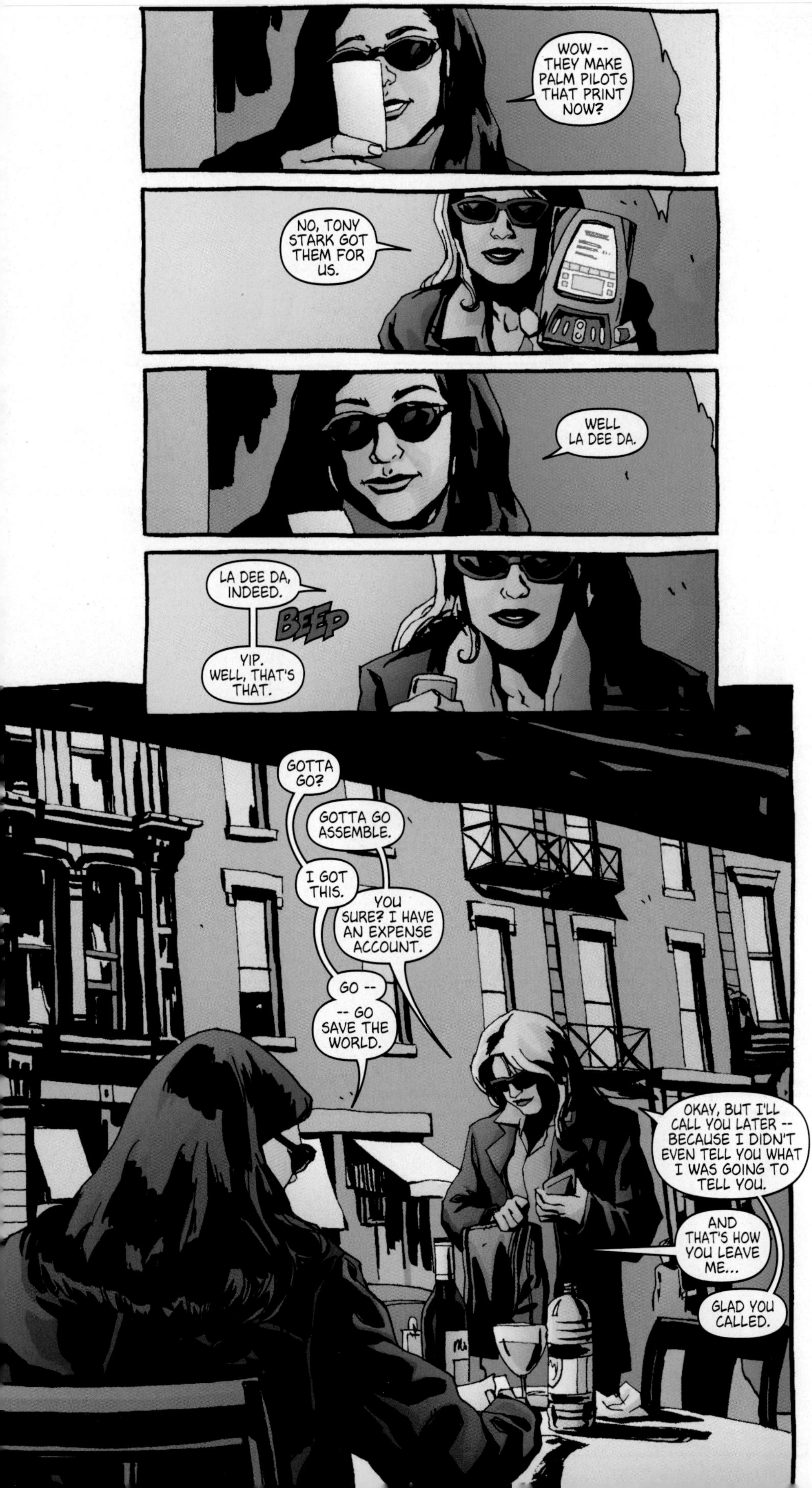
WOW -- THEY MAKE PALM PILOTS THAT PRINT NOW?
NO, TONY STARK GOT THEM FOR US.
WELL LA DEE DA.
LA DEE DA, INDEED.
BEEP
YIP. WELL, THAT'S THAT.
GOTTA GO?
GOTTA GO ASSEMBLE.
I GOT THIS.
YOU SURE? I HAVE AN EXPENSE ACCOUNT.
GO --
-- GO SAVE THE WORLD.
OKAY, BUT I'LL CALL YOU LATER -- BECAUSE I DIDN'T EVEN TELL YOU WHAT I WAS GOING TO TELL YOU.
AND THAT'S HOW YOU LEAVE ME...
GLAD YOU CALLED.

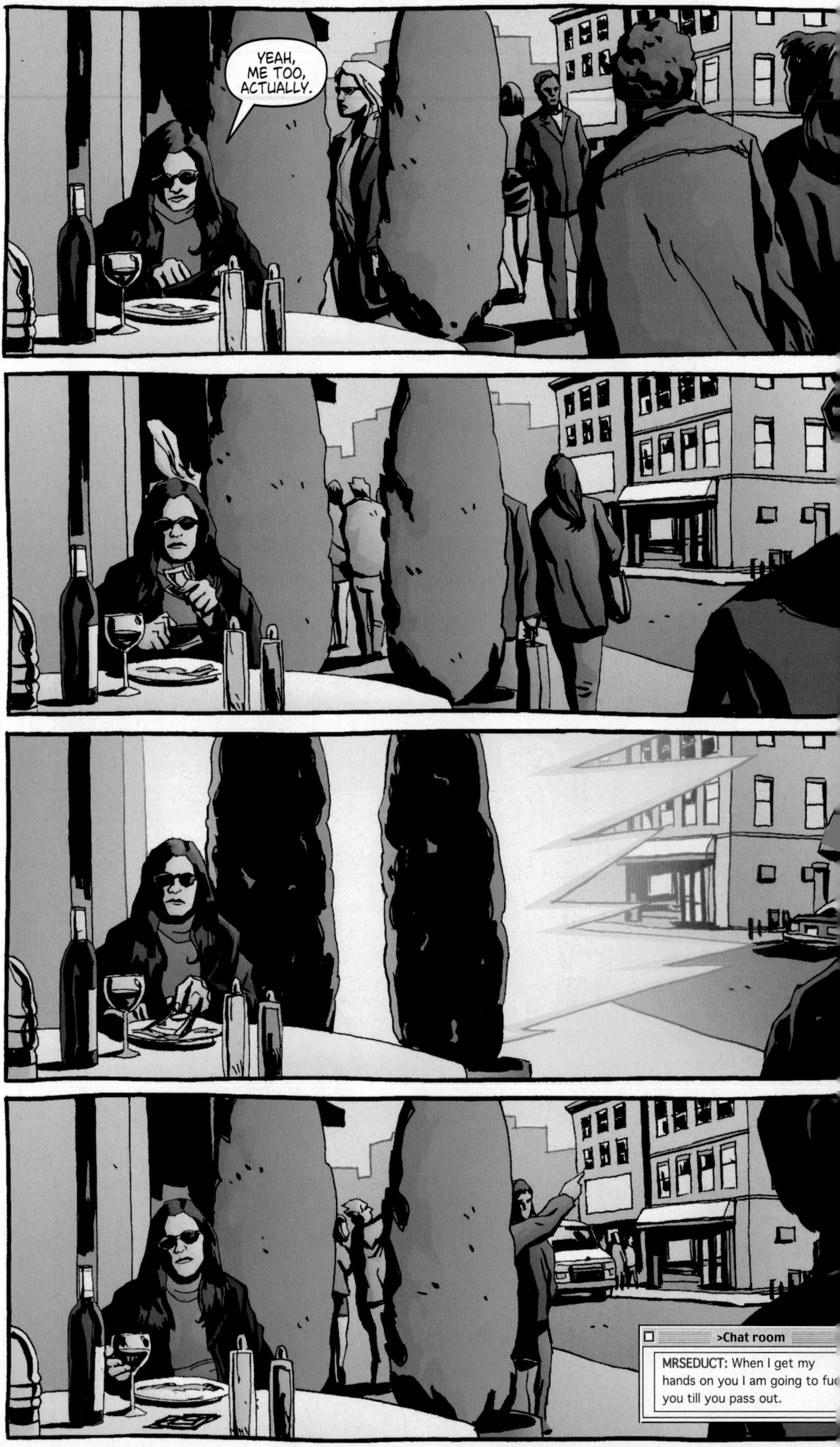
YEAH, ME TOO, ACTUALLY.
>Chat room
MRSEDUCT: When I get my hands on you I am going to fu
you till you pass out.

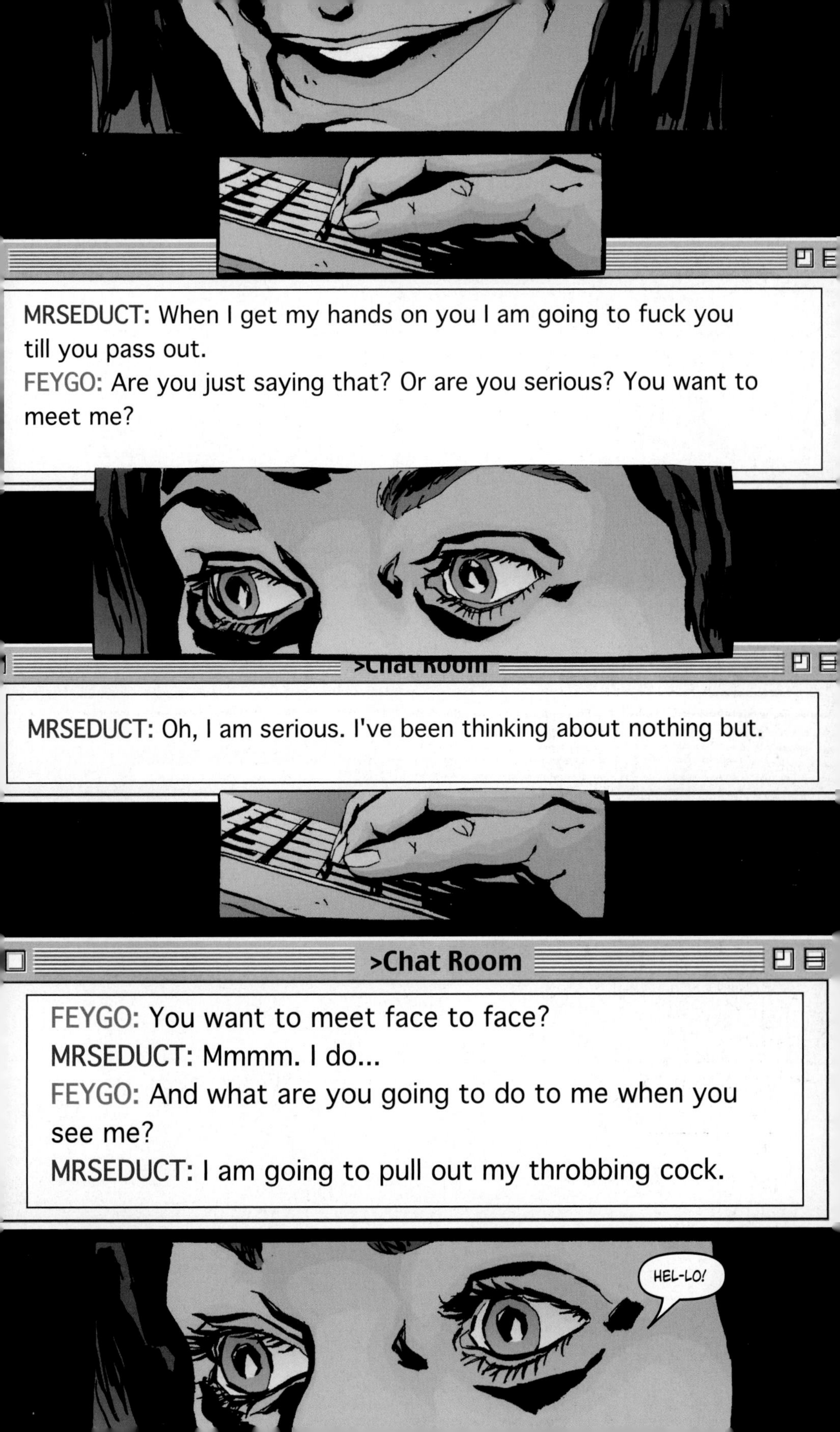
MRSEDUCT: When I get my hands on you I am going to fuck you till you pass out.
FEYGO: Are you just saying that? Or are you serious? You want to meet me?
>Chat Room
MRSEDUCT: Oh, I am serious. I've been thinking about nothing but.
>Chat Room
FEYGO: You want to meet face to face?
MRSEDUCT: Mmmm. I do...
FEYGO: And what are you going to do to me when you see me?
MRSEDUCT: I am going to pull out my throbbing cock.
HEL-LO!

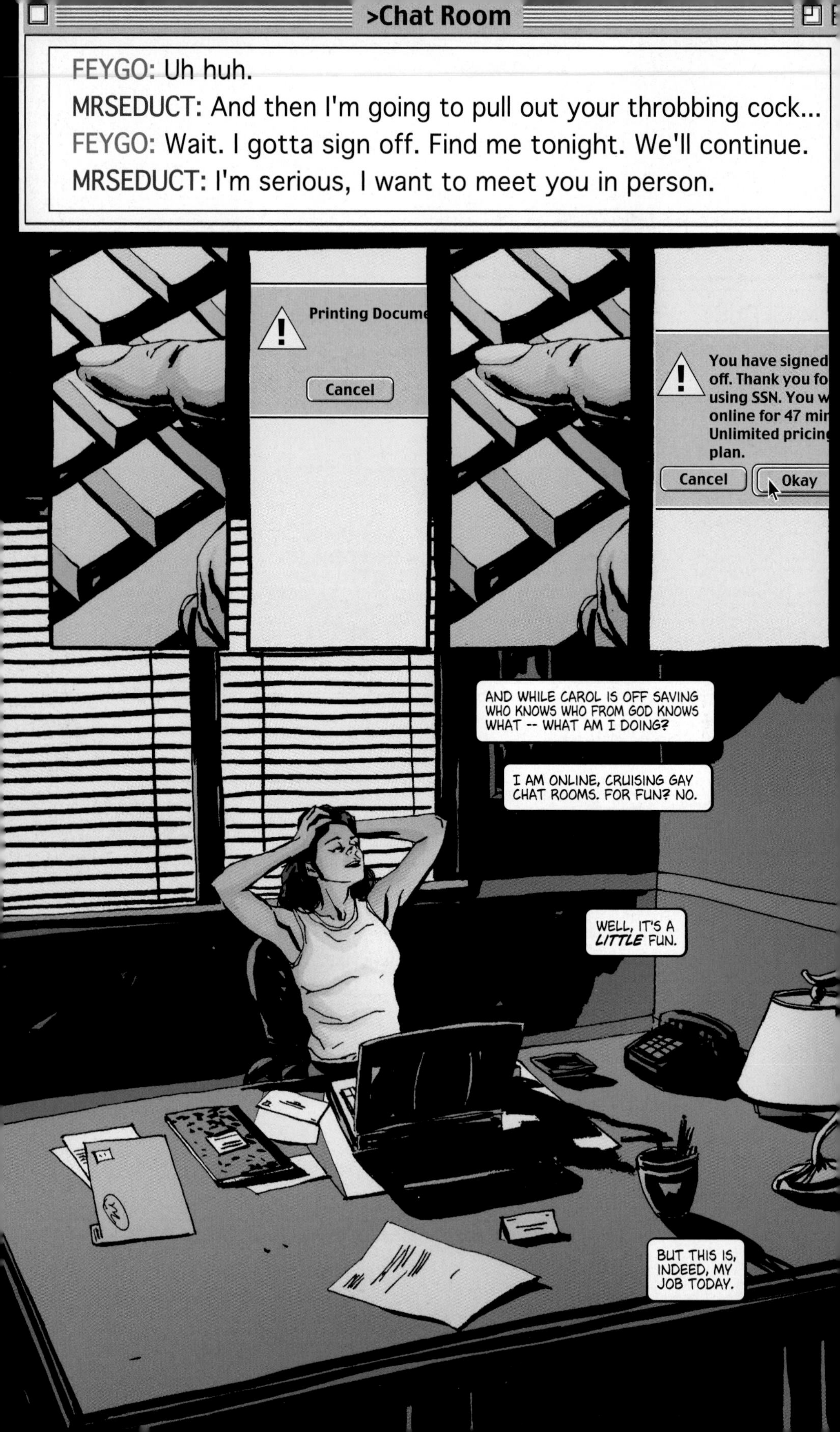
>Chat Room
FEYGO: Uh huh.
MRSEDUCT: And then I'm going to pull out your throbbing cock...
FEYGO: Wait. I gotta sign off. Find me tonight. We'll continue.
MRSEDUCT: I'm serious, I want to meet you in person.
Printing Docume
Cancel
You have signed off. Thank you fo using SSN. You w online for 47 mi Unlimited pricin plan.
Cancel
Okay
AND WHILE CAROL IS OFF SAVING WHO KNOWS WHO FROM GOD KNOWS WHAT -- WHAT AM I DOING?
I AM ONLINE, CRUISING GAY CHAT ROOMS. FOR FUN? NO.
WELL, IT'S A *LITTLE* FUN.
BUT THIS IS, INDEED, MY JOB TODAY.

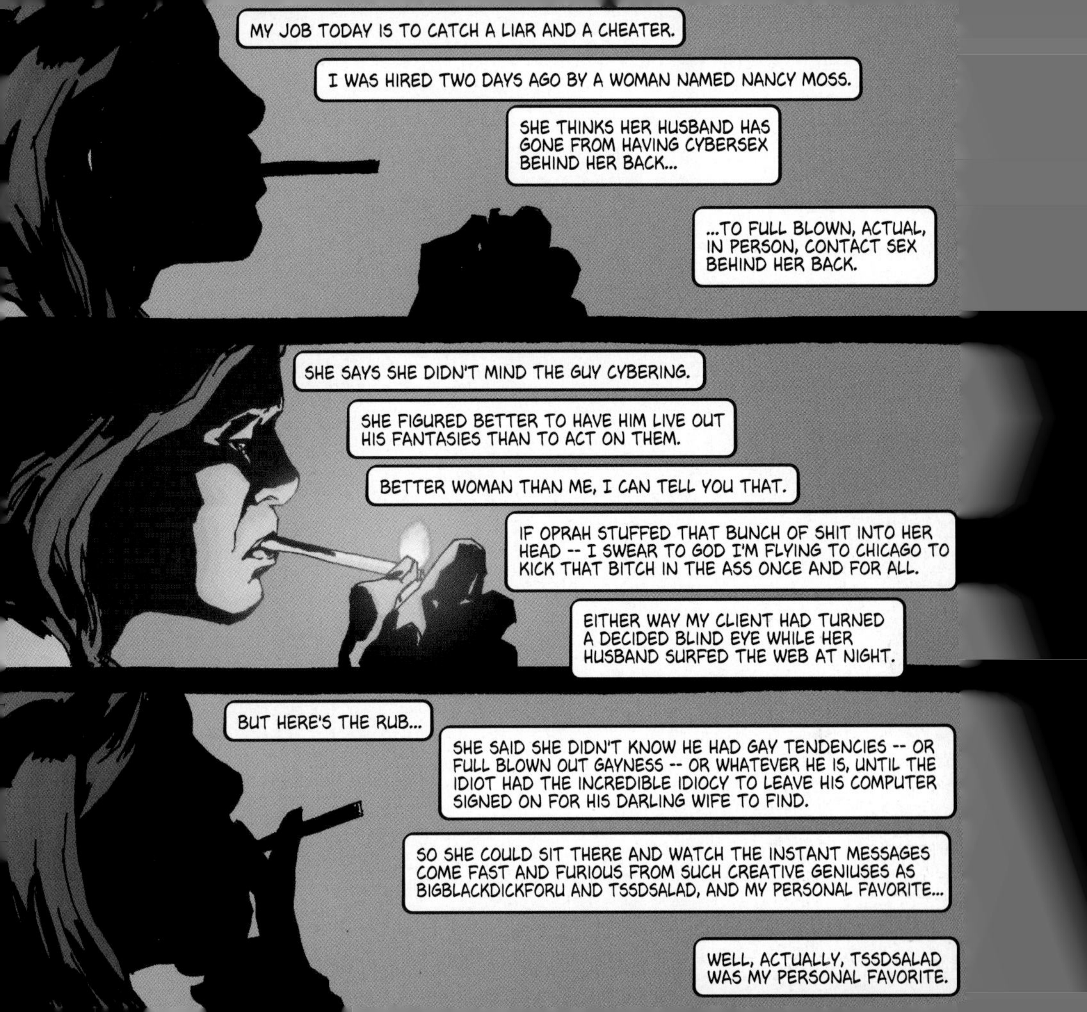
MY JOB TODAY IS TO CATCH A LIAR AND A CHEATER.
I WAS HIRED TWO DAYS AGO BY A WOMAN NAMED NANCY MOSS.
SHE THINKS HER HUSBAND HAS GONE FROM HAVING CYBERSEX BEHIND HER BACK...
...TO FULL BLOWN, ACTUAL, IN PERSON, CONTACT SEX BEHIND HER BACK.
SHE SAYS SHE DIDN'T MIND THE GUY CYBERING.
SHE FIGURED BETTER TO HAVE HIM LIVE OUT HIS FANTASIES THAN TO ACT ON THEM.
BETTER WOMAN THAN ME, I CAN TELL YOU THAT.
IF OPRAH STUFFED THAT BUNCH OF SHIT INTO HER HEAD -- I SWEAR TO GOD I'M FLYING TO CHICAGO TO KICK THAT BITCH IN THE ASS ONCE AND FOR ALL.
EITHER WAY MY CLIENT HAD TURNED A DECIDED BLIND EYE WHILE HER HUSBAND SURFED THE WEB AT NIGHT.
BUT HERE'S THE RUB...
SHE SAID SHE DIDN'T KNOW HE HAD GAY TENDENCIES -- OR FULL BLOWN OUT GAYNESS -- OR WHATEVER HE IS, UNTIL THE IDIOT HAD THE INCREDIBLE IDIOCY TO LEAVE HIS COMPUTER SIGNED ON FOR HIS DARLING WIFE TO FIND.
SO SHE COULD SIT THERE AND WATCH THE INSTANT MESSAGES COME FAST AND FURIOUS FROM SUCH CREATIVE GENIUSES AS BIGBLACKDICKFORU AND TSSDSALAD, AND MY PERSONAL FAVORITE...
WELL, ACTUALLY, TSSDSALAD WAS MY PERSONAL FAVORITE.

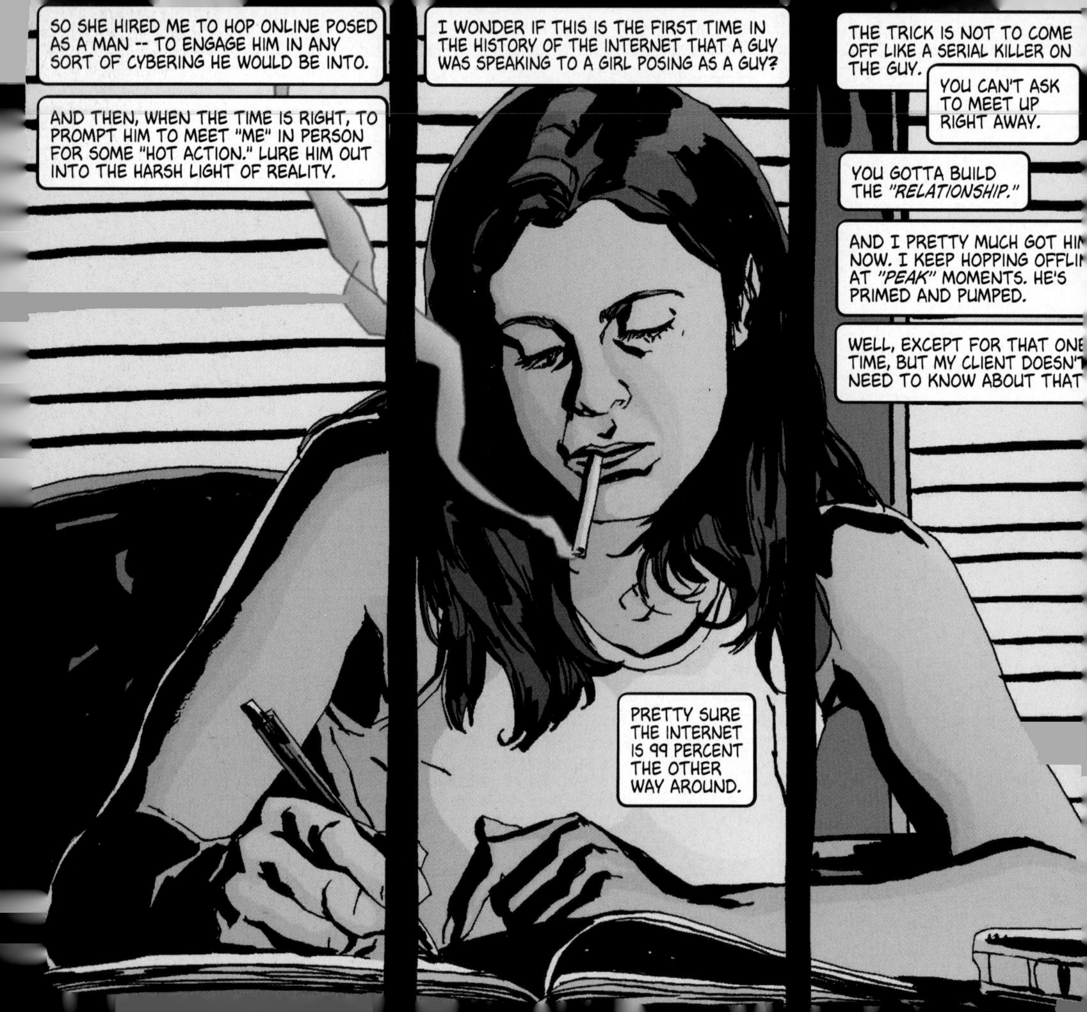
SO SHE HIRED ME TO HOP ONLINE POSED AS A MAN -- TO ENGAGE HIM IN ANY SORT OF CYBERING HE WOULD BE INTO.
AND THEN, WHEN THE TIME IS RIGHT, TO PROMPT HIM TO MEET "ME" IN PERSON FOR SOME "HOT ACTION." LURE HIM OUT INTO THE HARSH LIGHT OF REALITY.
I WONDER IF THIS IS THE FIRST TIME IN THE HISTORY OF THE INTERNET THAT A GUY WAS SPEAKING TO A GIRL POSING AS A GUY?
PRETTY SURE THE INTERNET IS 99 PERCENT THE OTHER WAY AROUND.
THE TRICK IS NOT TO COME OFF LIKE A SERIAL KILLER ON THE GUY.
YOU CAN'T ASK TO MEET UP RIGHT AWAY.
YOU GOTTA BUILD THE *"RELATIONSHIP."*
AND I PRETTY MUCH GOT HI NOW. I KEEP HOPPING OFFLI AT *"PEAK"* MOMENTS. HE'S PRIMED AND PUMPED.
WELL, EXCEPT FOR THAT ONE TIME, BUT MY CLIENT DOESN'T NEED TO KNOW ABOUT THAT

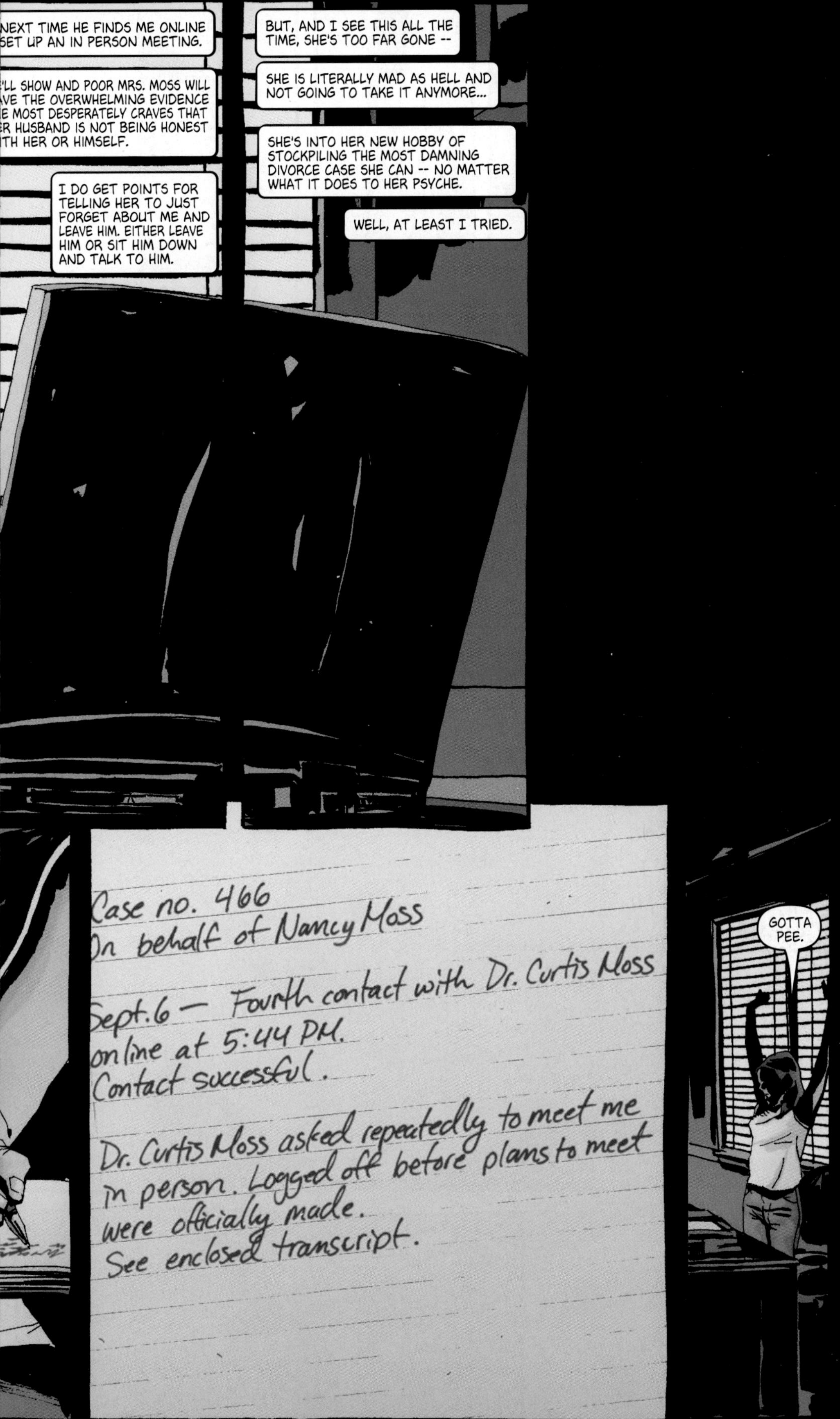
NEXT TIME HE FINDS ME ONLINE
SET UP AN IN PERSON MEETING.
'LL SHOW AND POOR MRS. MOSS WILL
AVE THE OVERWHELMING EVIDENCE
E MOST DESPERATELY CRAVES THAT
R HUSBAND IS NOT BEING HONEST
TH HER OR HIMSELF.
I DO GET POINTS FOR TELLING HER TO JUST FORGET ABOUT ME AND LEAVE HIM. EITHER LEAVE HIM OR SIT HIM DOWN AND TALK TO HIM.
BUT, AND I SEE THIS ALL THE TIME, SHE'S TOO FAR GONE --
SHE IS LITERALLY MAD AS HELL AND NOT GOING TO TAKE IT ANYMORE...
SHE'S INTO HER NEW HOBBY OF STOCKPILING THE MOST DAMNING DIVORCE CASE SHE CAN -- NO MATTER WHAT IT DOES TO HER PSYCHE.
WELL, AT LEAST I TRIED.
Case no. 466
On behalf of Nancy Moss
Sept. 6 — Fourth contact with Dr. Curtis Moss
online at 5:44 PM.
Contact successful.
Dr. Curtis Moss asked repeatedly to meet me
in person. Logged off before plans to meet
were officially made.
See enclosed transcript.
GOTTA PEE.

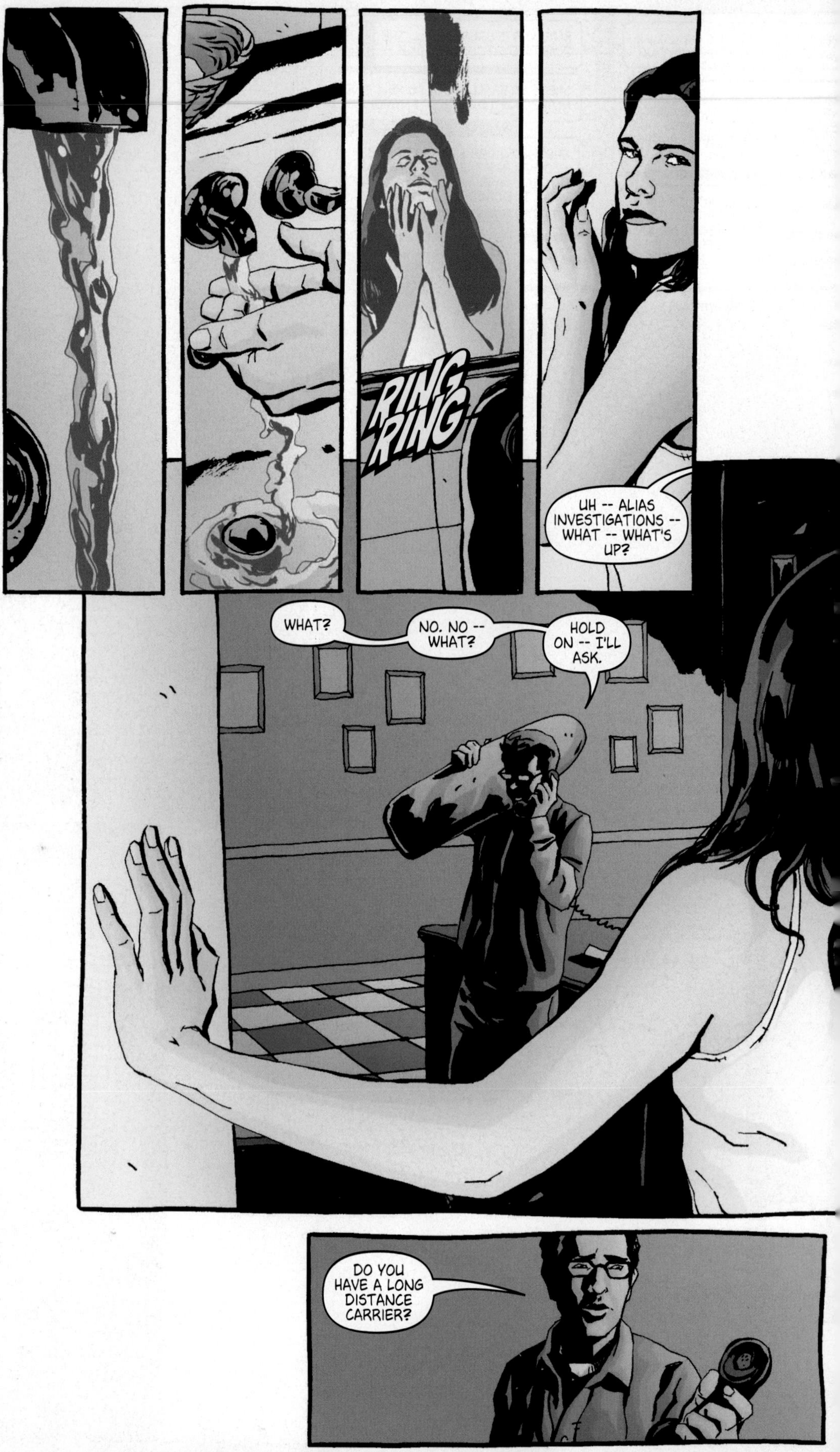
RING RING
UH -- ALIAS INVESTIGATIONS -- WHAT -- WHAT'S UP?
WHAT?
NO. NO -- WHAT?
HOLD ON -- I'LL ASK.
DO YOU HAVE A LONG DISTANCE CARRIER?

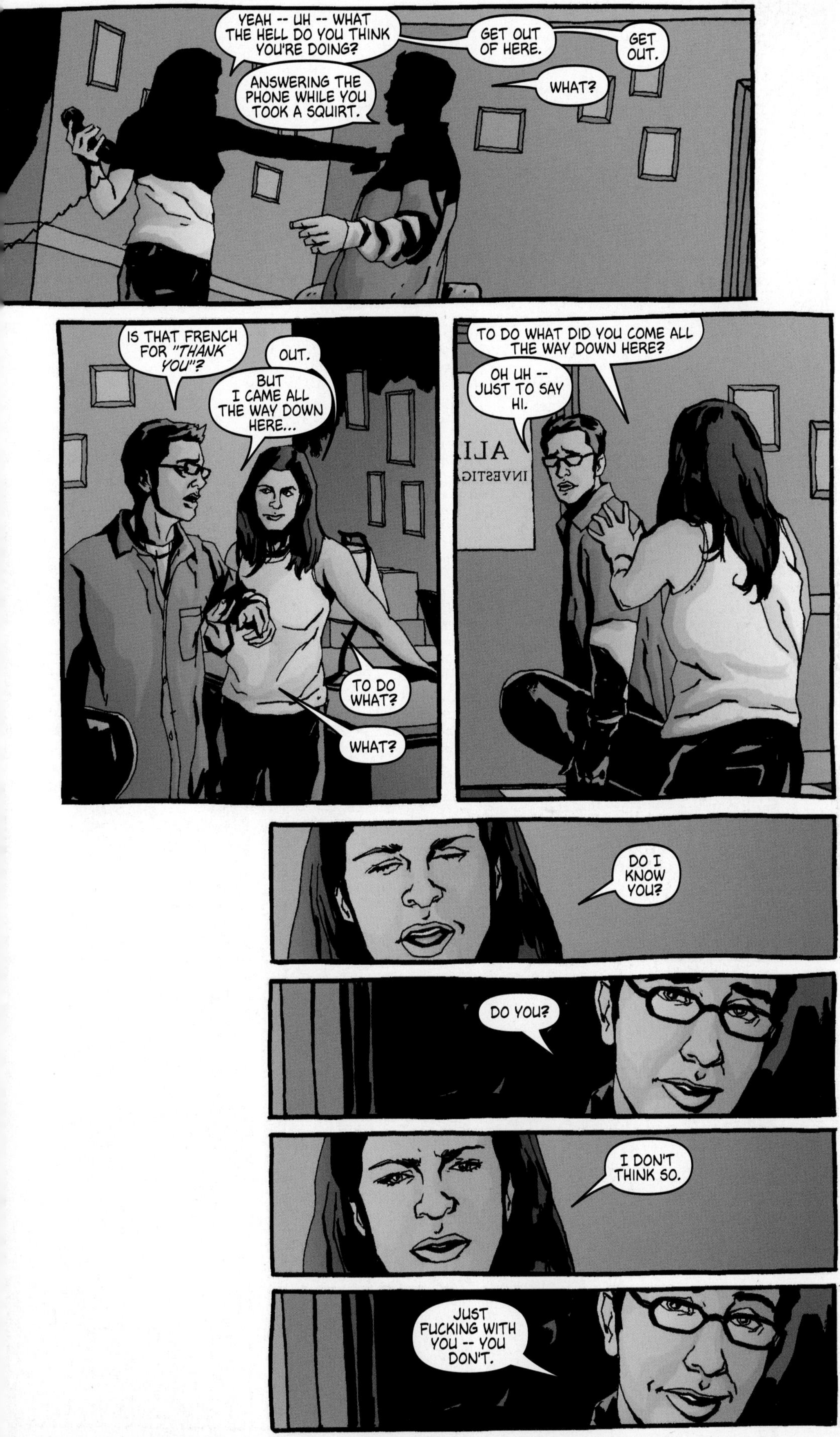
YEAH -- UH -- WHAT THE HELL DO YOU THINK YOU'RE DOING?
GET OUT OF HERE.
GET OUT.
ANSWERING THE PHONE WHILE YOU TOOK A SQUIRT.
WHAT?
IS THAT FRENCH FOR "THANK YOU"?
OUT.
BUT I CAME ALL THE WAY DOWN HERE...
TO DO WHAT?
WHAT?
TO DO WHAT DID YOU COME ALL THE WAY DOWN HERE?
OH UH -- JUST TO SAY HI.
ALI
INVESTIG
DO I KNOW YOU?
DO YOU?
I DON'T THINK SO.
JUST FUCKING WITH YOU -- YOU DON'T.

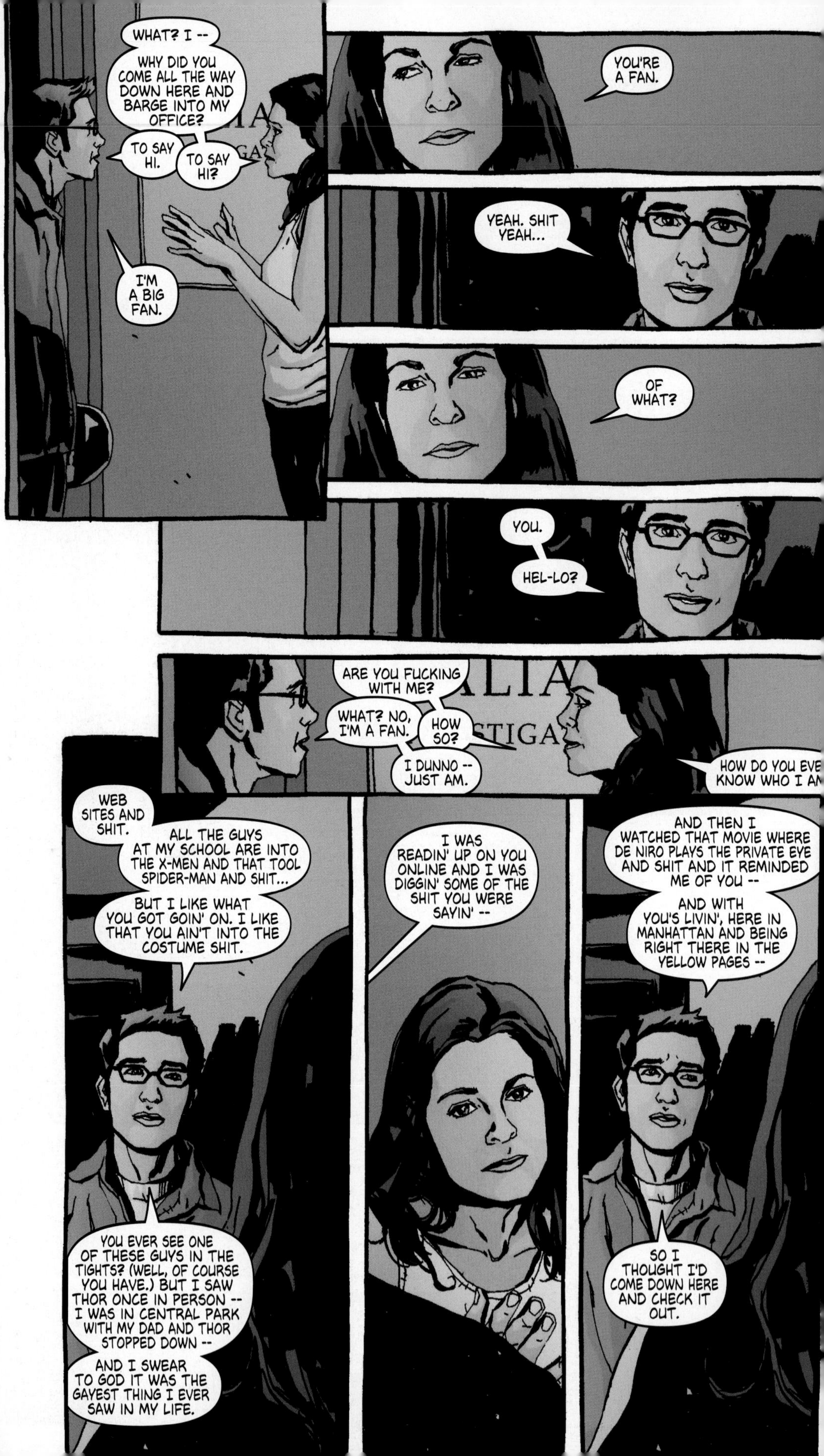
WHAT? I --
WHY DID YOU COME ALL THE WAY DOWN HERE AND BARGE INTO MY OFFICE?
TO SAY HI.
TO SAY HI?
I'M A BIG FAN.
YOU'RE A FAN.
YEAH. SHIT YEAH...
OF WHAT?
YOU.
HEL-LO?
ARE YOU FUCKING WITH ME?
WHAT? NO, I'M A FAN.
HOW SO?
I DUNNO -- JUST AM.
HOW DO YOU EVE
KNOW WHO I A
WEB SITES AND SHIT.
ALL THE GUYS AT MY SCHOOL ARE INTO THE X-MEN AND THAT TOOL SPIDER-MAN AND SHIT...
BUT I LIKE WHAT YOU GOT GOIN' ON. I LIKE THAT YOU AIN'T INTO THE COSTUME SHIT.
YOU EVER SEE ONE OF THESE GUYS IN THE TIGHTS? (WELL, OF COURSE YOU HAVE.) BUT I SAW THOR ONCE IN PERSON -- I WAS IN CENTRAL PARK WITH MY DAD AND THOR STOPPED DOWN --
AND I SWEAR TO GOD IT WAS THE GAYEST THING I EVER SAW IN MY LIFE.
I WAS READIN' UP ON YOU ONLINE AND I WAS DIGGIN' SOME OF THE SHIT YOU WERE SAYIN' --
AND THEN I WATCHED THAT MOVIE WHERE DE NIRO PLAYS THE PRIVATE EYE AND SHIT AND IT REMINDED ME OF YOU --
AND WITH YOU'S LIVIN', HERE IN MANHATTAN AND BEING RIGHT THERE IN THE YELLOW PAGES --
SO I THOUGHT I'D COME DOWN HERE AND CHECK IT OUT.

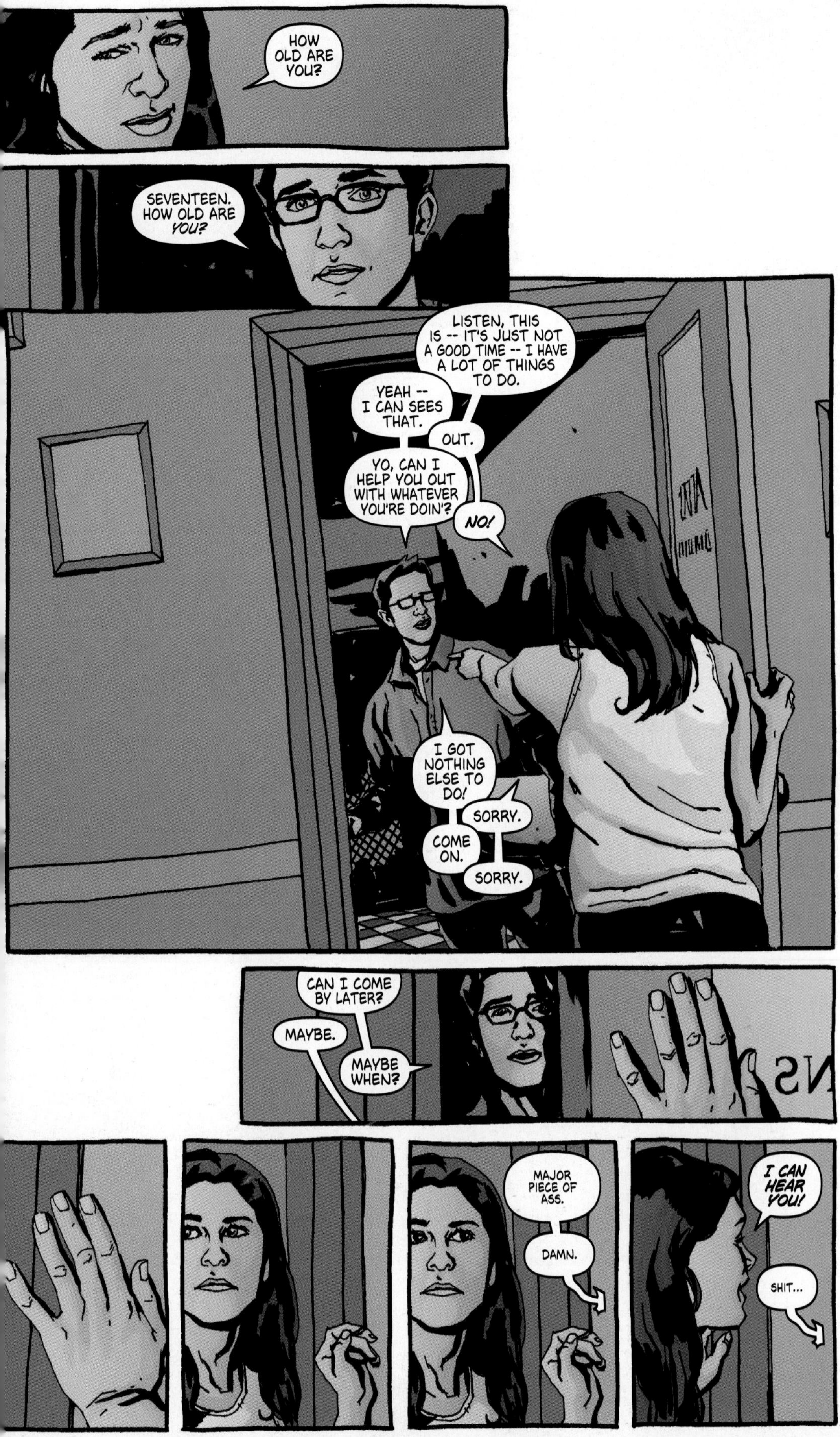
HOW OLD ARE YOU?
SEVENTEEN. HOW OLD ARE *YOU?*
LISTEN, THIS IS -- IT'S JUST NOT A GOOD TIME -- I HAVE A LOT OF THINGS TO DO.
YEAH -- I CAN SEES THAT.
OUT.
YO, CAN I HELP YOU OUT WITH WHATEVER YOU'RE DOIN'?
NO!
I GOT NOTHING ELSE TO DO!
SORRY.
COME ON.
SORRY.
CAN I COME BY LATER?
MAYBE.
MAYBE WHEN?
MAJOR PIECE OF ASS.
DAMN.
I CAN HEAR YOU!
SHIT...

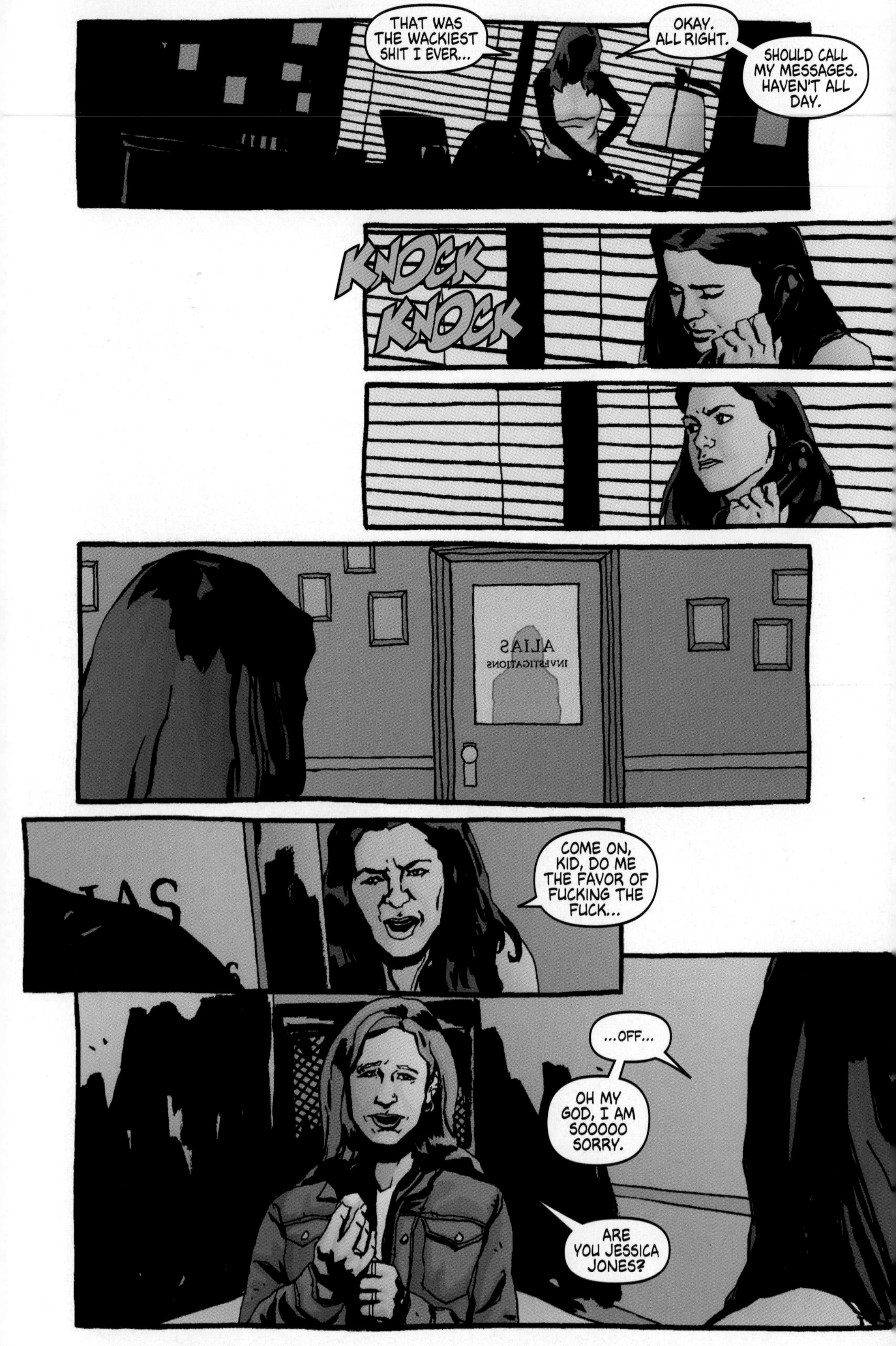
THAT WAS THE WACKIEST SHIT I EVER...
OKAY. ALL RIGHT.
SHOULD CALL MY MESSAGES. HAVEN'T ALL DAY.
KNOCK KNOCK
ALIAS INVESTIGATIONS
COME ON, KID, DO ME THE FAVOR OF FUCKING THE FUCK...
...OFF...
OH MY GOD, I AM SOOOOO SORRY.
ARE YOU JESSICA JONES?

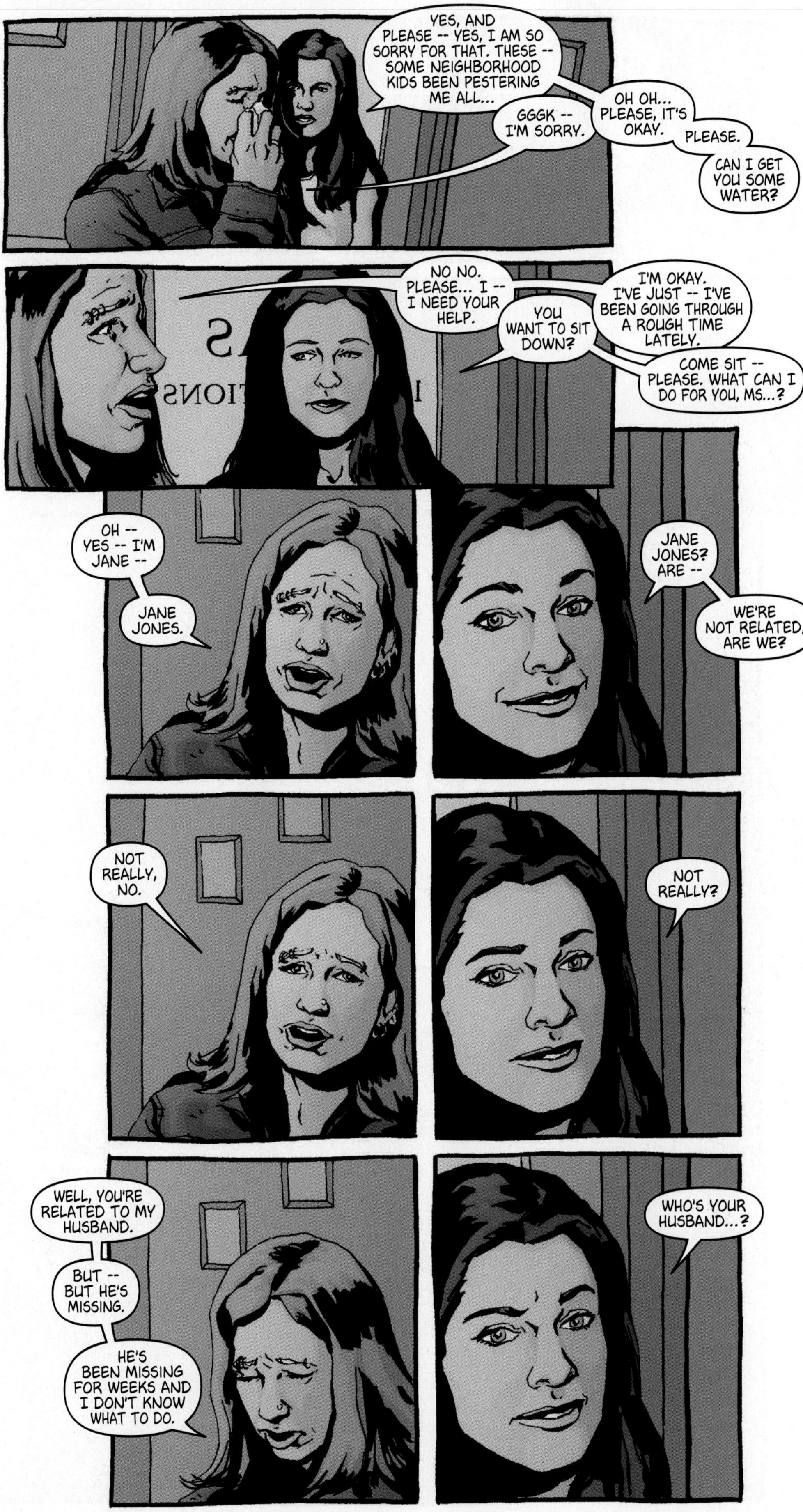

YES, AND PLEASE -- YES, I AM SO SORRY FOR THAT. THESE -- SOME NEIGHBORHOOD KIDS BEEN PESTERING ME ALL...
OH OH... PLEASE, IT'S OKAY.
GGGK -- I'M SORRY.
PLEASE.
CAN I GET YOU SOME WATER?
NO NO. PLEASE... I -- I NEED YOUR HELP.
I'M OKAY. I'VE JUST -- I'VE BEEN GOING THROUGH A ROUGH TIME LATELY.
YOU WANT TO SIT DOWN?
COME SIT -- PLEASE. WHAT CAN I DO FOR YOU, MS...?
OH -- YES -- I'M JANE --
JANE JONES.
JANE JONES? ARE --
WE'RE NOT RELATED, ARE WE?
NOT REALLY, NO.
NOT REALLY?
WELL, YOU'RE RELATED TO MY HUSBAND.
BUT -- BUT HE'S MISSING.
HE'S BEEN MISSING FOR WEEKS AND I DON'T KNOW WHAT TO DO.
WHO'S YOUR HUSBAND...?

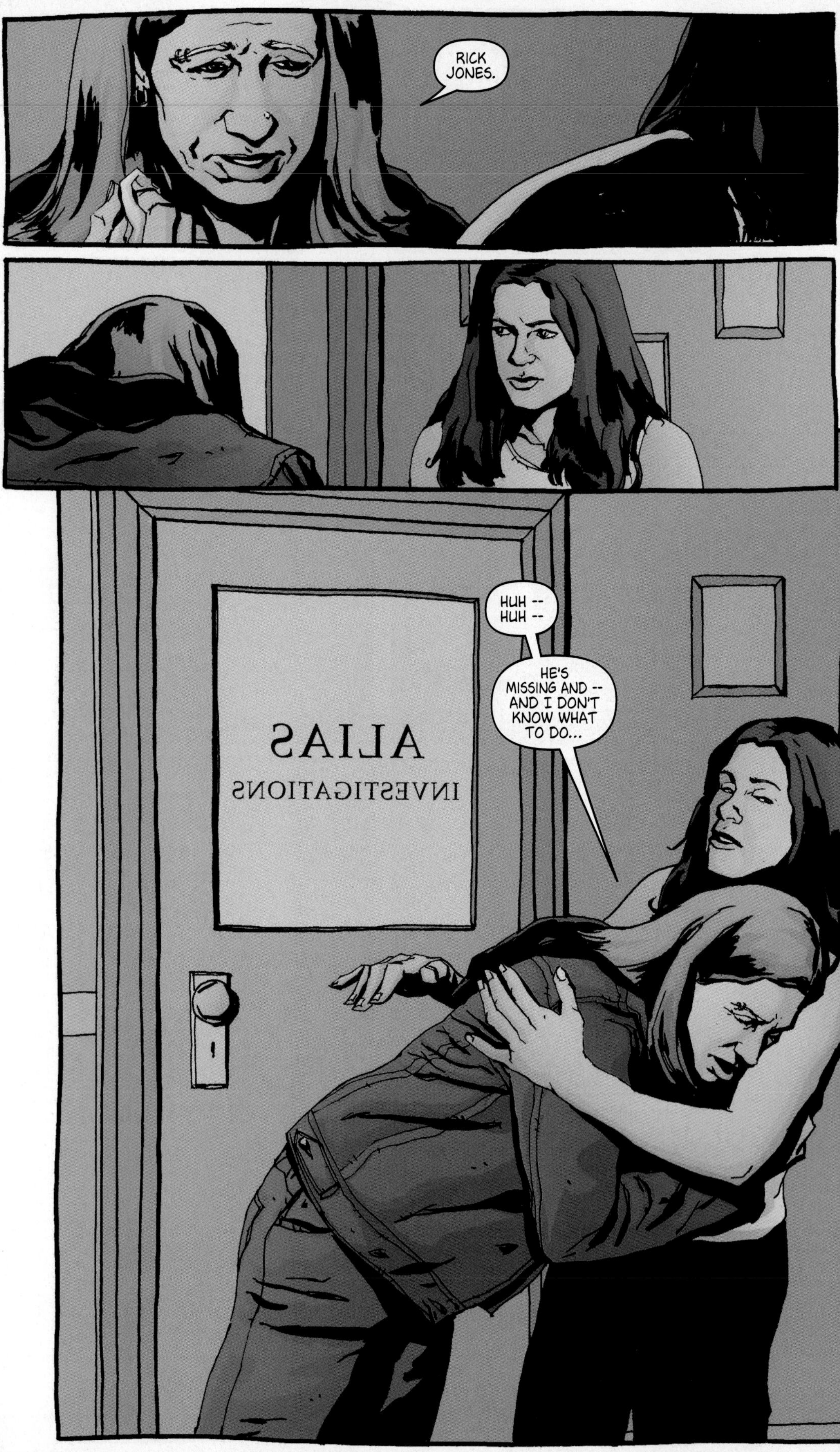
RICK JONES.
HUH -- HUH --
HE'S MISSING AND -- AND I DON'T KNOW WHAT TO DO...
ALIAS INVESTIGATIONS

C[redacted]

ISSUE #7

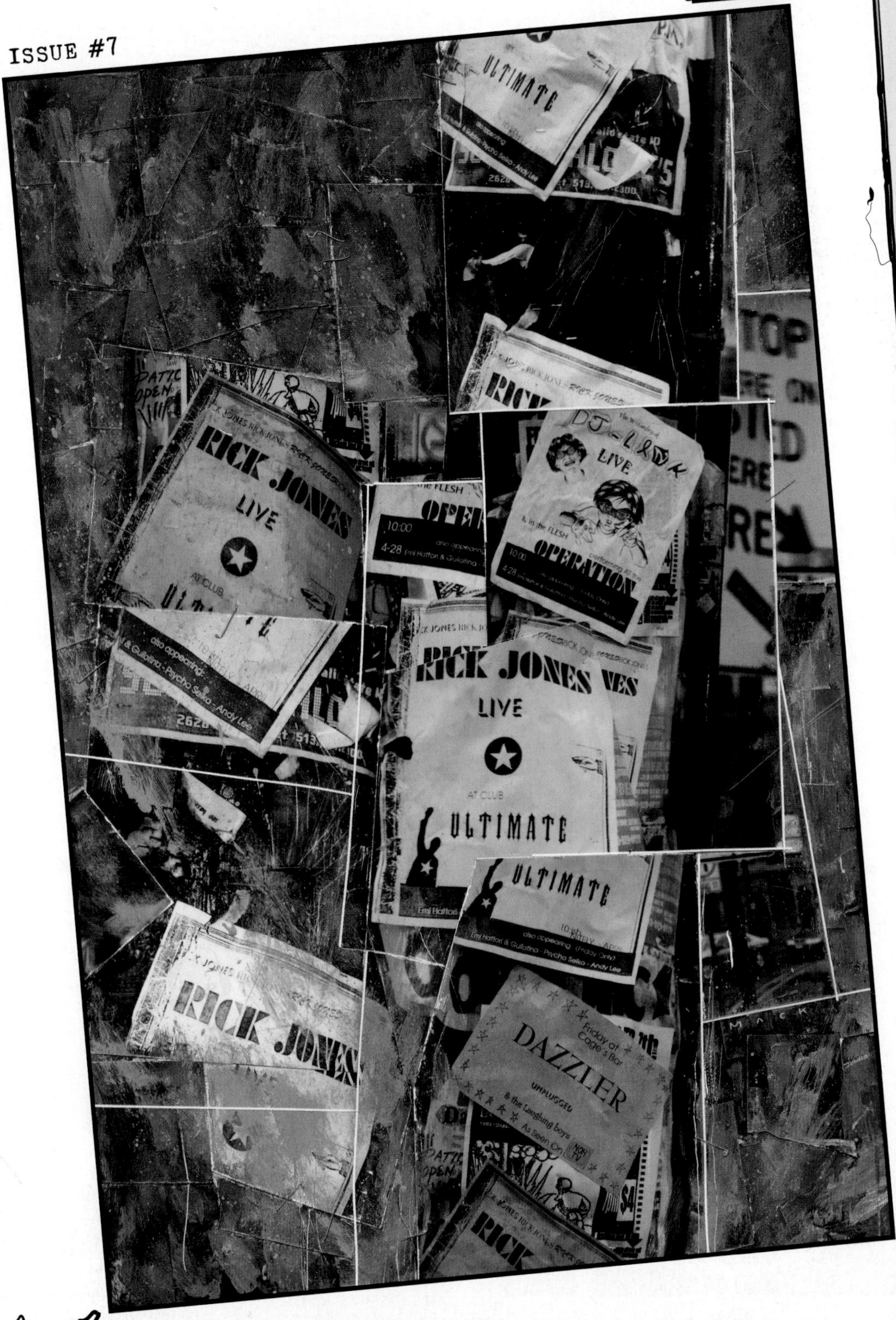

RICK JONES
LIVE
AT CLUB
ULTIMATE
also appearing
Psycho Seiko - Andy Lee
OPERATION
& in the FLESH
10:00
4-28
Emil Hatton & Guillotina
DJ-
LIVE
ULTIMATE
also appearing (Friday Only)
Emil Hatton & Guillotina - Psycho Seiko - Andy Lee
DAZZLER
Friday at Cage's Bar
UNPLUGGED
& the Laughing boys
As Seen On
MACK

JUST -- JUST START AT THE BEGINNING.

TAKE YOUR TIME.

MAAAN.

WELL, LIKE I SAID -- RICK JONES, MY HUSBAND -- MY LITTLE CUTIE OF A HUSBAND -- IS MISSING.

THE WORDS SOUND WRONG -- MY HUSBAND IS MISSING. I DON'T KNOW IF IT'S SINKING IN CORRECTLY.

I DON'T KNOW WHERE HE IS AND I DON'T HAVE A CLUE WHERE TO BEGIN LOOKING.

HE'S BEEN MISSING FOR OVER A MONTH NOW AND IT'S JUST KILLING ME -- BECAUSE I DON'T KNOW WHAT'S GOING ON.

I DIDN'T KNOW WHERE TO TURN TO. THE AVENGERS DON'T ANSWER THEIR DOOR...

I MEAN -- IT -- IT -- IT --

OKAY -- I -- HE'S GONE MISSING BEFORE, BUT NEVER AS LONG AS THIS.

NEVER AS LONG AS THIS.

SEE, WE'VE BEEN MARRIED FOR SIX MONTHS.

I MET HIM AT ONE OF HIS SHOWS.

EVER BEEN TO ONE OF HIS SHOWS, THE VOICE OF AN ANGEL, HE HAS. I MEAN IT -- AN ANGEL.

IF HE HADN'T GOTTEN ALL CAUGHT UP IN ALL THIS SUPER HERO SHIT -- HE REALLY COULDA GONE ALL THE WAY.

AND LISTEN, I KNEW WHEN I STA GOING OUT WITH HIM THAT -- THAT ISN'T YOUR USUAL WORKING JO

HE TOLD ME STRAIGHT UP -- THAT HIS LIFE IS COMPLICATED.

I MEAN, DID YOU KNOW THAT HE STOPPED THE *"KREE-SKRULL WAR"* ALL BY HIMSELF?

NOT A LOT OF PEOPLE KNOW THAT, BUT HE DID.

HE DID AN HE NEVER ASK FOR CREDIT ANYTHING.

YEAH, I KNEW HE WAS A SPECIAL -- AND I'LL ADMIT THAT IN THE BEGINNING IT WAS A BIG TURNON.

BEING WITH A MAN WHO -- WHO RAN WITH SUCH AN AMAZING CROWD.

I MEAN, YOU KNOW, RIGHT? IT'S EXCITING.

WELL, *I* NEVER GOT TO MEET ANY OF THEM -- ANY OF THE SUPER HEROES.

THAT WAS *HIS* THING -- BECAUSE, YOU KNOW, THE AVENGERS HAVE A PRETTY TIGHT SECURITY SITUATION THING --

-- BUT I RESPECT THAT. I DO.

AND HE'D ALWAYS COME HOME AND TELL ME ALL THE STORIES.

SO, OKAY, I FOUND THE PERFECT MAN... BUT I HAD TO SHARE HIM WITH THE WORLD EVERY ONCE IN A WHILE.

I MEAN, I HAVE FRIENDS WHO ARE MARRIED -- THEY CAN'T EVEN STAND THEIR HUSBANDS.

THEY HATE THEM.

BUT -- BUT I *LOVE* RICK.

I *DO*.

AND NOT KNOWING WHERE HE IS -- IS MAKING ME SICK TO MY STOMACH. I CAN'T TAKE IT ANYMORE.

I MEAN, HE JUST -- JUST DISAPPEARED ONE DAY AND NOW I DON'T KNOW WHAT TO DO...

SO -- SO I LOOKED YOU UP AND CAME HERE.

I MEAN, IF ANYONE CAN FIND HIM, IT'S YOU.

HE ALWAYS SPOKE HIGHLY OF YOU.

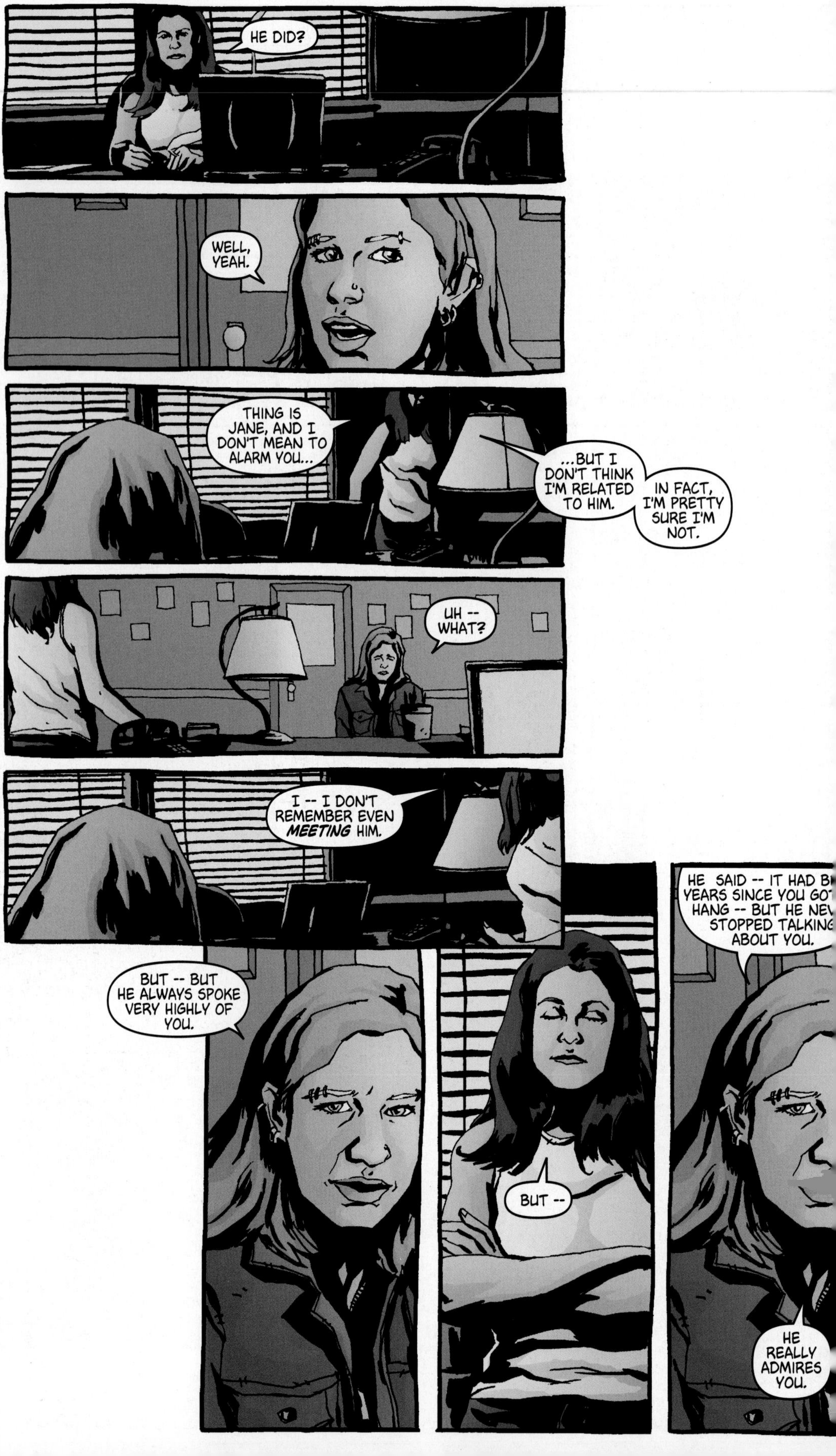
HE DID?
WELL, YEAH.
THING IS JANE, AND I DON'T MEAN TO ALARM YOU...
...BUT I DON'T THINK I'M RELATED TO HIM.
IN FACT, I'M PRETTY SURE I'M NOT.
UH -- WHAT?
I -- I DON'T REMEMBER EVEN *MEETING* HIM.
BUT -- BUT HE ALWAYS SPOKE VERY HIGHLY OF YOU.
BUT --
HE SAID -- IT HAD B YEARS SINCE YOU GOT HANG -- BUT HE NEV STOPPED TALKING ABOUT YOU.
HE REALLY ADMIRES YOU.

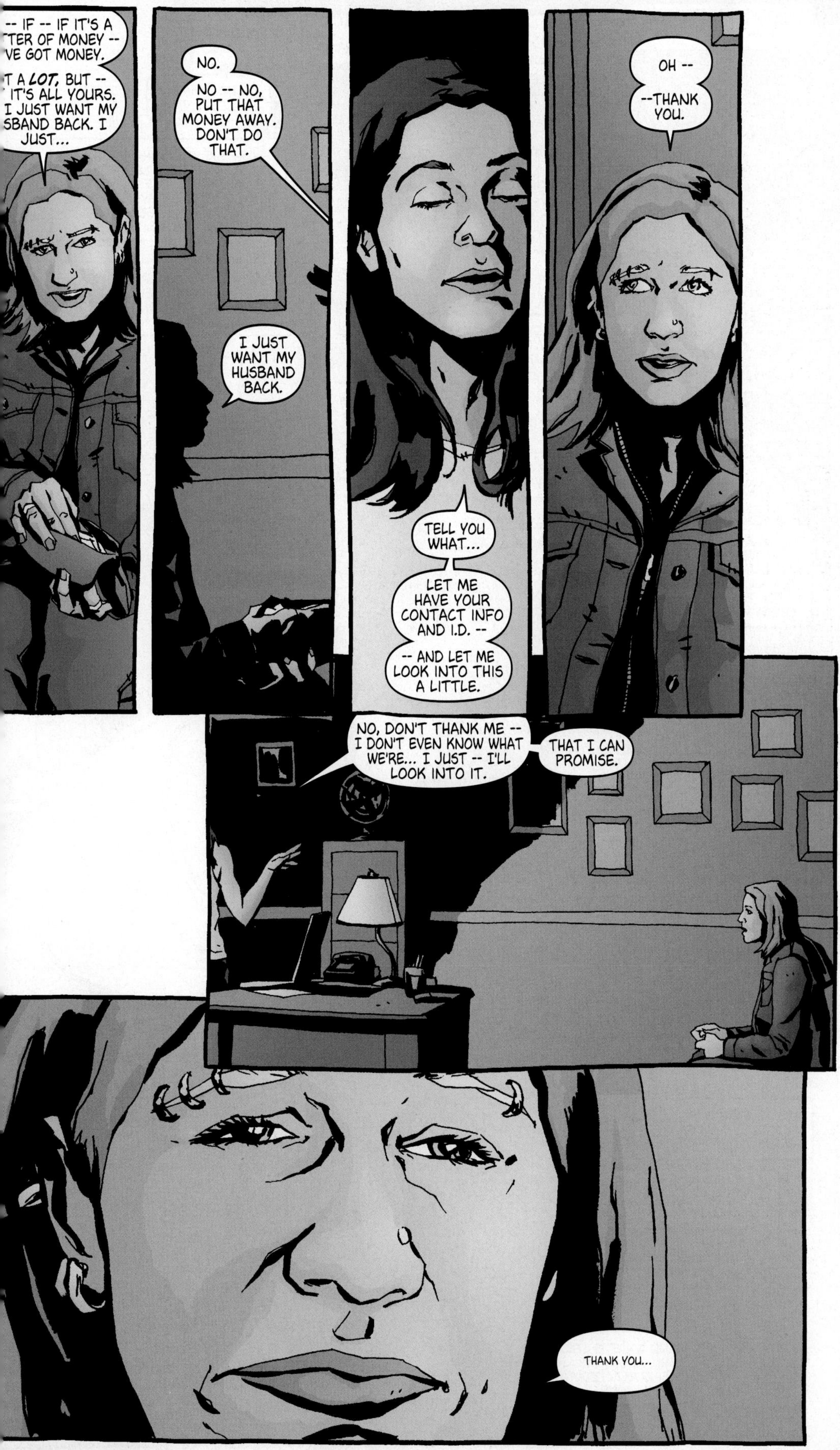
-- IF -- IF IT'S A
TTER OF MONEY --
VE GOT MONEY.
T A LOT, BUT --
IT'S ALL YOURS.
I JUST WANT MY
SBAND BACK. I
JUST...
NO.
NO -- NO, PUT THAT MONEY AWAY. DON'T DO THAT.
I JUST WANT MY HUSBAND BACK.
TELL YOU WHAT...
LET ME HAVE YOUR CONTACT INFO AND I.D. --
-- AND LET ME LOOK INTO THIS A LITTLE.
OH --
--THANK YOU.
NO, DON'T THANK ME -- I DON'T EVEN KNOW WHAT WE'RE... I JUST -- I'LL LOOK INTO IT.
THAT I CAN PROMISE.
THANK YOU...

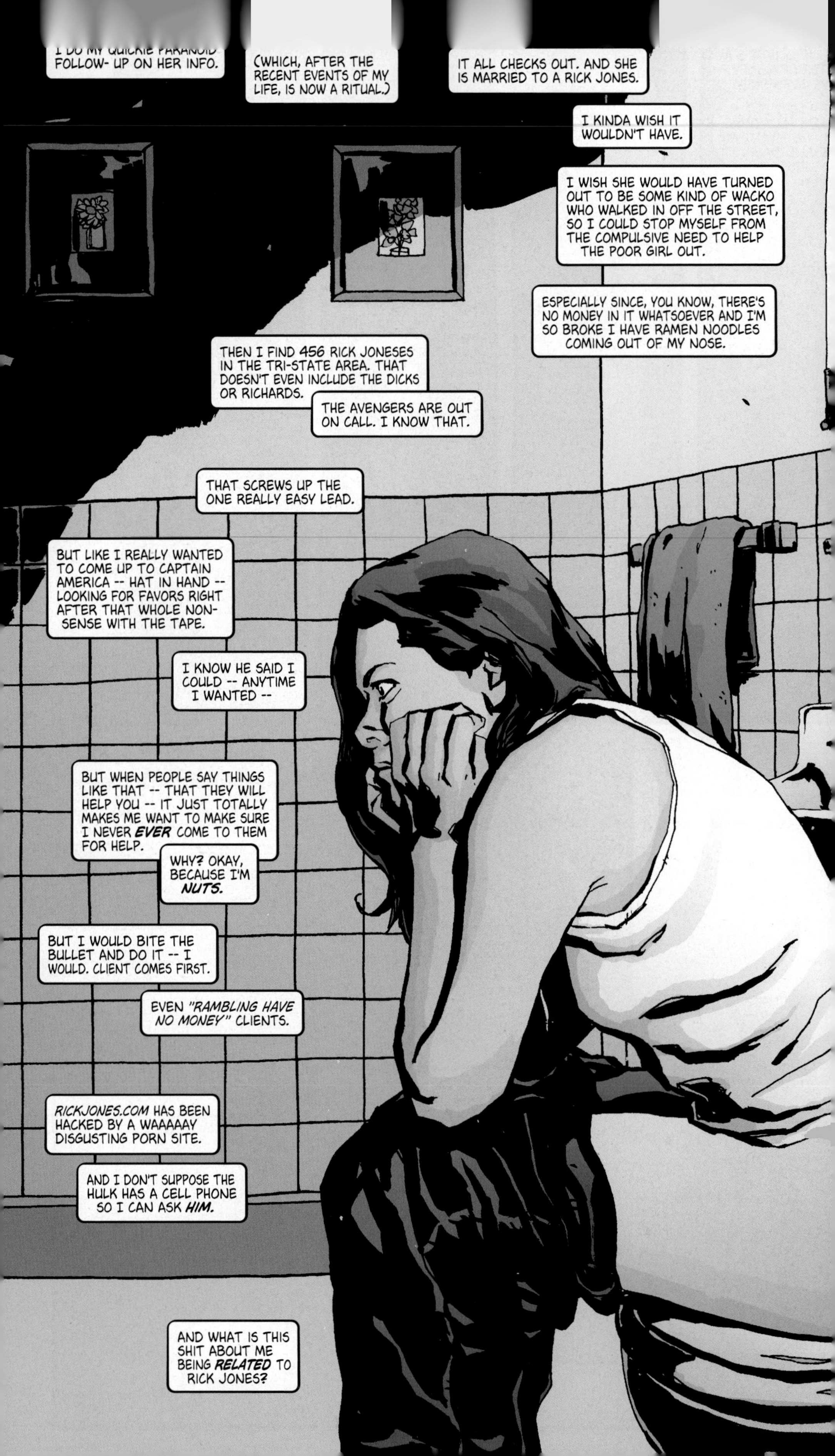
I DO MY QUICKIE PARANOID FOLLOW- UP ON HER INFO.
(WHICH, AFTER THE RECENT EVENTS OF MY LIFE, IS NOW A RITUAL.)
IT ALL CHECKS OUT. AND SHE IS MARRIED TO A RICK JONES.
I KINDA WISH IT WOULDN'T HAVE.
I WISH SHE WOULD HAVE TURNED OUT TO BE SOME KIND OF WACKO WHO WALKED IN OFF THE STREET, SO I COULD STOP MYSELF FROM THE COMPULSIVE NEED TO HELP THE POOR GIRL OUT.
ESPECIALLY SINCE, YOU KNOW, THERE'S NO MONEY IN IT WHATSOEVER AND I'M SO BROKE I HAVE RAMEN NOODLES COMING OUT OF MY NOSE.
THEN I FIND 456 RICK JONESES IN THE TRI-STATE AREA. THAT DOESN'T EVEN INCLUDE THE DICKS OR RICHARDS.
THE AVENGERS ARE OUT ON CALL. I KNOW THAT.
THAT SCREWS UP THE ONE REALLY EASY LEAD.
BUT LIKE I REALLY WANTED TO COME UP TO CAPTAIN AMERICA -- HAT IN HAND -- LOOKING FOR FAVORS RIGHT AFTER THAT WHOLE NON-SENSE WITH THE TAPE.
I KNOW HE SAID I COULD -- ANYTIME I WANTED --
BUT WHEN PEOPLE SAY THINGS LIKE THAT -- THAT THEY WILL HELP YOU -- IT JUST TOTALLY MAKES ME WANT TO MAKE SURE I NEVER ***EVER*** COME TO THEM FOR HELP.
WHY? OKAY, BECAUSE I'M ***NUTS.***
BUT I WOULD BITE THE BULLET AND DO IT -- I WOULD. CLIENT COMES FIRST.
EVEN *"RAMBLING HAVE NO MONEY"* CLIENTS.
RICKJONES.COM HAS BEEN HACKED BY A WAAAAAY DISGUSTING PORN SITE.
AND I DON'T SUPPOSE THE HULK HAS A CELL PHONE SO I CAN ASK ***HIM.***
AND WHAT IS THIS SHIT ABOUT ME BEING ***RELATED*** TO RICK JONES?

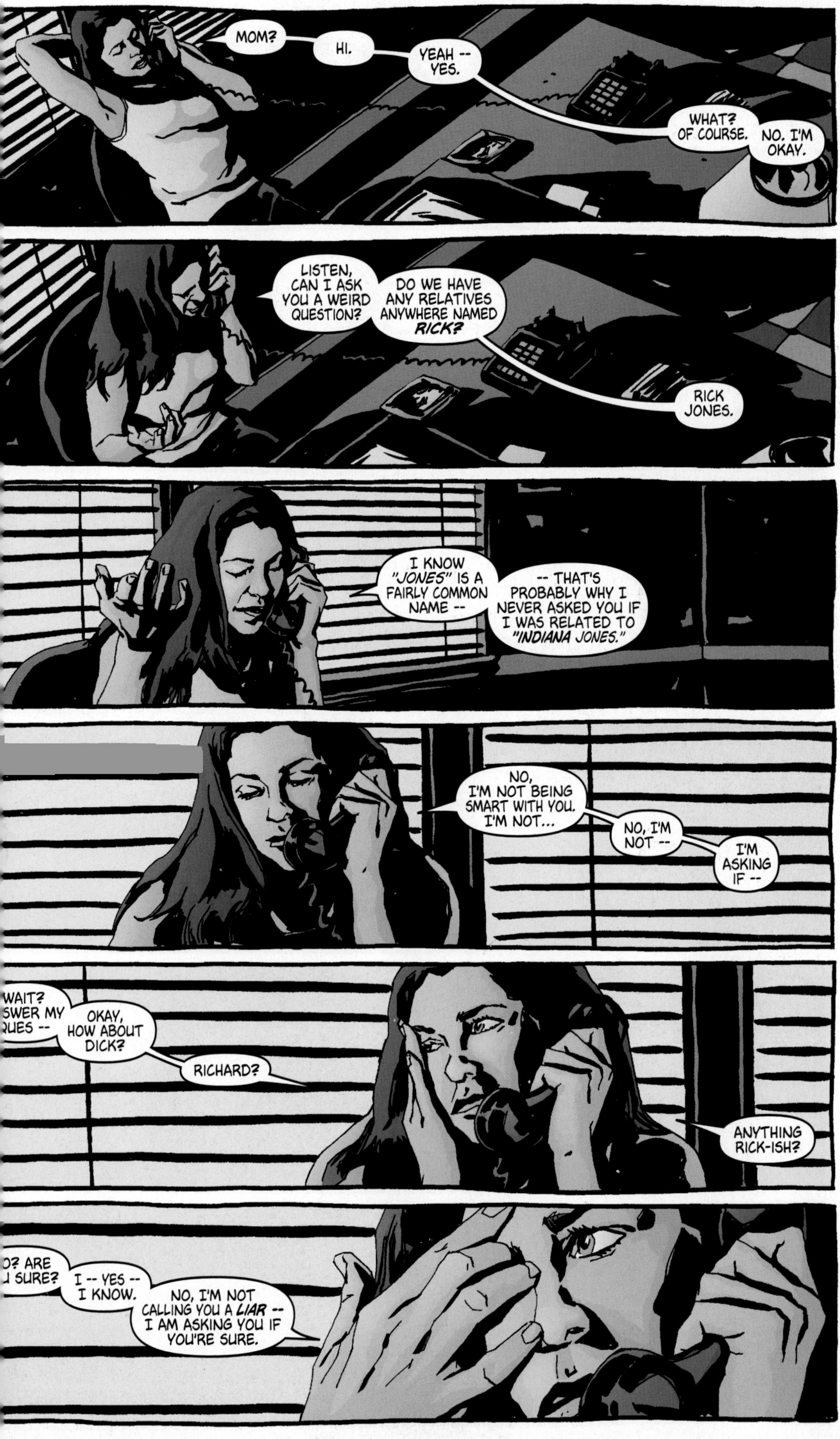
MOM?
HI.
YEAH -- YES.
WHAT? OF COURSE.
NO. I'M OKAY.
LISTEN, CAN I ASK YOU A WEIRD QUESTION?
DO WE HAVE ANY RELATIVES ANYWHERE NAMED *RICK?*
RICK JONES.
I KNOW *"JONES"* IS A FAIRLY COMMON NAME --
-- THAT'S PROBABLY WHY I NEVER ASKED YOU IF I WAS RELATED TO *"INDIANA JONES."*
NO, I'M NOT BEING SMART WITH YOU. I'M NOT...
NO, I'M NOT --
I'M ASKING IF --
WAIT? SWER MY QUES --
OKAY, HOW ABOUT DICK?
RICHARD?
ANYTHING RICK-ISH?
O? ARE SURE?
I -- YES -- I KNOW.
NO, I'M NOT CALLING YOU A *LIAR* -- I AM ASKING YOU IF YOU'RE SURE.

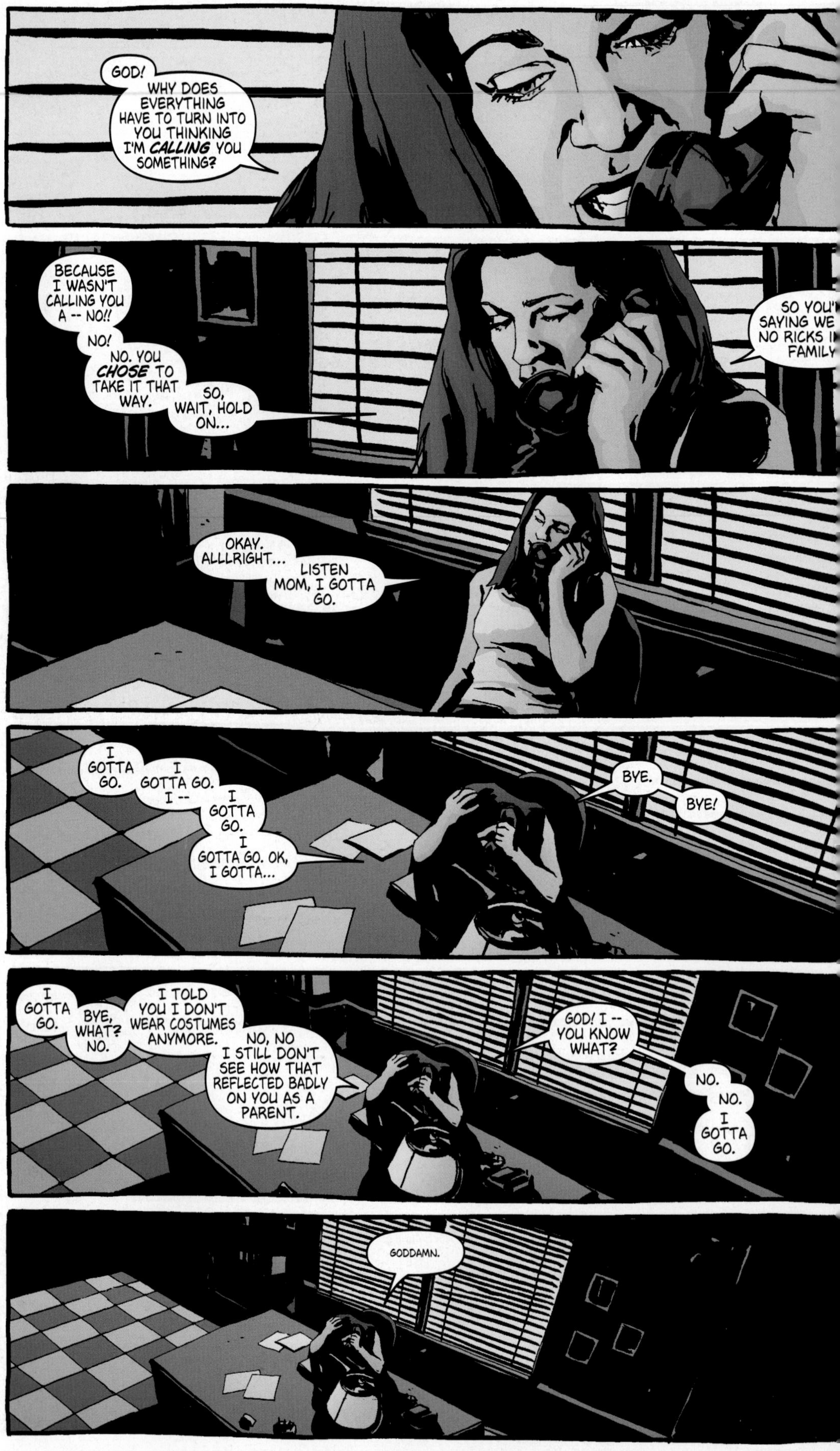
GOD! WHY DOES EVERYTHING HAVE TO TURN INTO YOU THINKING I'M *CALLING* YOU SOMETHING?
BECAUSE I WASN'T CALLING YOU A -- NO!!
NO!
NO. YOU *CHOSE* TO TAKE IT THAT WAY.
SO, WAIT, HOLD ON...
OKAY. ALLLRIGHT...
LISTEN MOM, I GOTTA GO.
I GOTTA GO.
I GOTTA GO. I --
I GOTTA GO.
I GOTTA GO. OK, I GOTTA...
BYE.
BYE!
I GOTTA GO.
BYE, WHAT? NO.
I TOLD YOU I DON'T WEAR COSTUMES ANYMORE.
NO, NO I STILL DON'T SEE HOW THAT REFLECTED BADLY ON YOU AS A PARENT.
GOD! I -- YOU KNOW WHAT?
NO.
NO.
I GOTTA GO.
GODDAMN.

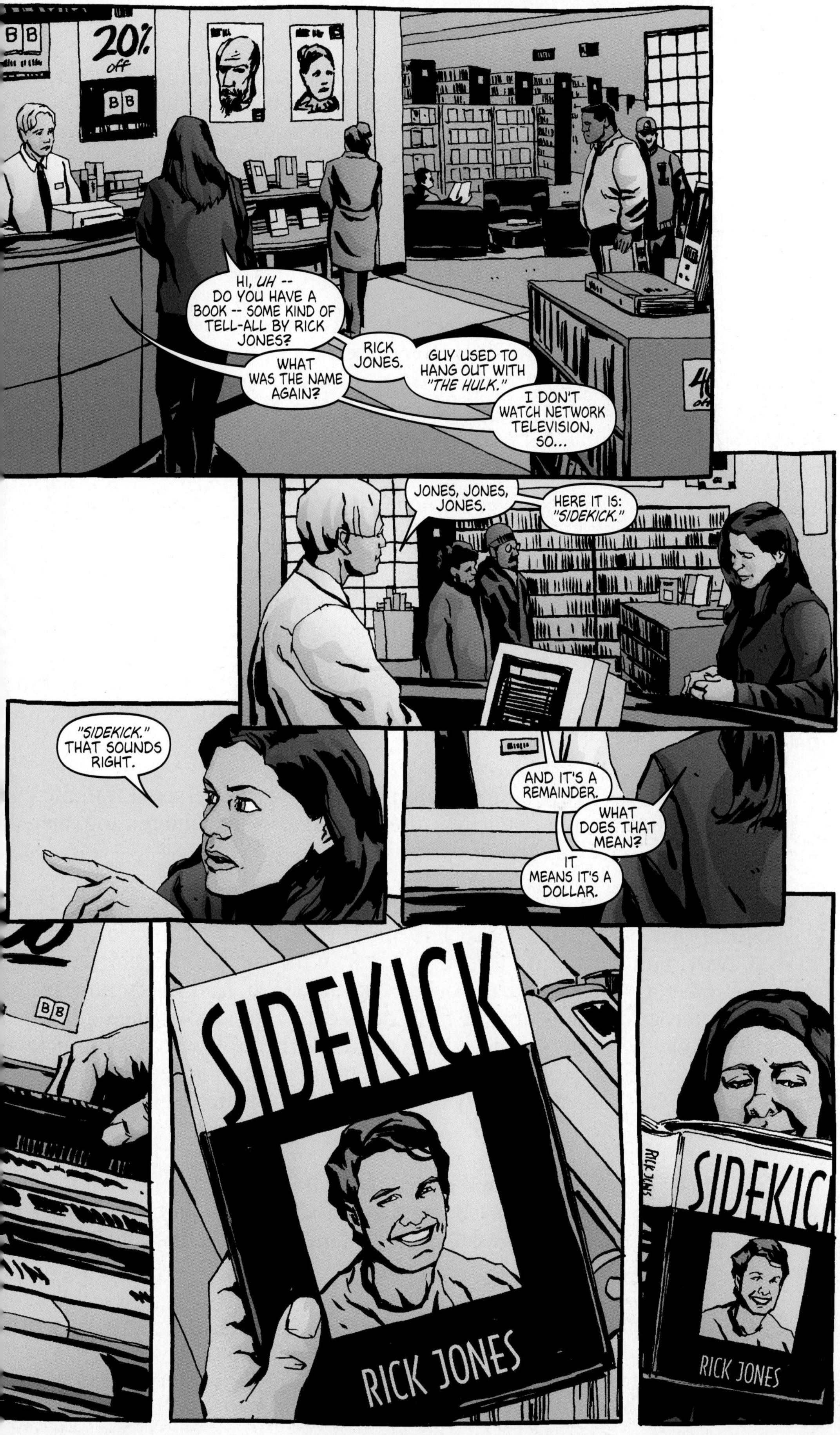
20% off
HI, UH -- DO YOU HAVE A BOOK -- SOME KIND OF TELL-ALL BY RICK JONES?
WHAT WAS THE NAME AGAIN?
RICK JONES.
GUY USED TO HANG OUT WITH "THE HULK."
I DON'T WATCH NETWORK TELEVISION, SO...
JONES, JONES, JONES.
HERE IT IS: "SIDEKICK."
"SIDEKICK." THAT SOUNDS RIGHT.
AND IT'S A REMAINDER.
WHAT DOES THAT MEAN?
IT MEANS IT'S A DOLLAR.
SIDEKICK
RICK JONES
SIDEKICK
RICK JONES

a great man, no denying it. Captain America probably will end up being remembered as one of the greatest men in American history. I know this is not the most original observation in the world, but having spent time with the man thought just the fact that he definitely lives up to the hype was worth sharing.

But during the time when I was hanging out with him, when I was his partner I think it's safe to say that he was going through one of the worst periods in life.

When I was training to replace Bucky Barnes, Cap's incredibly talented partner during his World War Two adventures, Cap was still very much Rip V Winkle. He had recently awoken from a decades-long deep freeze. You know the story. He was awoken into a modern world he had no way of understanding. Can you imagine going through something like that? I can't. But picked up his shield and, like the country he represents, he pushed on as best could.

And since both he and I were brought in under the incredibly genero Avengers umbrella provided by Stark Industries — both of us men with families, without direction—I guess it seemed a natural fit. And at this point my life I badly wanted a 'promotion' in the super hero ranks. I was a hanger-I knew that. And this was my big chance to get into the game for real, under tutelage of a real living legend. At first, I was honored. Honored and flatte to be asked to be Captain America's brand new partner. All of a sudden I was list.

I gave it my all. I gave Cap's intense bootcamp-style personal training eve thing I had. But as time went on, after a couple of adventures together, I member starting to feel a little dirty inside.

The whole thing reminded me of this guy I knew in high school who despondent that his girlfriend had left him. The very first love of his life moved away with her family forever. Later in the summer he started going with this other girl, who sort of looked like his ex. And every day he wo subtly ask the girl to do things a little different to her appearance. He wo make her wear her hair down. He would ask her to wear a certain kind lipstick. And we all watched as he slowly turned this innocent girl into his girlfriend. It was sad, and doubly so because the guy didn't even realize he doing it.

Well, that's pretty much how I ended up feeling about that time in my life eventually realized that I wasn't being Captain America's partner. What I doing was helping a grieving man come to terms with the incredible loss in life. I was a phase.

I also realized that the reason some people can put on a costume and fi crime and others can't is because it ain't easy. Sure, it looks easy when you it, but that's what makes them larger than life heroes. Have you ever trie throw your body over a four-foot wall? Ever just try to climb a fence? Eve

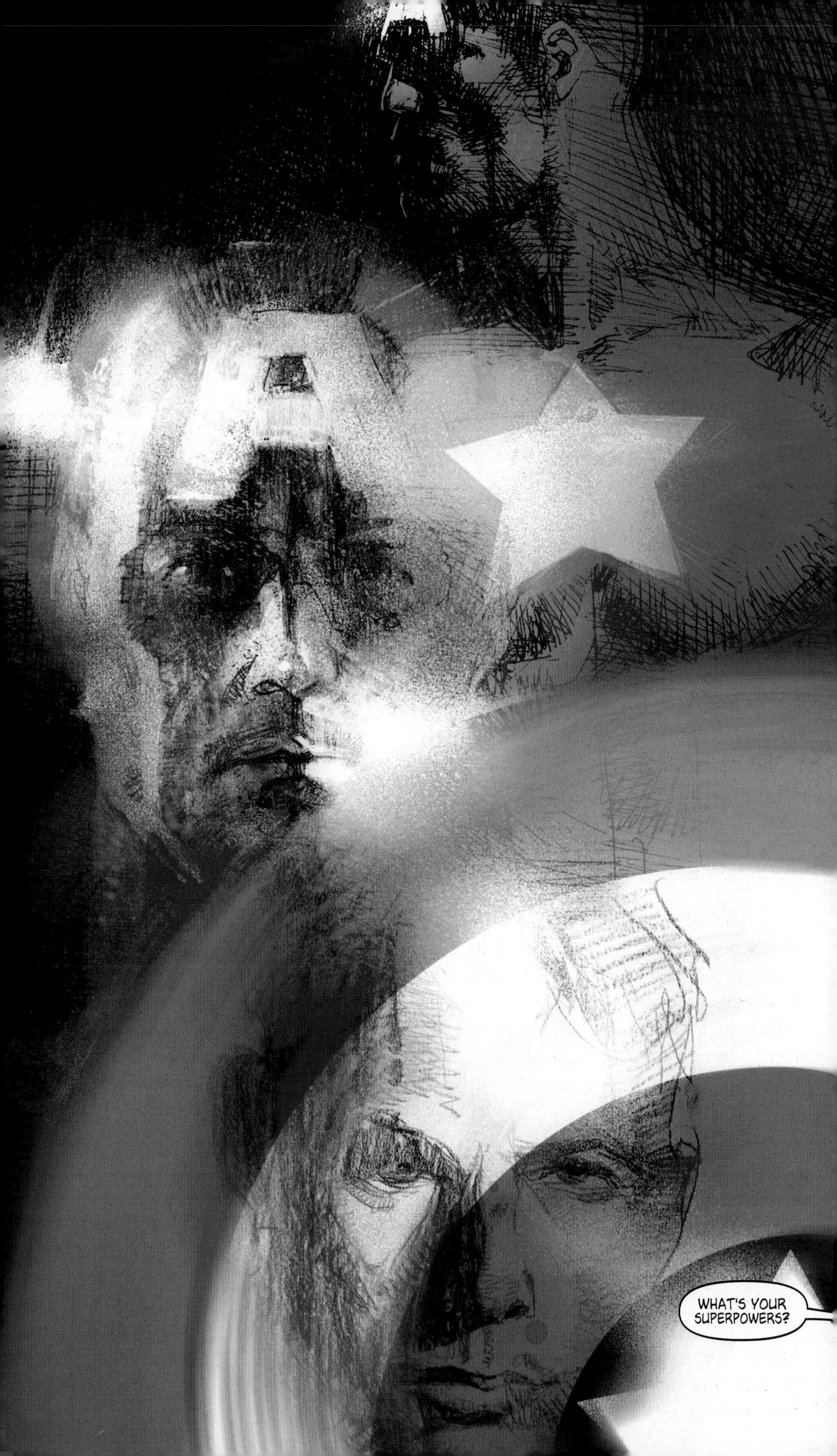
WHAT'S YOUR SUPERPOWERS?

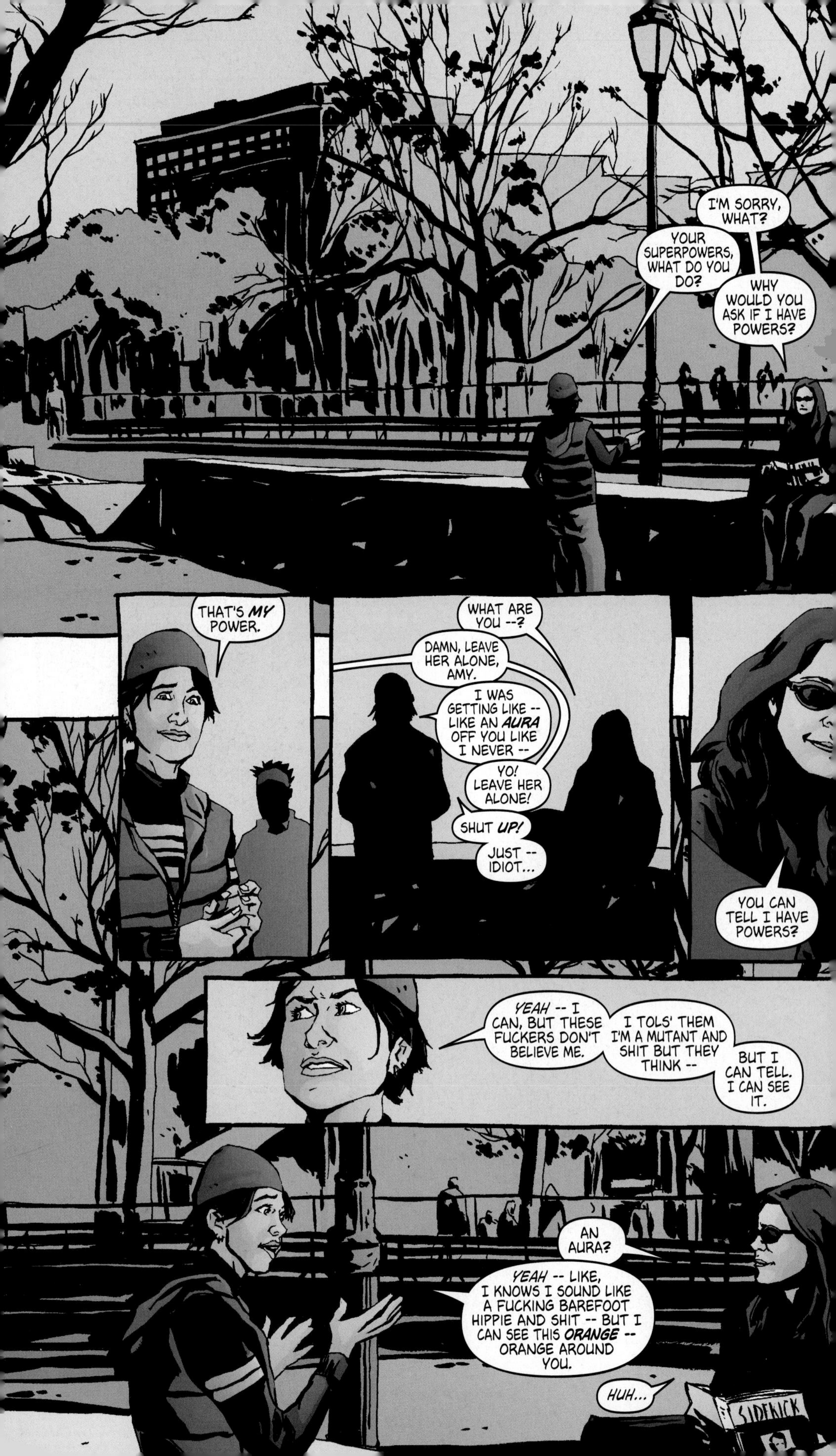

I'M SORRY, WHAT?
YOUR SUPERPOWERS, WHAT DO YOU DO?
WHY WOULD YOU ASK IF I HAVE POWERS?
THAT'S MY POWER.
WHAT ARE YOU --?
DAMN, LEAVE HER ALONE, AMY.
I WAS GETTING LIKE -- LIKE AN AURA OFF YOU LIKE I NEVER --
YO! LEAVE HER ALONE!
SHUT UP!
JUST -- IDIOT...
YOU CAN TELL I HAVE POWERS?
YEAH -- I CAN, BUT THESE FUCKERS DON'T BELIEVE ME.
I TOLS' THEM I'M A MUTANT AND SHIT BUT THEY THINK --
BUT I CAN TELL. I CAN SEE IT.
AN AURA?
YEAH -- LIKE, I KNOWS I SOUND LIKE A FUCKING BAREFOOT HIPPIE AND SHIT -- BUT I CAN SEE THIS ORANGE -- ORANGE AROUND YOU.
HUH...
SIDEKICK

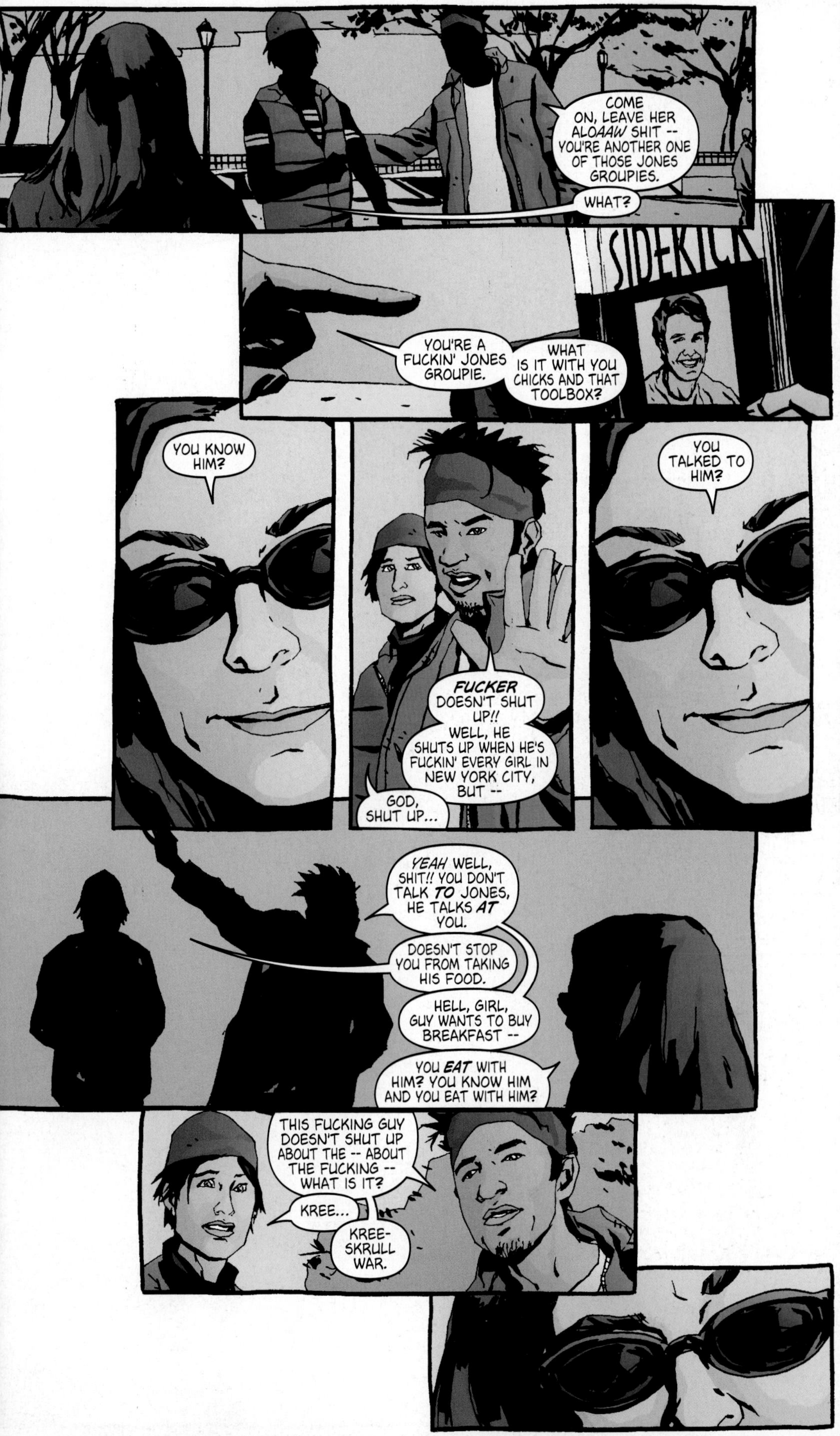

COME ON, LEAVE HER ALOAAW SHIT -- YOU'RE ANOTHER ONE OF THOSE JONES GROUPIES.
WHAT?
SIDEKICK
YOU'RE A FUCKIN' JONES GROUPIE.
WHAT IS IT WITH YOU CHICKS AND THAT TOOLBOX?
YOU KNOW HIM?
FUCKER DOESN'T SHUT UP!! WELL, HE SHUTS UP WHEN HE'S FUCKIN' EVERY GIRL IN NEW YORK CITY, BUT --
GOD, SHUT UP...
YOU TALKED TO HIM?
YEAH WELL, SHIT!! YOU DON'T TALK TO JONES, HE TALKS AT YOU.
DOESN'T STOP YOU FROM TAKING HIS FOOD.
HELL, GIRL, GUY WANTS TO BUY BREAKFAST --
YOU EAT WITH HIM? YOU KNOW HIM AND YOU EAT WITH HIM?
THIS FUCKING GUY DOESN'T SHUT UP ABOUT THE -- ABOUT THE FUCKING -- WHAT IS IT?
KREE...
KREE-SKRULL WAR.

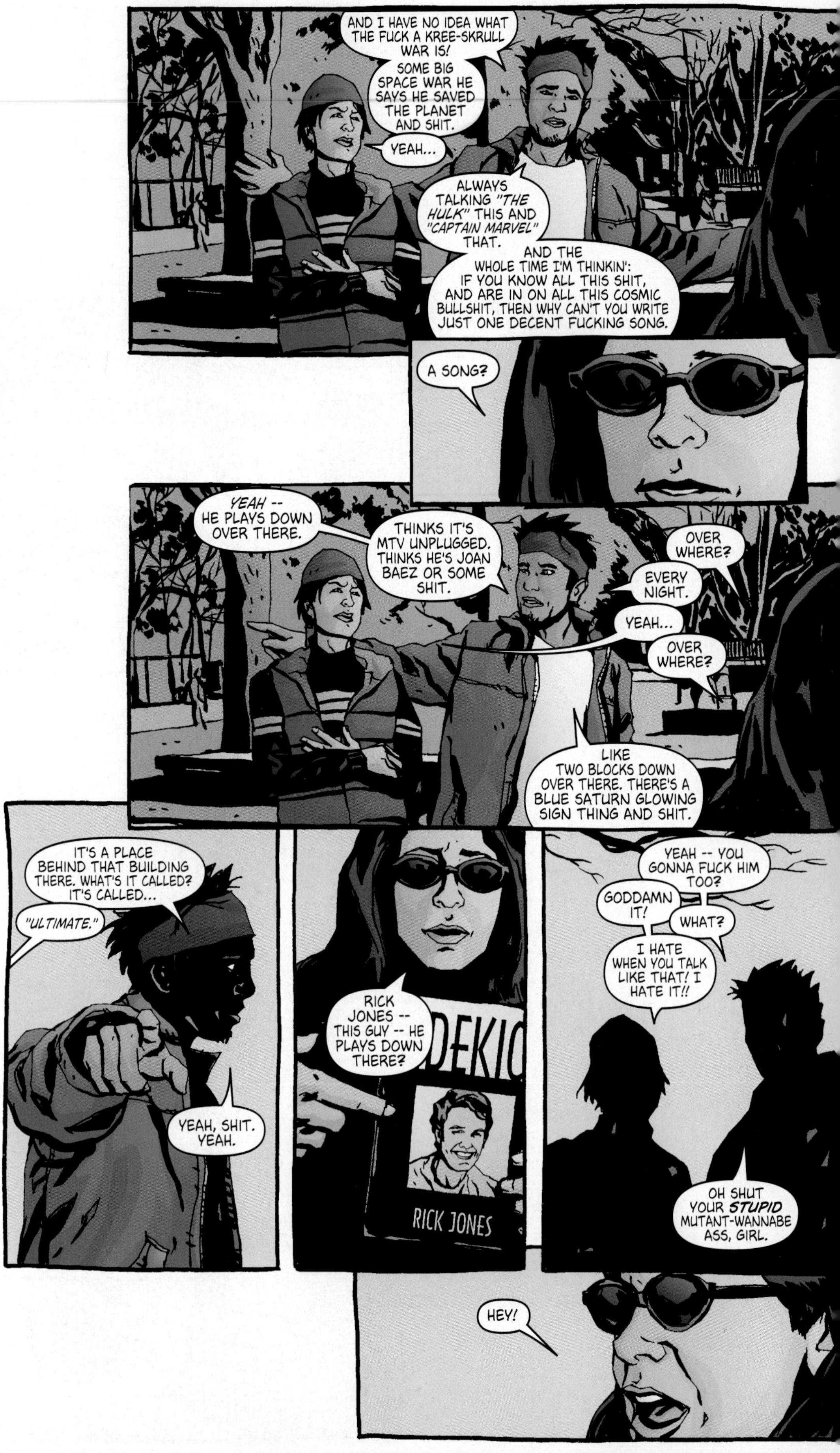
AND I HAVE NO IDEA WHAT THE FUCK A KREE-SKRULL WAR IS!
SOME BIG SPACE WAR HE SAYS HE SAVED THE PLANET AND SHIT.
YEAH...
ALWAYS TALKING "THE HULK" THIS AND "CAPTAIN MARVEL" THAT.
AND THE WHOLE TIME I'M THINKIN': IF YOU KNOW ALL THIS SHIT, AND ARE IN ON ALL THIS COSMIC BULLSHIT, THEN WHY CAN'T YOU WRITE JUST ONE DECENT FUCKING SONG.
A SONG?
YEAH -- HE PLAYS DOWN OVER THERE.
THINKS IT'S MTV UNPLUGGED. THINKS HE'S JOAN BAEZ OR SOME SHIT.
OVER WHERE?
EVERY NIGHT.
YEAH...
OVER WHERE?
LIKE TWO BLOCKS DOWN OVER THERE. THERE'S A BLUE SATURN GLOWING SIGN THING AND SHIT.
IT'S A PLACE BEHIND THAT BUILDING THERE. WHAT'S IT CALLED? IT'S CALLED...
"ULTIMATE."
YEAH, SHIT. YEAH.
RICK JONES -- THIS GUY -- HE PLAYS DOWN THERE?
DEKIO
RICK JONES
YEAH -- YOU GONNA FUCK HIM TOO?
GODDAMN IT!
WHAT?
I HATE WHEN YOU TALK LIKE THAT! I HATE IT!!
OH SHUT YOUR STUPID MUTANT-WANNABE ASS, GIRL.
HEY!

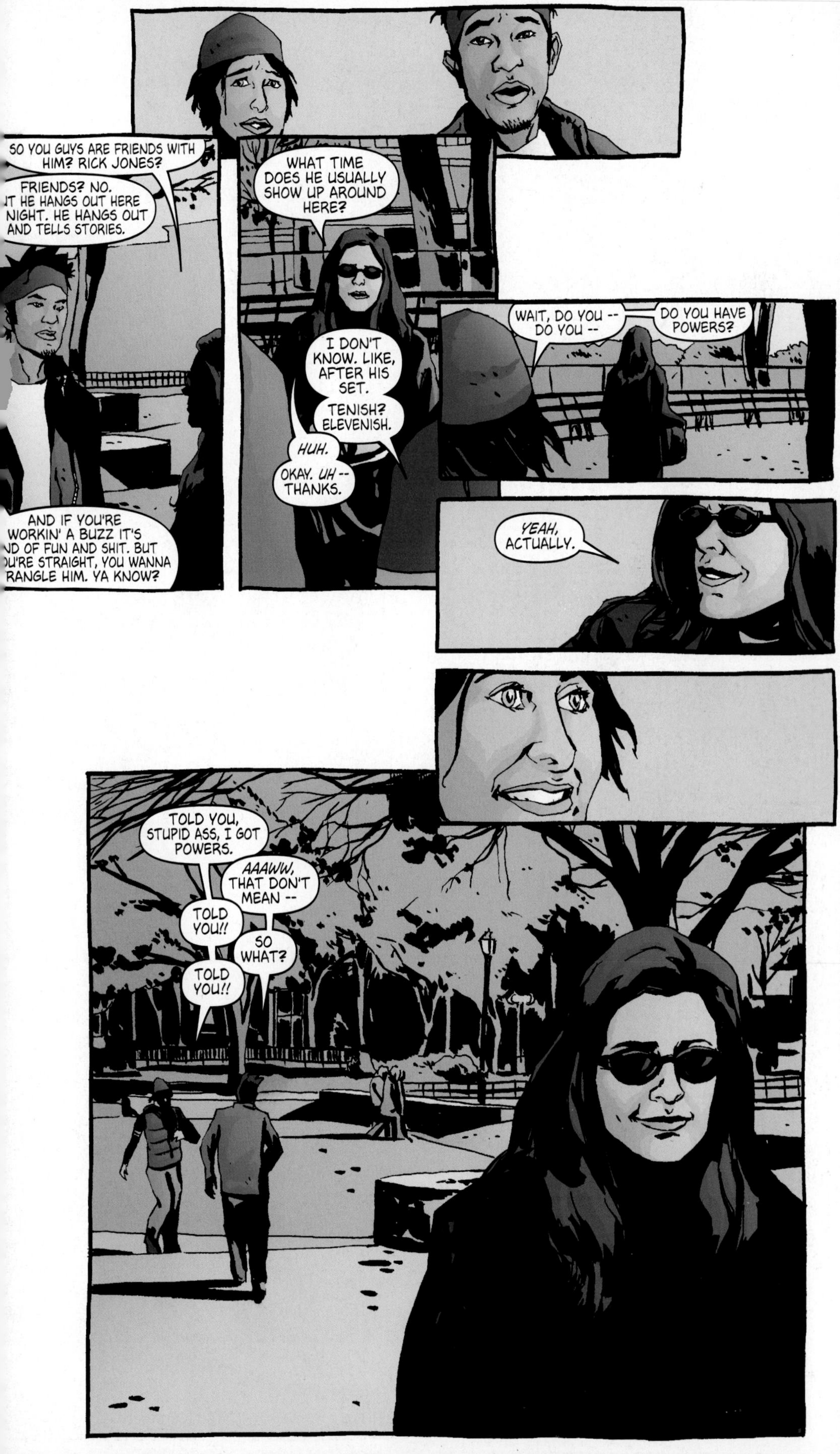

SO YOU GUYS ARE FRIENDS WITH HIM? RICK JONES?
FRIENDS? NO.
...T HE HANGS OUT HERE ...NIGHT. HE HANGS OUT AND TELLS STORIES.
AND IF YOU'RE WORKIN' A BUZZ IT'S ...ND OF FUN AND SHIT. BUT ...U'RE STRAIGHT, YOU WANNA ...RANGLE HIM. YA KNOW?
WHAT TIME DOES HE USUALLY SHOW UP AROUND HERE?
I DON'T KNOW. LIKE, AFTER HIS SET.
TENISH? ELEVENISH.
HUH.
OKAY. *UH* -- THANKS.
WAIT, DO YOU -- DO YOU --
DO YOU HAVE POWERS?
YEAH, ACTUALLY.
TOLD YOU, STUPID ASS, I GOT POWERS.
AAAWW, THAT DON'T MEAN --
TOLD YOU!!
SO WHAT?
TOLD YOU!!

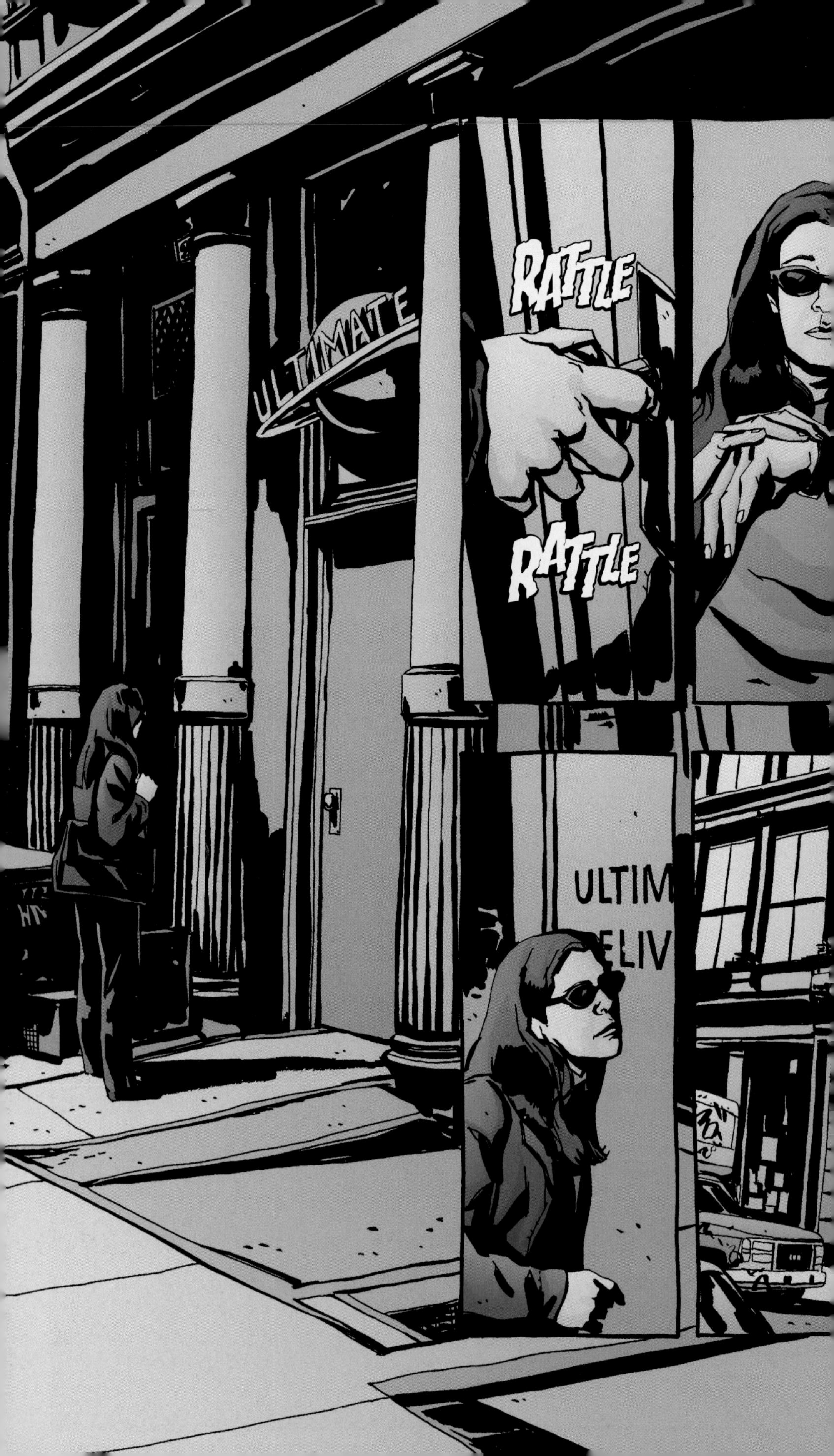
ULTIMATE
RATTLE
RATTLE
ULTIM
ELIV

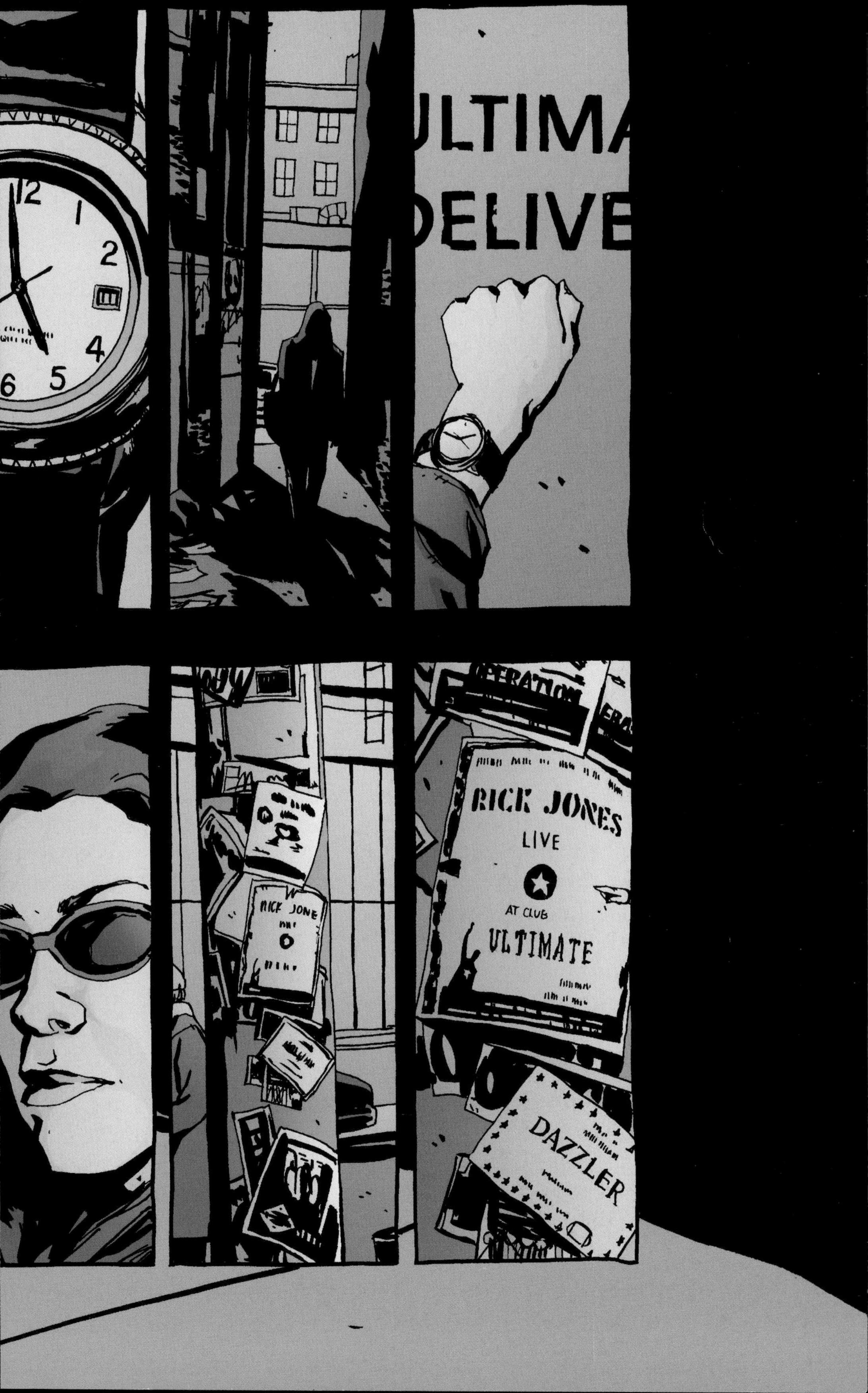

ULTIMA
DELIVE
OPERATION
RICK JONES
LIVE
AT CLUB
ULTIMATE
RICK JONE
DAZZLER

fact of the matter is that this day still haunts my dreams.

In the world of the super-powered, a lot of people like to pla "what if?" What if Bruce Banner hadn't tried to save me from the gamm bomb testing? What if I'd turned into a radiation mutation like The Hu instead of Banner? What if I'd just melted on the spot? You know, like person should when a bomb goes off in his face.

Well, let me tell you something, no one on this planet has playe "what if?" more than me. So believe me when I say, it does no good.

Do I blame myself? Do I think that I created The Hulk in the stupidi of my youth? Do I think that I ruined Bruce Banner's life? Do I think am responsible for whatever damage The Hulk causes? For a great, loi time I did. I did feel very responsible. And, yes, I will admit that part the reason why I hung around with The Hulk for so long was that I was ha hoping that, eventually, he would put me out of my misery. Accidental or otherwise.

I wrestled with these ideas for such a long, long time. And I do blan myself. Of course I do. So now you ask, how can I live with mysel Because Bruce Banner told me to.

It was Bruce who convinced me that, though I was in the wror place at the wrong time for about as wrong a reason as you cou possibly imagine, it still wasn't my fault that Bruce made th conscious decision to run out into the desert and try to save m Bruce knew what he was doing more than anyone alive cou have known. Bruce knew he was putting his life in jeopardy. Do yc know why he did it? Because he's a hero. That's what heroes do. The put you before themselves. If there's anything truly tragic about wh happened to Bruce, it's that the soul of a hero, a brilliant hero, is trappe inside the body of a monster-child.

And to look into Bruce Banner's face, even after all the sh he has been through, and to hear him say that he doesn't regr saving my life that first time, is to truly know what it takes to be hero. I think about this a lot, what it means to be a hero. I certain have been around enough of them.

I think you're born with it. You have to be. There's no oth explanation. You just have it or you do not. I have met a lot of colorf

HERE YOU GO.

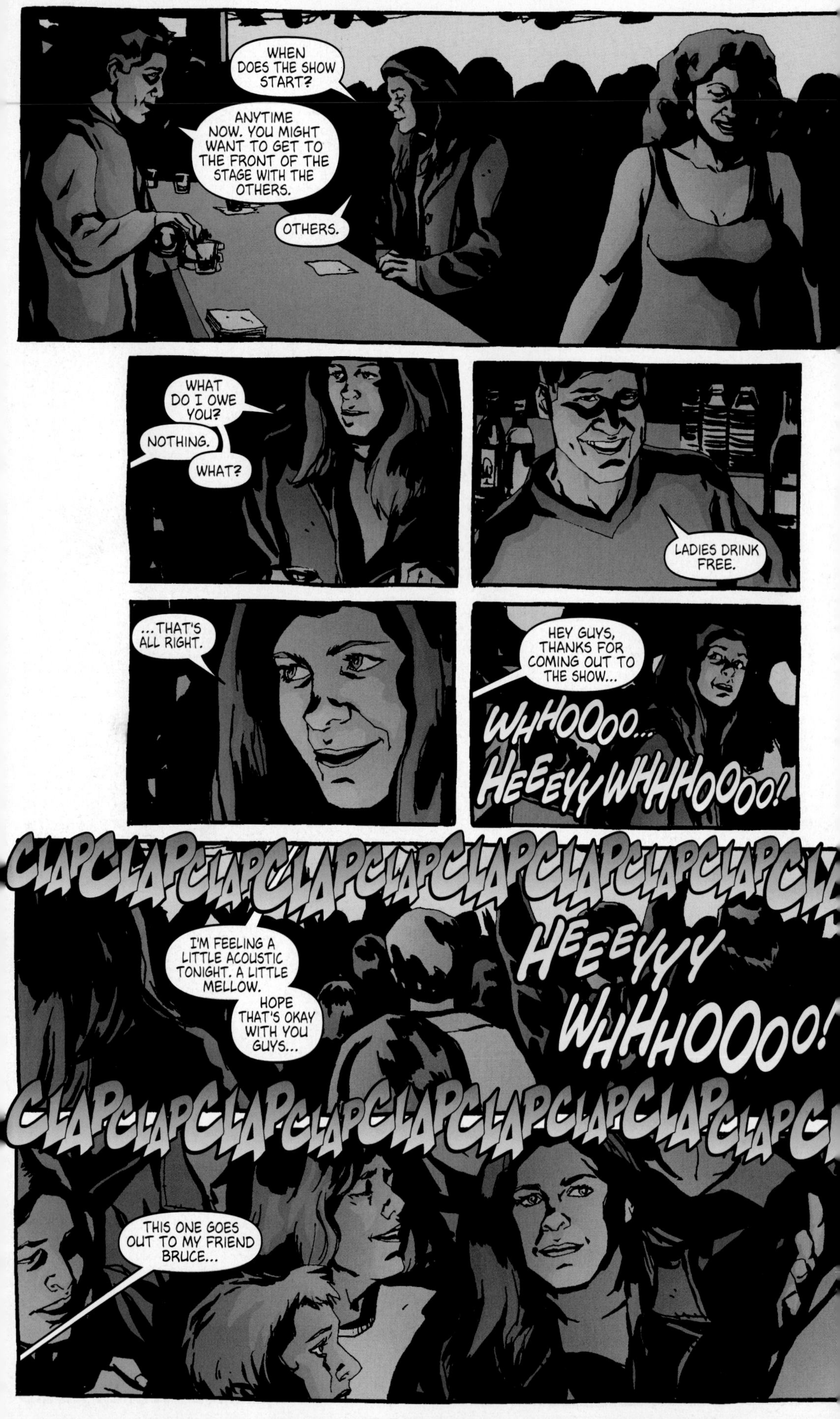
WHEN DOES THE SHOW START?
ANYTIME NOW. YOU MIGHT WANT TO GET TO THE FRONT OF THE STAGE WITH THE OTHERS.
OTHERS.
WHAT DO I OWE YOU?
NOTHING.
WHAT?
LADIES DRINK FREE.
...THAT'S ALL RIGHT.
HEY GUYS, THANKS FOR COMING OUT TO THE SHOW...
WHHOOOO... HEEEYY WHHHOOOOO!
CLAPCLAPCLAPCLAPCLAPCLAPCLAPCLAPCLAPCLAPCLAPCLA
HEEEYYY WHHHOOOOO!
I'M FEELING A LITTLE ACOUSTIC TONIGHT. A LITTLE MELLOW.
HOPE THAT'S OKAY WITH YOU GUYS...
CLAPCLAPCLAPCLAPCLAPCLAPCLAPCLAPCLAPCLAPCLAPCL
THIS ONE GOES OUT TO MY FRIEND BRUCE...

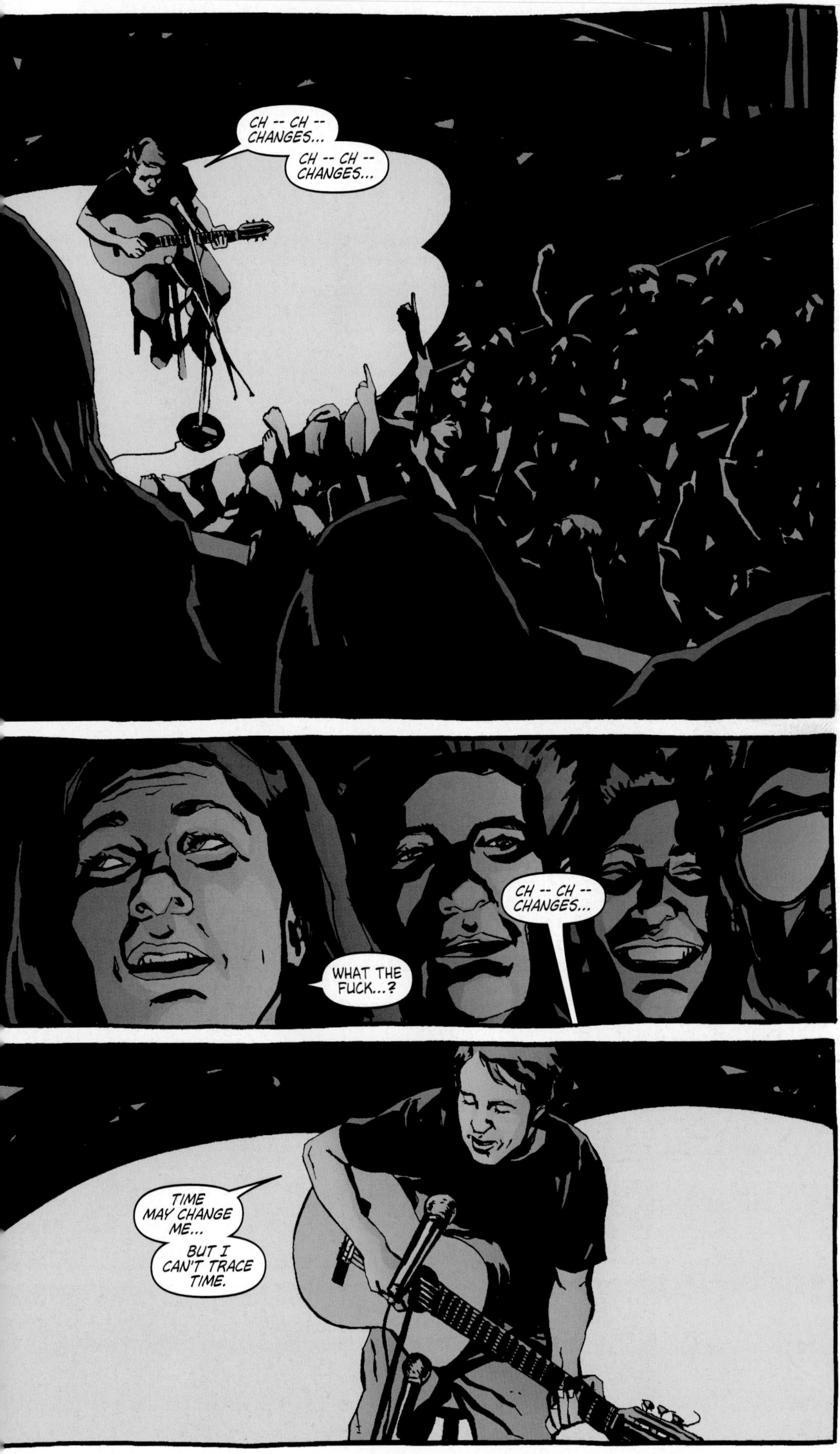
CH -- CH -- CHANGES...
CH -- CH -- CHANGES...
CH -- CH -- CHANGES...
WHAT THE FUCK...?
TIME MAY CHANGE ME...
BUT I CAN'T TRACE TIME.

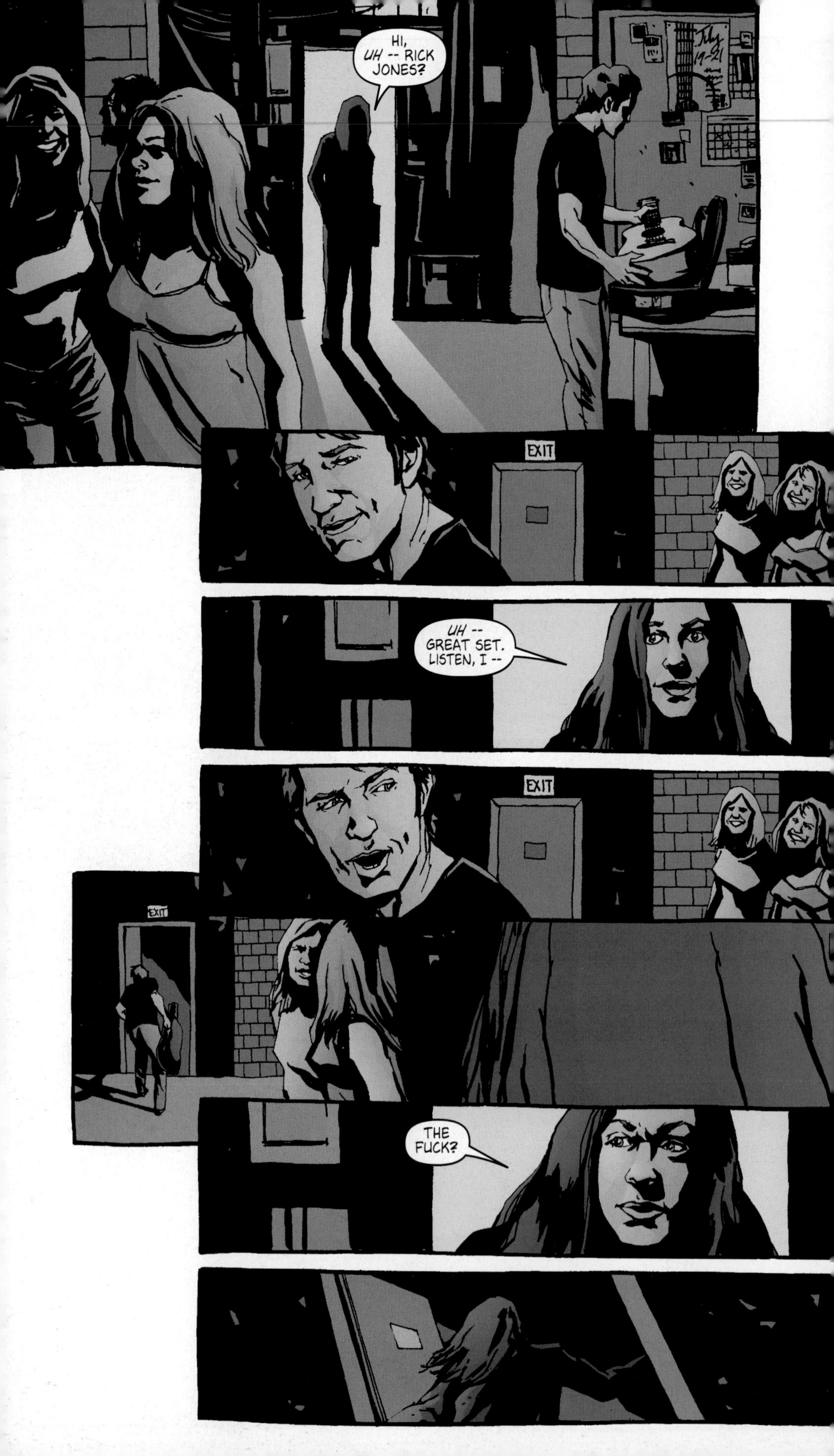
HI, UH -- RICK JONES?
July 19-21
EXIT
UH -- GREAT SET. LISTEN, I --
EXIT
EXIT
THE FUCK?

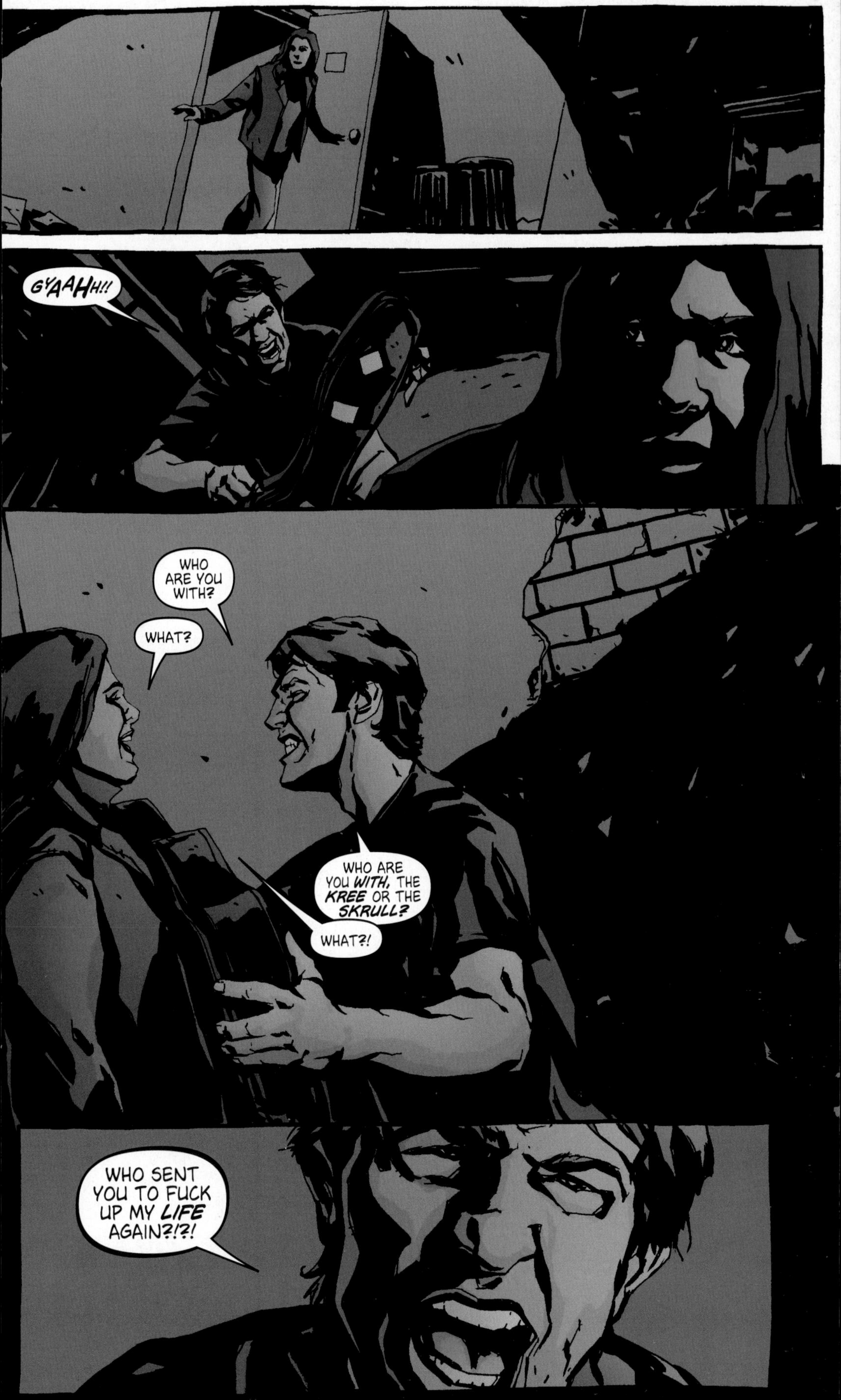
GYAAHH!!
WHO ARE YOU WITH?
WHAT?
WHO ARE YOU WITH, THE KREE OR THE SKRULL?
WHAT?!
WHO SENT YOU TO FUCK UP MY LIFE AGAIN?!?!

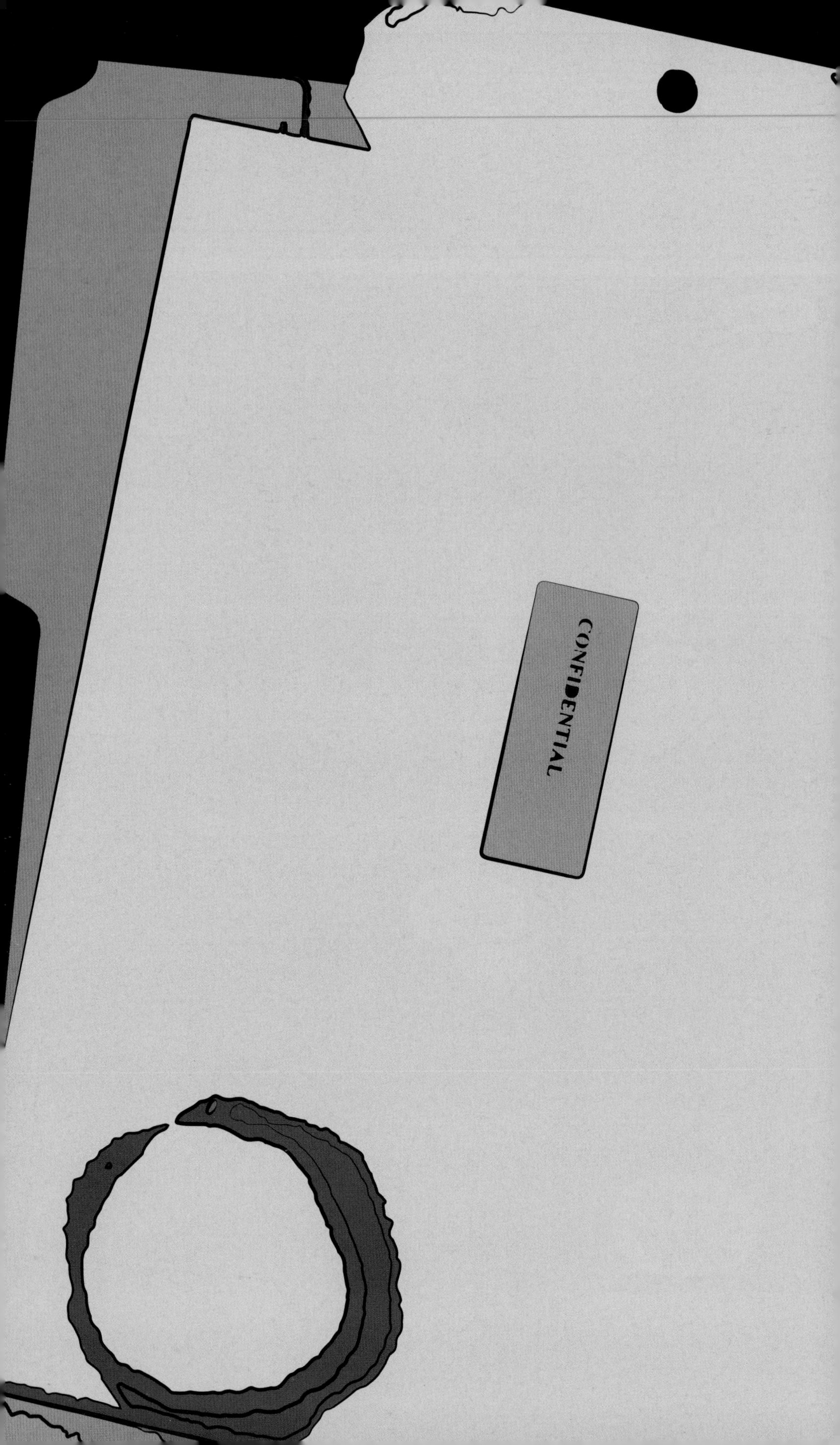
CONFIDENTIAL

ISSUE #8 B[redacted]

[redacted]

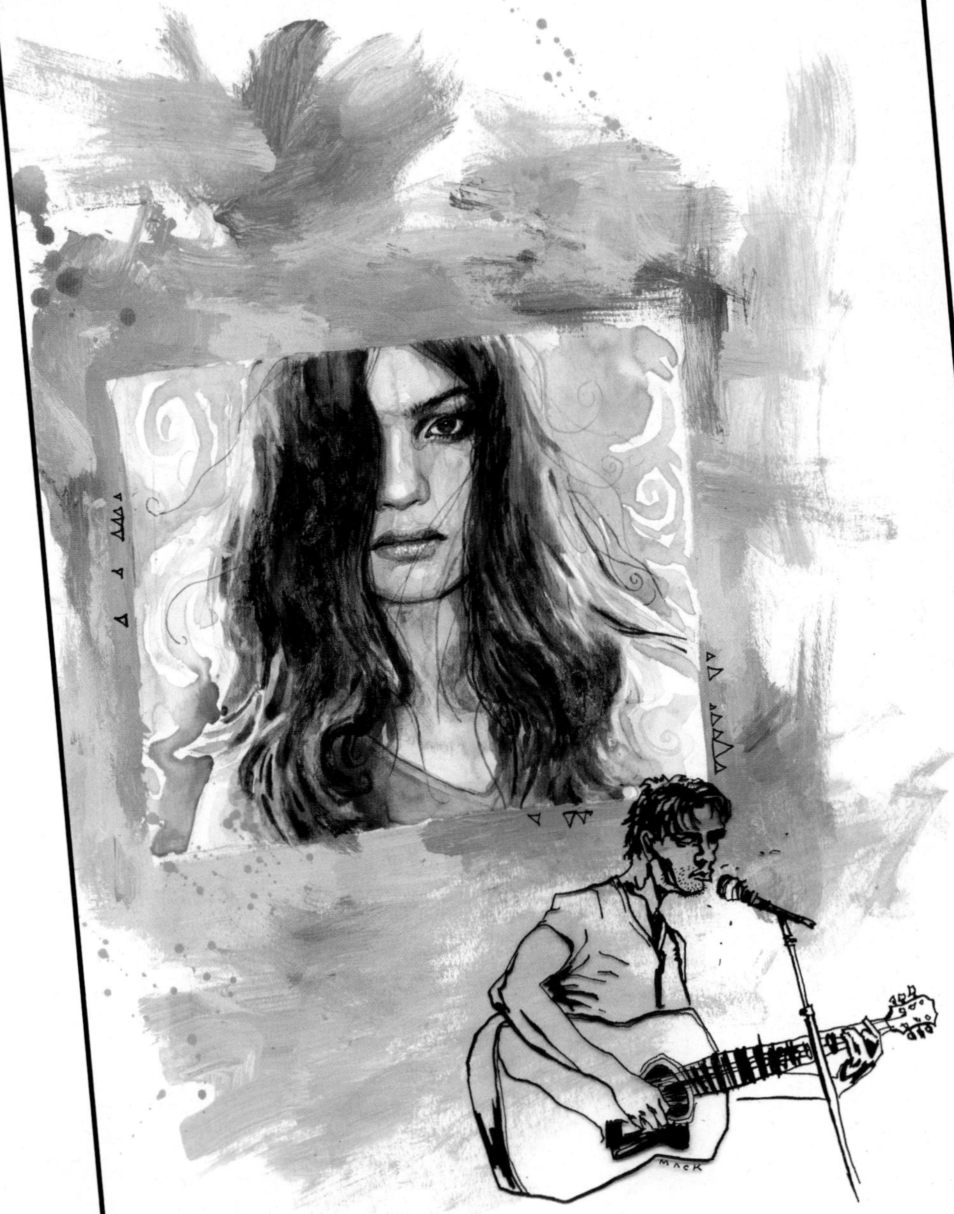

MACK

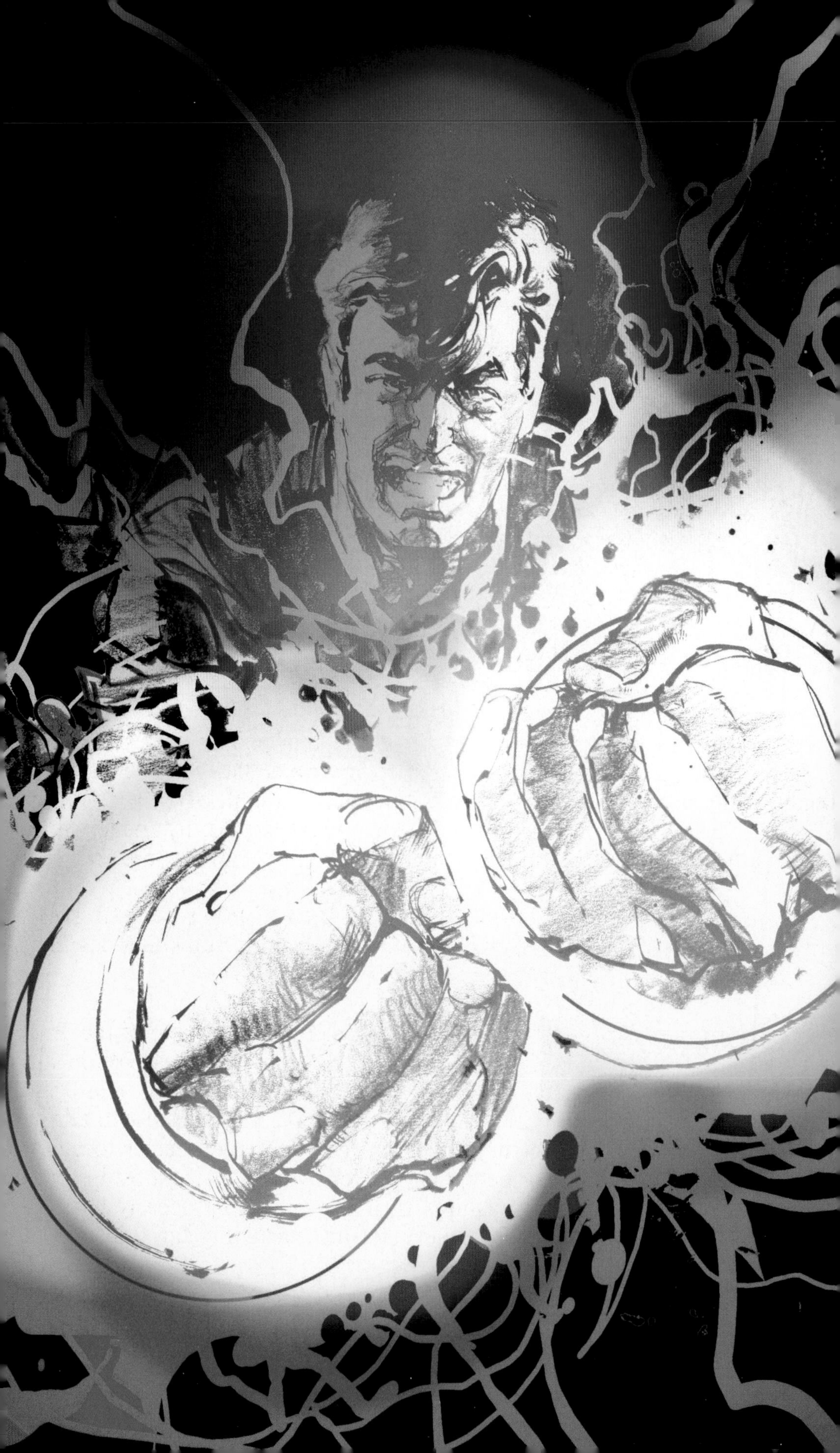

't know how much I'm going to feel like talking about my relationship
1 a guy you people know as Captain Marvel. Firstly, I don't really know
'm an experienced enough writer to adequately create the proper mind
ure that was my complicated life when I was sharing it with him; and
ondly, to be frank, it still hurts to talk about him — let alone write about
1.

Captain Mar-Vell of the Kree Empire, a stoic society if you want to use
 polite word, and I became connected to each other by a couple of
sterious metal arm bands I found accidentally.

And before I continue, I know what you're thinking: So Rick Jones is
·e when Bruce Banner becomes cursed as The Hulk, then he stumbles his
/ into a half-assed partnership with none other than Captain America,
. now he just happens to find a couple of arm bands that, when touched
ether, have the unexplainable ability over time and space to actually
tch one body from one dimension to another body in another dimension?

What do you want me to say? Yes. Yes! I keep Forrest Gump-ing
self into these bizarre and spectacular situations.

And no, I cannot explain it. There are guys I know, like Stephen
inge, who firmly believe with all their hearts that people's fates are pre-
tten and pre-determined. That there are some people who are literally
n to follow a certain path. A path of greatness, a path of destruction, a
h of mediocrity. A path. And no matter what you do, no matter how
ch you think you control your destiny, your destiny controls you.

To be honest, I don't know how I feel about it. I don't know if I am
owing a path or if I am subconsciously putting myself into situations like
se. I don't know. It hurts my head to think about it.

The only thing Mar-Vell and I had in common was the curse of the arm
ids. Mar-Vell was a true warrior. A war hero to his people with an
vavering commitment that his fight was worth fighting. It was this
ity of spirit that made the time I had to spend in a literal limbo, to allow
 corporeal form to be here in your existence, that much easier to bear.
of this writing I have never been married, or even in a relationship long
ugh to identify it as a relationship, but if I ever am, I sincerely hope it
ls up being half as rewarding as my partnership was with Mar-Vell.

It's too bad he wouldn't allow himself to become more of a public figure
e on Earth. He just wasn't that kind of hero. Because I think that Mar-
ll really would have sparked people's imagination and ideals in a positive
y. At his funeral I heard someone say that he was a heroes' hero. That

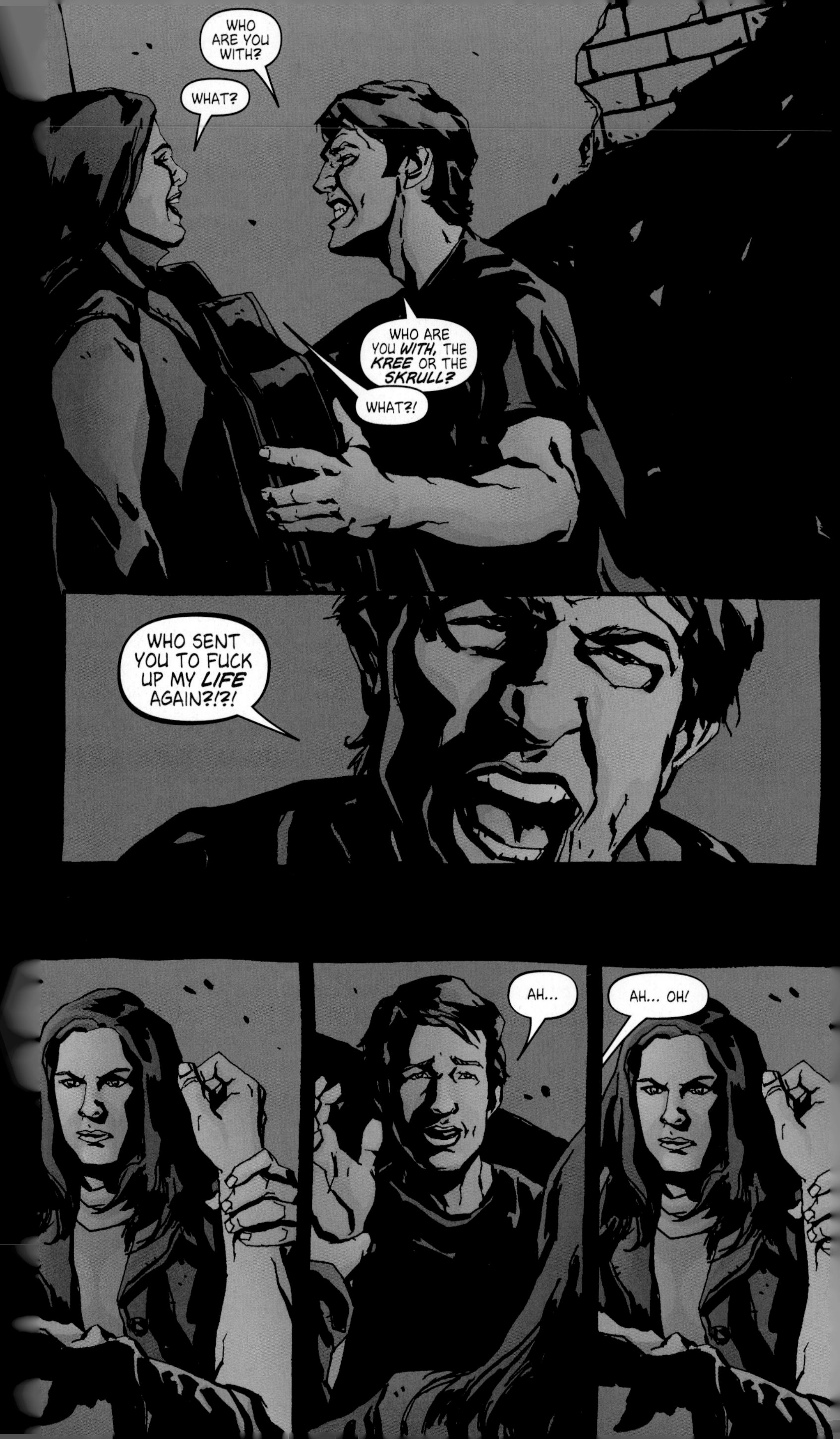
WHO ARE YOU WITH?
WHAT?
WHO ARE YOU WITH, THE KREE OR THE SKRULL?
WHAT?!
WHO SENT YOU TO FUCK UP MY LIFE AGAIN?!?!
AH...
AH... OH!

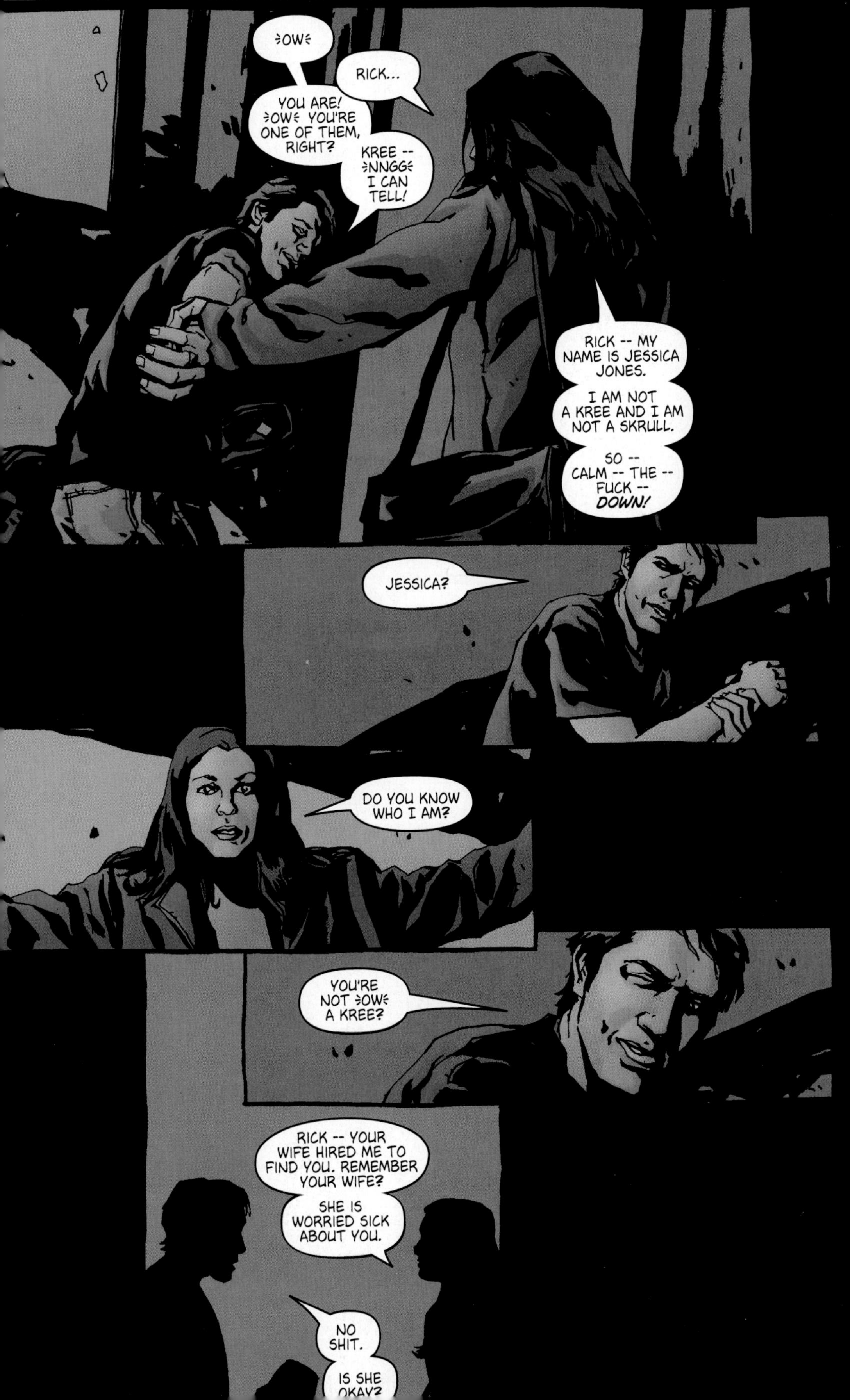

OW
RICK...
YOU ARE! OW YOU'RE ONE OF THEM, RIGHT?
KREE -- NNGG I CAN TELL!
RICK -- MY NAME IS JESSICA JONES.
I AM NOT A KREE AND I AM NOT A SKRULL.
SO -- CALM -- THE -- FUCK -- *DOWN!*
JESSICA?
DO YOU KNOW WHO I AM?
YOU'RE NOT OW A KREE?
RICK -- YOUR WIFE HIRED ME TO FIND YOU. REMEMBER YOUR WIFE?
SHE IS WORRIED SICK ABOUT YOU.
NO SHIT.

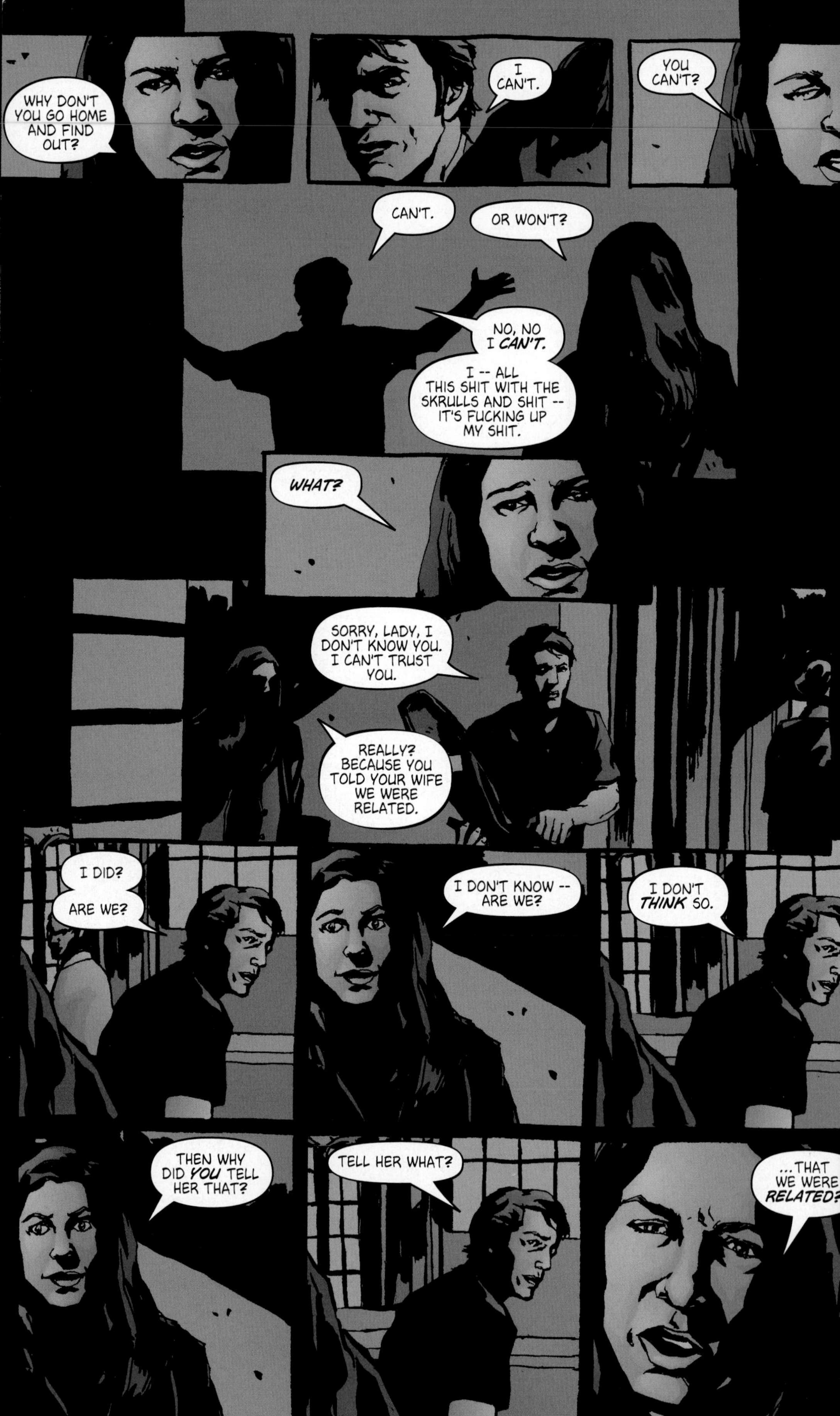
WHY DON'T YOU GO HOME AND FIND OUT?
I CAN'T.
YOU CAN'T?
CAN'T.
OR WON'T?
NO, NO I *CAN'T.*
I -- ALL THIS SHIT WITH THE SKRULLS AND SHIT -- IT'S FUCKING UP MY SHIT.
WHAT?
SORRY, LADY, I DON'T KNOW YOU. I CAN'T TRUST YOU.
REALLY? BECAUSE YOU TOLD YOUR WIFE WE WERE RELATED.
I DID?
ARE WE?
I DON'T KNOW -- ARE WE?
I DON'T *THINK* SO.
THEN WHY DID *YOU* TELL HER THAT?
TELL HER WHAT?
...THAT WE WERE *RELATED?*

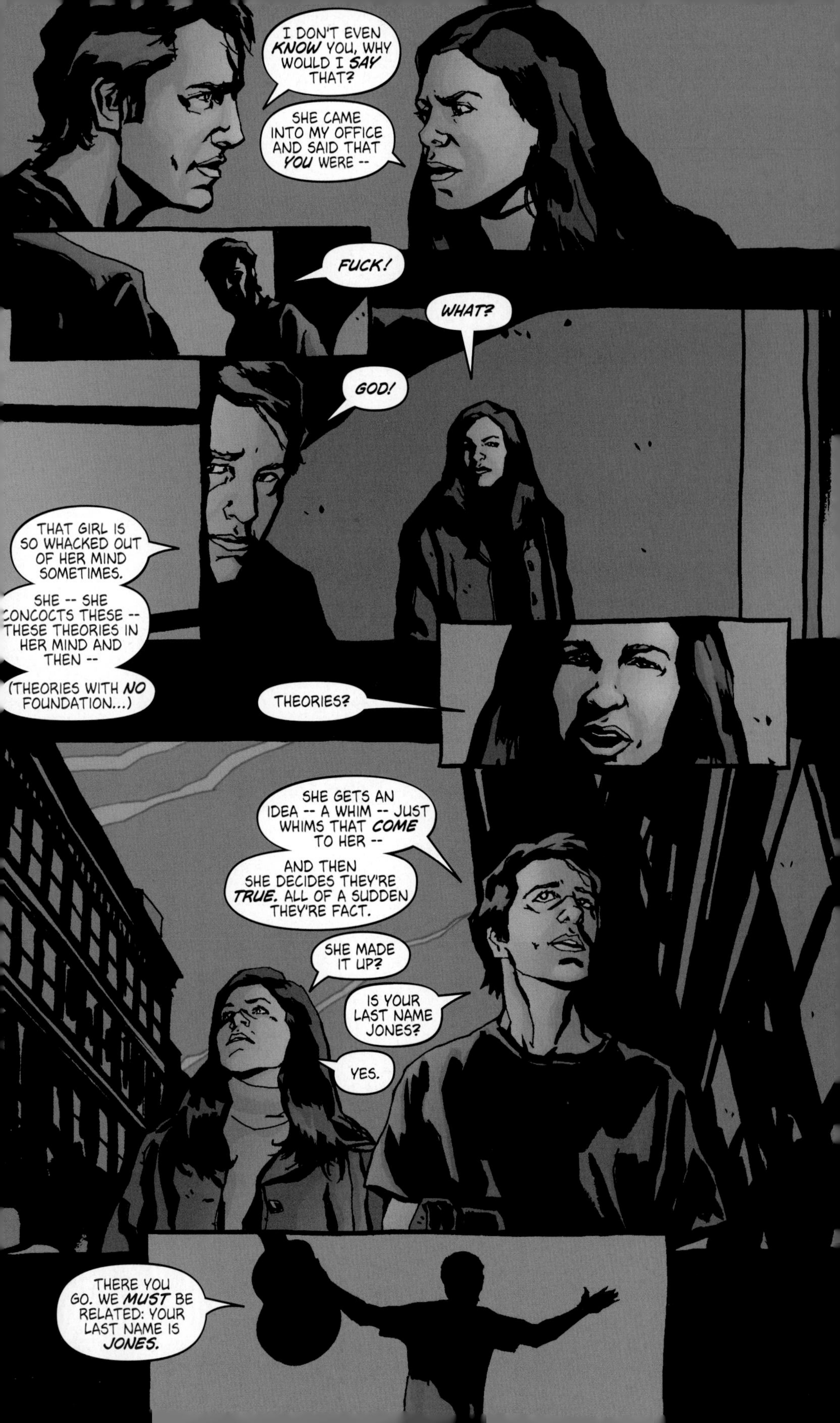
I DON'T EVEN KNOW YOU, WHY WOULD I SAY THAT?
SHE CAME INTO MY OFFICE AND SAID THAT YOU WERE --
FUCK!
WHAT?
GOD!
THAT GIRL IS SO WHACKED OUT OF HER MIND SOMETIMES.
SHE -- SHE CONCOCTS THESE -- THESE THEORIES IN HER MIND AND THEN --
(THEORIES WITH NO FOUNDATION...)
THEORIES?
SHE GETS AN IDEA -- A WHIM -- JUST WHIMS THAT COME TO HER --
AND THEN SHE DECIDES THEY'RE TRUE. ALL OF A SUDDEN THEY'RE FACT.
SHE MADE IT UP?
IS YOUR LAST NAME JONES?
YES.
THERE YOU GO. WE MUST BE RELATED: YOUR LAST NAME IS JONES.

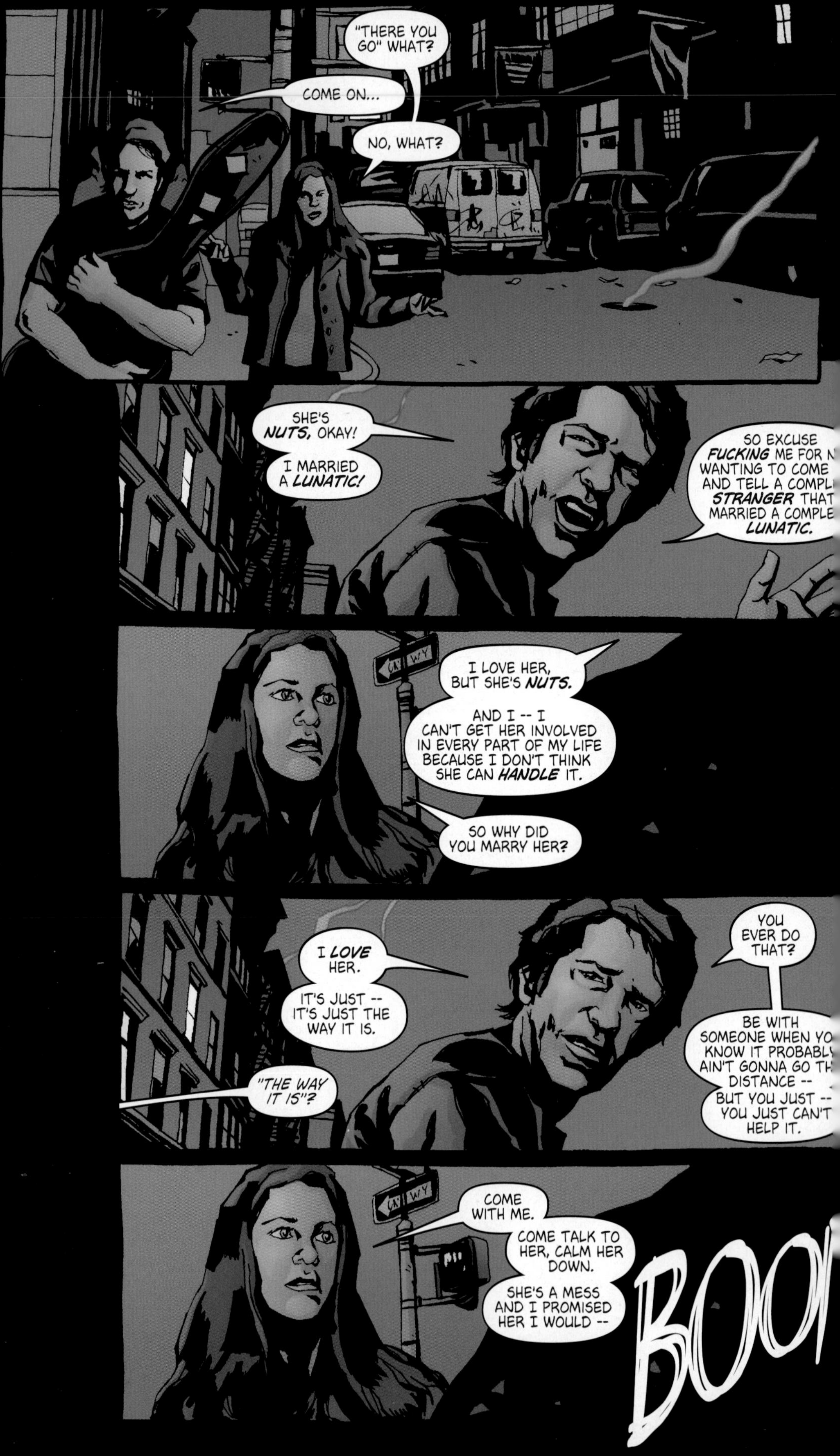
"THERE YOU GO" WHAT?
COME ON...
NO, WHAT?
SHE'S *NUTS,* OKAY!
I MARRIED A *LUNATIC!*
SO EXCUSE *FUCKING* ME FOR N WANTING TO COME AND TELL A COMPL *STRANGER* THAT MARRIED A COMPLE *LUNATIC.*
I LOVE HER, BUT SHE'S *NUTS.*
AND I -- I CAN'T GET HER INVOLVED IN EVERY PART OF MY LIFE BECAUSE I DON'T THINK SHE CAN *HANDLE* IT.
SO WHY DID YOU MARRY HER?
I *LOVE* HER.
IT'S JUST -- IT'S JUST THE WAY IT IS.
"THE WAY IT IS"?
YOU EVER DO THAT?
BE WITH SOMEONE WHEN YO KNOW IT PROBABL AIN'T GONNA GO TH DISTANCE -- BUT YOU JUST -- YOU JUST CAN'T HELP IT.
COME WITH ME.
COME TALK TO HER, CALM HER DOWN.
SHE'S A MESS AND I PROMISED HER I WOULD --
BOO

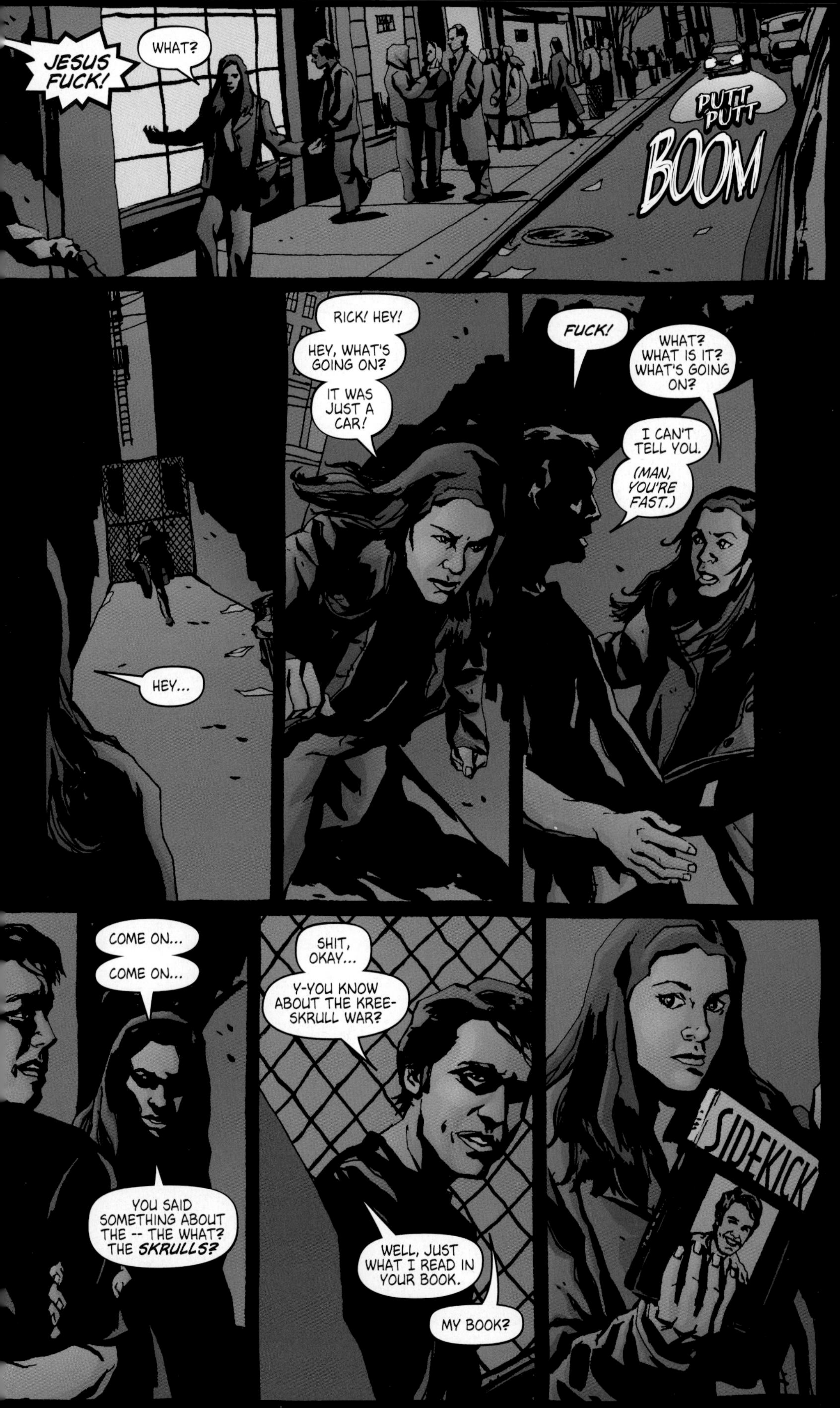
JESUS FUCK!
WHAT?
PUTT PUTT
BOOM
HEY...
RICK! HEY!
HEY, WHAT'S GOING ON?
IT WAS JUST A CAR!
FUCK!
WHAT? WHAT IS IT? WHAT'S GOING ON?
I CAN'T TELL YOU.
(MAN, YOU'RE FAST.)
COME ON...
COME ON...
YOU SAID SOMETHING ABOUT THE -- THE WHAT? THE SKRULLS?
SHIT, OKAY...
Y-YOU KNOW ABOUT THE KREE-SKRULL WAR?
WELL, JUST WHAT I READ IN YOUR BOOK.
MY BOOK?
SIDEKICK

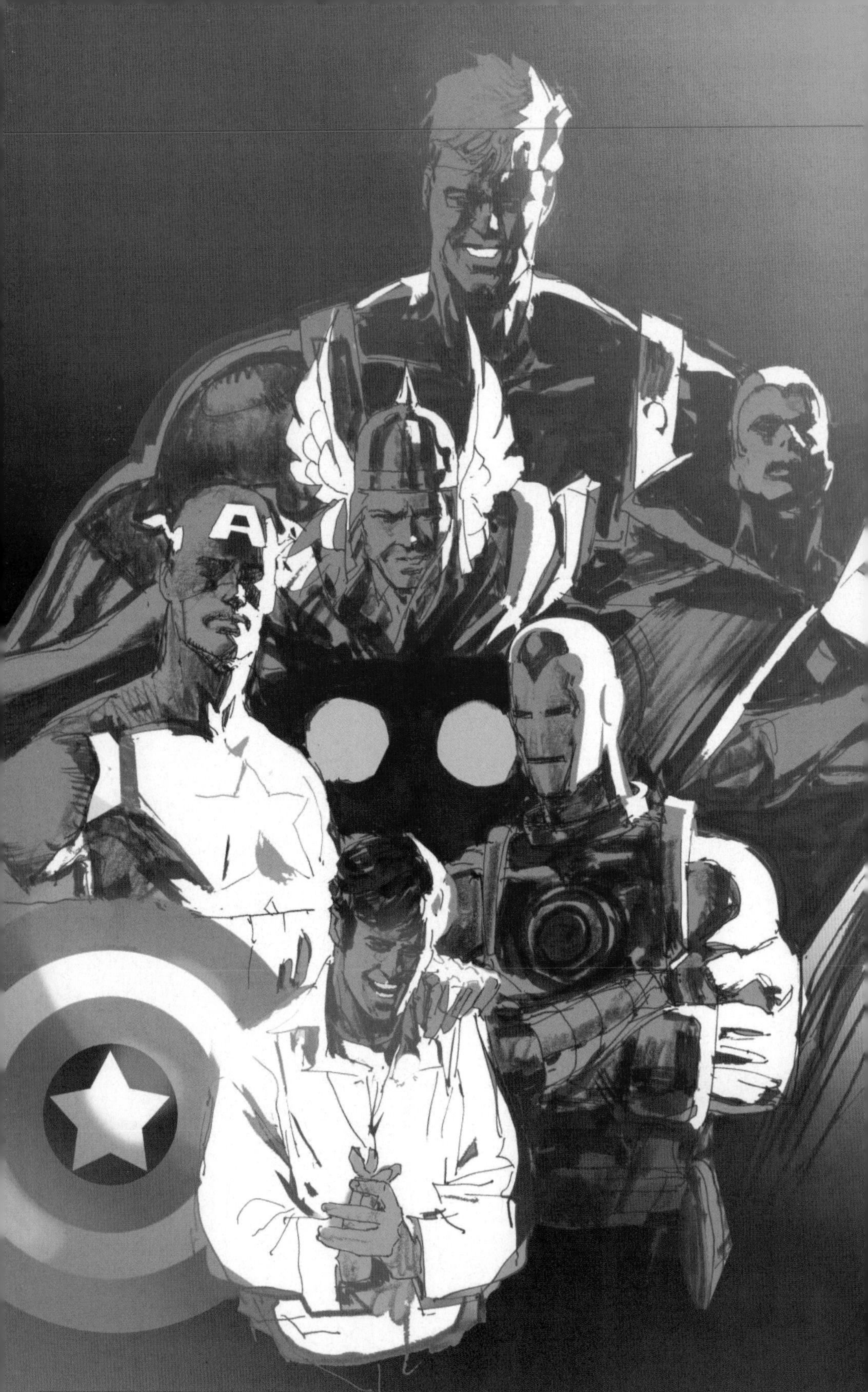

Yes, that's me actually winning the day at the end of the Kree-Skrull War. It didn't happe
often, so indulge me the cheesy photo.

Opposite: The only decent photo I ever took of a spacecraft, and it isn't even a decent pho

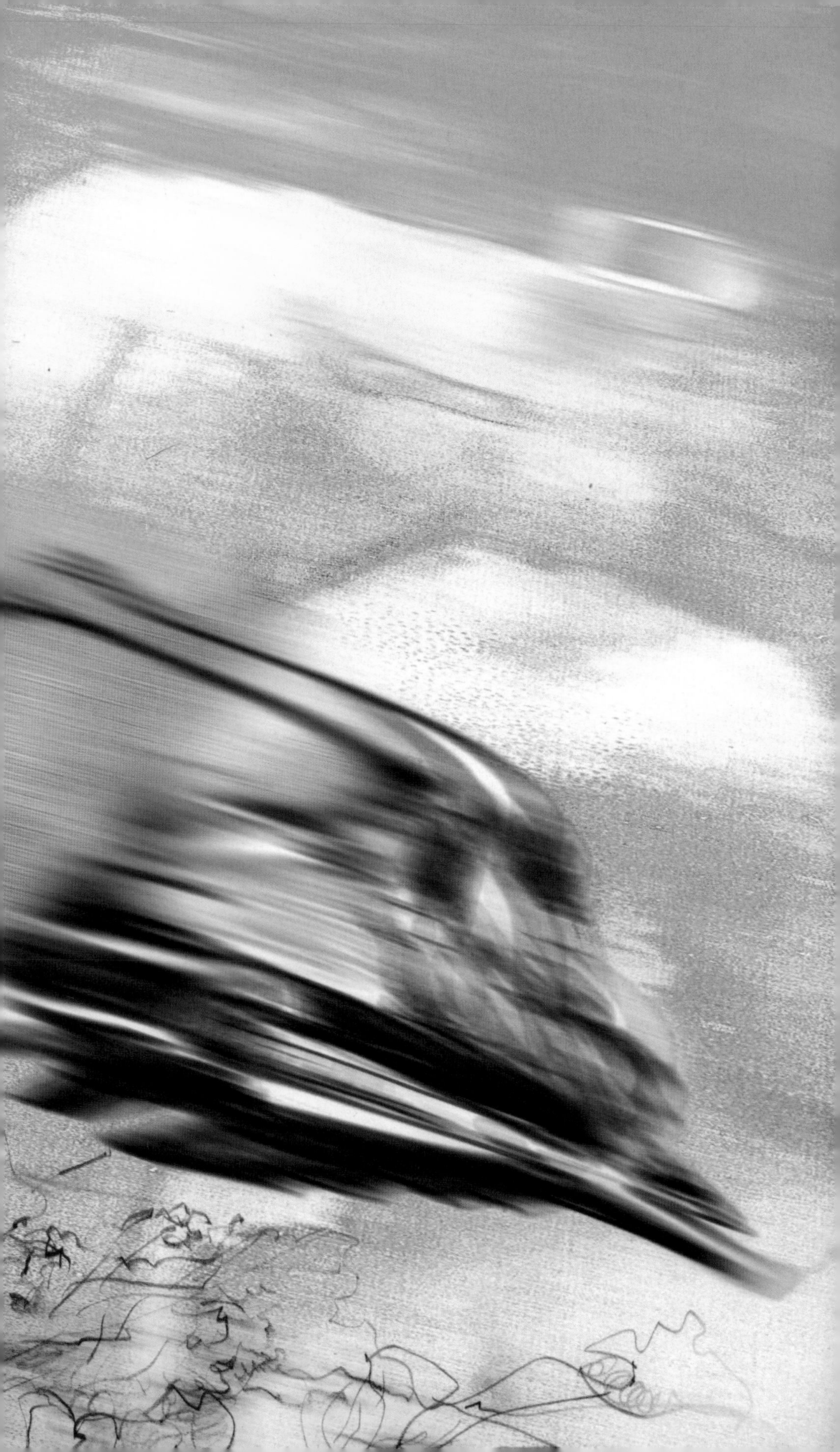

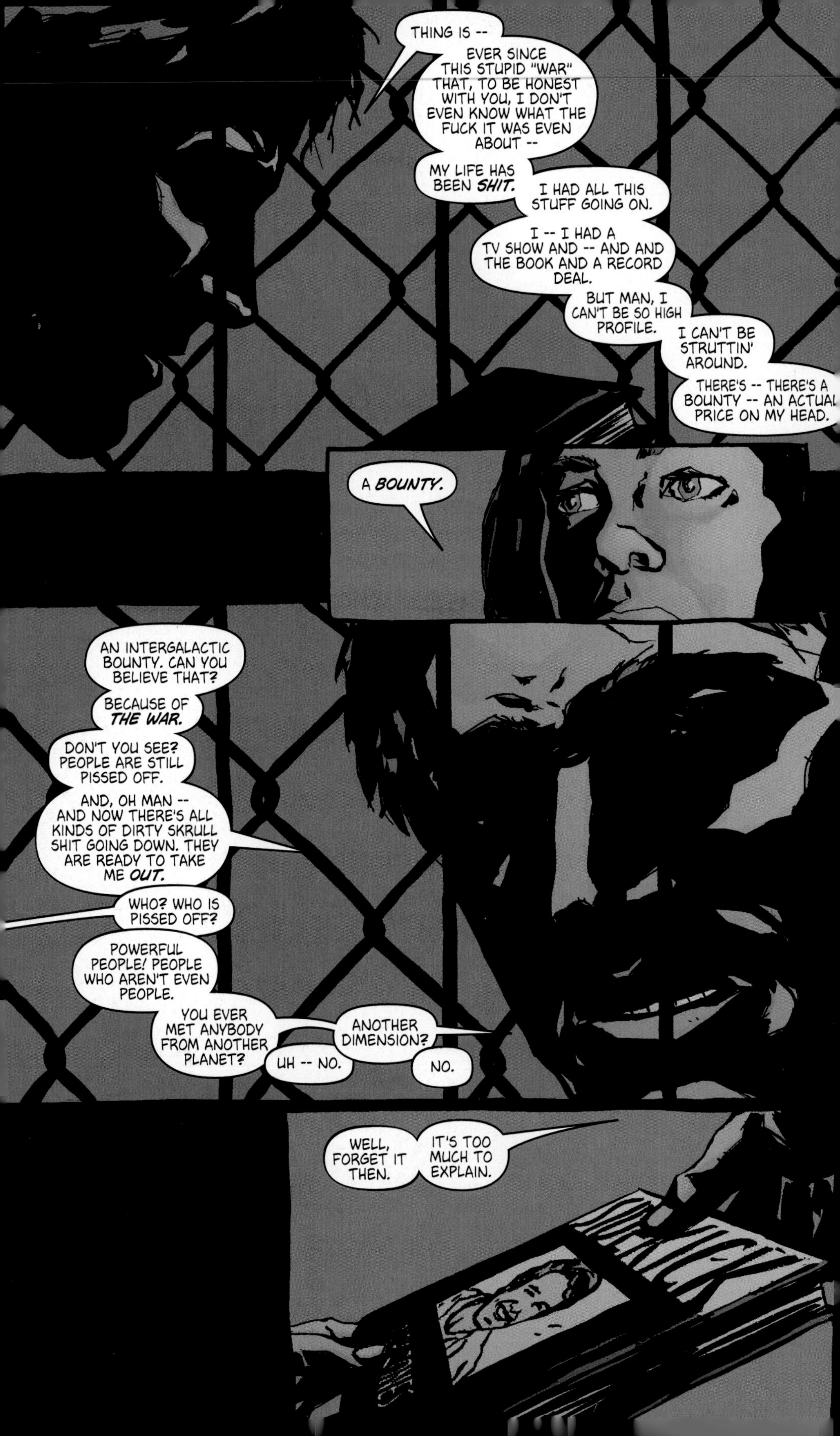
THING IS --
EVER SINCE THIS STUPID "WAR" THAT, TO BE HONEST WITH YOU, I DON'T EVEN KNOW WHAT THE FUCK IT WAS EVEN ABOUT --
MY LIFE HAS BEEN SHIT.
I HAD ALL THIS STUFF GOING ON.
I -- I HAD A TV SHOW AND -- AND AND THE BOOK AND A RECORD DEAL.
BUT MAN, I CAN'T BE SO HIGH PROFILE.
I CAN'T BE STRUTTIN' AROUND.
THERE'S -- THERE'S A BOUNTY -- AN ACTUAL PRICE ON MY HEAD.
A BOUNTY.
AN INTERGALACTIC BOUNTY. CAN YOU BELIEVE THAT?
BECAUSE OF THE WAR.
DON'T YOU SEE? PEOPLE ARE STILL PISSED OFF.
AND, OH MAN -- AND NOW THERE'S ALL KINDS OF DIRTY SKRULL SHIT GOING DOWN. THEY ARE READY TO TAKE ME OUT.
WHO? WHO IS PISSED OFF?
POWERFUL PEOPLE! PEOPLE WHO AREN'T EVEN PEOPLE.
YOU EVER MET ANYBODY FROM ANOTHER PLANET?
UH -- NO.
ANOTHER DIMENSION?
NO.
WELL, FORGET IT THEN.
IT'S TOO MUCH TO EXPLAIN.

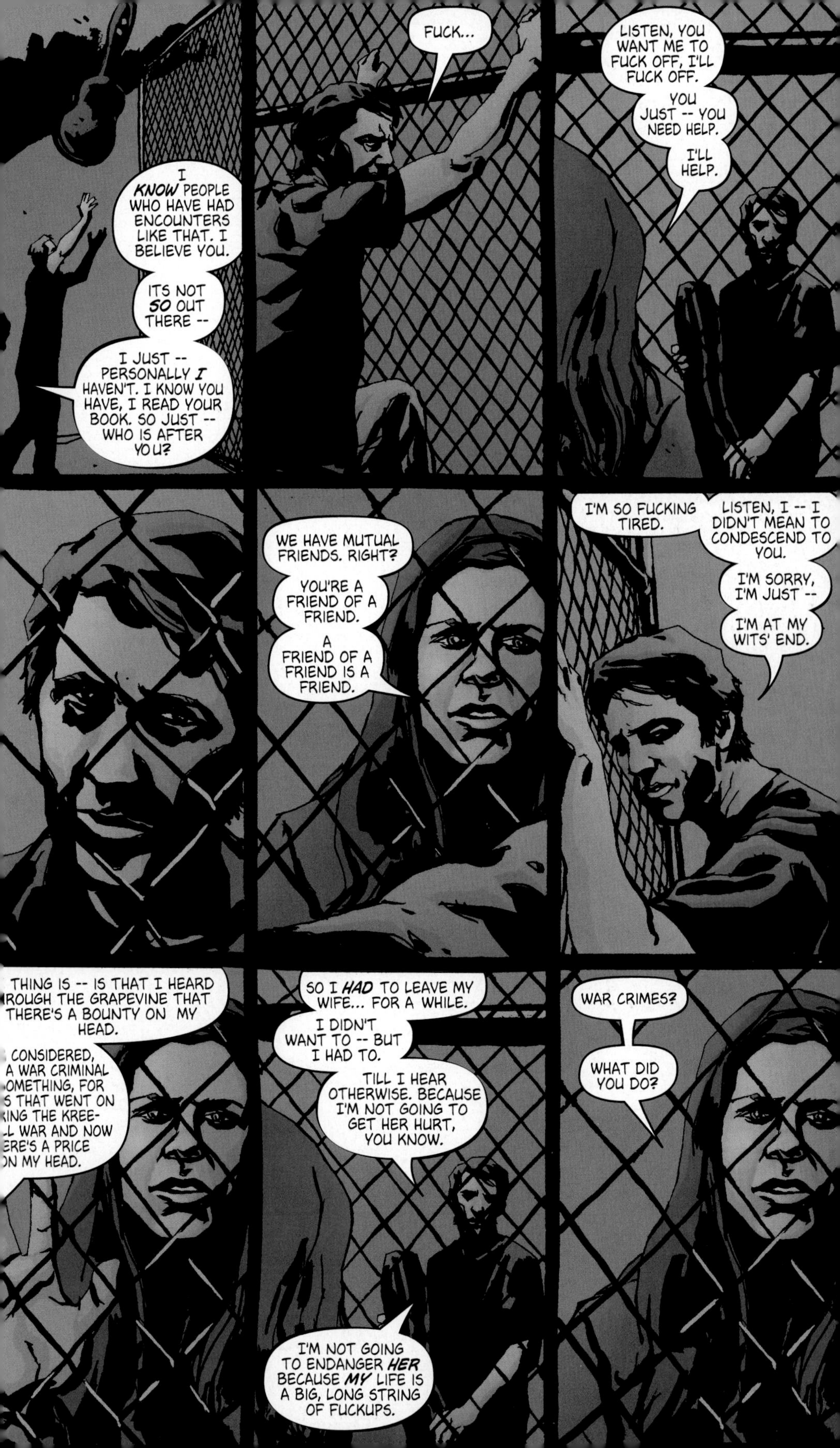
I KNOW PEOPLE WHO HAVE HAD ENCOUNTERS LIKE THAT. I BELIEVE YOU.
ITS NOT SO OUT THERE --
I JUST -- PERSONALLY I HAVEN'T. I KNOW YOU HAVE, I READ YOUR BOOK. SO JUST -- WHO IS AFTER YOU?
FUCK...
LISTEN, YOU WANT ME TO FUCK OFF, I'LL FUCK OFF.
YOU JUST -- YOU NEED HELP.
I'LL HELP.
WE HAVE MUTUAL FRIENDS. RIGHT?
YOU'RE A FRIEND OF A FRIEND.
A FRIEND OF A FRIEND IS A FRIEND.
I'M SO FUCKING TIRED.
LISTEN, I -- I DIDN'T MEAN TO CONDESCEND TO YOU.
I'M SORRY, I'M JUST --
I'M AT MY WITS' END.
THING IS -- IS THAT I HEARD ROUGH THE GRAPEVINE THAT THERE'S A BOUNTY ON MY HEAD.
CONSIDERED, A WAR CRIMINAL OMETHING, FOR S THAT WENT ON ING THE KREE- L WAR AND NOW ERE'S A PRICE ON MY HEAD.
SO I HAD TO LEAVE MY WIFE... FOR A WHILE.
I DIDN'T WANT TO -- BUT I HAD TO.
TILL I HEAR OTHERWISE. BECAUSE I'M NOT GOING TO GET HER HURT, YOU KNOW.
I'M NOT GOING TO ENDANGER HER BECAUSE MY LIFE IS A BIG, LONG STRING OF FUCKUPS.
WAR CRIMES?
WHAT DID YOU DO?

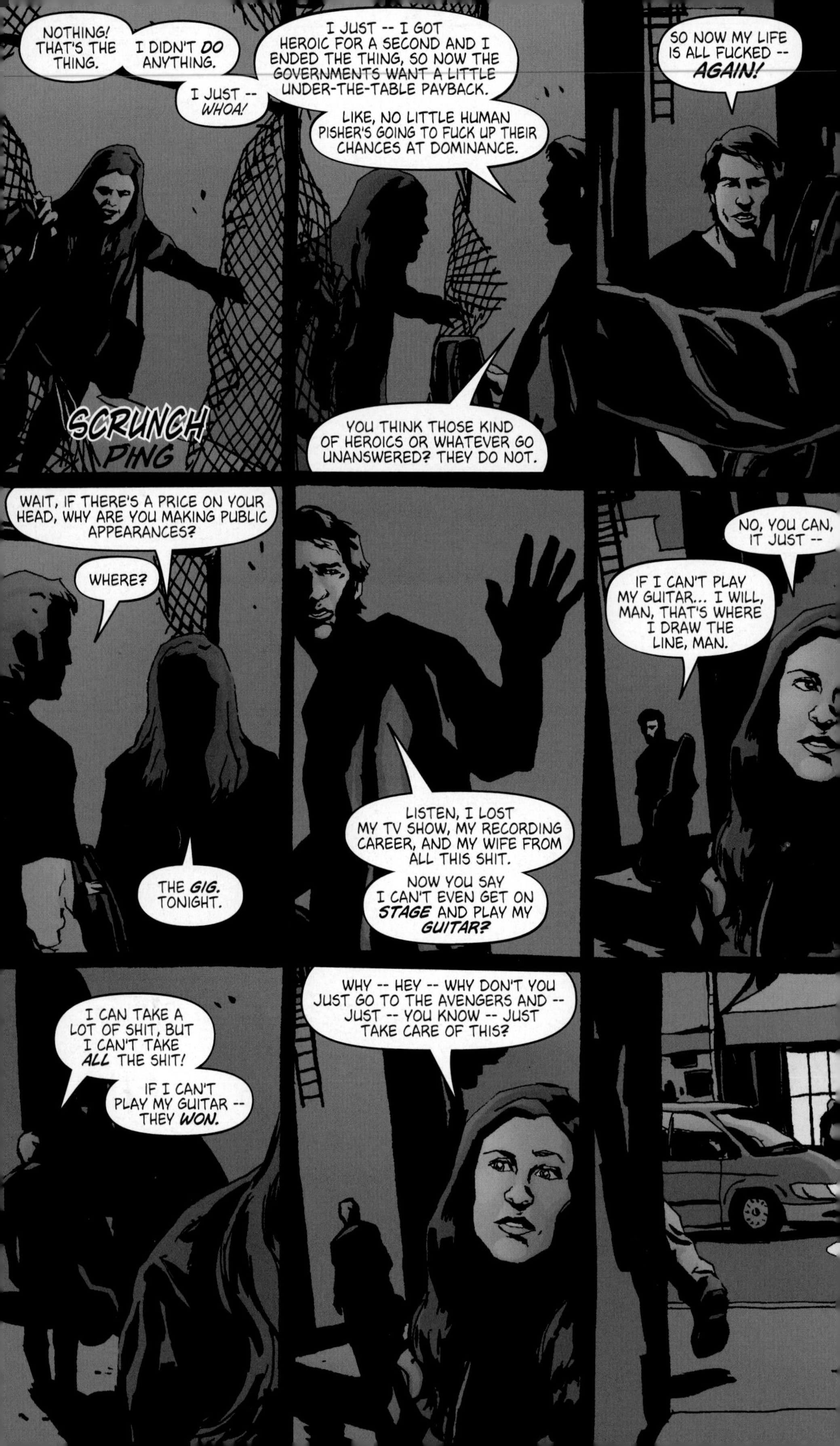
NOTHING! THAT'S THE THING.
I DIDN'T *DO* ANYTHING.
I JUST -- *WHOA!*
SCRUNCH
PING
I JUST -- I GOT HEROIC FOR A SECOND AND I ENDED THE THING, SO NOW THE GOVERNMENTS WANT A LITTLE UNDER-THE-TABLE PAYBACK.
LIKE, NO LITTLE HUMAN PISHER'S GOING TO FUCK UP THEIR CHANCES AT DOMINANCE.
YOU THINK THOSE KIND OF HEROICS OR WHATEVER GO UNANSWERED? THEY DO NOT.
SO NOW MY LIFE IS ALL FUCKED -- ***AGAIN!***
WAIT, IF THERE'S A PRICE ON YOUR HEAD, WHY ARE YOU MAKING PUBLIC APPEARANCES?
WHERE?
THE *GIG.* TONIGHT.
LISTEN, I LOST MY TV SHOW, MY RECORDING CAREER, AND MY WIFE FROM ALL THIS SHIT.
NOW YOU SAY I CAN'T EVEN GET ON ***STAGE*** AND PLAY MY ***GUITAR?***
NO, YOU CAN, IT JUST --
IF I CAN'T PLAY MY GUITAR... I WILL, MAN, THAT'S WHERE I DRAW THE LINE, MAN.
I CAN TAKE A LOT OF SHIT, BUT I CAN'T TAKE ***ALL*** THE SHIT!
IF I CAN'T PLAY MY GUITAR -- THEY ***WON.***
WHY -- HEY -- WHY DON'T YOU JUST GO TO THE AVENGERS AND -- JUST -- YOU KNOW -- JUST TAKE CARE OF THIS?

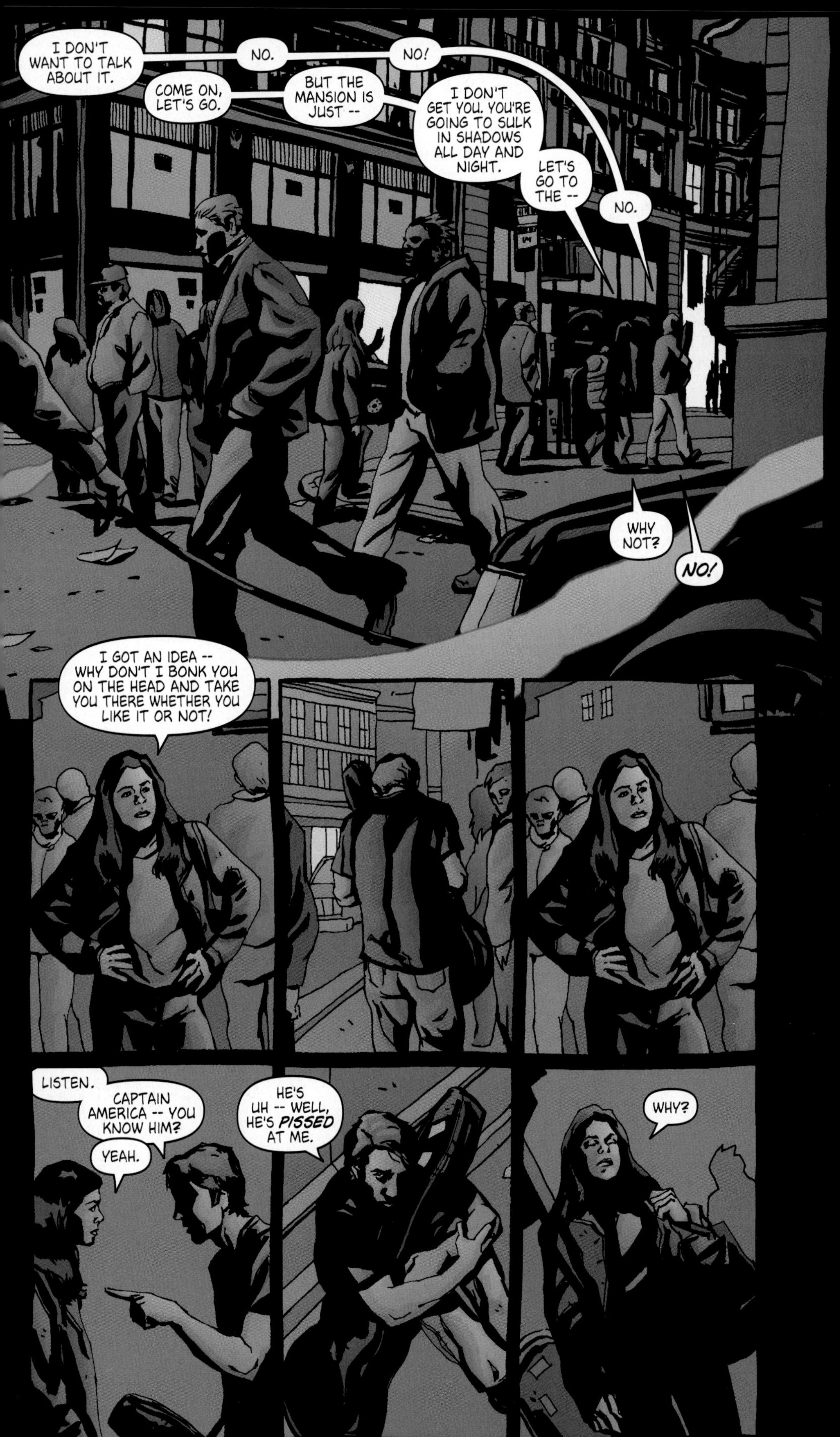
I DON'T WANT TO TALK ABOUT IT.
NO.
NO!
COME ON, LET'S GO.
BUT THE MANSION IS JUST --
I DON'T GET YOU. YOU'RE GOING TO SULK IN SHADOWS ALL DAY AND NIGHT.
LET'S GO TO THE --
NO.
WHY NOT?
NO!
I GOT AN IDEA -- WHY DON'T I BONK YOU ON THE HEAD AND TAKE YOU THERE WHETHER YOU LIKE IT OR NOT!
LISTEN.
CAPTAIN AMERICA -- YOU KNOW HIM?
YEAH.
HE'S UH -- WELL, HE'S PISSED AT ME.
WHY?

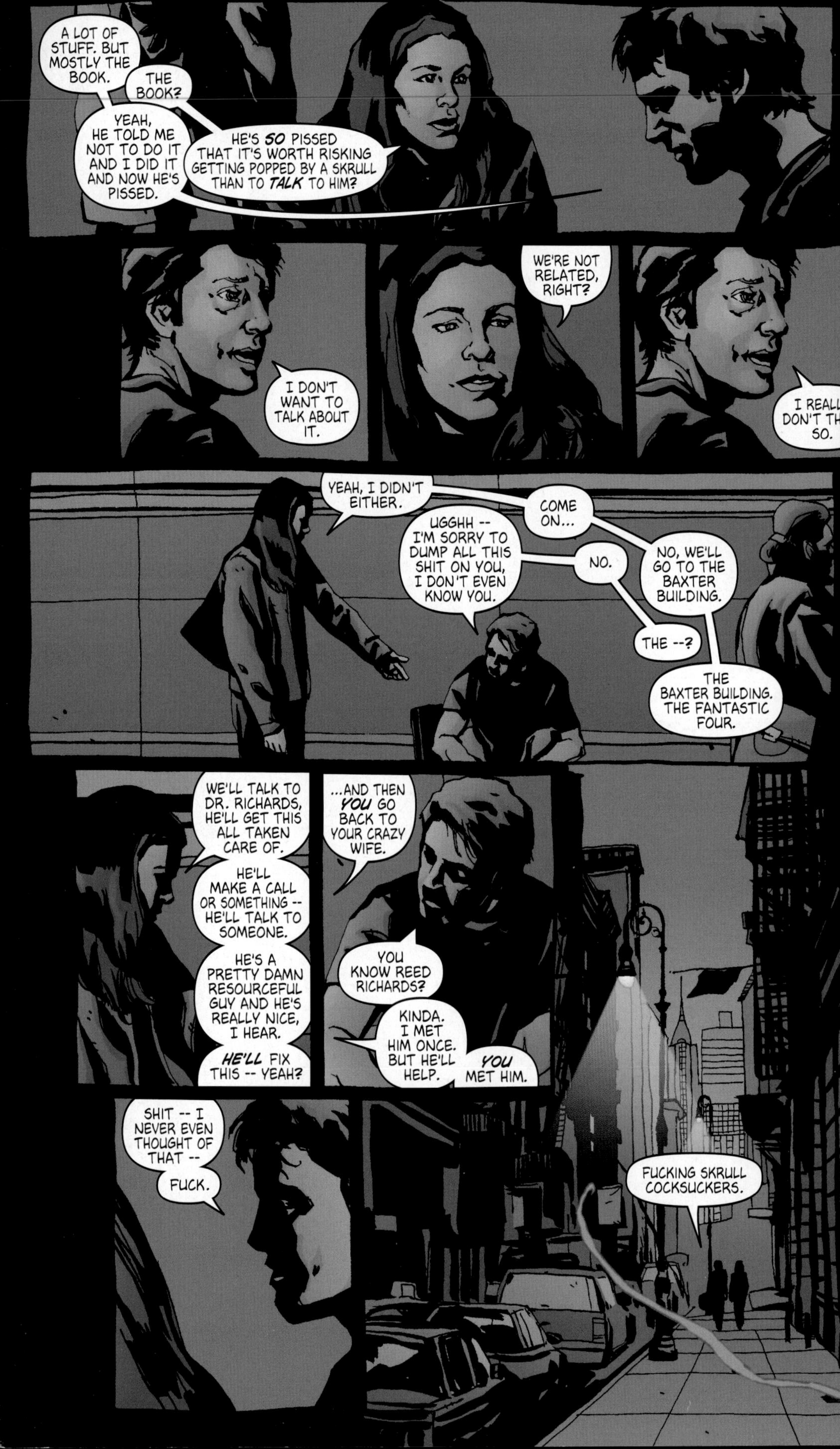
A LOT OF STUFF. BUT MOSTLY THE BOOK.
THE BOOK?
YEAH, HE TOLD ME NOT TO DO IT AND I DID IT AND NOW HE'S PISSED.
HE'S SO PISSED THAT IT'S WORTH RISKING GETTING POPPED BY A SKRULL THAN TO TALK TO HIM?
I DON'T WANT TO TALK ABOUT IT.
WE'RE NOT RELATED, RIGHT?
I REALL DON'T TH SO.
YEAH, I DIDN'T EITHER.
UGGHH -- I'M SORRY TO DUMP ALL THIS SHIT ON YOU, I DON'T EVEN KNOW YOU.
COME ON...
NO.
NO, WE'LL GO TO THE BAXTER BUILDING.
THE --?
THE BAXTER BUILDING. THE FANTASTIC FOUR.
WE'LL TALK TO DR. RICHARDS, HE'LL GET THIS ALL TAKEN CARE OF.
HE'LL MAKE A CALL OR SOMETHING -- HE'LL TALK TO SOMEONE.
HE'S A PRETTY DAMN RESOURCEFUL GUY AND HE'S REALLY NICE, I HEAR.
HE'LL FIX THIS -- YEAH?
...AND THEN YOU GO BACK TO YOUR CRAZY WIFE.
YOU KNOW REED RICHARDS?
KINDA. I MET HIM ONCE. BUT HE'LL HELP.
YOU MET HIM.
SHIT -- I NEVER EVEN THOUGHT OF THAT --
FUCK.
FUCKING SKRULL COCKSUCKERS.

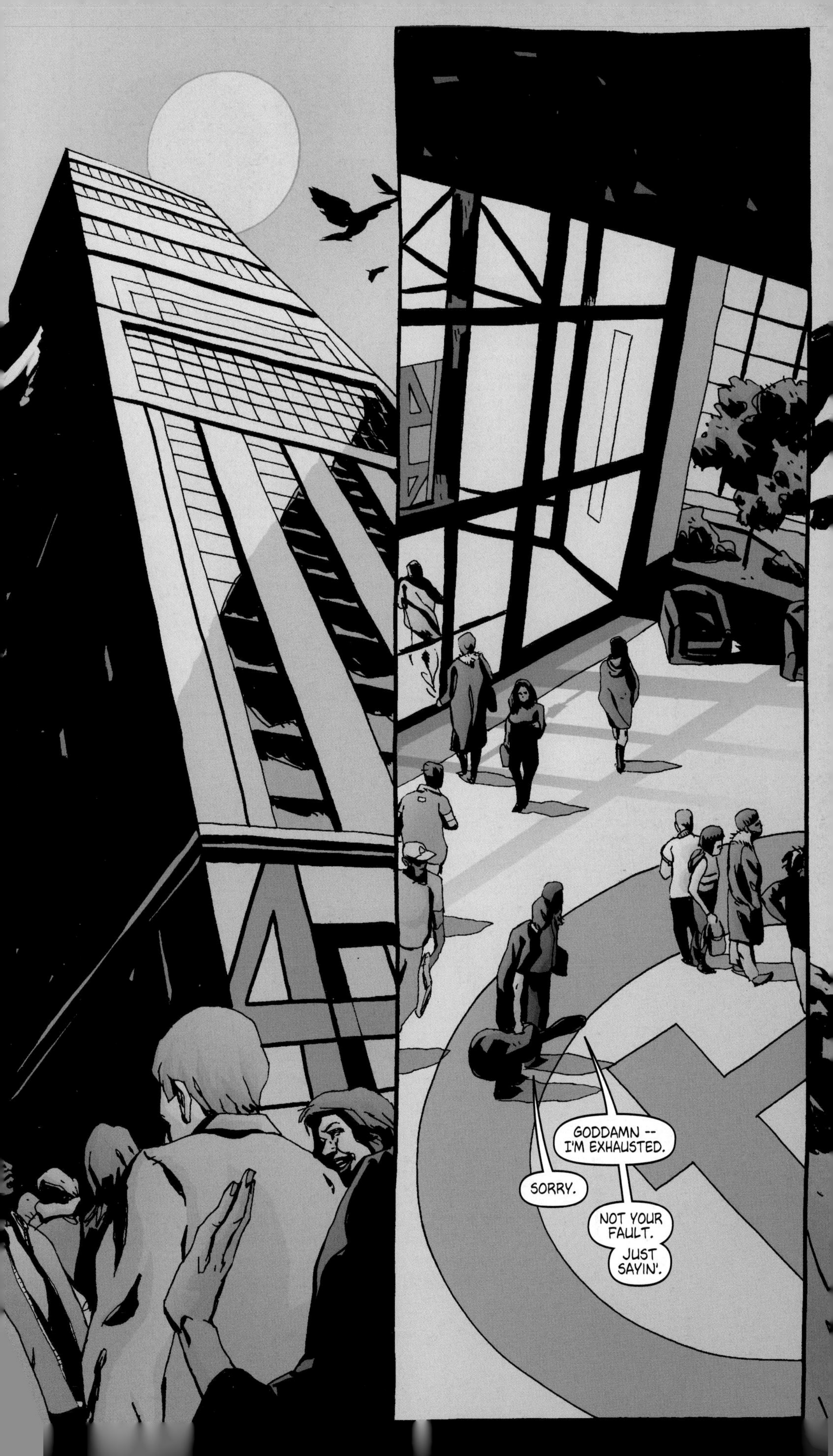
GODDAMN -- I'M EXHAUSTED.
SORRY.
NOT YOUR FAULT.
JUST SAYIN'.

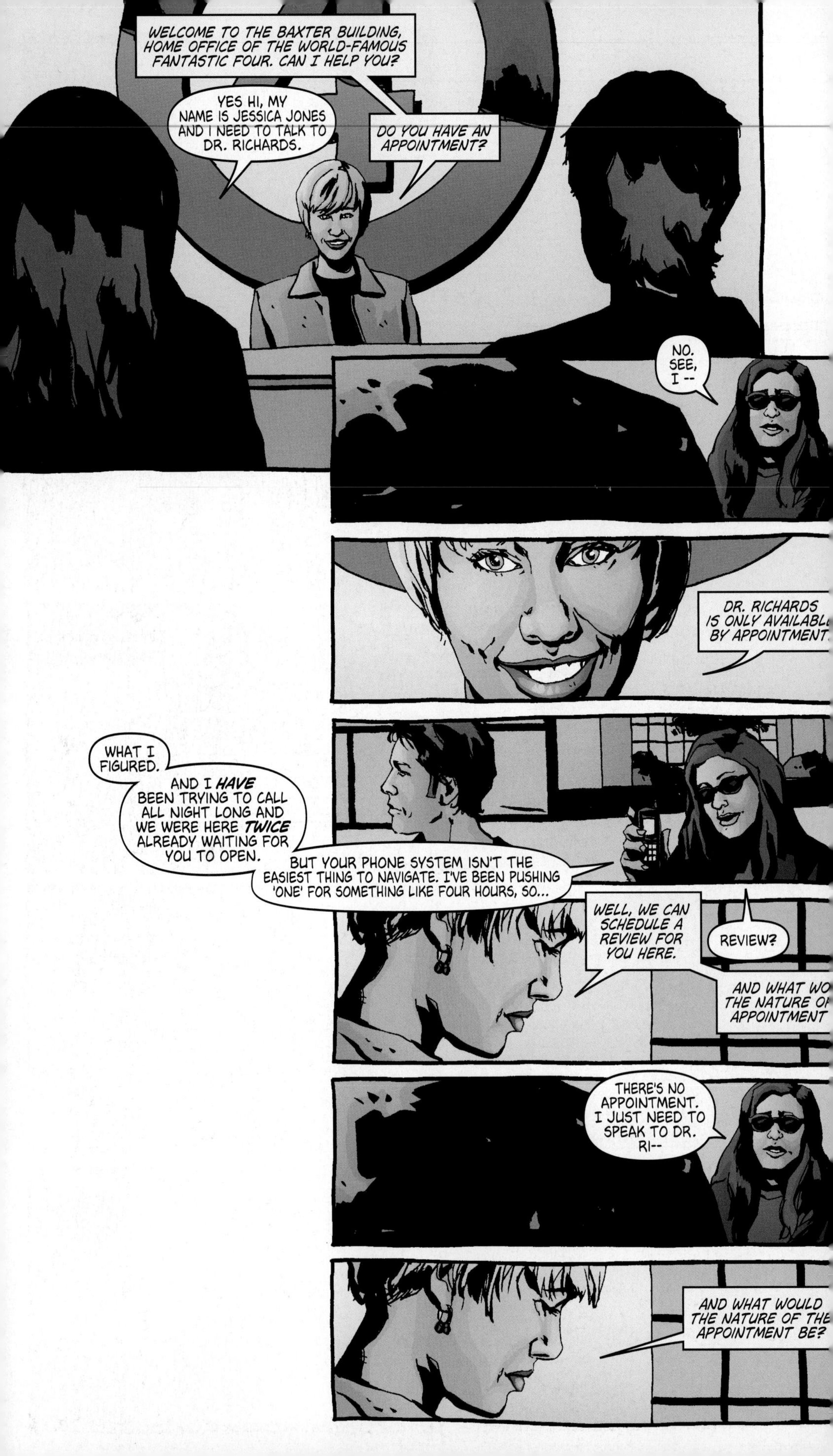
WELCOME TO THE BAXTER BUILDING, HOME OFFICE OF THE WORLD-FAMOUS FANTASTIC FOUR. CAN I HELP YOU?
YES HI, MY NAME IS JESSICA JONES AND I NEED TO TALK TO DR. RICHARDS.
DO YOU HAVE AN APPOINTMENT?
NO. SEE, I --
DR. RICHARDS IS ONLY AVAILABL BY APPOINTMENT
WHAT I FIGURED.
AND I HAVE BEEN TRYING TO CALL ALL NIGHT LONG AND WE WERE HERE TWICE ALREADY WAITING FOR YOU TO OPEN.
BUT YOUR PHONE SYSTEM ISN'T THE EASIEST THING TO NAVIGATE. I'VE BEEN PUSHING 'ONE' FOR SOMETHING LIKE FOUR HOURS, SO...
WELL, WE CAN SCHEDULE A REVIEW FOR YOU HERE.
REVIEW?
AND WHAT WO THE NATURE OF APPOINTMENT
THERE'S NO APPOINTMENT. I JUST NEED TO SPEAK TO DR. RI--
AND WHAT WOULD THE NATURE OF THE APPOINTMENT BE?

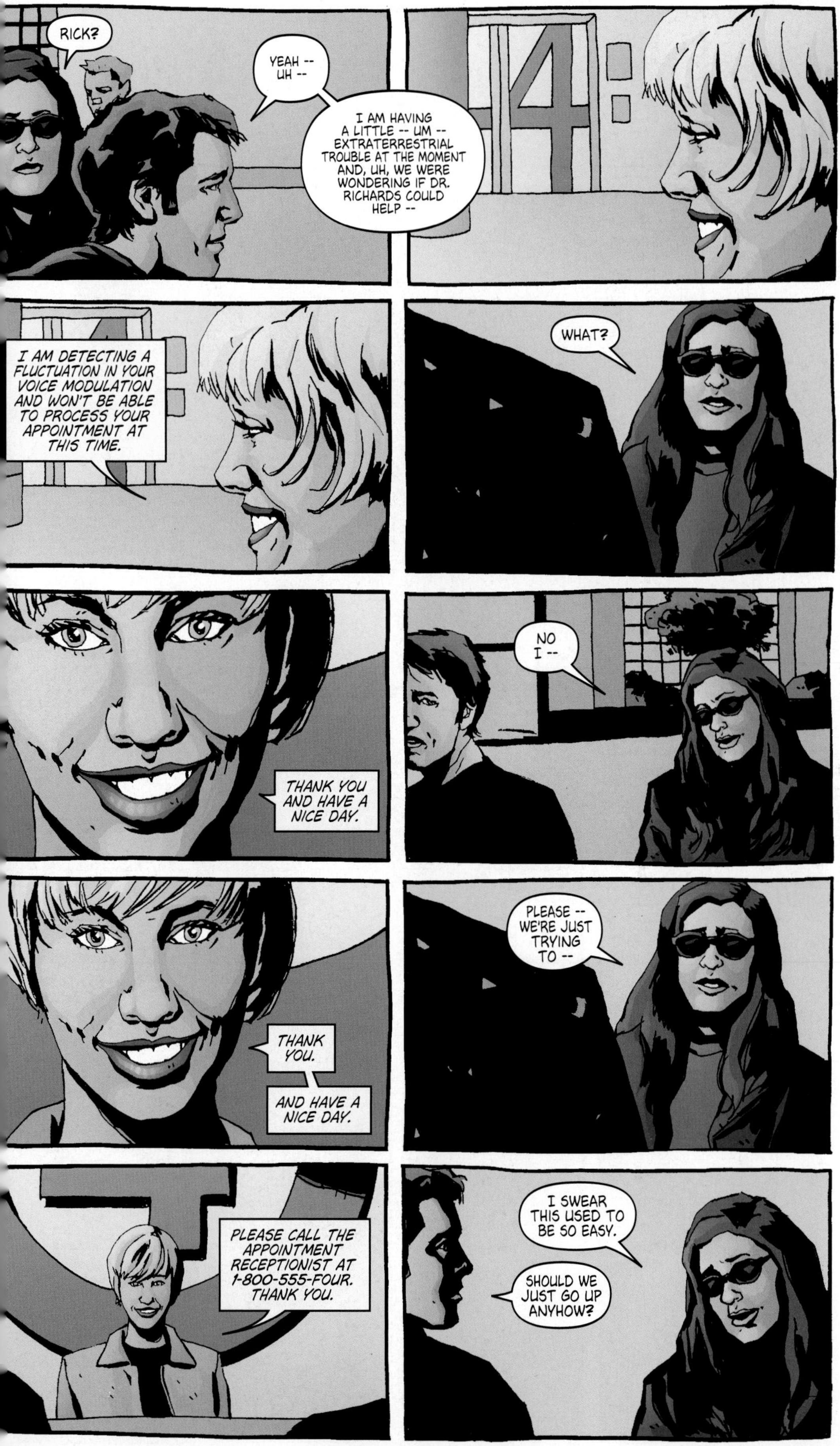
RICK?
YEAH -- UH --
I AM HAVING A LITTLE -- UM -- EXTRATERRESTRIAL TROUBLE AT THE MOMENT AND, UH, WE WERE WONDERING IF DR. RICHARDS COULD HELP --
I AM DETECTING A FLUCTUATION IN YOUR VOICE MODULATION AND WON'T BE ABLE TO PROCESS YOUR APPOINTMENT AT THIS TIME.
WHAT?
THANK YOU AND HAVE A NICE DAY.
NO I --
THANK YOU.
AND HAVE A NICE DAY.
PLEASE -- WE'RE JUST TRYING TO --
PLEASE CALL THE APPOINTMENT RECEPTIONIST AT 1-800-555-FOUR. THANK YOU.
I SWEAR THIS USED TO BE SO EASY.
SHOULD WE JUST GO UP ANYHOW?

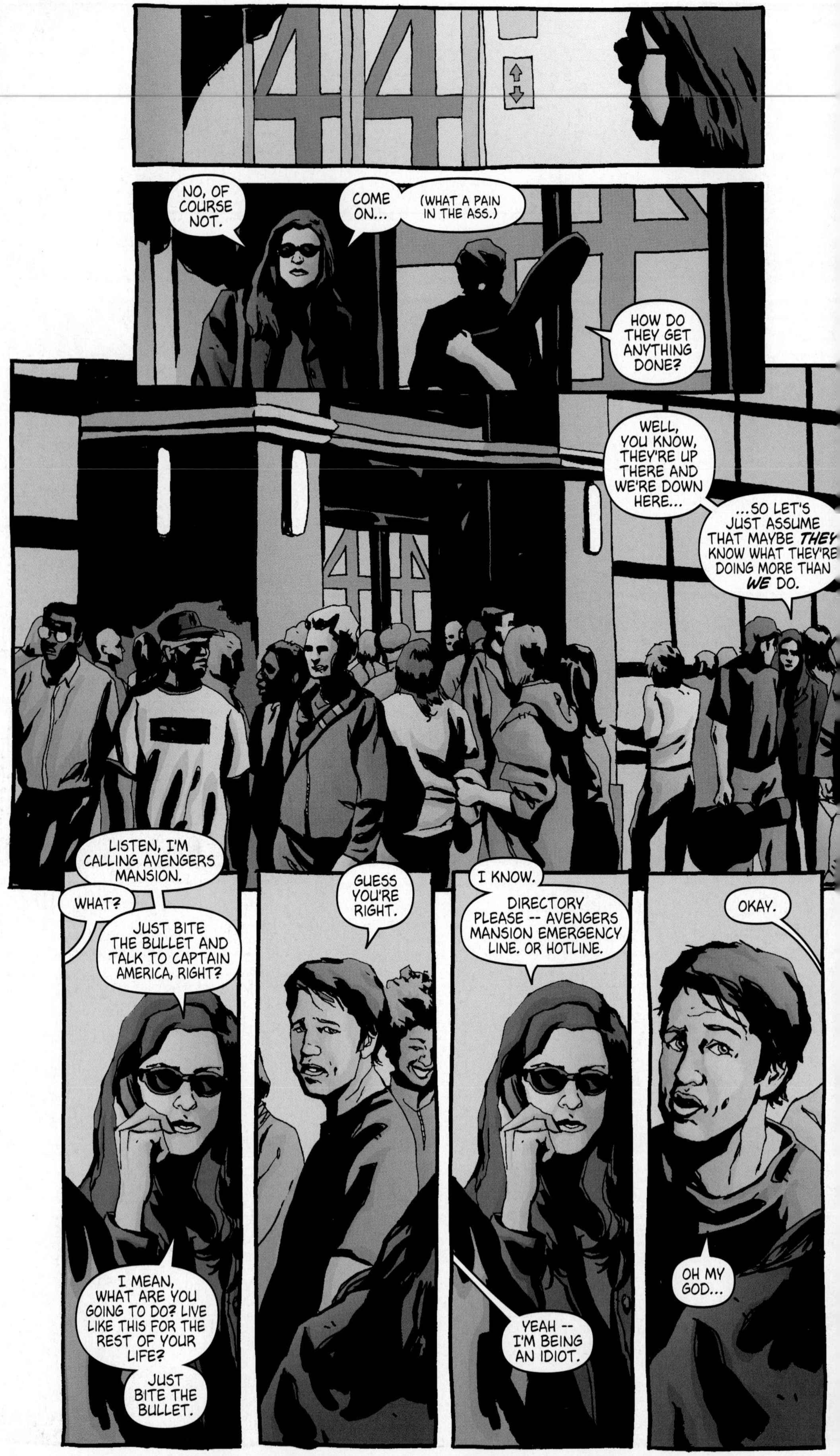

NO, OF COURSE NOT.
COME ON...
(WHAT A PAIN IN THE ASS.)
HOW DO THEY GET ANYTHING DONE?
WELL, YOU KNOW, THEY'RE UP THERE AND WE'RE DOWN HERE...
...SO LET'S JUST ASSUME THAT MAYBE THEY KNOW WHAT THEY'RE DOING MORE THAN WE DO.
LISTEN, I'M CALLING AVENGERS MANSION.
WHAT?
JUST BITE THE BULLET AND TALK TO CAPTAIN AMERICA, RIGHT?
I MEAN, WHAT ARE YOU GOING TO DO? LIVE LIKE THIS FOR THE REST OF YOUR LIFE?
JUST BITE THE BULLET.
GUESS YOU'RE RIGHT.
I KNOW.
DIRECTORY PLEASE -- AVENGERS MANSION EMERGENCY LINE. OR HOTLINE.
YEAH -- I'M BEING AN IDIOT.
OKAY.
OH MY GOD...

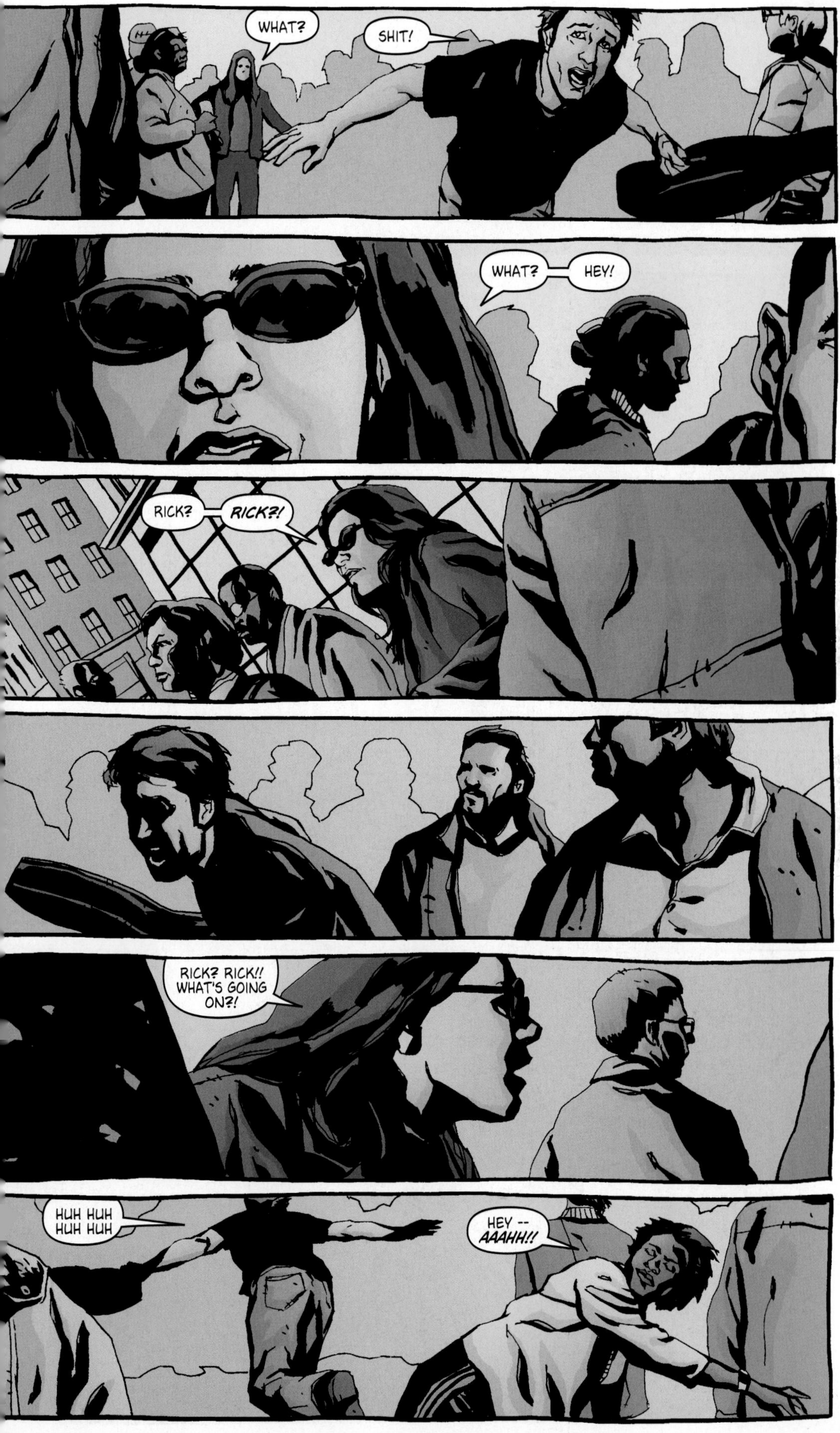
WHAT?
SHIT!
WHAT?
HEY!
RICK?
RICK?!
RICK? RICK!! WHAT'S GOING ON?!
HUH HUH HUH HUH
HEY -- AAAHH!!

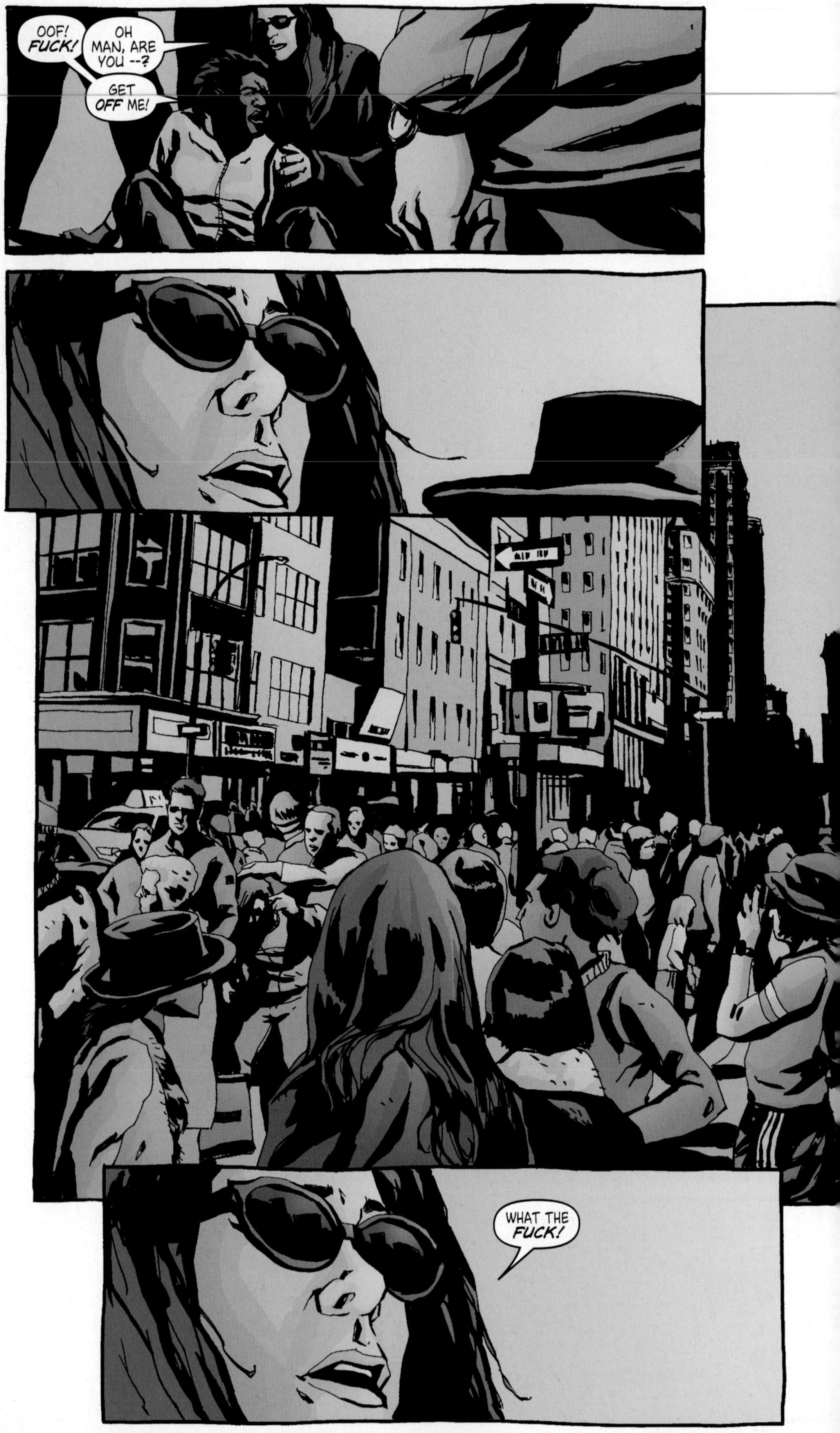
OOF! FUCK!
OH MAN, ARE YOU --?
GET OFF ME!
WHAT THE FUCK!

CONFIDENTIAL

R[redacted]MI[redacted]

ISSUE #9

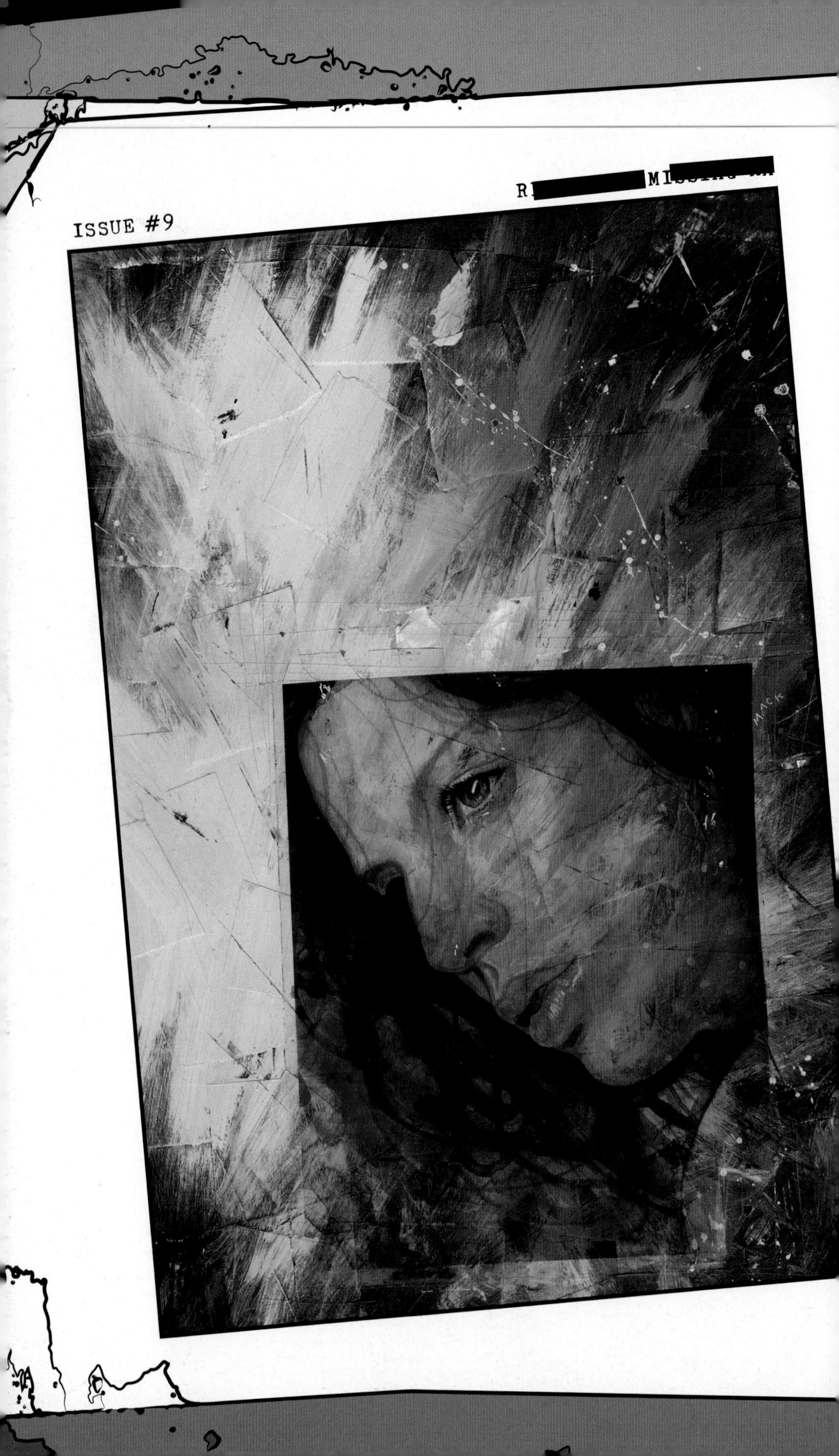
MACK

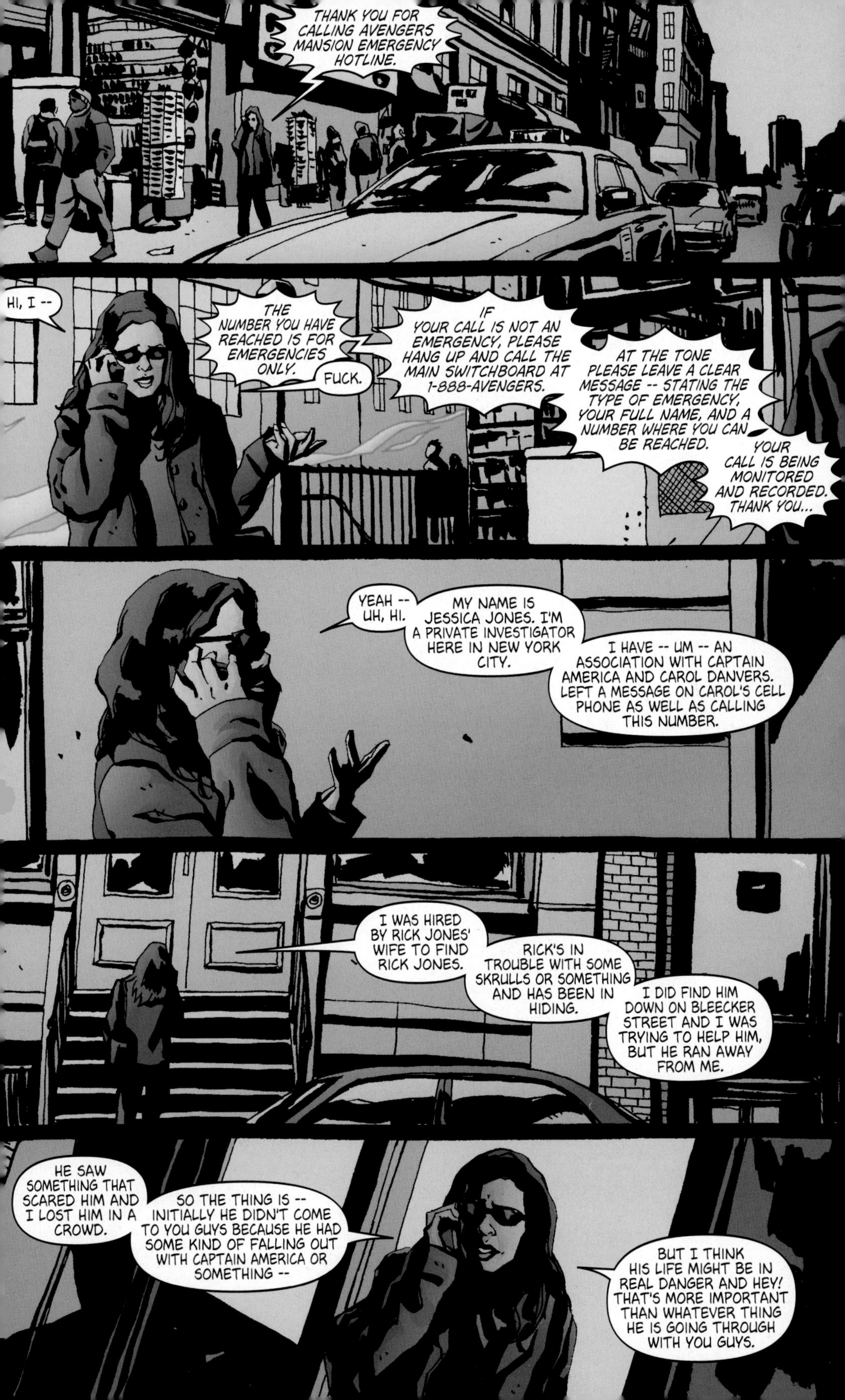
THANK YOU FOR CALLING AVENGERS MANSION EMERGENCY HOTLINE.
HI, I --
THE NUMBER YOU HAVE REACHED IS FOR EMERGENCIES ONLY.
FUCK.
IF YOUR CALL IS NOT AN EMERGENCY, PLEASE HANG UP AND CALL THE MAIN SWITCHBOARD AT 1-888-AVENGERS.
AT THE TONE PLEASE LEAVE A CLEAR MESSAGE -- STATING THE TYPE OF EMERGENCY, YOUR FULL NAME, AND A NUMBER WHERE YOU CAN BE REACHED.
YOUR CALL IS BEING MONITORED AND RECORDED. THANK YOU...
YEAH -- UH, HI.
MY NAME IS JESSICA JONES. I'M A PRIVATE INVESTIGATOR HERE IN NEW YORK CITY.
I HAVE -- UM -- AN ASSOCIATION WITH CAPTAIN AMERICA AND CAROL DANVERS. LEFT A MESSAGE ON CAROL'S CELL PHONE AS WELL AS CALLING THIS NUMBER.
I WAS HIRED BY RICK JONES' WIFE TO FIND RICK JONES.
RICK'S IN TROUBLE WITH SOME SKRULLS OR SOMETHING AND HAS BEEN IN HIDING.
I DID FIND HIM DOWN ON BLEECKER STREET AND I WAS TRYING TO HELP HIM, BUT HE RAN AWAY FROM ME.
HE SAW SOMETHING THAT SCARED HIM AND I LOST HIM IN A CROWD.
SO THE THING IS -- INITIALLY HE DIDN'T COME TO YOU GUYS BECAUSE HE HAD SOME KIND OF FALLING OUT WITH CAPTAIN AMERICA OR SOMETHING --
BUT I THINK HIS LIFE MIGHT BE IN REAL DANGER AND HEY! THAT'S MORE IMPORTANT THAN WHATEVER THING HE IS GOING THROUGH WITH YOU GUYS.

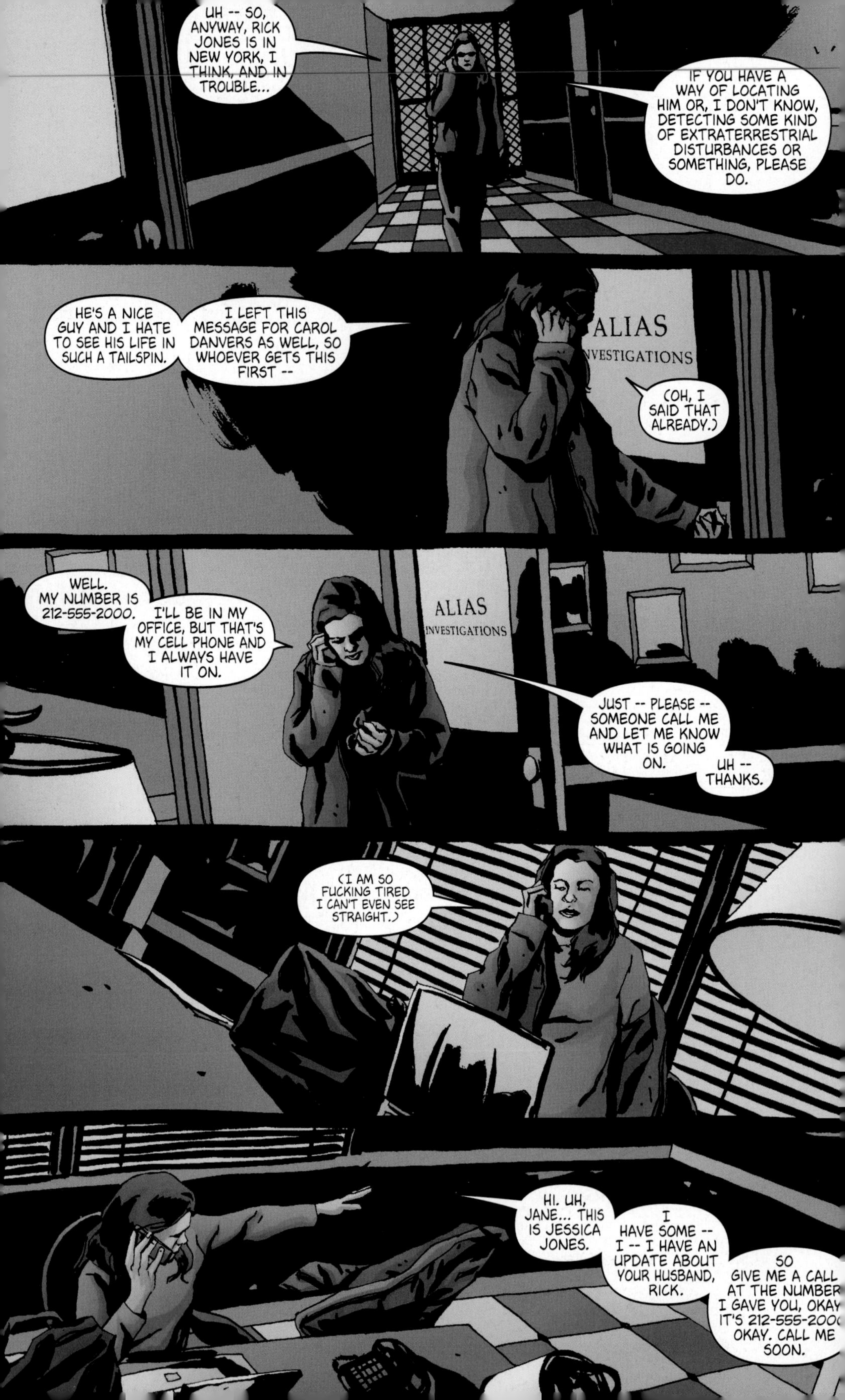

UH -- SO, ANYWAY, RICK JONES IS IN NEW YORK, I THINK, AND IN TROUBLE...
IF YOU HAVE A WAY OF LOCATING HIM OR, I DON'T KNOW, DETECTING SOME KIND OF EXTRATERRESTRIAL DISTURBANCES OR SOMETHING, PLEASE DO.
HE'S A NICE GUY AND I HATE TO SEE HIS LIFE IN SUCH A TAILSPIN.
I LEFT THIS MESSAGE FOR CAROL DANVERS AS WELL, SO WHOEVER GETS THIS FIRST --
ALIAS INVESTIGATIONS
(OH, I SAID THAT ALREADY.)
WELL. MY NUMBER IS 212-555-2000.
I'LL BE IN MY OFFICE, BUT THAT'S MY CELL PHONE AND I ALWAYS HAVE IT ON.
ALIAS INVESTIGATIONS
JUST -- PLEASE -- SOMEONE CALL ME AND LET ME KNOW WHAT IS GOING ON.
UH -- THANKS.
(I AM SO FUCKING TIRED I CAN'T EVEN SEE STRAIGHT.)
HI. UH, JANE... THIS IS JESSICA JONES.
I HAVE SOME -- I -- I HAVE AN UPDATE ABOUT YOUR HUSBAND, RICK.
SO GIVE ME A CALL AT THE NUMBER I GAVE YOU, OKAY IT'S 212-555-200 OKAY. CALL ME SOON.

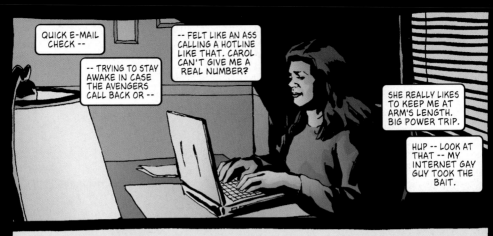

QUICK E-MAIL CHECK --

-- TRYING TO STAY AWAKE IN CASE THE AVENGERS CALL BACK OR --

-- FELT LIKE AN ASS CALLING A HOTLINE LIKE THAT. CAROL CAN'T GIVE ME A REAL NUMBER?

SHE REALLY LIKES TO KEEP ME AT ARM'S LENGTH. BIG POWER TRIP.

HUP -- LOOK AT THAT -- MY INTERNET GAY GUY TOOK THE BAIT.

NO MORE GAMES. ITS TIME TO MEET, DYING TO MEET YOU. LETS BE ADVENTUROUS. MEET ME AT THE STARBUCKS AT 43RD AND LEXINGTON. I'LL BE WEARING A BLUE SWEATER WITH

HIS WIFE HIRED ME TO CATCH HIM IN THE ACT. I JUST CAUGHT HIM IN THE ACT.

HE'S CHEATING ON HER AND HE'S GAY AND WON'T EVEN HAVE THE BALLS TO JUST COME OUT AND TELL HER --

AND HE GOES SNEAKING AROUND LIKE THIS -- HOOKING UP WITH GUYS ON THE INTERNET.

I'VE BEEN TOYING WITH HIM ONLINE WITH AN ALIAS.

HE THINKS I'M A HOT GAY GUY -- *UHGH* -- I WISH. HE WANTS TO MEET.

OOOOH, AT A STARBUCKS. HOW INCREDIBLY UNINTERESTING ON EVERY LEVEL.

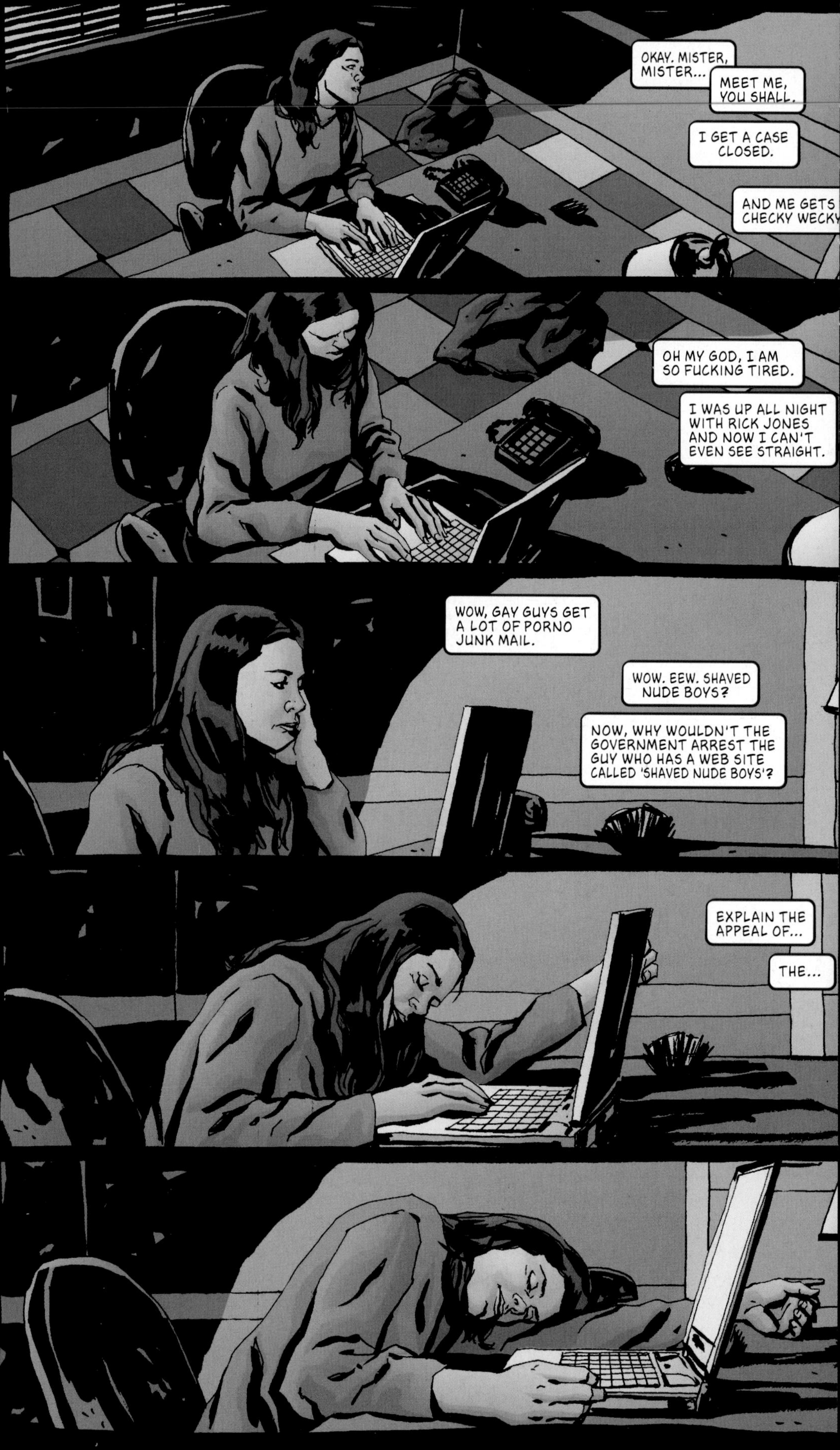
OKAY. MISTER, MISTER...
MEET ME, YOU SHALL.
I GET A CASE CLOSED.
AND ME GETS CHECKY WECKY
OH MY GOD, I AM SO FUCKING TIRED.
I WAS UP ALL NIGHT WITH RICK JONES AND NOW I CAN'T EVEN SEE STRAIGHT.
WOW, GAY GUYS GET A LOT OF PORNO JUNK MAIL.
WOW. EEW. SHAVED NUDE BOYS?
NOW, WHY WOULDN'T THE GOVERNMENT ARREST THE GUY WHO HAS A WEB SITE CALLED 'SHAVED NUDE BOYS'?
EXPLAIN THE APPEAL OF...
THE...

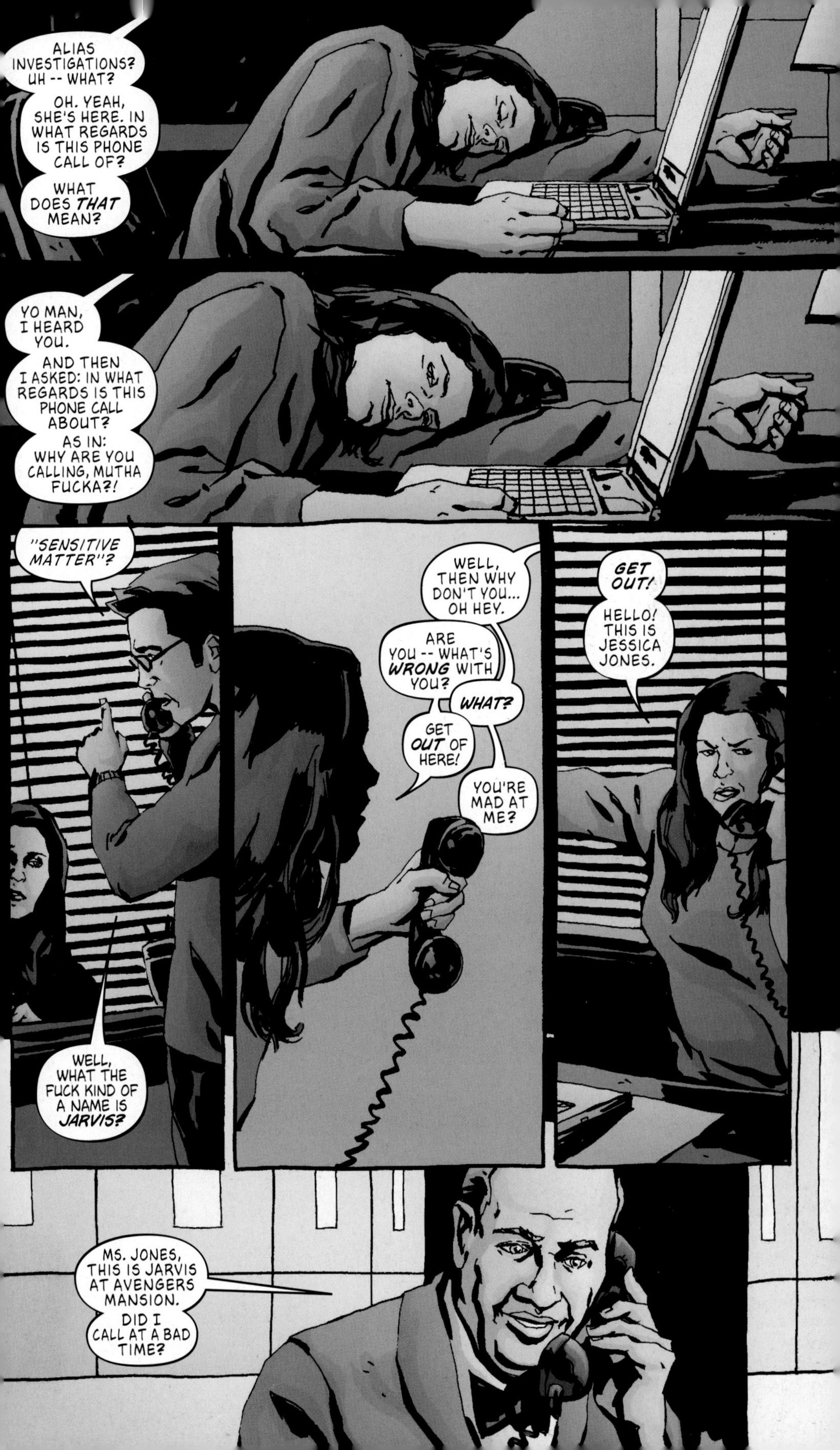
ALIAS INVESTIGATIONS? UH -- WHAT?
OH. YEAH, SHE'S HERE. IN WHAT REGARDS IS THIS PHONE CALL OF?
WHAT DOES *THAT* MEAN?
YO MAN, I HEARD YOU.
AND THEN I ASKED: IN WHAT REGARDS IS THIS PHONE CALL ABOUT?
AS IN: WHY ARE YOU CALLING, MUTHA FUCKA?!
"SENSITIVE MATTER"?
WELL, WHAT THE FUCK KIND OF A NAME IS *JARVIS?*
WELL, THEN WHY DON'T YOU... OH HEY.
ARE YOU -- WHAT'S *WRONG* WITH YOU?
WHAT?
GET *OUT* OF HERE!
YOU'RE MAD AT ME?
GET OUT!
HELLO! THIS IS JESSICA JONES.
MS. JONES, THIS IS JARVIS AT AVENGERS MANSION.
DID I CALL AT A BAD TIME?

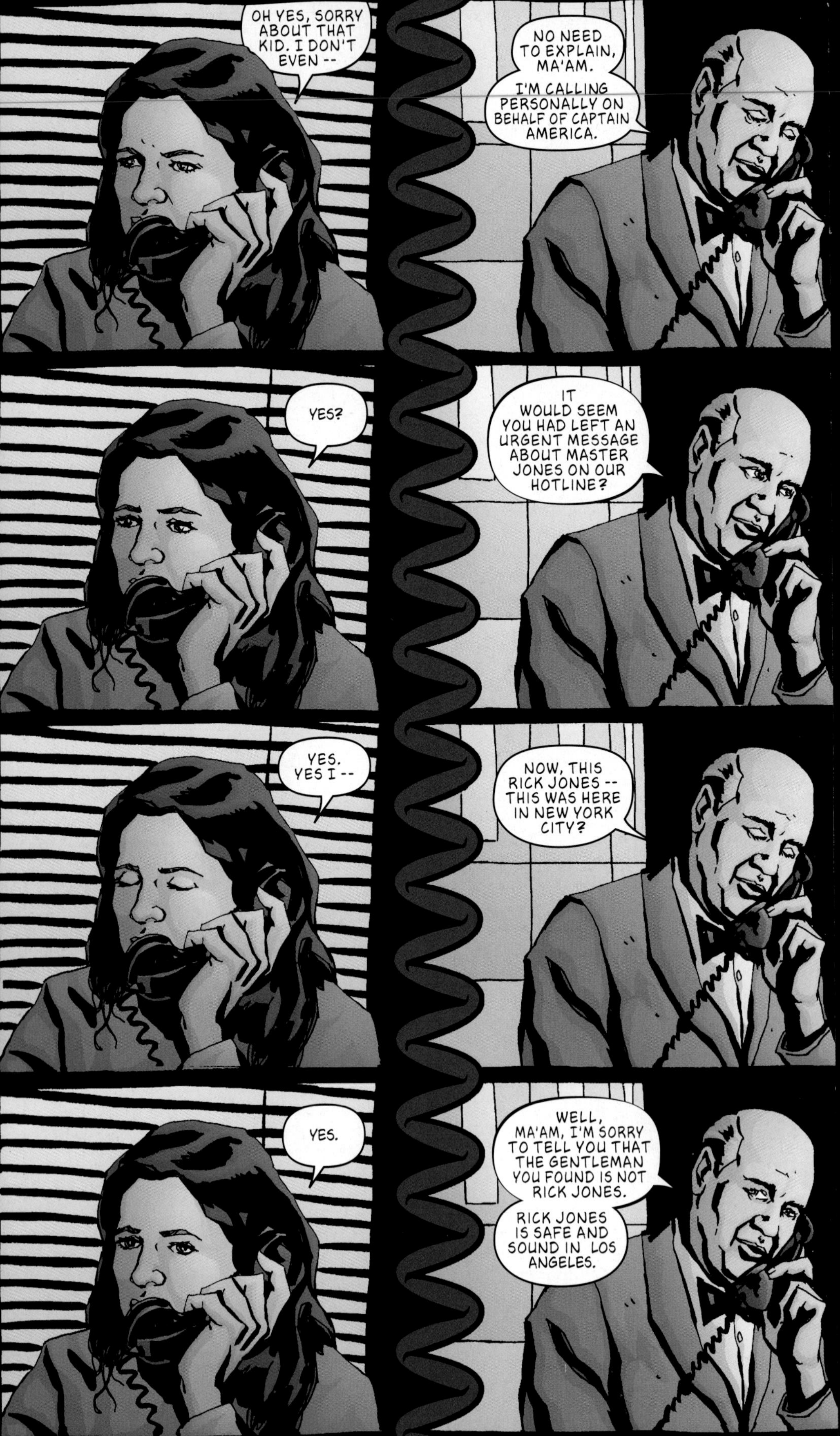
OH YES, SORRY ABOUT THAT KID. I DON'T EVEN --
NO NEED TO EXPLAIN, MA'AM.
I'M CALLING PERSONALLY ON BEHALF OF CAPTAIN AMERICA.
YES?
IT WOULD SEEM YOU HAD LEFT AN URGENT MESSAGE ABOUT MASTER JONES ON OUR HOTLINE?
YES. YES I --
NOW, THIS RICK JONES -- THIS WAS HERE IN NEW YORK CITY?
YES.
WELL, MA'AM, I'M SORRY TO TELL YOU THAT THE GENTLEMAN YOU FOUND IS NOT RICK JONES.
RICK JONES IS SAFE AND SOUND IN LOS ANGELES.

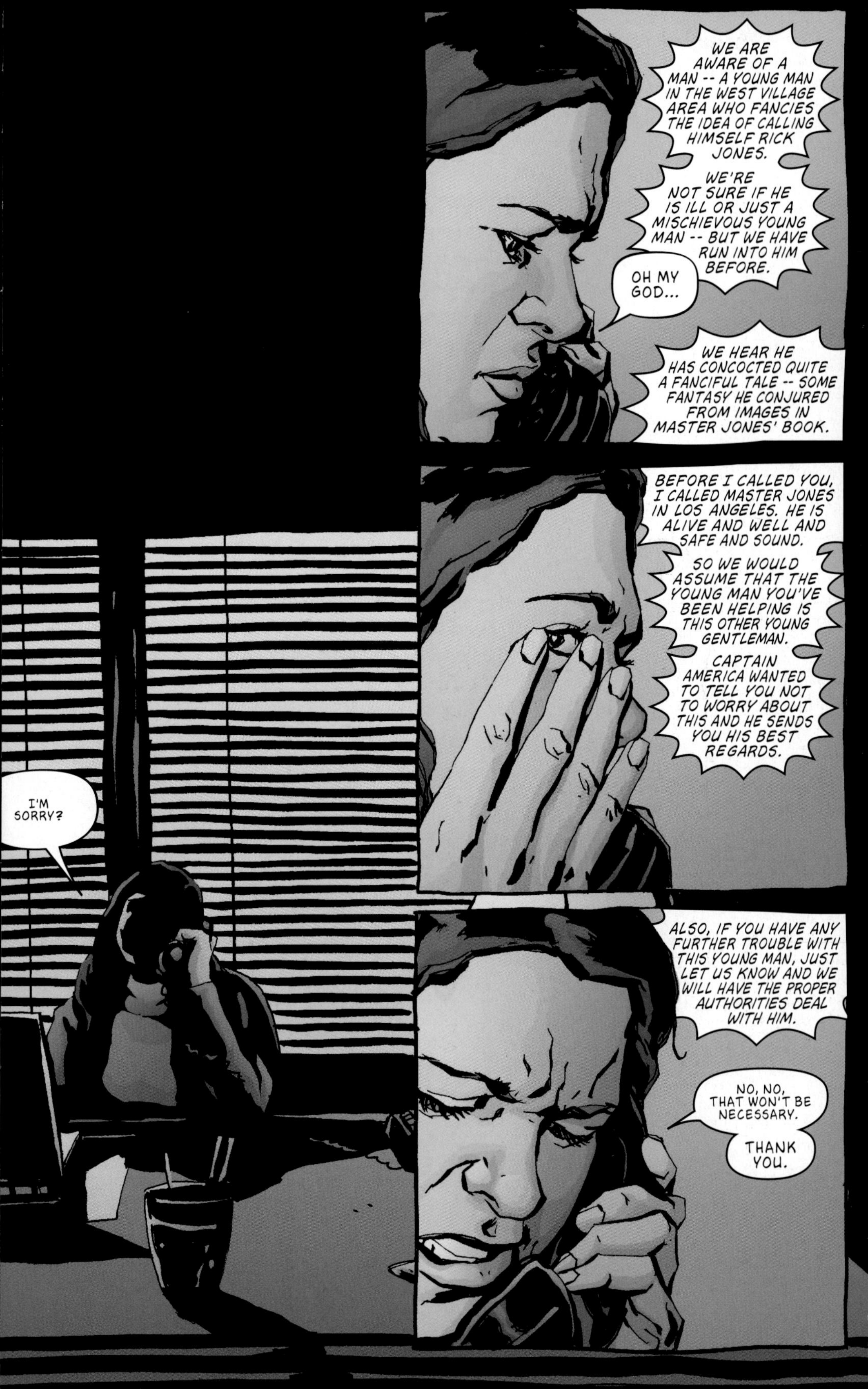
WE ARE AWARE OF A MAN -- A YOUNG MAN IN THE WEST VILLAGE AREA WHO FANCIES THE IDEA OF CALLING HIMSELF RICK JONES.
WE'RE NOT SURE IF HE IS ILL OR JUST A MISCHIEVOUS YOUNG MAN -- BUT WE HAVE RUN INTO HIM BEFORE.
OH MY GOD...
WE HEAR HE HAS CONCOCTED QUITE A FANCIFUL TALE -- SOME FANTASY HE CONJURED FROM IMAGES IN MASTER JONES' BOOK.
BEFORE I CALLED YOU, I CALLED MASTER JONES IN LOS ANGELES. HE IS ALIVE AND WELL AND SAFE AND SOUND.
SO WE WOULD ASSUME THAT THE YOUNG MAN YOU'VE BEEN HELPING IS THIS OTHER YOUNG GENTLEMAN.
CAPTAIN AMERICA WANTED TO TELL YOU NOT TO WORRY ABOUT THIS AND HE SENDS YOU HIS BEST REGARDS.
I'M SORRY?
ALSO, IF YOU HAVE ANY FURTHER TROUBLE WITH THIS YOUNG MAN, JUST LET US KNOW AND WE WILL HAVE THE PROPER AUTHORITIES DEAL WITH HIM.
NO, NO, THAT WON'T BE NECESSARY.
THANK YOU.

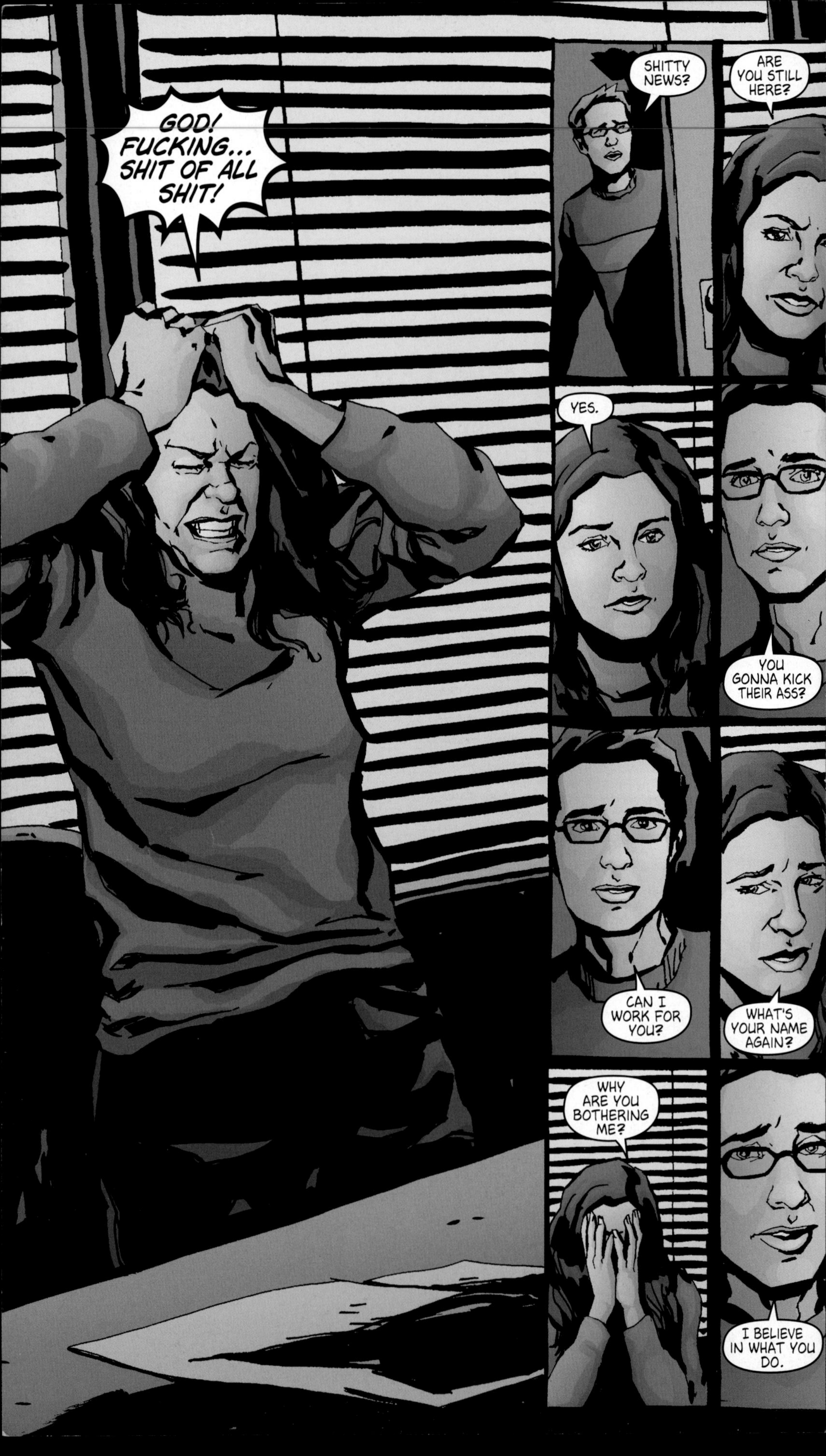
GOD! FUCKING... SHIT OF ALL SHIT!
SHITTY NEWS?
ARE YOU STILL HERE?
YES.
YOU GONNA KICK THEIR ASS?
CAN I WORK FOR YOU?
WHAT'S YOUR NAME AGAIN?
WHY ARE YOU BOTHERING ME?
I BELIEVE IN WHAT YOU DO.

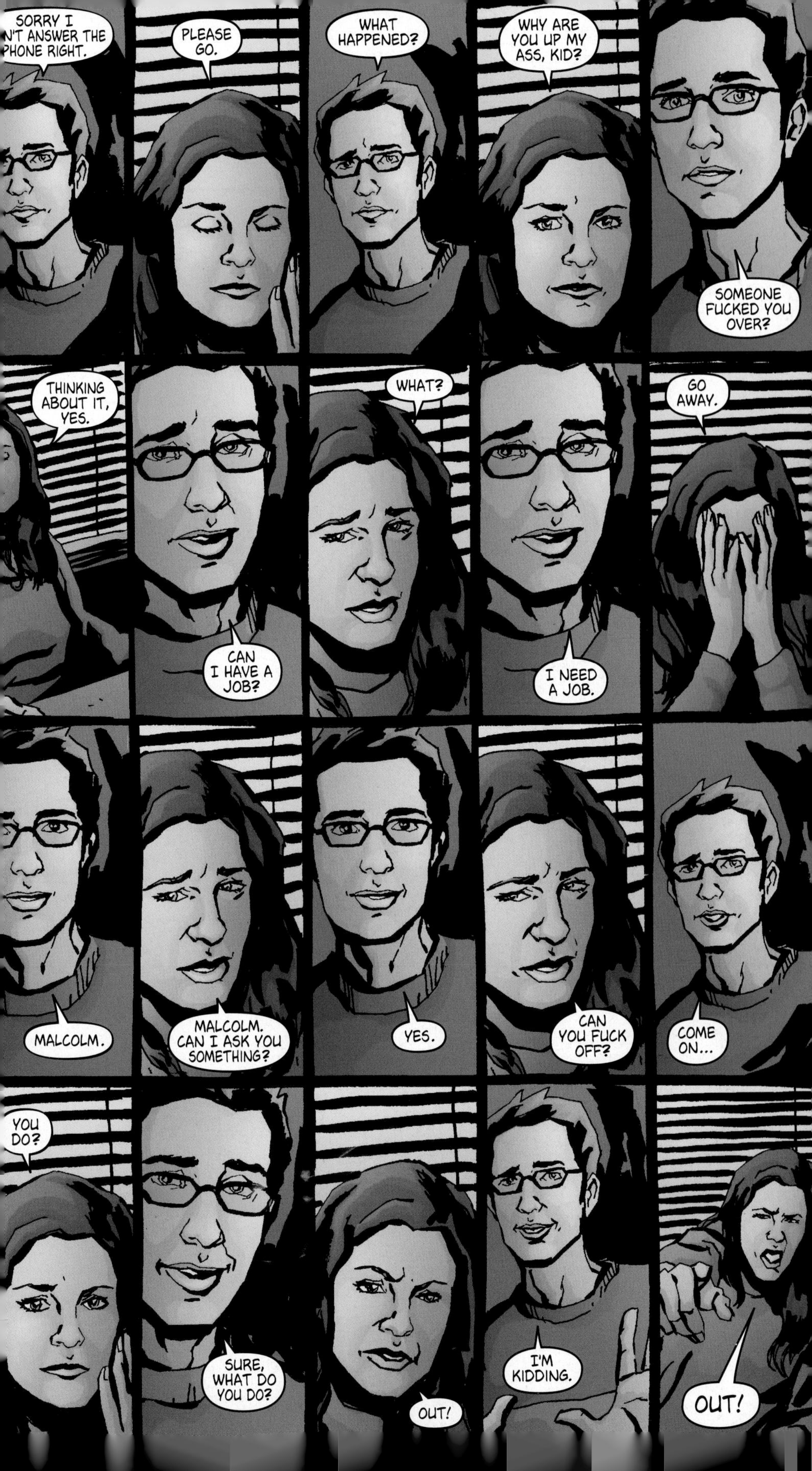
SORRY I N'T ANSWER THE PHONE RIGHT.
PLEASE GO.
WHAT HAPPENED?
WHY ARE YOU UP MY ASS, KID?
SOMEONE FUCKED YOU OVER?
THINKING ABOUT IT, YES.
CAN I HAVE A JOB?
WHAT?
I NEED A JOB.
GO AWAY.
MALCOLM.
MALCOLM. CAN I ASK YOU SOMETHING?
YES.
CAN YOU FUCK OFF?
COME ON...
YOU DO?
SURE, WHAT DO YOU DO?
OUT!
I'M KIDDING.
OUT!

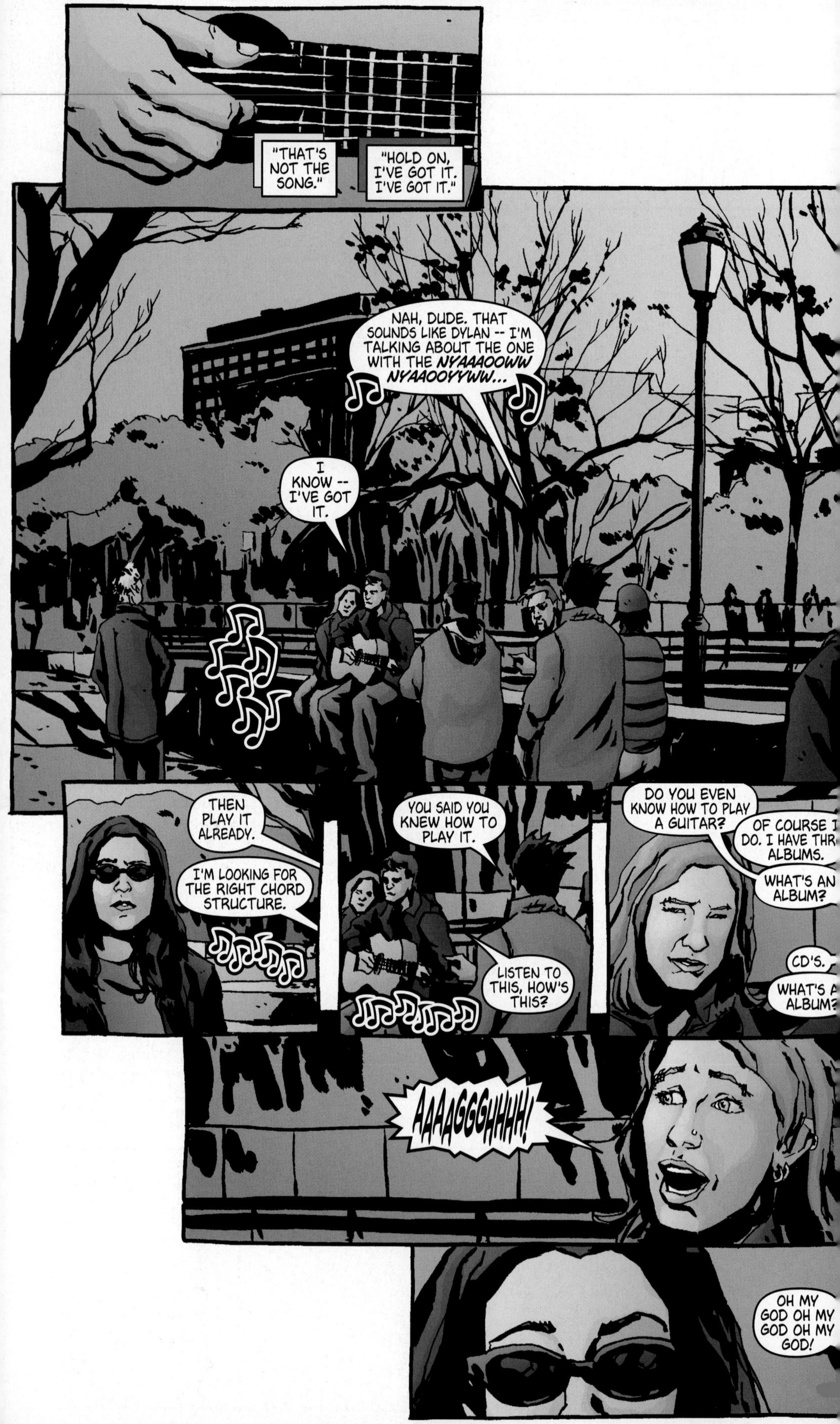
"THAT'S NOT THE SONG."
"HOLD ON, I'VE GOT IT. I'VE GOT IT."
NAH, DUDE. THAT SOUNDS LIKE DYLAN -- I'M TALKING ABOUT THE ONE WITH THE NYAAAOOWW NYAAOOYYWW...
I KNOW -- I'VE GOT IT.
THEN PLAY IT ALREADY.
I'M LOOKING FOR THE RIGHT CHORD STRUCTURE.
YOU SAID YOU KNEW HOW TO PLAY IT.
LISTEN TO THIS, HOW'S THIS?
DO YOU EVEN KNOW HOW TO PLAY A GUITAR?
WHAT'S AN ALBUM?
CD'S.
AAAAGGGHHHH!
OH MY GOD OH MY GOD OH MY GOD!

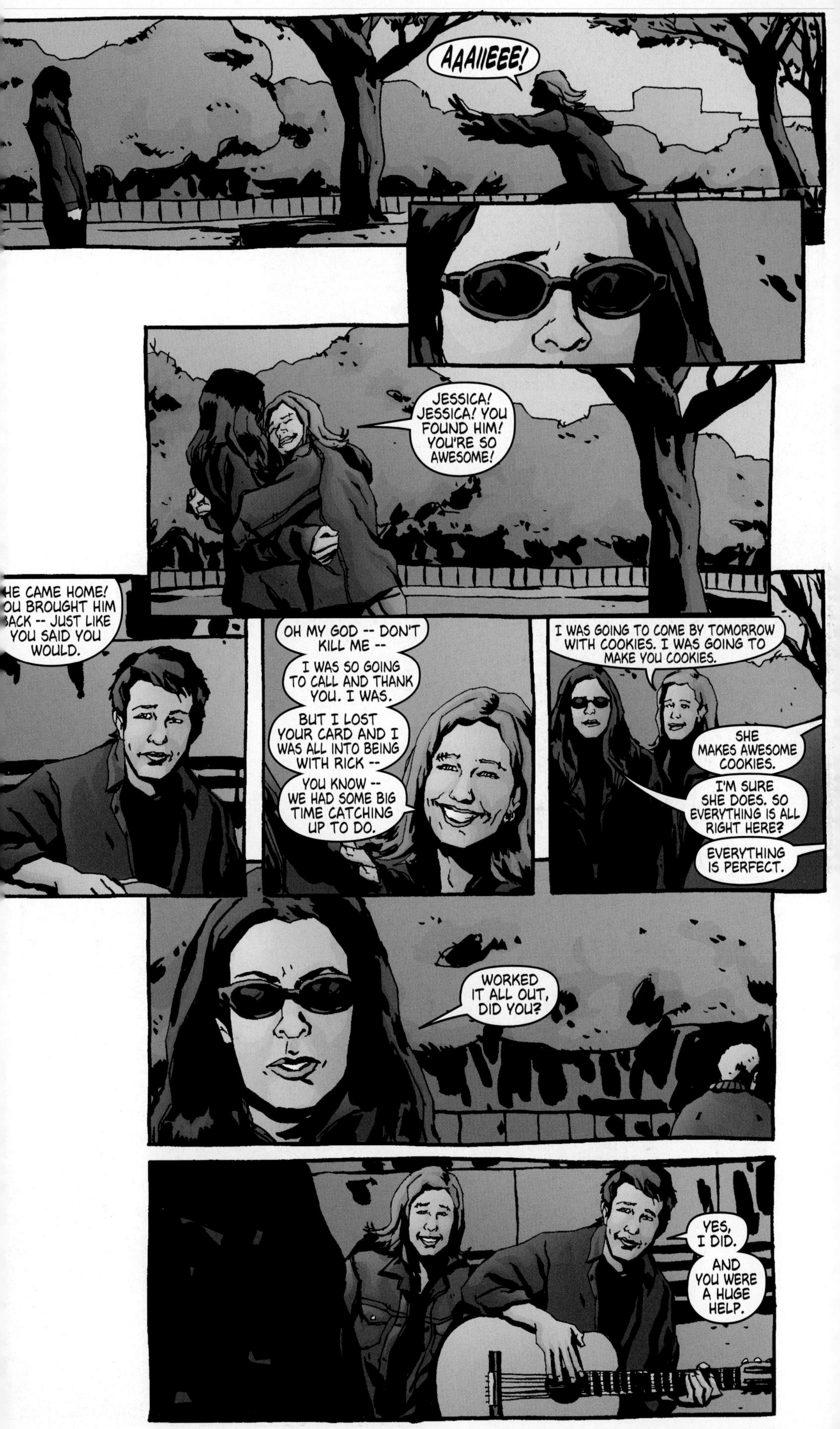
AAAIIEEE!
JESSICA! JESSICA! YOU FOUND HIM! YOU'RE SO AWESOME!
HE CAME HOME! YOU BROUGHT HIM BACK -- JUST LIKE YOU SAID YOU WOULD.
OH MY GOD -- DON'T KILL ME --
I WAS SO GOING TO CALL AND THANK YOU. I WAS.
BUT I LOST YOUR CARD AND I WAS ALL INTO BEING WITH RICK --
YOU KNOW -- WE HAD SOME BIG TIME CATCHING UP TO DO.
I WAS GOING TO COME BY TOMORROW WITH COOKIES. I WAS GOING TO MAKE YOU COOKIES.
SHE MAKES AWESOME COOKIES.
I'M SURE SHE DOES. SO EVERYTHING IS ALL RIGHT HERE?
EVERYTHING IS PERFECT.
WORKED IT ALL OUT, DID YOU?
YES, I DID.
AND YOU WERE A HUGE HELP.

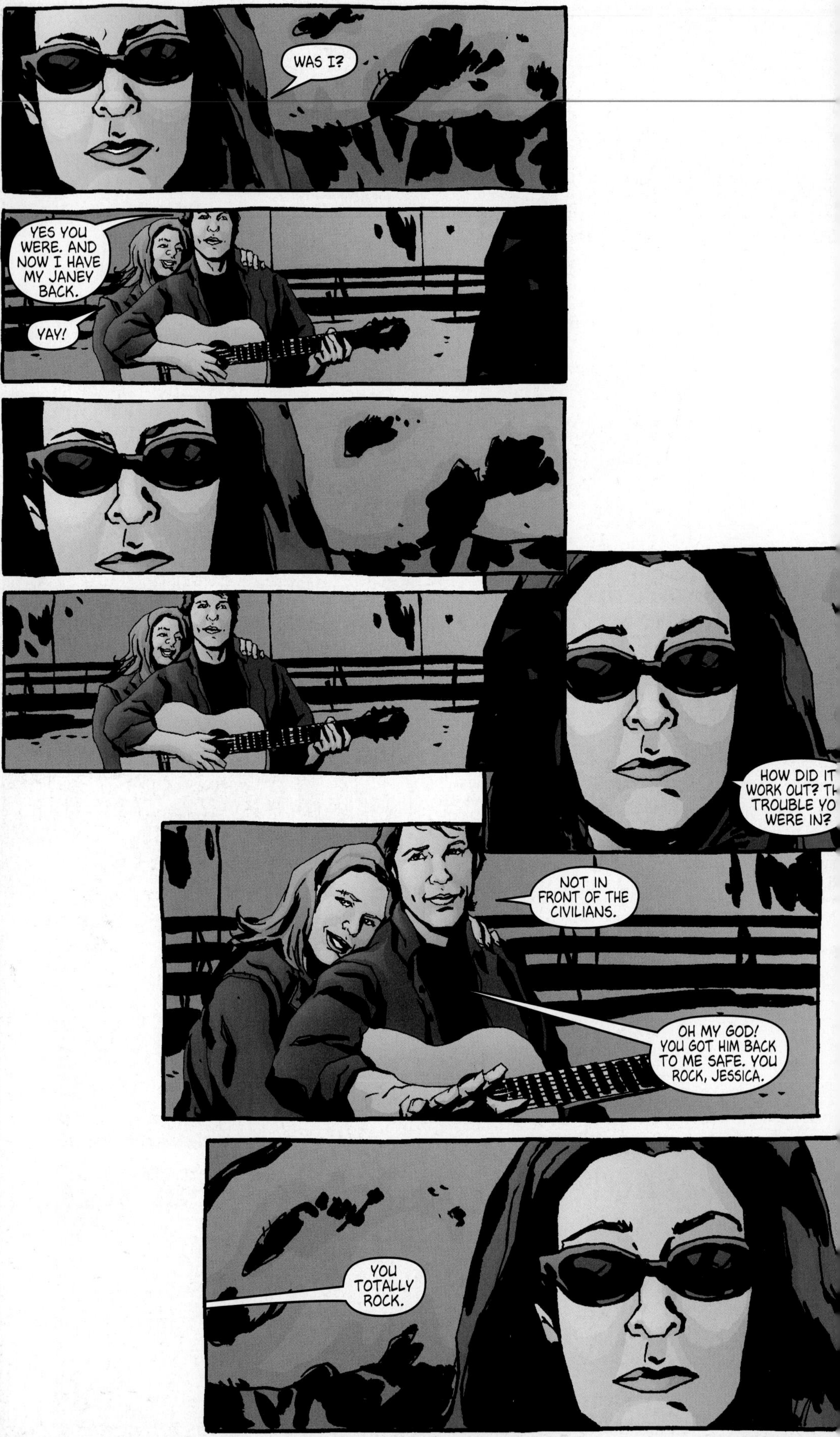

WAS I?
YES YOU WERE. AND NOW I HAVE MY JANEY BACK.
YAY!
HOW DID IT WORK OUT? TH TROUBLE YO WERE IN?
NOT IN FRONT OF THE CIVILIANS.
OH MY GOD! YOU GOT HIM BACK TO ME SAFE. YOU ROCK, JESSICA.
YOU TOTALLY ROCK.

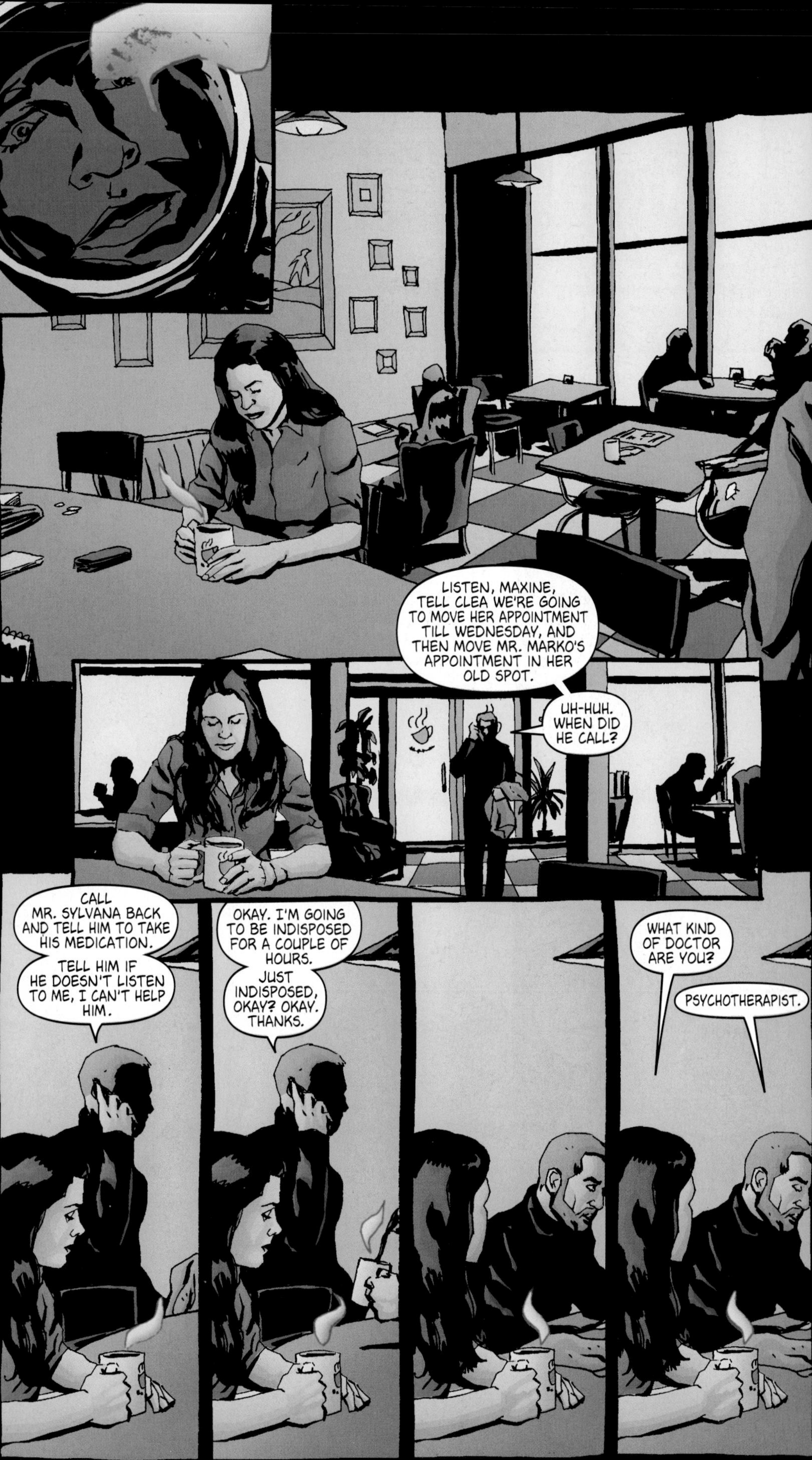
LISTEN, MAXINE, TELL CLEA WE'RE GOING TO MOVE HER APPOINTMENT TILL WEDNESDAY, AND THEN MOVE MR. MARKO'S APPOINTMENT IN HER OLD SPOT.
UH-HUH. WHEN DID HE CALL?
CALL MR. SYLVANA BACK AND TELL HIM TO TAKE HIS MEDICATION.
TELL HIM IF HE DOESN'T LISTEN TO ME, I CAN'T HELP HIM.
OKAY. I'M GOING TO BE INDISPOSED FOR A COUPLE OF HOURS.
JUST INDISPOSED, OKAY? OKAY. THANKS.
WHAT KIND OF DOCTOR ARE YOU?
PSYCHOTHERAPIST.

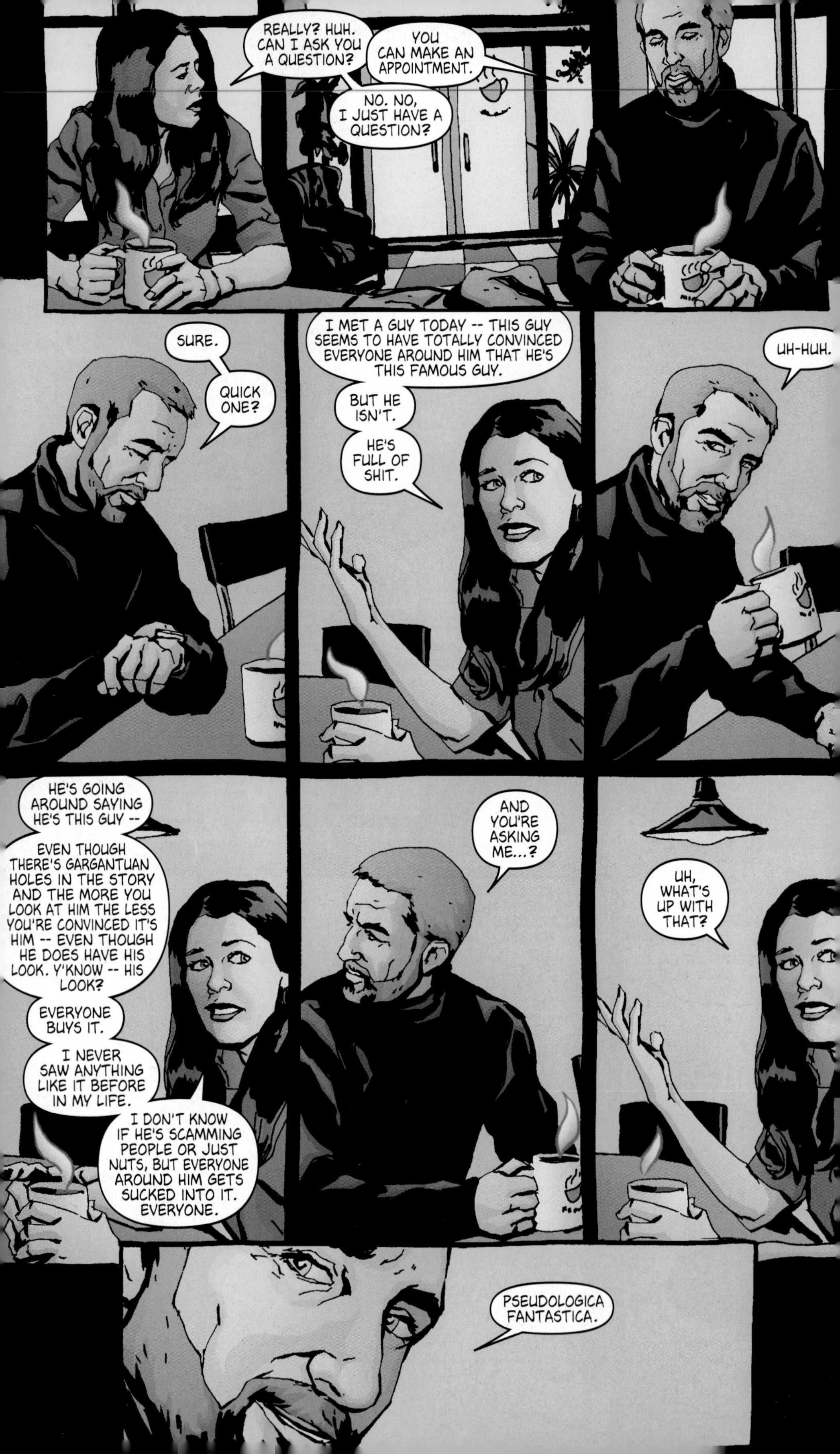

REALLY? HUH. CAN I ASK YOU A QUESTION?
YOU CAN MAKE AN APPOINTMENT.
NO. NO, I JUST HAVE A QUESTION?
SURE.
QUICK ONE?
I MET A GUY TODAY -- THIS GUY SEEMS TO HAVE TOTALLY CONVINCED EVERYONE AROUND HIM THAT HE'S THIS FAMOUS GUY.
BUT HE ISN'T.
HE'S FULL OF SHIT.
UH-HUH.
HE'S GOING AROUND SAYING HE'S THIS GUY --
EVEN THOUGH THERE'S GARGANTUAN HOLES IN THE STORY AND THE MORE YOU LOOK AT HIM THE LESS YOU'RE CONVINCED IT'S HIM -- EVEN THOUGH HE DOES HAVE HIS LOOK. Y'KNOW -- HIS LOOK?
EVERYONE BUYS IT.
I NEVER SAW ANYTHING LIKE IT BEFORE IN MY LIFE.
I DON'T KNOW IF HE'S SCAMMING PEOPLE OR JUST NUTS, BUT EVERYONE AROUND HIM GETS SUCKED INTO IT. EVERYONE.
AND YOU'RE ASKING ME...?
UH, WHAT'S UP WITH THAT?
PSEUDOLOGICA FANTASTICA.

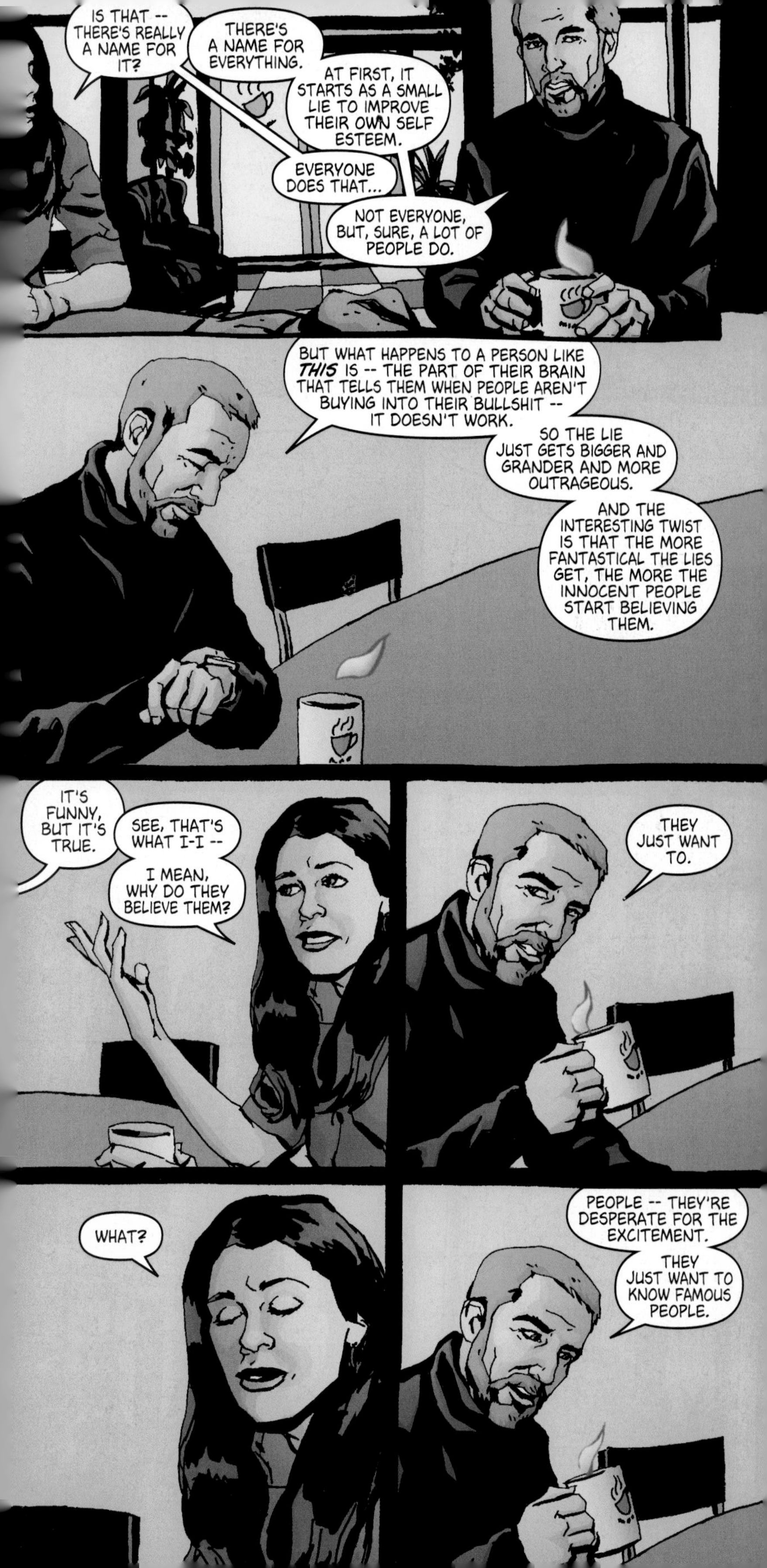
IS THAT -- THERE'S REALLY A NAME FOR IT?
THERE'S A NAME FOR EVERYTHING.
AT FIRST, IT STARTS AS A SMALL LIE TO IMPROVE THEIR OWN SELF ESTEEM.
EVERYONE DOES THAT...
NOT EVERYONE, BUT, SURE, A LOT OF PEOPLE DO.
BUT WHAT HAPPENS TO A PERSON LIKE *THIS* IS -- THE PART OF THEIR BRAIN THAT TELLS THEM WHEN PEOPLE AREN'T BUYING INTO THEIR BULLSHIT -- IT DOESN'T WORK.
SO THE LIE JUST GETS BIGGER AND GRANDER AND MORE OUTRAGEOUS.
AND THE INTERESTING TWIST IS THAT THE MORE FANTASTICAL THE LIES GET, THE MORE THE INNOCENT PEOPLE START BELIEVING THEM.
IT'S FUNNY, BUT IT'S TRUE.
SEE, THAT'S WHAT I-I --
I MEAN, WHY DO THEY BELIEVE THEM?
THEY JUST WANT TO.
WHAT?
PEOPLE -- THEY'RE DESPERATE FOR THE EXCITEMENT.
THEY JUST WANT TO KNOW FAMOUS PEOPLE.

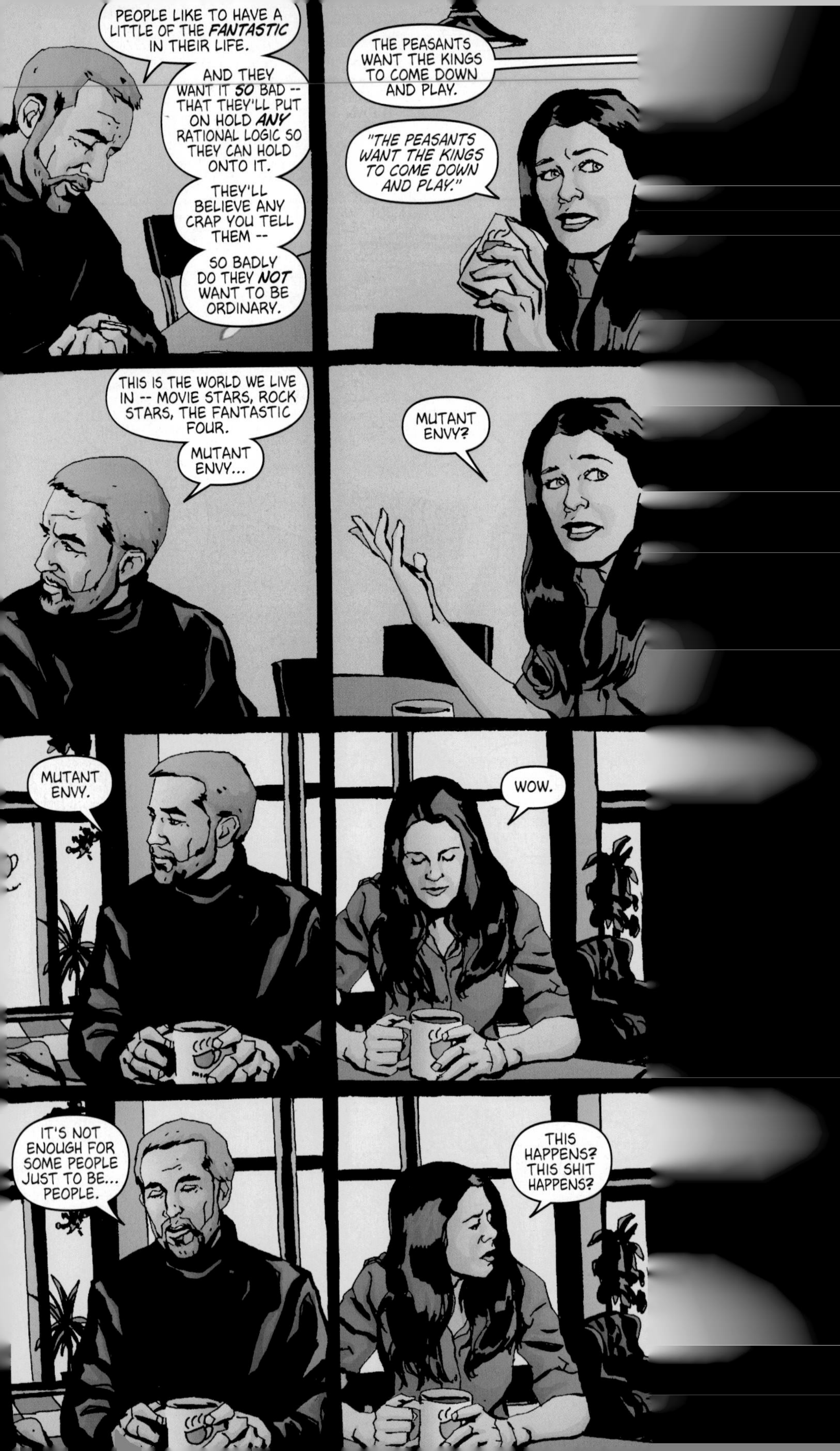
PEOPLE LIKE TO HAVE A LITTLE OF THE FANTASTIC IN THEIR LIFE.
AND THEY WANT IT SO BAD -- THAT THEY'LL PUT ON HOLD ANY RATIONAL LOGIC SO THEY CAN HOLD ONTO IT.
THEY'LL BELIEVE ANY CRAP YOU TELL THEM --
SO BADLY DO THEY NOT WANT TO BE ORDINARY.
THE PEASANTS WANT THE KINGS TO COME DOWN AND PLAY.
"THE PEASANTS WANT THE KINGS TO COME DOWN AND PLAY."
THIS IS THE WORLD WE LIVE IN -- MOVIE STARS, ROCK STARS, THE FANTASTIC FOUR.
MUTANT ENVY...
MUTANT ENVY?
MUTANT ENVY.
WOW.
IT'S NOT ENOUGH FOR SOME PEOPLE JUST TO BE... PEOPLE.
THIS HAPPENS? THIS SHIT HAPPENS?

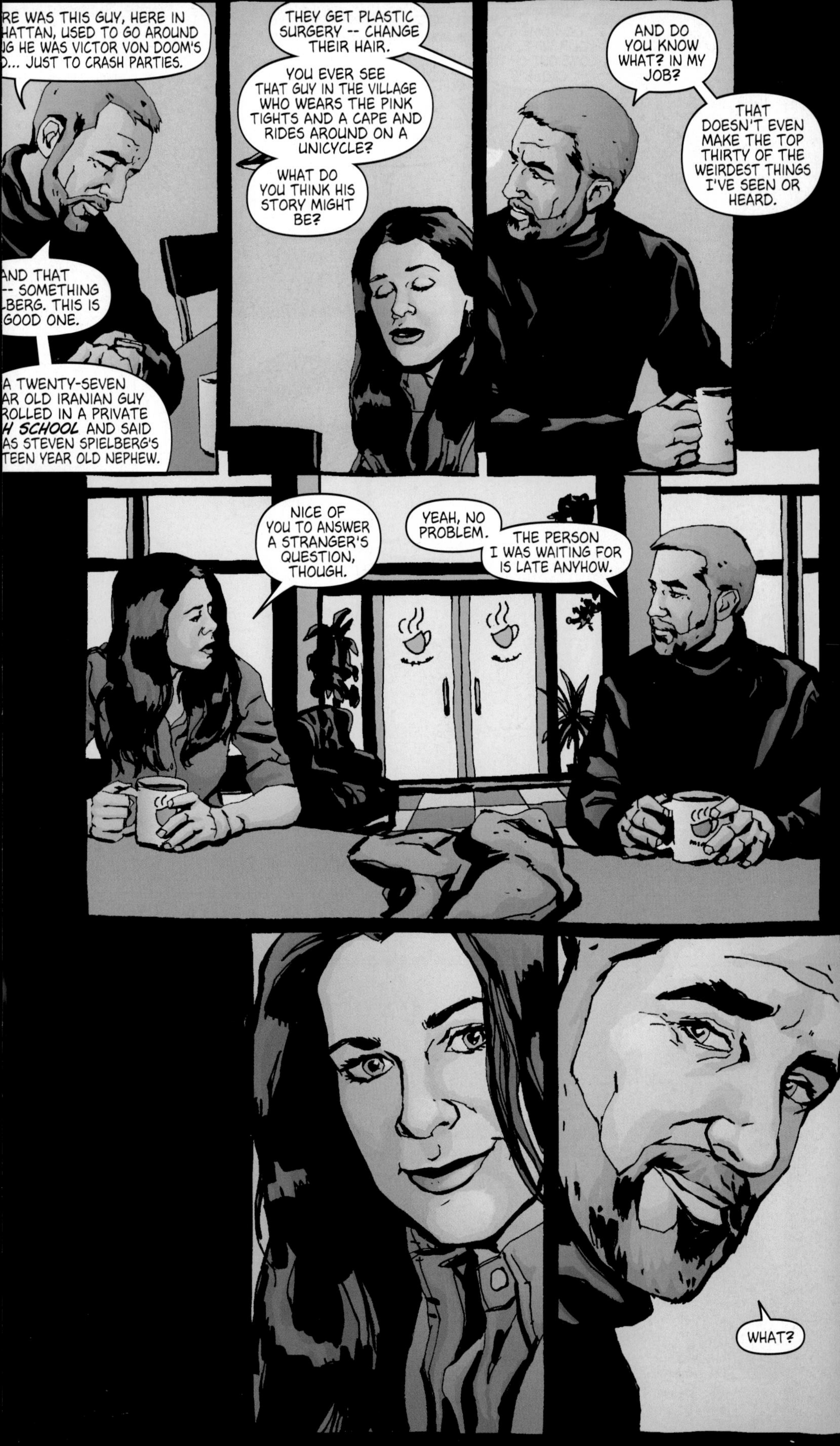
RE WAS THIS GUY, HERE IN HATTAN, USED TO GO AROUND IG HE WAS VICTOR VON DOOM'S D... JUST TO CRASH PARTIES.
AND THAT -- SOMETHING LBERG. THIS IS GOOD ONE.
A TWENTY-SEVEN AR OLD IRANIAN GUY ROLLED IN A PRIVATE H SCHOOL AND SAID AS STEVEN SPIELBERG'S TEEN YEAR OLD NEPHEW.
THEY GET PLASTIC SURGERY -- CHANGE THEIR HAIR.
YOU EVER SEE THAT GUY IN THE VILLAGE WHO WEARS THE PINK TIGHTS AND A CAPE AND RIDES AROUND ON A UNICYCLE?
WHAT DO YOU THINK HIS STORY MIGHT BE?
AND DO YOU KNOW WHAT? IN MY JOB?
THAT DOESN'T EVEN MAKE THE TOP THIRTY OF THE WEIRDEST THINGS I'VE SEEN OR HEARD.
NICE OF YOU TO ANSWER A STRANGER'S QUESTION, THOUGH.
YEAH, NO PROBLEM.
THE PERSON I WAS WAITING FOR IS LATE ANYHOW.
WHAT?

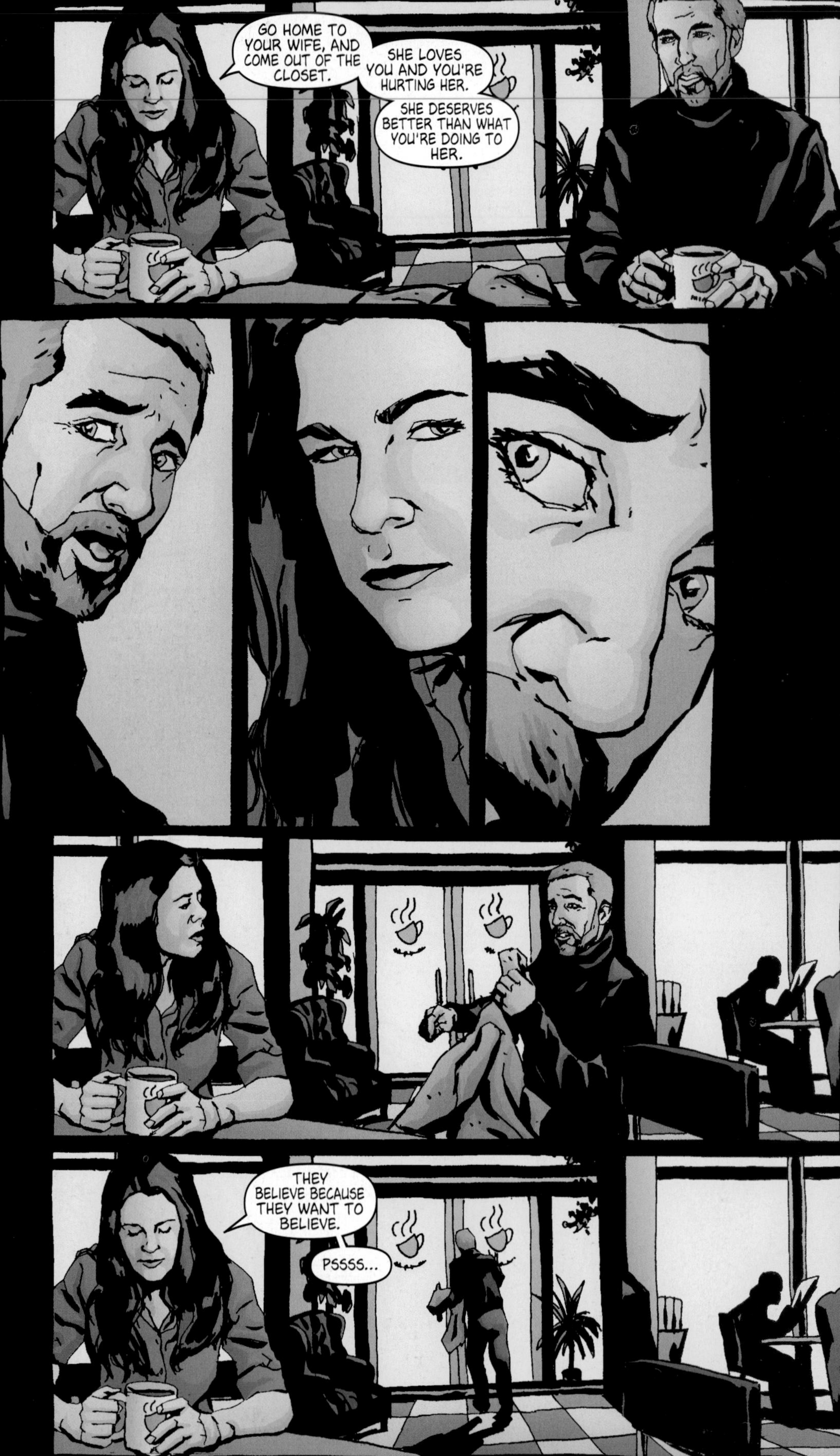
GO HOME TO YOUR WIFE, AND COME OUT OF THE CLOSET.
SHE LOVES YOU AND YOU'RE HURTING HER.
SHE DESERVES BETTER THAN WHAT YOU'RE DOING TO HER.
THEY BELIEVE BECAUSE THEY WANT TO BELIEVE.
PSSSS...

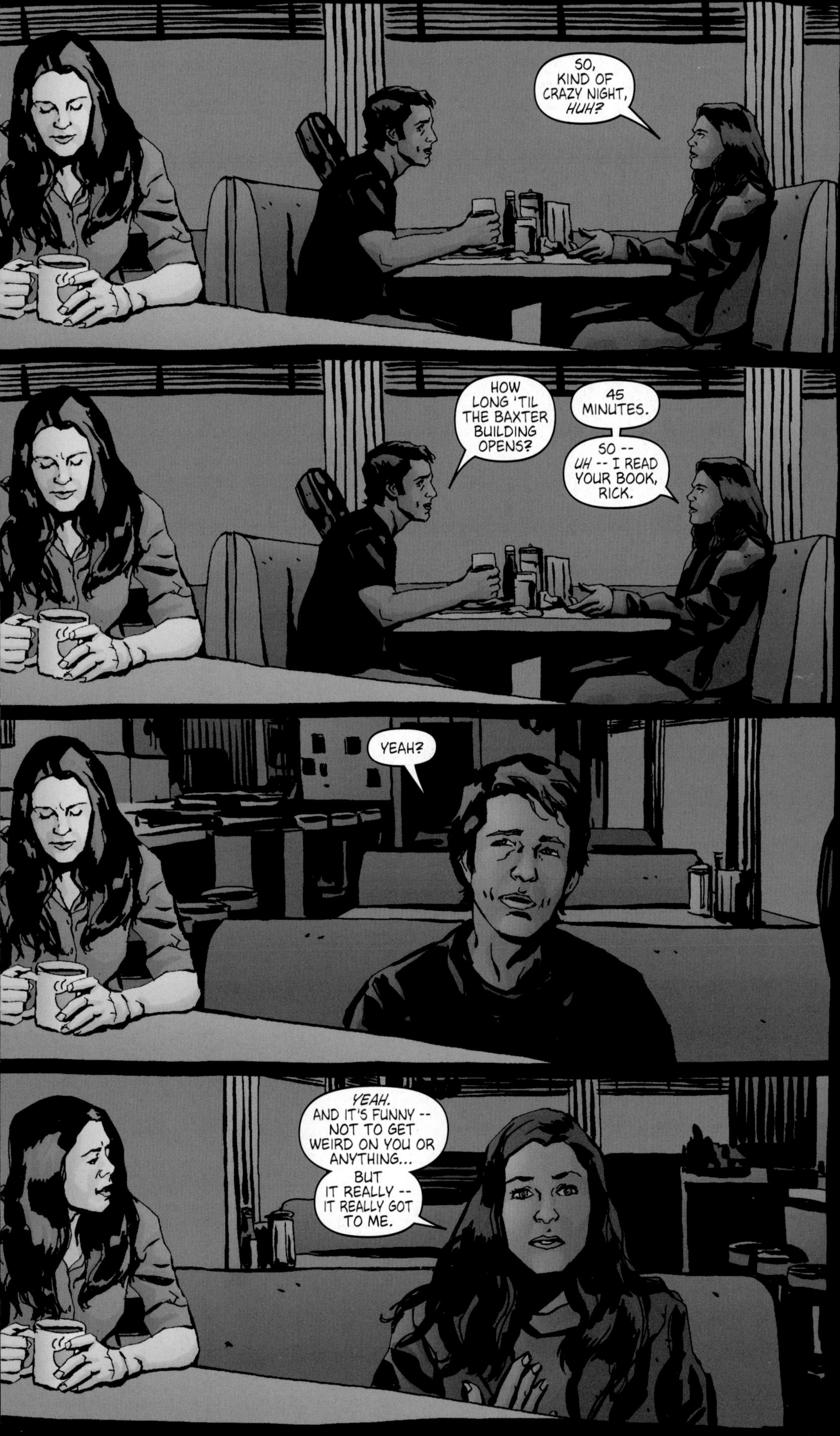
SO, KIND OF CRAZY NIGHT, *HUH?*
HOW LONG 'TIL THE BAXTER BUILDING OPENS?
45 MINUTES.
SO -- *UH* -- I READ YOUR BOOK, RICK.
YEAH?
YEAH. AND IT'S FUNNY -- NOT TO GET WEIRD ON YOU OR ANYTHING...
BUT IT REALLY -- IT REALLY GOT TO ME.

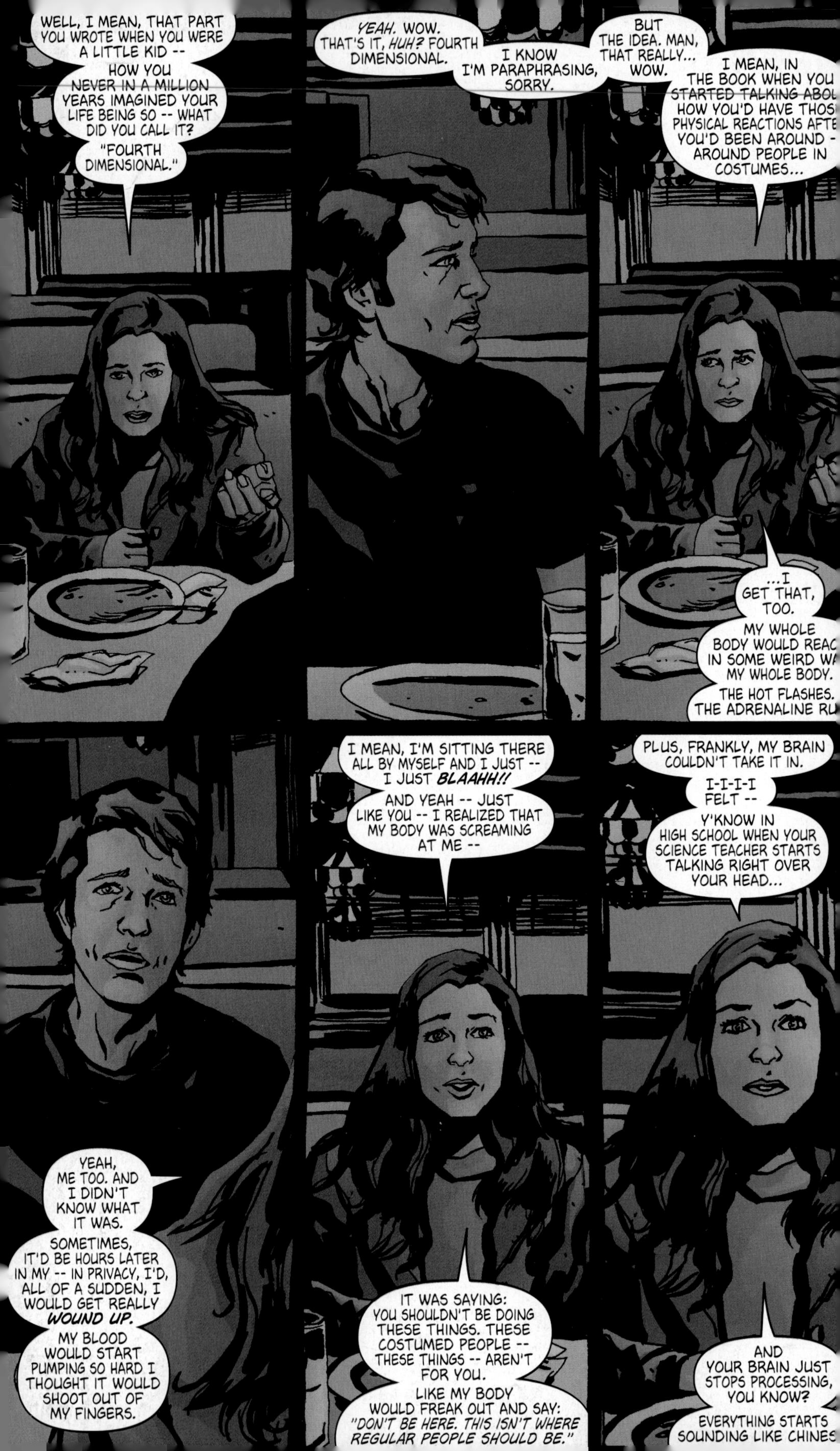
WELL, I MEAN, THAT PART YOU WROTE WHEN YOU WERE A LITTLE KID --
HOW YOU NEVER IN A MILLION YEARS IMAGINED YOUR LIFE BEING SO -- WHAT DID YOU CALL IT?
"FOURTH DIMENSIONAL."
YEAH. WOW. THAT'S IT, HUH? FOURTH DIMENSIONAL.
I KNOW I'M PARAPHRASING, SORRY.
BUT THE IDEA. MAN, THAT REALLY... WOW.
I MEAN, IN THE BOOK WHEN YOU STARTED TALKING ABOU HOW YOU'D HAVE THOS PHYSICAL REACTIONS AFTE YOU'D BEEN AROUND - AROUND PEOPLE IN COSTUMES...
...I GET THAT, TOO.
MY WHOLE BODY WOULD REAC IN SOME WEIRD WA MY WHOLE BODY.
THE HOT FLASHES. THE ADRENALINE RU
YEAH, ME TOO. AND I DIDN'T KNOW WHAT IT WAS.
SOMETIMES, IT'D BE HOURS LATER IN MY -- IN PRIVACY, I'D, ALL OF A SUDDEN, I WOULD GET REALLY WOUND UP.
MY BLOOD WOULD START PUMPING SO HARD I THOUGHT IT WOULD SHOOT OUT OF MY FINGERS.
I MEAN, I'M SITTING THERE ALL BY MYSELF AND I JUST -- I JUST BLAAHH!!
AND YEAH -- JUST LIKE YOU -- I REALIZED THAT MY BODY WAS SCREAMING AT ME --
IT WAS SAYING: YOU SHOULDN'T BE DOING THESE THINGS. THESE COSTUMED PEOPLE -- THESE THINGS -- AREN'T FOR YOU.
LIKE MY BODY WOULD FREAK OUT AND SAY: "DON'T BE HERE. THIS ISN'T WHERE REGULAR PEOPLE SHOULD BE."
PLUS, FRANKLY, MY BRAIN COULDN'T TAKE IT IN.
I-I-I-I FELT --
Y'KNOW IN HIGH SCHOOL WHEN YOUR SCIENCE TEACHER STARTS TALKING RIGHT OVER YOUR HEAD...
AND YOUR BRAIN JUST STOPS PROCESSING, YOU KNOW?
EVERYTHING STARTS SOUNDING LIKE CHINES

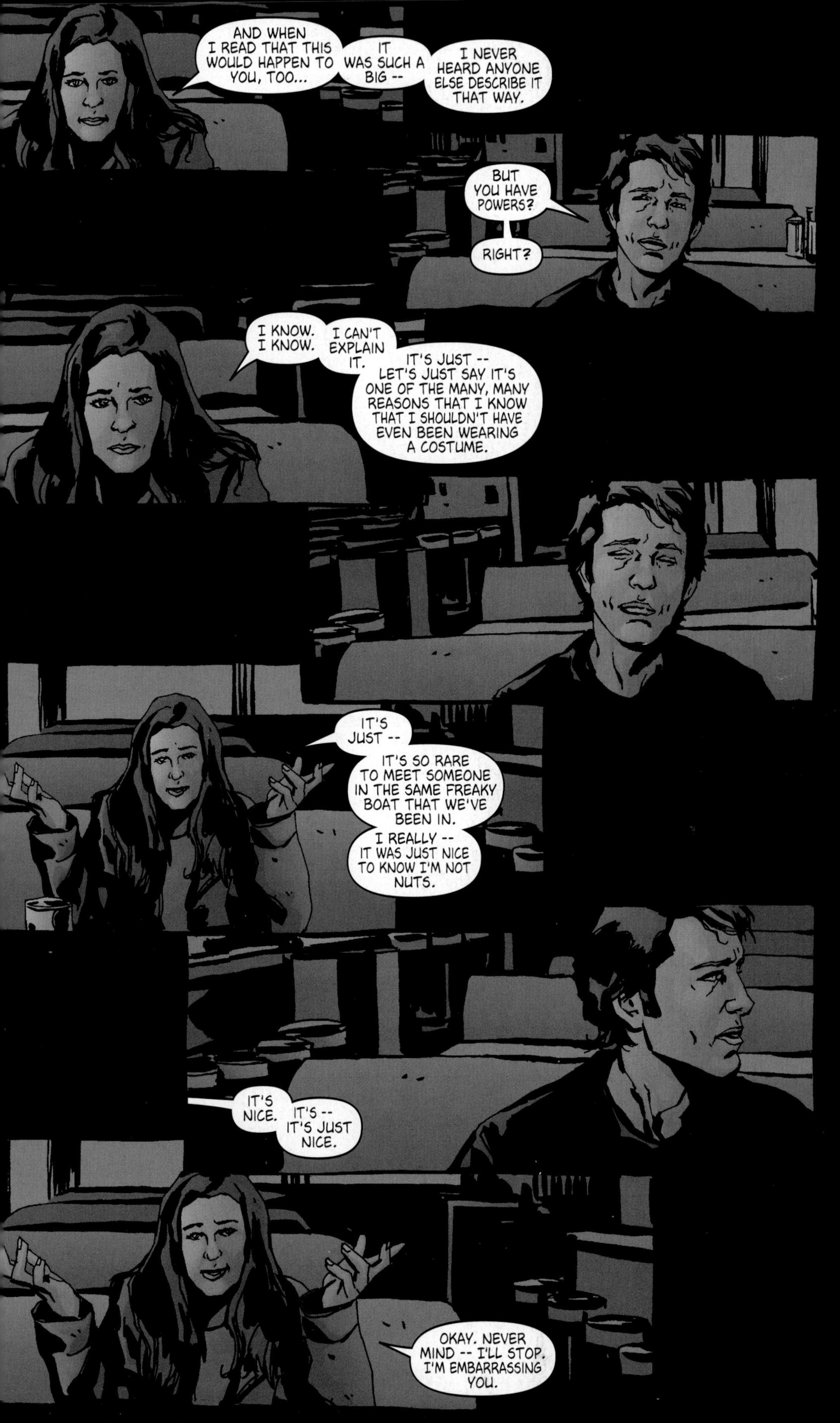
AND WHEN I READ THAT THIS WOULD HAPPEN TO YOU, TOO...
IT WAS SUCH A BIG --
I NEVER HEARD ANYONE ELSE DESCRIBE IT THAT WAY.
BUT YOU HAVE POWERS?
RIGHT?
I KNOW. I KNOW.
I CAN'T EXPLAIN IT.
IT'S JUST -- LET'S JUST SAY IT'S ONE OF THE MANY, MANY REASONS THAT I KNOW THAT I SHOULDN'T HAVE EVEN BEEN WEARING A COSTUME.
IT'S JUST --
IT'S SO RARE TO MEET SOMEONE IN THE SAME FREAKY BOAT THAT WE'VE BEEN IN.
I REALLY -- IT WAS JUST NICE TO KNOW I'M NOT NUTS.
IT'S NICE.
IT'S -- IT'S JUST NICE.
OKAY. NEVER MIND -- I'LL STOP. I'M EMBARRASSING YOU.

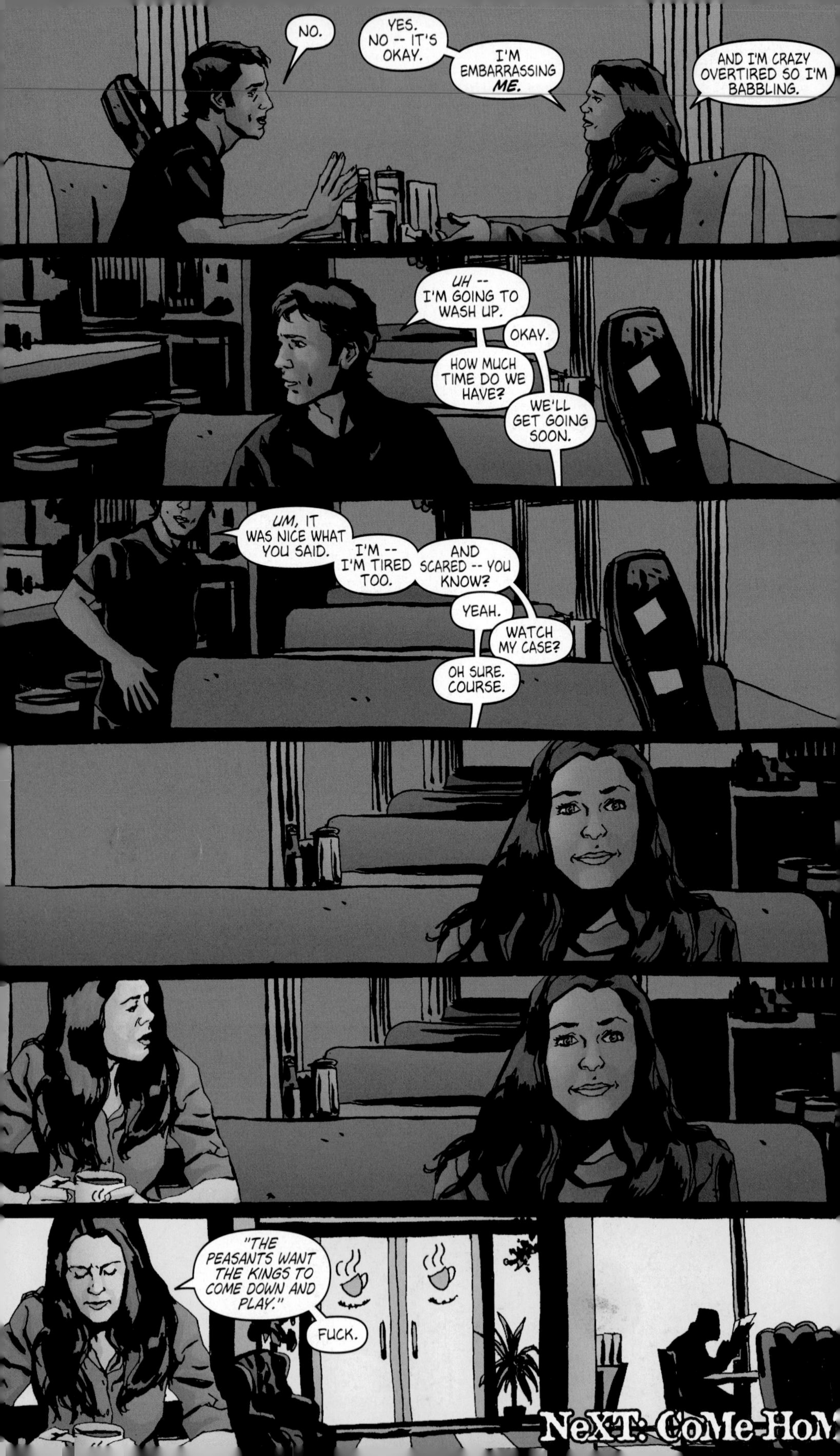
NO.
YES. NO -- IT'S OKAY.
I'M EMBARRASSING *ME.*
AND I'M CRAZY OVERTIRED SO I'M BABBLING.
UH -- I'M GOING TO WASH UP.
OKAY.
HOW MUCH TIME DO WE HAVE?
WE'LL GET GOING SOON.
UM, IT WAS NICE WHAT YOU SAID.
I'M -- I'M TIRED TOO.
AND SCARED -- YOU KNOW?
YEAH.
WATCH MY CASE?
OH SURE. COURSE.
"THE PEASANTS WANT THE KINGS TO COME DOWN AND PLAY."
FUCK.
NeXT: CoMe-HoM

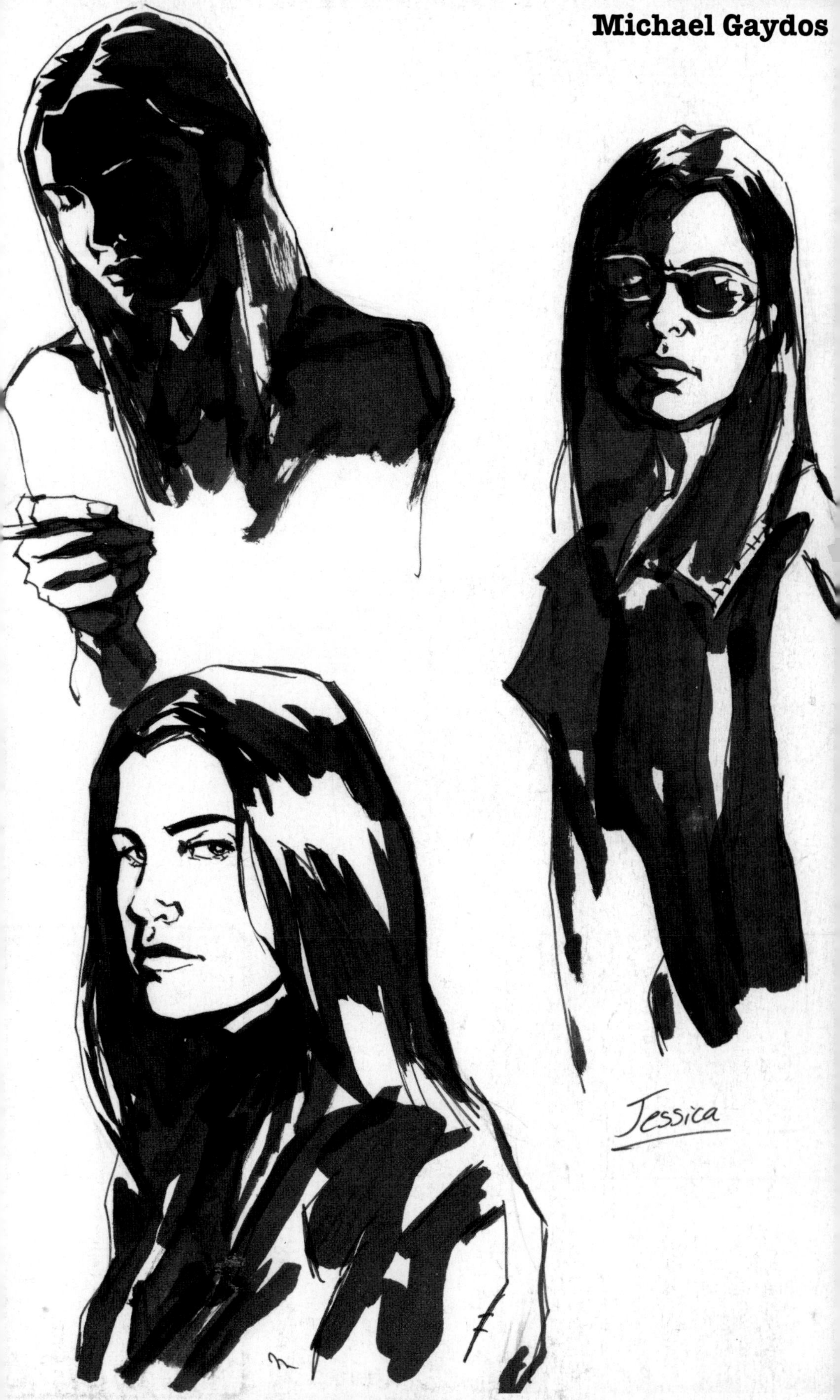
Jessica

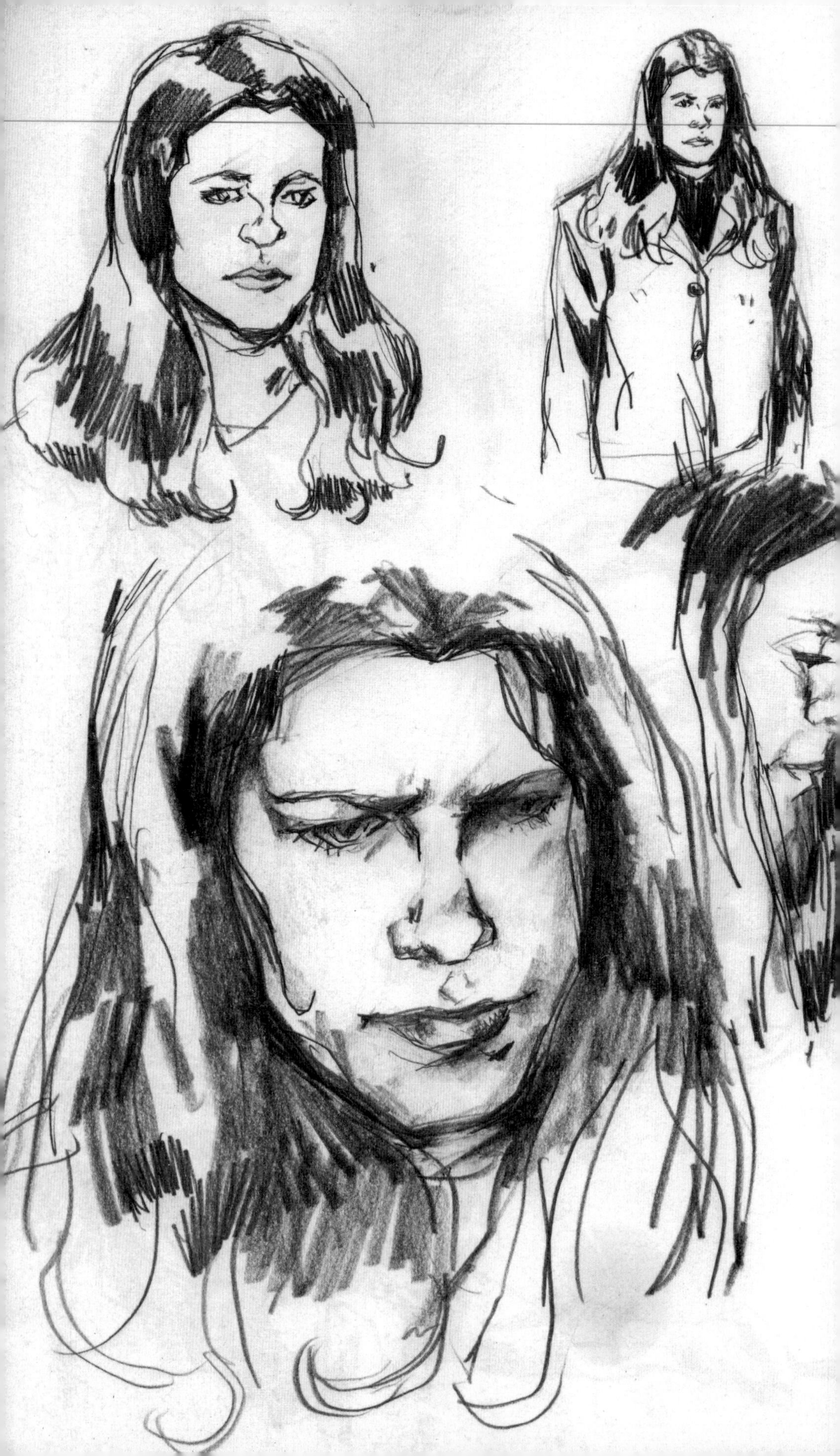